BEGINNING iOS GAME DEVELOPMENT

BEGINNING

iOS Game Development

BEGINNING

iOS Game Development

Patrick Alessi

WILEY

Wiley Publishing, Inc.

Beginning iOS Game Development

Published by
John Wiley & Sons, Inc.
10475 Crosspoint Boulevard
Indianapolis, IN 46256
www.wiley.com

Copyright © 2012 by Patrick Alessi

Published by John Wiley & Sons, Inc., Indianapolis, Indiana

Published simultaneously in Canada

ISBN: 978-1-118-10732-4
ISBN: 978-1-118-22408-3 (ebk)
ISBN: 978-1-118-23161-6 (ebk)
ISBN: 978-1-118-26231-3 (ebk)

Manufactured in the United States of America

10 9 8 7 6 5 4 3 2 1

For general information on our other products and services please contact our Customer Care Department within the United States at (877) 762-2974, outside the United States at (317) 572-3993 or fax (317) 572-4002.

Wiley publishes in a variety of print and electronic formats and by print-on-demand. Some material included with standard print versions of this book may not be included in e-books or in print-on-demand. If this book refers to media such as a CD or DVD that is not included in the version you purchased, you may download this material at http://booksupport.wiley.com. For more information about Wiley products, visit www.wiley.com.

Library of Congress Control Number: 2011940541

For Morgan — I hope that watching me take on and conquer a difficult task inspires you to do the same.

ABOUT THE AUTHOR

PATRICK ALESSI has been fascinated with writing computer programs since he first saw his name flash across a terminal in 1980. Since then, he has written software using every language and hardware platform that he could get his hands on, including a brief and painful foray into Fortran on a VAX system during his engineering education. Patrick holds a B.S. degree in Civil Engineering from Rutgers University and an M.S. in Computer Science from Stevens Institute of Technology.

Professionally, Patrick has built data-centric applications for clients ranging from small business databases to large-scale systems for the United States Air Force. He has also developed a variety of real-time systems, graphics intensive desktop applications, and games. Currently, he is focused on developing connected applications and games for mobile devices such as the iPhone and iPad.

When he can back away from the computer, Patrick enjoys photography, traveling, gaming on his Xbox and doing just about anything with his family. You can follow him on Twitter at @pwalessi and read his blog at iphonedevsphere.blogspot.com.

ABOUT THE TECHNICAL EDITOR

MICHAEL GILBERT is a long-time systems programmer for various engineering firms. He got his start developing games for the Atari ST, and was a frequent contributing editor for *STart* magazine. Over the years, he has developed gaming software on the PC and Mac for clients worldwide. He's also an expert Flash ActionScript programmer and has produced a popular Internet gaming environment called HigherGames; you can check it out at www.highergames.com. He now enjoys developing games for the iPhone and iPad, and currently has four games in the AppStore (Woridgo, Jumpin' Java, Kings Battlefield, and Set Pro HD). In his spare time, he enjoys trying to defeat his wife, Janeen, in a friendly game of Scrabble. You can follow him on Twitter at @mija711.

CREDITS

ACQUISITIONS EDITOR
Mary James

PROJECT EDITOR
Brian MacDonald

TECHNICAL EDITOR
Michael Gilbert

PRODUCTION EDITOR
Rebecca Anderson

COPY EDITOR
Mike La Bonne

EDITORIAL MANAGER
Mary Beth Wakefield

FREELANCER EDITORIAL MANAGER
Rosemarie Graham

ASSOCIATE DIRECTOR OF MARKETING
David Mayhew

MARKETING MANAGER
Ashley Zurcher

BUSINESS MANAGER
Amy Knies

PRODUCTION MANAGER
Tim Tate

VICE PRESIDENT AND EXECUTIVE GROUP PUBLISHER
Richard Swadley

VICE PRESIDENT AND EXECUTIVE PUBLISHER
Neil Edde

ASSOCIATE PUBLISHER
Jim Minatel

PROJECT COORDINATOR, COVER
Katie Crocker

PROOFREADER
Nancy Carrasco

INDEXER
Robert Swanson

COVER DESIGNER
Ryan Sneed

COVER IMAGE
© Adeline Lim / iStockPhoto

ACKNOWLEDGMENTS

I WOULD LIKE TO take this opportunity to thank everyone who made this book possible. Mary James, my acquisitions editor, encouraged me to get back to writing and fostered this book through the acquisitions process. My project editor, Brian MacDonald, was instrumental in turning my stream of consciousness into a cohesive work. Mike Gilbert, my technical editor, gave up valuable app development and gaming time to review my work. I would also like to thank all of the other editorial and production staff that put many hours into this project to help get it to print.

The most important people in the writing process are my wife, Cheryl, and my stepdaughter, Morgan. They pick up the slack for me when I can't keep up with my other duties, ensuring that life goes on as normal. They also put up with my fits, general crankiness, and lack of time for fun family activities as I worked my way through writing this book. Your patience with me is astounding. Finally, I'd like to thank my parents for molding me into the semi-mature adult that I've turned into.

CONTENTS

INTRODUCTION

IOS DEVICES PROVIDE DEVELOPERS with a unique and exciting platform for making games. The iPhone gives gamers a tiny computer in their pocket that they have with them all the time. The iPad provides a similar gameplay experience but with a larger screen, more processing power, and more memory. The devices allow for unique control schemes with their touch-sensitive displays, accelerometer, and even a gyroscope on the latest devices.

According to Scott Forstall at Apple's 2011 World Wide Developer Conference, there are over 200 million iOS devices. This represents a huge audience for games. In the first 14 months after the release of the iPad, Apple sold 25 million devices. Forstall also said that in the App Store's three years, 14 billion apps have been downloaded. Developers have been paid a total of $2.5 billion for their efforts.

According to market research firms NewZoo and Distimo (http://www.distimo.com/blog/2011_05_distimo-and-newzoo%C2%A0partner-on-games-data-over-5-million-ios-games-downloaded-per-day-by-63-million-ios-gamers-in-us-eu/), games are the largest category of applications on the app store. A full half of all downloads of free and paid apps are games. According to the National Gamers Survey in March 2011, there were more than 60 million iOS gamers in the US and Europe.

As you can see, there is a huge financial incentive to write games for the iOS platform. But, there is more to it than that. Writing games is fun! If you like to write interesting programs and solve difficult problems, you will enjoy writing games. Also, games are a very expressive form of programming. As a corporate programmer in my day job, I sometimes feel like I've built the same three-tier database/web application a hundred times. But, with games, every one is different.

With the right tools, you can make a game out of just about anything that you could possibly imagine. Apple provides some terrific, and free, tools for building games for iOS. Xcode, the development environment, is one of the best that I have ever worked with. If you are familiar with Visual Studio, Eclipse, or any of the other industry standard IDEs, you will feel right at home with Xcode. Apple also put a lot of thought into creating well-designed APIs to help you to take advantage of the features of the iOS platform. Once you learn some of the key fundamentals, you should be able to pick up and run with any of the core technologies and this book will help you to get there. Most chapters in this book feature real, working games that you will build. I think that the best way to learn is by doing, and by working along with the game examples in this book, you will learn how to use Apple's tools to build games.

WHO THIS BOOK IS FOR

This book will teach anyone with any type of programming background how to write basic games for iOS devices such as the iPhone, iPod touch, and iPad. Even though the book assumes some programming experience, I feel that someone with very little to no experience could pick this title up and use it as a starting point for beginning the journey into the world of game programming.

If you already have experience with Java, C#, or another object-oriented programming language, so much the better. If you already know C and/or Objective-C, feel free to skim over Chapters 3 and 4 as they will probably be old hat for you. However, I may have a little nugget in there that could teach you something new.

The book assumes no experience in writing for the Mac or iOS. That was a major factor in my decision to write this book. Every other book that I have seen on iOS game development assumes a foundation in basic iOS programming. I have not done that. I start from the beginning and guide you through the whole process of writing games for iOS from start to finish. By the end of this book, you will have written several games and you will have experience with many of the frameworks that you can use to draw graphics, perform animation, work with sound, and handle user input.

Keep in mind that this is a "Beginner" level title. If you have already published dozens of games for iOS, this book probably is not for you. In order to keep the book accessible for beginners, I have steered clear of the more difficult APIs. For example, I do not cover using OpenGL to render graphics. However, I do mention that advanced tools exist, explain their use, and attempt to point readers in the right direction if they decide that the technology may be appropriate for their project.

Finally, in addition to aspiring game developers, I think that this book would be handy for all developers of iOS applications. After all, the APIs for graphics, animation, sound, and user input are just as applicable to a boring database application as they are to games. You might be able to spice up your next business tool and wow your customers and clients with eye-popping animations or you may be able to accept input in a way that you never thought of before reading this book.

WHAT THIS BOOK COVERS

As I mentioned, this is a beginner-level book, so I cover all of the technologies that a reader new to the iOS platform needs to get started writing games.

In the first part of the book, I cover the absolute basics that you need to know in order to write any iOS program, game or not. I cover the IDE, Xcode, which every iOS programmer uses, including those at Apple, to write, debug, and test their programs. Then, I go on to cover the C and Objective-C programming languages, which you will use to create native iOS applications. Finally, I cover the Cocoa Foundation framework that provides basic functionality that you need to write iOS programs.

In the second part, after you have the basics nailed down, I cover the tools that you will need to write games. You will learn how to use Apple's frameworks to perform the basic functions necessary for games. I've broken it down into four areas: graphics, user interaction, animation, and sound. Once you have finished with part two, you will certainly be capable of developing your own games from scratch.

Additionally, each chapter in this section features a playable game. After you are finished working through the examples, you can enhance these games on your own to learn more about the technologies discussed in the chapter. You can think of the example games as a starting point for your exploration into iOS game development.

HOW THIS BOOK IS STRUCTURED

I have organized the book so that a reader new to iOS development can work through the book in order from start to finish. I would recommend working through the book in order, as each chapter builds upon concepts covered in the previous chapters. I organized the book this way to provide a tutorial type of experience for the reader as opposed to a referential one. Sure, you can use the book as a reference guide to the APIs that I cover when you are done, but I tried to write the book in a way that gently guides the reader from one topic to the next. If you learn how to use the Apple documentation effectively, you already have a terrific reference. What I aim to do is be your guide through the APIs.

WHAT YOU NEED TO USE THIS BOOK

In order to build applications for iOS, you will need an Apple computer with Mac OS X. Additionally, you need to install the Xcode development environment. Xcode 4 is a free download that you can get from the Mac App Store.

If you intend to run your games on a device such as the iPhone or iPad, as opposed to running your code in the iPhone simulator, you will need to join the iOS developer program. At the time of this writing, joining the program costs $99 annually and entitles you to build and run programs on your device and to submit your finished applications to the Apple App Store for sale. If you are not currently part of the developer program, don't worry. There is very little in the book that requires you to run on an actual device. Nearly everything will work correctly in the simulator. Where there is a need to run on the device, I have noted that in the text.

CONVENTIONS

To help you get the most from the text and keep track of what's happening, we've used a number of conventions throughout the book.

TRY IT OUT

The *Try It Out* is an exercise you should work through, following the text in the book.

1. They usually consist of a set of steps.
2. Each step has a number.
3. Follow the steps on your copy of Xcode.

How It Works

After each Try It Out, the code you've typed will be explained in detail.

As for styles in the text:

➤ We *highlight* new terms and important words when we introduce them.

➤ We show keyboard strokes like this: Ctrl+A.

➤ We show file names, URLs, and code within the text like so: `persistence.properties`.

We present code in two different ways:

```
We use a monofont type with no highlighting for most code examples.
We use bold to emphasize code that's particularly important in the present context.
```

Also, Xcode's code editor provides a rich color scheme to indicate various parts of code syntax. That's a great tool to help you learn language features in the editor and to help prevent mistakes as you code. To reinforce Xcode's colors, the code listings in this book are colorized, using colors similar to what you would see on screen in Xcode working with the book's code. In order to optimize print clarity, some colors have a slightly different hue in print than what you see on screen. But all of the colors for the code in this book should be close enough to the default Xcode colors to give you an accurate representation of the colors.

SOURCE CODE

As you work through the examples in this book, you may choose either to type in all the code manually or to use the source code files that accompany the book. All of the source code used in this book is available for download at `www.wrox.com`. You will find the code snippets from the source code are accompanied by a note indicating the name of the program, so you know it's available for download and can easily locate it in the download file. Once at the site, simply locate the book's title (either by using the Search box or by using one of the title lists) and click the Download Code link on the book's detail page to obtain all the source code for the book.

 NOTE *Because many books have similar titles, you may find it easiest to search by ISBN; this book's ISBN is 978-1-118-10732-4.*

Once you download the code, just decompress it with your favorite compression tool. Alternately, you can go to the main Wrox code download page at `www.wrox.com/dynamic/books/download .aspx` to see the code available for this book and all other Wrox books.

ERRATA

We make every effort to ensure that there are no errors in the text or in the code. However, no one is perfect, and mistakes do occur. If you find an error in one of our books, like a spelling mistake or faulty piece of code, we would be very grateful for your feedback. By sending in errata you may save another reader hours of frustration and at the same time you will be helping us provide even higher quality information.

To find the errata page for this book, go to www.wrox.com and locate the title using the Search box or one of the title lists. Then, on the book details page, click the Book Errata link. On this page you can view all errata that has been submitted for this book and posted by Wrox editors. A complete book list including links to each book's errata is also available at www.wrox.com/misc-pages/booklist.shtml.

If you don't spot "your" error on the Book Errata page, go to www.wrox.com/contact/techsupport.shtml and complete the form there to send us the error you have found. We'll check the information and, if appropriate, post a message to the book's errata page and fix the problem in subsequent editions of the book.

P2P.WROX.COM

For author and peer discussion, join the P2P forums at p2p.wrox.com. The forums are a web-based system for you to post messages relating to Wrox books and related technologies and interact with other readers and technology users. The forums offer a subscription feature to e-mail you topics of interest of your choosing when new posts are made to the forums. Wrox authors, editors, other industry experts, and your fellow readers are present on these forums.

At p2p.wrox.com you will find a number of different forums that will help you not only as you read this book, but also as you develop your own applications. To join the forums, just follow these steps:

1. Go to p2p.wrox.com and click the Register link.

2. Read the terms of use and click Agree.

3. Complete the required information to join as well as any optional information you wish to provide and click Submit.

4. You will receive an e-mail with information describing how to verify your account and complete the joining process.

 NOTE *You can read messages in the forums without joining P2P but in order to post your own messages, you must join.*

Once you join, you can post new messages and respond to messages other users post. You can read messages at any time on the Web. If you would like to have new messages from a particular forum e-mailed to you, click the Subscribe to this Forum icon by the forum name in the forum listing.

For more information about how to use the Wrox P2P, be sure to read the P2P FAQs for answers to questions about how the forum software works as well as many common questions specific to P2P and Wrox books. To read the FAQs, click the FAQ link on any P2P page.

PART I
The Tools to Get Started

1

Games on iOS

WHAT YOU WILL LEARN IN THIS CHAPTER:

➤ Examining the unique features of games on iOS

➤ Documenting and developing your idea

➤ Prototyping and preparing your game for coding

➤ Getting an overview of the game-related frameworks in iOS

Since you have picked up this book and are reading this, you must be interested in writing a game for iOS. Why do you want to write a game? There are some great reasons to write a game for iOS, first and foremost is that writing a game is fun! You can escape all of the constraints of reality in a game. In your game, you make the rules.

Writing games for iOS can be particularly fun because of the amazing capabilities of the device. You can include using a GPS, camera, accelerometer, and even a gyroscope in your game. Writing games for iOS can also be financially rewarding. With the ubiquity of iOS devices, millions of people can play your game. Moreover, since you will distribute your game in Apple's App Store, you do not have to worry about setting up your own storefront to distribute your creations. In January of 2011, Apple released a list of the top-selling applications on the App Store:

➤ Doodle Jump

➤ Tap Tap Revenge 3

➤ Pocket God

➤ Angry Birds

➤ Tap Tap Revenge 2.6

➤ Bejeweled 2 + Blitz

➤ Traffic Rush

➤ Tap Tap Revenge Classic

➤ AppBox Pro Alarm

➤ Flight Control

Notice that nine of the ten best-selling applications of all time for the iOS platform are games. Therefore, your choice to start investing your valuable time as an iOS game developer is a good one.

But, before worrying about making millions in the App Store, you need to think about not just making any iOS game, but making a good game.

WHAT MAKES A GOOD IOS GAME?

As an aspiring iOS game developer, the first question that you need to ask yourself is, "What makes a good iOS game?" In this section, I'll try to give you some ideas that you can think about while you are designing your game.

Device Usage

As you start to formulate your ideas on your iOS game, you need to keep several things in mind. The first is how people use iOS devices and how that relates to the way that they play games.

Take another look at the top iOS applications. You could categorize each of the games as a casual game. There are no 100-hour RPGs or first person shooters on the list. All of the games on the list are easy to pick up for first-time gamers. Additionally, all of these games let you get in and out quickly in short bursts.

Think about how people use games or other applications in general on a mobile device. When you take out your phone to game, or use the address book, calendar, or text messaging, you want to get into the application and do what you want to do and get out quickly. Mobile users generally do not have a lot of time to dig into all of the features that may be present in a full-featured desktop application. The same is true for games. The most successful games for iOS are simple, with easy-to-learn rules and short levels that can be played in a few minutes. This may change as the iPad becomes a more prevalent gaming platform; but for now, short levels and simple rules are the best way to start the design of a successful game.

Use Unique Features of iOS

Some other factors that you should consider when designing your iOS game is how a player will control the game and how you can take advantage of the advanced features of iOS devices.

The most successful games on iOS have very simple control schemes. There are no physical buttons available on an iOS device. Therefore, designing a game that needs a controller like that of an Xbox 360 with dozen of buttons will not work in iOS. The control scheme needs to be simple. The most successful game controls allow the player to interact directly with the game actors themselves, and not through an intermediary controller like a D-pad or joystick. Apple clearly lays this point out in its Human Interface Guidelines (HIG), which I recommend that you read. The HIG is available online at `http://developer.apple.com/library/ios/#documentation/userexperience/conceptual/mobilehig/Introduction/Introduction.html`.

You can use the touch capability of iOS devices to immerse the player in the game. When you allow a player to control a game by interacting directly with the parts of the game, the player feels more involved with the game. Think about building a board game like chess. It is more intuitive and immersive for a player to move the chess pieces as opposed to using an onscreen joystick and buttons to move the pieces.

You can also use some of the other features of iOS devices to make your games more immersive. All iOS devices contain an accelerometer that you can use to determine the orientation of the device. Consider how you can use this to enhance the controls of your game. Imagine a game that the player controls by tilting a device. You will learn how to build this type of game later in the book. This control scheme allows you to incorporate the physical world of the player with the imaginary world of your game.

Another feature widely available is GPS. Think about how you could incorporate the location of a player into your game. Perhaps you could build a game that gives a player points for going to certain locations. On the other hand, maybe, if a player were in a certain location he or she would be able to get a special weapon.

Make Your Game Fun

Your most important consideration while you are designing your game should be to make the game fun. If the game is not fun, no one will want to play it. Keep in mind that you will be playing the game very often as you are developing it. If the game is not fun, you will not enjoy the development process and this will show through in the game. Think about what makes games fun and apply those things to your game. Different people have different ideas of fun, and your perception of fun may not be the same as everyone else's. It is helpful to have as many other people as possible try out your game during the development process. These testers can often provide valuable feedback that you can use to make your game better.

First, the game should be easily approachable. Games with rules that are difficult to understand are often difficult for new players to pick up. You do not want to do anything to deter players from playing your game. Instead, use a simple set of rules that players will readily understand. If you have to write 10 pages of help to explain the rules of your game, it is probably too complex for a hand-held device. If you do decide to make a complex game, you should be prepared to offer players a tutorial. Players are far more inclined to work through an in-game experience as opposed to reading a document to learn the rules.

Next, balance the game to challenge your players. It is not fun to play a game that is too easy nor is it fun to play a game that is too difficult. As the game designer, you need to find a balance that challenges your players but does not discourage them from playing. To do this, you will need to play-test your game often during the development cycle. Puzzle games often use another technique. That is, to start slowly with easy levels and gradually work the player up to the more difficult levels. That way, the player can get a feel for the game mechanics on the easier levels and apply those lessons to the more difficult ones.

Finally, reward the player. When a player accomplishes something of note in your game, reward him. You can do this by showing an animated cut scene. You can also award achievements by using the GameKit APIs. You can also use Game Center Leader boards to foster competition between players of your game.

The most important thing is that you have fun developing your game. If the game is not fun for you to develop, it likely will not be fun for players. Let your enthusiasm and excitement for the game show through.

Graphics and Design

Do not underestimate the value of graphics in your game. A wonderful icon may be the only thing that a potential buyer of your game sees in the iTunes store. If you plan to sell your game in the iTunes store, spend the time, or money, to develop a beautiful icon for your game.

Aside from the icon, pay close attention to the graphics and motif of your game. Nice graphics can make the difference between App Store success and failure. There are many physics-based destruction games on the App Store; however, Angry Birds reigns supreme because the graphic design of the bird and pig characters makes Angry Birds stand out from its competition. The gameplay is identical to many other games in the genre, but the characters in Angry Birds stand out from the crowd.

Unfortunately, I am not a graphic artist or designer, so you may notice that the quality of the graphics in this book is sub par. This is fine for instructional purposes; however, if your graphic skills are as weak as mine and you intend on selling your game, you would do well to hire a professional to develop your graphics.

DEVELOPING YOUR IDEA

After you have come up with the basic idea for your game, you need to start developing it further. At this stage, you should not be thinking about writing code. Instead, you need to focus on what your game will do, not how you will do it.

Documenting Your Game

The first step is to commit the concepts for your game to writing. I know that this may seem like a painful and tedious chore, but the specifications that you create in this phase will guide the entire development process. This step is particularly important if you are developing the game for a customer and not just for yourself. In this case, the specification will serve as a sort of contract that both you and your customer can use to measure the success of your efforts and to evaluate how far along you are on the game.

You should start your specification with an application definition statement. This single sentence describes the overall concept of your game and its intended audience. You will use this statement to help guide the rest of your decisions throughout the development process. In this section, I will walk you through the process of building a specification for a beginner's chess game. Therefore, a good application definition statement may be something like: "The purpose of this project is to implement the game of chess with features geared toward teaching a beginner the basics of the game."

Once you have your application definition statement, you are ready to start defining the features that you will implement in your game. You can do this in a formal document, or you can just write a checklist. For a beginner's chess game, you may come up with a feature list like this:

➤ Implement the correct rules of chess.

➤ Provide the ability for the player to undo moves.

➤ Give the player a way to ask the computer for suggested moves.

➤ Show the player legal moves for any selected piece.

➤ Build a computer opponent that can adapt to the player's skill level.

There is no need to specify every tiny detail of your game in this document. You need only worry about the key features that define the game or make your implementation of the game special. Notice that this list is very high level. At this point, there is no need to go into deep detail. This list will serve as a checklist that you can use to gauge your progress in the development process.

I like to use the feature list as an outline during the development process. As you learn more about each feature in the list, you can flesh out each item. For example, for the first item, "Implement the correct rules of Chess," you may want to add separate sub items as you get into the development process. Some of these may be:

➤ Enforce rules for each piece.

➤ Correctly allow castling when appropriate.

➤ Do not let a player move the king into "check."

➤ Implement the en-passant rule.

Once you have finished documenting all of your game's features, go back and evaluate it against your application definition statement. If you have features that conflict with the application definition, eliminate them from the game, or put them off as enhancements that you may build later. In the chess example, perhaps you decided that one of the features should be an extensive library of openings. Most beginners at chess do not understand the myriad openings, so this may not be an important feature for a game targeted at beginners. It is critical to keep your target audience in mind as you decide on the features that you want to include with your game.

Prototyping Your Game

Once you have defined the features and audience for your game, you are ready to do some prototyping. This may not be necessary for a well-understood game like chess, but for a new idea, it is critical.

At this stage, you may want to build a simple version of your game with pen and paper. Draw the board or background for your game and make cutouts of the pieces or other actors in your game. Then, use these clips of paper to simulate playing your game. Figure 1-1 shows my pen-and-paper prototype for the Blocker game that you will build later in the book.

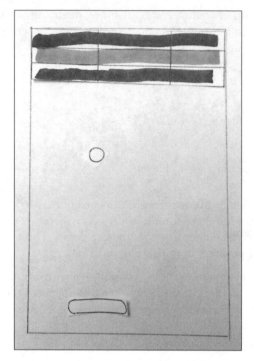

FIGURE 1-1: A pen-and-paper prototype

In the best case, do this with a friend or two. This is especially important for original ideas because you will learn a lot about the flow and gameplay of your game before you write your first line of code. You may discover that the game's rules are difficult to understand or that the game is too easy. You may even realize that the game is just not fun and you have to go back to the drawing board. You are much better off learning this after you spent an hour making paper game pieces as opposed to discovering that your game is not fun after spending weeks or months writing code.

Preparing to Code

When you are convinced that your game is fun and meets the goals stated in your application definition statement, you are just about ready to start working on the software. At this point, I would recommend building a mockup of your game in a graphics or layout program. You can use any program that you are comfortable with such as Illustrator, Photoshop, or OmniGraffle.

Using a graphics editor, you can get a feel for the pixel dimensions of your game objects and see how the objects will relate to each other on screen. You need not be a great artist to do this. The graphics that you build at this point are only for your personal use.

To start, create a new document that matches the screen size and resolution of your target device, as shown in Table 1-1.

TABLE 1-1: Screen Resolution Sizes

DEVICE	RESOLUTION
iPad	1024 × 768
iPhone 4	960 × 640
Other iPhones and iPod touch	480 × 320

Now, start drawing your game graphics and add them to your document. Continue to work with this document to refine the size of your game elements. When you are finished, you will have a file that you can use to estimate the correct size and position for the graphics in your game.

GAME-RELATED FRAMEWORKS

Now that you have a fundamental idea for a game, you need to think about how you will build your game. The iOS technologies that you will use to build games are the primary focus of this book. In this section, I hope to give you a broad overview of the components that you will piece together to build your games. Then, later in the book, you will learn how to implement these components to bring your game to life.

In order to build just about any game, you will need an understanding of several key components: graphics, sound, and user interaction. Without these components, you really cannot create an interesting game. Before you can get into any of that, however, you need to learn about the basic framework that you will use to build any iOS application, game, or otherwise: Cocoa.

Cocoa

The very first step for anyone new to iOS programming is an explanation of Cocoa. According to Apple, "Cocoa is a set of object-oriented frameworks that provides a runtime environment for applications running in Mac OS X and iOS." In its most basic sense, Cocoa is a library of classes that you can use to build your games. Additionally, Cocoa includes the runtime environment that presents the user interface that you see on iOS devices, which enables your games to run.

The libraries in Cocoa encompass everything you need to build just about any program for the iOS platform. In cases where the libraries do not meet your needs, you can extend them to work for you. Cocoa provides the building blocks, which you will combine to build your games.

Cocoa dates back to the NeXT computer company and the late 1980s. Steve Jobs founded NeXT after his first stint at Apple. The Cocoa library was originally called NeXTSTEP. When you learn more about Cocoa in the upcoming chapters, you will see classes like NSString and NSArray. The NS is short for NeXTSTEP.

The Cocoa libraries are written in Objective-C. Objective-C is a superset of the C programming language, which the programmers have extended to include object-oriented features. You will use the Objective-C language with Cocoa throughout this book to build games for iOS. Do not worry if you do not already know C and Objective-C. You will learn more about both languages later on in the book. The important thing to take away here is that you will use the Cocoa frameworks with the Objective-C language to develop games for iOS.

The two most important Cocoa frameworks for building iOS applications are Foundation and UIKit.

The Foundation framework provides many low-level classes that are used in every iOS program, hence the name Foundation. Foundation includes object-oriented versions of base types such as strings and dates; collections such as arrays, dictionaries, and sets; along with utility classes for working with I/O, URLs, autorelease pools, and timers.

The UIKit framework contains the classes that you use to build the user interface of your programs. UIKit contains classes that implement buttons, images, text, tables, search bars, and myriad other user interface widgets. UIKit also provides classes that you can use to handle user interaction such as gesture recognizers and an interface to the hardware accelerometer. UIKit also provides you with the canvas on which you will draw your games: the View.

Figure 1-2 shows how the Cocoa framework fits into the overall picture of the iOS environment. Everything below your game in the figure is provided by iOS.

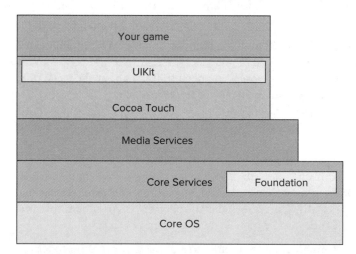

FIGURE 1-2: Cocoa in iOS

At the bottom of the iOS stack is the Core OS. This layer contains the most basic components of the iOS operating system including the Kernel, file system, networking components, and device drivers.

The Core Services layer is built upon the Core OS layer. This layer provides access to the hardware features in the Core OS layer and contains the Foundation framework. As such, this layer provides you with the most basic building blocks that you will need to build any iOS application such as Strings, Arrays, and many other common data types. You will explore the Foundation framework in detail in Chapter 5.

The Media Services layer is next up the stack. The media layer is responsible for providing the graphics and sound APIs that you will use to build your games. These APIs include Core Graphics, Core Animation, and Core Audio. You will learn more about using these APIs to build your game graphics, animation, and sound in Part II of this book.

The highest level APIs in the iOS ecosystem are in the Cocoa Touch layer. This layer includes the UIKit framework, which you learned about earlier. It is atop the Cocoa Touch layer that you build your software.

One of the great things about Cocoa is that it provides frameworks that allow you to work at various levels of abstraction allowing you to choose the level that is right for your application. For example, there are different APIs for drawing graphics that you can choose among based on the complexity of your application. This allows you to use simple APIs when it is appropriate, but gives you the flexibility to work with more powerful and therefore complex APIs when needed.

Drawing: UIKit and Core Graphics

The idea that Cocoa provides different APIs to help you reach your program goals based on the complexity of your application, is evidenced by the drawing APIs. Figure 1-3 shows a simplified stack of the iOS drawing APIs.

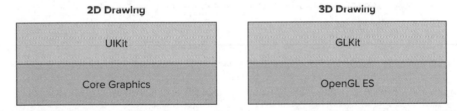

FIGURE 1-3: iOS Drawing APIs

The first choice that you need to make is to determine if you will render your game in 2D or 3D. To keep the examples in this book simple, I have decided to build all of the games in 2D. However, iOS provides excellent support for 3D games.

When you are working with 2D graphics, you should start with the top layer of the 2D graphics stack in Figure 1-3: UIKit. Since UIKit sits atop Core Graphics, it supports most of the features of Core Graphics in a simplified way. Both UIKit and Core Graphics help you create and manipulate Bezier paths, images, bitmaps, colors, and fonts. Core Graphics extends the capabilities in UIKit by giving you the ability to directly work with line attributes, color spaces, pattern colors, gradients, shadings, and image masks.

Since UIKit is built on top of Core Graphics, UIKit and Core Graphics work together seamlessly. This allows you to begin your project by using the easiest API (UIKit) and only dropping down to the lower level API (Core Graphics) when you need access to features that are not supported by UIKit. You will learn to use the 2D APIs in Chapter 6.

If you decide to build a 3D game, iOS has full support for OpenGL ES. OpenGL is a C-based graphics library that you can use to build high-performance 2D and 3D graphics. In iOS 5, Apple has introduced a new framework called GLKit that sits atop the OpenGL ES layer. GLKit promises to simplify certain aspects of 3D development for iOS developers.

Unfortunately, due to the size and scope of the OpenGL ES library, it is beyond the scope of this book. However, I wanted to make you aware of the capability to use OpenGL on iOS. If you build a game by using the native drawing APIs, and discover that the performance is not good enough to support your game, you can migrate your drawing code to OpenGL for a performance boost.

User Interaction: Cocoa Touch

Handling user interaction in iOS is straightforward using the classes in UIKit. Like working with graphics, you can handle user interaction in several ways based on the level of granularity that you need. For example, there are several ways that you can work with a user tapping the screen.

The most straightforward method for handling this sort of input is by using the UIButton class. Buttons provide the capability to react when a player taps them. Therefore, if you are only concerned with when a player taps a button, the simplest solution is to use a button.

If your game demands more precise control of the timing of when the player taps the screen, you can monitor *touch events*. These touch events represent every action that occurs when a player touches the screen. Touch events include the player touching down on the screen, the player moving his finger while touching the screen, and the player lifting his finger from the screen.

A final way of dealing with user interaction with the screen is by using *gesture recognizers*. Gesture recognizers are pre-built classes that you can use to recognize specific motions that are common to iOS, such as pinching and swiping. Instead of having to monitor the touch events to determine if a user is performing a two-finger pinch, you can use a gesture recognizer. The gesture recognizer will collect all of the touch data for you, analyze it, and send a message when it detects that the user has performed a gesture.

You will learn all about using these methods of handling user interaction later in Chapter 7.

I have one final note on user interaction. As you are designing your game, keep in mind some of the other interesting ways that a user can interact with an iOS device aside from touch. iOS devices have a built-in accelerometer, which allows you to determine the physical orientation of the device. Therefore, you can build a game that the user interacts with by moving the actual device. You will learn how to access the accelerometer later as well.

Animation: Core Animation

Another core component of an interesting game is animation.

You perform frame-based animation for real-time action games by drawing each frame individually, with each frame differing slightly from the last. For instance, in the Blocker game that you will build later in the book, you will draw the ball in a slightly different position in each frame, giving your game the illusion of motion.

When you are building games that require precise coordination between the timing of the game and position of the game's objects, you will use frame-based animations. However, if your game is a turn-based game, you may not require this sort of precision. In that case, a much easier way to perform animation is through the Core Animation framework.

Core Animation is the framework behind the animations that you see in the iPhone user interface. You use Core Animation by changing properties on animatable objects. Then, Core Animation automatically animates the changes that you have made. For instance, if you want to animate the movement of an object from one point on the screen to another, you can specify the endpoint and tell Core Animation to move the object.

It is easy to create very complex animations by using Core Animation by linking animations together and performing more than one animation at a time. You will learn to use Core Animation to build a card game in Chapter 8.

Sound: Core Audio

As you have seen with the Drawing and User Interaction APIs, Cocoa provides many ways to achieve your goal. The sound APIs are no different. There are several different sound frameworks that you can use depending on the needs of your application.

The simplest way to play sounds is to use the System Sound Services. System Sound Services is part of the AudioToolbox framework. The purpose of the System Sound Services is to play notifications for UI events such as button clicks, so it is designed to play sounds that are 30 seconds or shorter. This API is very easy to use, so if you are interested in playing only short sound effects, you will want to try using System Sound Services.

When your game requires more than playing sound effects in response to UI actions, you will find yourself moving up to the AV Foundation framework. The AV Foundation framework provides an Objective-C interface with many more options and fewer limitations for playing sounds and video.

Perhaps you want to allow a user to access the music in his iPod library during your game. You can accomplish this by using the Media Player framework. The Media Player framework gives you access to the iPod library along with a rich set of APIs for media playback.

You will learn how to use System Sound, AV Foundation, and The Media Player framework in Chapter 9.

There are other sound APIs in iOS that are even more detailed. Although I will not cover them in this book, they bear mentioning here in case you need them in your game or are simply interested in learning more about them.

First of these APIs is the Audio Toolbox framework. Audio Toolbox is a step deeper than AV Foundation. Using Audio Toolbox, you can precisely synchronize audio playback with your application. This would be especially important in a music simulation game like Rock Band or Guitar Hero where you need the player's action to be in exact sync with the music. You can also use Audio Toolbox to access individual packets of audio, parse audio streams, and record audio at the packet level.

The Audio Unit framework allows your application to host audio processing plug-ins called audio units. There are pre-made audio units for mixing, equalization, format conversion, and real-time input/output. It is even possible to build your own audio units for advanced sound processing.

Finally, you can use the OpenAL framework to create positional-based stereo sound playback. By using OpenAL, you can accurately position the sounds in your game in three-dimensional space.

Game Kit

Each of the frameworks described previously help you to build the basic features of your game: graphics, sound, animation, and user interaction. There is one final framework that you can use to take your games farther and add advanced features that will take your games to the next level. That framework is called Game Kit.

Game Kit enables three core pieces of functionality: Peer-to-peer networking, In-game voice chat, and Game Center.

Peer-to-peer networking lets you set up an ad hoc network between devices. You can use either Bluetooth or a wireless network to enable this communication. The peer-to-peer networking capabilities in Game Kit helps you create a connection between devices running your game and enables you to share information between these devices. The peer-to-peer network framework does not specify the format of the data that you can exchange between the devices on the network, so you have a large amount of flexibility in developing a data format that works for your game.

In-game voice chat enables you to allow players of your game to chat with each other during a game.

Finally, Game Center helps you add a social aspect to your games. Game Center is a social gaming service that includes Leader Boards, Achievements Friends Lists, Turn-based Gaming, and Auto-matching to anonymous players.

You can use Leader Boards and Achievements to repeatedly encourage players to come back to your game. Leader Boards show player scores for your game. Many players will constantly check the leader boards in an effort to outdo their friend's high scores. Achievements are awards that you can give to players for completing certain goals in your game. Players can track their achievements by using Game Center and comparing their achievements to those of their friends.

Turn-Based Gaming lets you set up a game that your players can play over a period of time. Turn-Based Gaming allows your players to compete against each other even if they are not connected to Game Center at the same time. Additionally, the Turn-Based Gaming framework classes support players competing in multiple instances of your game simultaneously.

SUMMARY

In this chapter, you had a brief overview of building games for iOS. First, you looked at the features of iOS that make it a great platform for gaming. Then, you familiarized yourself with the process of developing your idea into a game, including documentation and prototyping. Finally, you took a high-level look at the frameworks that you will learn in this book.

Now that you have an idea of where the book is heading, you are probably itching to get started developing games. Before you can start writing code, however, you first need to take a look at the primary tool that you will be using to write your games: Xcode.

▶ **WHAT YOU LEARNED IN THIS CHAPTER**

TOPIC	MAIN POINTS
Unique features of iOS	Allow players to interact directly with your game by using the touch screen. Integrate features such as the Accelerometer and Gyroscope where appropriate.
Developing your idea	Write an application definition statement to define the concept of your game. Build prototypes of your game by using pencil and paper and graphics software to refine your game idea.
Cocoa framework	Includes fundamental classes that you will use to build all types of iOS applications including games. Support for strings, collections, and other basic programming constructs.
Drawing APIs	In this book, you will use UIKit and Core Graphics for your drawing. iOS supports 3D drawing with OpenGL ES.
User Interaction	The Cocoa Touch framework classes provide support for dealing with user interaction. You can handle complex interactions with Gesture Recognizers.
Animation	You can perform interesting animations to enhance your games by using the Core Animation framework.
Sound	You can use the System Sound Services API to create short sounds for UI actions. For more complex audio, you will use AV Foundation. You can play music from a user's iPod library by using the Media Player framework.
Game Kit	The Game Kit API includes libraries to enable social interaction in your games. You can add interest to your games by enabling leader boards and achievements.

The Xcode Programming Environment

WHAT YOU WILL LEARN IN THIS CHAPTER:

➤ Using Xcode to write and debug programs

➤ Navigating your project's code and assets by using the Navigation area and the Jump bars

➤ Creating and editing code effectively by using the Editor area

➤ Debugging your code by using breakpoints

➤ Stepping through your code and inspecting variable values

➤ Building a simple user interface by using Interface Builder

Once you have the idea for your game planned out and you are ready to start writing code, you need to think about how you are going to get your code into the computer. You could use a simple text editor like emacs, vi, TextEdit, or BB Edit to write your code because code files are just basic ASCII text files. However, there is a better way, the Xcode Integrated Development Environment or IDE.

You may be familiar with using an IDE on other platforms. For example, Visual Studio is the most prevalent IDE for building software based on the .Net platform on Windows. Eclipse is an open source IDE that you can use to develop software in many languages including Java. Xcode is the IDE for building software for the Mac and iOS platform.

Aside from the capabilities of an advanced text editor, a good IDE provides you with additional tools that help you with the software development process. The typical tools include file management, integration with the code compiler, UI design functionality, and debugging features. In this chapter, you will see how Xcode incorporates all of these features to provide you with a top-quality development environment.

I realize that this is a book about writing games and that you are probably very excited to start working on some games. However, you will do all of your development for iOS using the Xcode IDE, so it is very important that you take the time now to learn how to use it. Just as you cannot become a master carpenter without learning about your tools, you cannot become a great iOS developer without learning about Xcode. The time that you spend learning Xcode now will help you to develop and debug your code for years to come.

THE CODING ENVIRONMENT

In order to build applications for the iPhone, you will use Apple's Xcode integrated development environment (IDE). Xcode is a powerful integrated development environment that has all of the features of a modern IDE. It integrates many powerful features including code editing, debugging, version control, and software profiling.

You can obtain a copy of Xcode from the Mac App Store by selecting "App Store..." from the Apple menu in the menu bar and searching the store for Xcode. At the time of this writing, Xcode is a free download from the App Store.

Once you have your copy of Xcode and you start it up for the first time, you will see the "Welcome to Xcode" window as you can see in Figure 2-1.

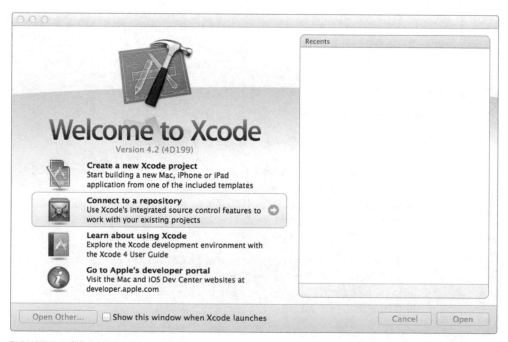

FIGURE 2-1: Welcome to Xcode!

The welcome screen offers you options to create a new project, connect to a source code repository, jump into the Xcode documentation, or log on to Apple's developer portal. The screen also shows a list of your recent projects so that you can quickly get back to your most recent work. You can prevent this dialog from showing each time that you open Xcode by unchecking the box at the bottom of the window that says, "Show this window when Xcode launches."

It is easiest to show how Xcode works by working with it. Therefore, in the next section, you will create a very simple project in Xcode to get you started.

Creating a Project

In this section, you will get started with Xcode by creating a new project and building a very simple program.

Start up Xcode and select "Create a new Xcode project" from the "Welcome to Xcode" window. If you have already dismissed the welcome window or if you have chosen not to show the welcome window when Xcode starts, select New ⇨ New Project ... from the File menu.

After choosing to start a new project, Xcode will present a dialog box asking you to choose a template for your new project as you can see in Figure 2-2. This dialog shows you all of the templates that you have installed for the various types of coding projects that you will likely undertake.

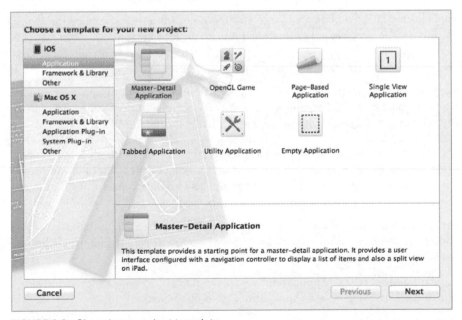

FIGURE 2-2: Choosing a project template

Xcode divides the left side of the dialog into sections for templates for building software for iOS and for Mac OS X. Since you are reading this book, you are probably most interested in developing games for iOS. So, you will generally choose among the templates presented in the top section.

Xcode divides the iOS templates into three groups: Application, Framework & Library, and Other.

The Application group consists of the following templates:

➤ **Master-Detail Application:** This template provides a starting point for a master-detail application. It provides a user interface configured with a navigation controller to display a list of items and also a split view on iPad. You probably will not use this template for game development.

➤ **OpenGL Game:** This template provides a starting point for an OpenGL ES-based game. It provides a view into which you render your OpenGL ES scene, and a timer to allow you to animate the view. Game developers commonly use OpenGL ES for game development, but using OpenGL ES to develop games is beyond the scope of this book.

➤ **Page-Based Application:** This template provides a starting point for a page-based application that uses a page view controller. You will generally not use this template for games.

➤ **Single View Application:** This template provides a starting point for an application that uses a single view. It provides a view controller to manage the view, and a storyboard or nib file that contains the view. Because of its simplicity, you will use this template for most of the games in this book.

➤ **Tabbed Application:** This template provides a starting point for an application that uses a tab bar. It provides a user interface configured with a tab bar controller, and view controllers for the tab bar items. You will not generally use this template for games.

➤ **Utility Application:** This template provides a starting point for a utility application that has a main view and an alternate view. For iPhone, it sets up an Info button to flip the main view to the alternate view. For iPad, it sets up an Info bar button that shows the alternate view in a popover. You will not generally use this template for games.

➤ **Empty Application:** This template provides a starting point for any application. It provides just an application delegate and a window. You can use this template if you want to build your game entirely from scratch without very much template code.

The Framework & Library template set consists of a single template: Cocoa Touch Static Library. You can use this template to build static libraries of code that link against the Foundation framework. You will not use this template in this book. However, this template is useful for building libraries of code that you can share amongst multiple projects.

The Other template set also consists of only a single template: Empty. The Empty template is just an empty project waiting for you to fill it up with code. You will not use this template in this book, but it is useful if you want to start a new project and none of the existing templates are appropriate.

In the Choose Template dialog, select "Application" under the iOS section on the left-hand side. Then, in the right pane, select "Single View Application," and click Next.

The next dialog asks you to choose some options for your new project.

The Product Name is self-explanatory. Come up with a clever name for your project and type it into the Product Name text box. I used FirstProgram.

The company identifier identifies your company. Usually you would use the reverse of your company's domain name, for example, com.google, but you can really put anything that you want in here. I use com.patalessi, but you should use your own name.

The device family drop-down defines the device for which you want to write your program, the iPhone, iPad, or Universal. Universal applications work on both the iPhone and the iPad. For this example, select iPhone.

The Use Storyboard checkbox enables you to storyboard your application. Storyboarding lets you use Interface Builder to lay out all of the screens in your program and define the transitions between them. You will not use storyboarding for this example, so ensure that the Use Storyboard checkbox is not checked.

The Use Automatic Reference Counting checkbox enables automatic reference counting for your application. You will learn about memory management and reference counting in Chapter 4. For now, just ensure that this box is checked.

The Include Unit Tests checkbox allows you to include unit test code with your project. Unit tests are useful for testing the logic of your program. Since you will not be using unit tests in this example, ensure that the Include Unit Tests checkbox is not checked, and then click Next.

Next, Xcode will prompt you for a location to save your program. Pick a location that you will remember because this is where all of your source code will be stored.

Uncheck the "Create local git repository for this project," checkbox. A git repository stores your source code and version control information. An in-depth examination of git and source code control is beyond the scope of this book. You can read more about source control and git in the Xcode 4 user guide. In particular, there is a section called, "Keep Track of Changes with Source Control" at http://developer.apple.com/library/mac/#documentation/ ToolsLanguages/Conceptual/Xcode4UserGuide/SCM/SCM.html.

Finally, click Create, and Xcode will create your new project.

Believe it or not, you have just created your first functioning iOS program. Pretty nice considering that you have not even typed in a line of code yet; unfortunately, it does not do anything except display a gray screen. If you select Product ➪ Run from the menu bar, the iOS Simulator will launch and run your new app. The simulator should look like Figure 2-3.

FIGURE 2-3: iOS Simulator running your program

You use the iOS simulator to run iOS programs on your computer. You can specify whether to use the iPhone simulator or the iPad simulator in the scheme dropdown at the top of the Xcode interface. The simulator uses the resources of your computer to run, so you should be aware that the results of running your games in the simulator are not identical to what you see when running your games on a device. This is especially important to realize in game development because you will see far greater performance in the simulator than you will see on a device. This applies to both the game logic, which is CPU dependent, and to graphics operations which are GPU dependent. As a result, you should absolutely test your games on actual devices as much as possible during the development process, particularly when you are doing performance testing.

Navigating Your Project

Now that you have created your first Xcode project, you are ready to take a closer look at the IDE. With all of the Views open and the editor set to show the Assistant editor, your screen will look like Figure 2-4, but without the color and labels.

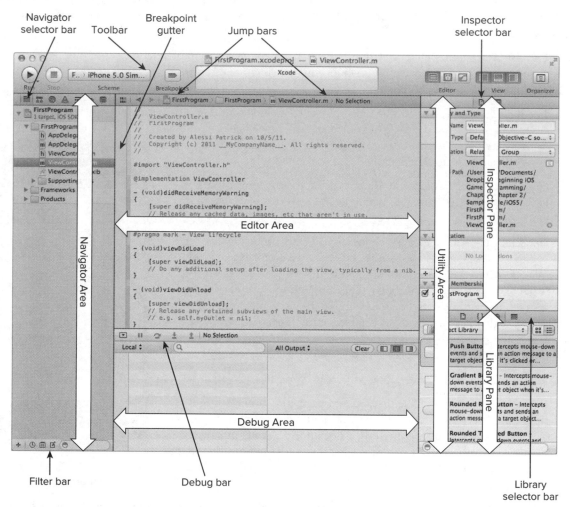

FIGURE 2-4: The Xcode interface

The Navigator Area

The first bit of the IDE that you will explore is the Navigator area, shown in blue on the left side of Figure 2-4. The Navigator simplifies navigation through various aspects of your project. The selector bar at the top of the navigator area allows you to select the specific area that you want to navigate. There are seven different navigators that you can use.

The first icon in the Navigator selector bar represents the Project Navigator. You use the Project Navigator to view the files that are part of your project. You can organize your files in folders and use the Project Navigator to drill down through these folders to get to the file that you want to edit.

Whatever item you select in the Project Navigator appears in the Editor area. Selecting a source code file (a file with the .m extension) will result in Xcode opening that file in the Editor area. If you select a user interface file (a file with the .xib extension), Interface Builder will open in the Editor area allowing you to work on the user interface file. You will learn more about Interface Builder later on in this chapter.

You can change various configuration settings for your project by selecting the project node at the top of the Project Navigator to open the project settings in the Editor area. You can try navigation by using the FirstProgram project by selecting various files in the Project Navigator and observing what Xcode displays in the Editor area.

There is also another way to navigate to files in your project by using the Jump bars at the top of the Editor window. You will learn about using the Jump bars in the section on editing your code later in this chapter.

Navigating by Symbol

The second icon is the Symbol Navigator. The Symbol Navigator allows you to navigate through your project based not on source code file, but by the symbols or program units themselves. In the Symbol Navigator, your code is organized by class. Each class in your project is like a folder with all of its methods underneath. Do not worry if you do not understand the terms *class* and *method*, you will learn more about them in Chapter 4. For now, just keep in mind that by using the Symbol Navigator, you can navigate directly to the class header or method that you want to work on by clicking the method name regardless of which source code file contains the method.

You can try this by using the FirstProgram project by opening a class in the Symbol Navigator and clicking on a method name. To see this in action, switch to the Symbol Navigator and expand the `ViewController` class by clicking on the arrow next to the class name. Then, click on the `-viewDidUnload` method under the `ViewController`. The Editor area should automatically switch to the `ViewController.m` source code file and highlight the `-(void)viewDidUnload` method.

Searching Your Code

The third icon is the Search Navigator. As you might expect, you use this navigator to execute searches on your code. You can type a search term in the blank text field at the top of the window and Xcode will display the search results below. If you click on the magnifying glass icon in the search field, you can turn on more search options by selecting, "Show Find Options," along with revisiting your recent searches. Clicking on any search result takes you to the point in your code where the result occurs. Figure 2-5 shows the results of a search of the FirstProgram project for the word "First." Feel free to experiment by searching through your FirstProgram project for various words and phrases.

FIGURE 2-5: Search Navigator results

Viewing Code Issues

The fourth option in the Navigator area is the Issue Navigator. This navigator informs you of any issues with your program. If Xcode discovers any issues with your code as you are typing, Xcode will report them in the Issue Navigator. Additionally, Xcode displays compiler errors and warnings in the Issue Navigator. To demonstrate, use the Project Navigator to open the `ViewController.m` file in the Editor area. In the `-(void)viewDidUnload` method under the line that reads `[super viewDidUnload];` add this bit of code:

```
[super noMethod];
```

Before you even attempt to compile your program, Xcode will report a problem in the Issue Navigator as you can see in Figure 2-6.

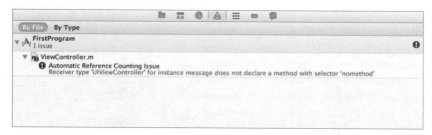

FIGURE 2-6: Issues reported in the Issue Navigator

The issue is an Automatic Reference Counting Issue. In the line of code, `[super noMethod]`, you tried calling the `noMethod` method on the `super` object. However, the `noMethod` method does not exist. Xcode warns you of this in the Issue Navigator with a message saying that the receiver does not declare the instance message that you are trying to call.

Clicking on an item in the Issue Navigator opens the appropriate code file and highlights the issue that it has identified. This makes it very easy to jump from issue to issue in your code, fixing them as you go along. Delete the new code that you added above and you will see the issue disappear from the Issue Navigator.

Examining Logs

The next two navigators are the Debug and Breakpoint Navigators. You will learn about how to use these panes in the section on debugging your programs later in this chapter.

The final navigator is the Log Navigator. You can find all of the Xcode log files in this pane. Xcode generates a log each time you build or run your program. You can click on any log in the list to open the log in the Editor area. Examining the build log can be helpful in tracking down problems when building your program. The Debug logs contain any output that your program sends to the console.

You can toggle showing or hiding the Navigator area by clicking the first icon in the View toolbar on the top right side of the Xcode window. You can also use the keyboard shortcut CMD-0 to do the same. You can also use the keyboard shortcuts CMD-1 through CMD-7 to change the

Navigator area to any one of the navigator panes that you have seen. You can also change navigators by using the View ⇨ Navigators menu from the menu bar.

Editing Your Code

Now that you know how to navigate to the files in your project, you need to know how to edit them. Xcode offers many features that can help you to write your code. These include: automatic code formatting with code coloring and indentation, code completion, and online documentation. Code completion and correction help you to identify the methods and functions that are available to you in context, helping you to avoid mistakes. The online documentation provides easy access to detailed information about the APIs in iOS. Let us look at each of these features in more detail.

Code Coloring

Open the FirstProgram project that you created in the last section. By default, the project navigator should be open in the left-hand pane of Xcode. If it is not, you can press CMD-1 or select View ⇨ Navigators ⇨ Show Project Navigator from the menu bar. In the project navigator pane, click on ViewController.m and you will see some of your program's source code in the editor area. The code should look like this:

```
#import "ViewController.h"

@implementation ViewController

- (void)didReceiveMemoryWarning
{
    [super didReceiveMemoryWarning];
    // Release any cached data, images, etc that aren't in use.
}

#pragma mark - View lifecycle

- (void)viewDidLoad
{
    [super viewDidLoad];
    // Do any additional setup after loading the view, typically from a nib.
}

- (void)viewDidUnload
{
    [super viewDidUnload];

    // Release any retained subviews of the main view.
    // e.g. self.myOutlet = nil;
}

- (void)viewWillAppear:(BOOL)animated
{
    [super viewWillAppear:animated];
}

- (void)viewDidAppear:(BOOL)animated
```

```
{
    [super viewDidAppear:animated];
}

- (void)viewWillDisappear:(BOOL)animated
{
    [super viewWillDisappear:animated];
}

- (void)viewDidDisappear:(BOOL)animated
{
    [super viewDidDisappear:animated];
}

- (BOOL)shouldAutorotateToInterfaceOrientation:
(UIInterfaceOrientation)interfaceOrientation
{
    // Return YES for supported orientations
    return (interfaceOrientation != UIInterfaceOrientationPortraitUpsideDown);
}

@end
```

The first thing that you should notice is how the code coloring helps you to identify the elements of your code. I have used the default code coloring scheme, but you can change the scheme or individual element colors by choosing Xcode ➪ Preferences... from the menu bar and selecting the Fonts & Colors button at the top of the preferences dialog.

You may be unfamiliar with the syntax, so do not worry too much about that right now. You will learn all about the C and Objective-C languages in upcoming chapters.

If you start at the top of the code, you will see that preprocessor statements like #import and #pragma are colored brown. The compiler does not compile these statements into your code. These directives serve as directions to the compiler's preprocessor.

Next, you should see that Xcode colors literal strings, or text, in your code red, like the text, "ViewController.h" in the first line. Xcode colors C and Objective-C language keywords like void and @implementation magenta. Non-executable text and comments like // Release any cached data, images, etc that aren't in use. are green.

Indentation and Snippets

Another nice feature of the text editor is the indentation. You can customize the indentation of your code in the Text Editing preference by using the Indentation tab. Xcode automatically indents your code to help make it easier to read.

You can force Xcode to re-indent sections of code by highlighting them and selecting Editor ➪ Structure ➪ Re-Indent from the menu bar.

Xcode will automatically indent your code as you type according to the syntax of your code. For example, programmers typically indent the code inside the braces in loops to visually separate the code that is executing in a loop.

Another nice feature is that Xcode will provide automatic code snippets to help you to write common code. To illustrate these points, type the word **for** in the `viewDidLoad` method after the line `[super viewDidLoad];`. As soon as you type the letter r in `for`, you should see something that looks like Figure 2-7.

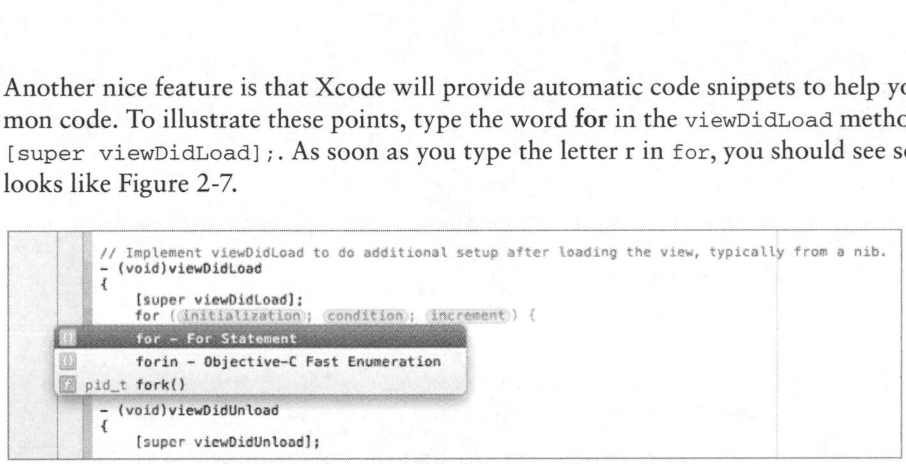

FIGURE 2-7: A code snippet for the `for` statement

While the code snippet is visible, press the Enter key to indicate that you would like to add the snippet to your code. You will see that Xcode highlights the initialization parameter. This shows you that Xcode is waiting for you to type in the initialization code for the `for` statement. Do not worry about how `for` statements work, you will learn about them in the next chapter. For now, just focus on how you can use the text editor to quickly write your code.

Type the text **int**. You will see another drop-down appear below that text that you have typed. This is the autocomplete feature. Xcode is providing you with a list of items that it thinks that you may want to insert into your code. Type a space to ignore the list and continue typing the text **i=0**.

To move on to the next element in the code snippet, the condition, press the Tab key. After you press Tab, you should see the condition highlighted. Type the letter i because you want to use the variable i that you declared in the initialization in your condition. After you type the i, you will see another autocomplete box. At the top is the variable i that you just created, denoted by the green letter V in the box at the left of the autocomplete box. Continue typing **<100** to complete your condition.

Press the Tab key again to move on to the increment. Type **i++** as the increment to add one to the value of the variable i each time through the loop.

Finally, press Tab again to move down into the statements that you want to execute each time through the loop. Type the following code:

```
NSLog(@"%i",i);
```

This statement logs the counter i to the debug console.

Your code should look like this:

```
- (void)viewDidLoad
{
    [super viewDidLoad];
    for (int i=0; i<100; i++) {
        NSLog(@"%i",i);
    }
}
```

Run your program by clicking the Run button at the top left corner of the Xcode window. Your program will still display a grey screen in the iOS simulator, but you should see the following text in the Debug area at the bottom of the screen:

```
2011-08-01 17:24:35.198 FirstProgram[1106:ef03] 0
2011-08-01 17:24:35.199 FirstProgram[1106:ef03] 1
2011-08-01 17:24:35.199 FirstProgram[1106:ef03] 2
2011-08-01 17:24:35.200 FirstProgram[1106:ef03] 3
...
2011-08-01 17:24:35.311 FirstProgram[1106:ef03] 96
2011-08-01 17:24:35.311 FirstProgram[1106:ef03] 97
2011-08-01 17:24:35.312 FirstProgram[1106:ef03] 98
2011-08-01 17:24:35.312 FirstProgram[1106:ef03] 99
```

You should notice how Xcode indented the NSLog statement inside of the braces {} of the for loop. Xcode will attempt to intelligently indent your code to make it easier to read.

Fix-it

Another particularly nice feature of Xcode is "Fix-it." Xcode will flag problems with your code as you type and offer to fix mistakes that it finds. Below the closing brace (}) for the for loop that you just wrote, add the following, incorrect, code:

```
ins n = 10;
```

You (purposely) mistakenly typed ins instead of int. Xcode recognizes this as a potential problem and puts a little, hollow, red octagon in the left-hand gutter of the editor window. Xcode also adds a red squiggle below the code that it believes is incorrect, just as you would see in a word processor like Microsoft Word under an incorrectly spelled word. If you click on the red octagon, you will see a popover appear as in Figure 2-8.

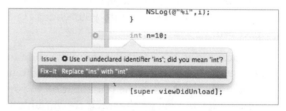

FIGURE 2-8: A Fix-it popover

This popover tells you that Xcode has found an issue. The issue is that you have used an undeclared identifier ins and Xcode believes that you may have meant int. Below, Xcode proposes to replace ins with int. If you press the Enter key to accept the correction, Xcode will replace the incorrect ins with the correct int.

If you are new to Xcode, I recommend that you type in the first few programs in this book as opposed to just downloading the source from the book's website. Typing the code will help you to get familiar with Xcode's text editing features including autocomplete and Fix-it.

Integrated Help

Another interesting feature of the Xcode editor is the integrated help system. You can get a quick help popover at any time by placing the cursor on a particular code element and pressing CTRL-CMD-? or by selecting Help ⇨ Quick Help for Selected Item from the menu bar. If you put the cursor in the code NSLog and press CTRL-CMD-?, you will see the quick help popover as in Figure 2-9.

FIGURE 2-9: Quick help popover

The quick help provides the name of the function, its declaration, which iOS versions support it, a short description of the method, the header in which the function is declared and a link to the complete reference documentation.

You can also keep quick help open all the time by opening the Utility area and displaying the Quick Help pane. You can do this by clicking the right-hand icon in the View toolbar and clicking the second icon in the Inspector selector bar. You can achieve the same thing by selecting View ➪ Utilities ➪ Show Quick Help Inspector from the menu bar. The quick help inspector shows the quick help information for the code at your cursor position. Try opening the Quick Help pane and moving the cursor around to various bits of your code. You should see the information in the pane change depending on the code under the cursor.

Using the Jump Bars

In the preceding section, you learned about using the Navigation area to find and open your source code files. You can also navigate your code by using the Jump bar at the top of the Editor area. Open the FirstProgram project and navigate to the ViewController.m file by using the navigation area. The jump bar at the top of the Editor area should look like Figure 2-10.

FIGURE 2-10: The Jump bar

The Jump bar shows the hierarchy that you have navigated to get to the code displayed in the Editor area. In this case, the ViewController.m file in the Editor area is contained in the project FirstProgram, in the FirstProgram folder, and the filename is ViewController.m.

The beauty of the Jump bar is that you can click on any heading in the bar to navigate from that point onward in a treelike manner. For example, if you click on the ViewController.m filename, you will see a list of all of the files that are at that point in the file hierarchy. You can easily switch to the AppDelegate.m file by selecting it from the Jump bar drop-down. You can also navigate directly to a method by clicking the text at the end of the Jump bar where it says, "No Selection," in Figure 2-10.

The Assistant Editor

As you will see in the upcoming chapters on C and Objective-C, a code file typically has an associated counterpart called a header file. You will often find yourself switching back and forth between the header and code files. Xcode makes this easy because it has the ability to show you your files side-by-side. In fact, the Xcode Assistant editor is smart enough to show you the corresponding file for whatever file you have open in the main editor area.

Open the ViewController.m code file in your FirstProgram project. Next, click on the tuxedo icon in the editor toolbar at the top right corner of the Xcode window or select View ⇨ Assistant Editor ⇨ Show Assistant Editor from the menu bar. Xcode will split the Editor area into two panes with your original code (.m) file on the left side and the corresponding header (.h) file on the right side.

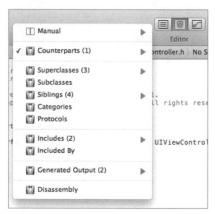

If you look in the Jump bar in the right-hand pane, you will see that the first entry in the Jump bar says, "Counterparts." This indicates that the Assistant editor is showing the counterpart to the file in the main editor. In addition to intelligently displaying a file's counterpart, you can also display various other files intelligently by clicking on the Counterparts label in the jump bar as you can see in Figure 2-11.

FIGURE 2-11: Other assistant editor options

You can verify that the Assistant editor is intelligently showing the main window's counterpart by changing the file in the main window. Select the file AppDelegate.h in the Navigator area and you will see the file AppDelegate.m displayed in the Assistant editor. This is because you chose to edit the header file and the Assistant is displaying its counterpart, the code file.

In addition to using the intelligent functionality, you can also select a file to display manually in the Assistant editor by selecting, "Manual" from the first element in the Assistant editor's jump bar. Then, you can just manually navigate to the file that you want to see in the Assistant editor. Holding down the option key and selecting a file in the Navigator area also opens that file in the Assistant editor.

Another nice feature of the assistant editor is that you can easily split the Assistant editor into multiple windows by clicking on the plus icon in the top right corner of the Assistant editor. You can also split each sub-window so you can have as many assistant editors open as you have room for on your screen. Figure 2-12 shows the ViewController.m file open in the main editor and each of its three superclasses open in individual panes in the Assistant editor.

FIGURE 2-12: Multiple panes open in the Assistant editor

XCODE DEBUGGING TOOLS

After you have written your code, you will need to run and debug it. To effectively debug your code, you will want to be able to step through your code line-by-line as it runs. It is also helpful to be able to stop execution at any time to inspect the values of variables in your program. Xcode provides these basic features and expands upon them with some excellent tools to help you find and fix the problems with your code.

Breaking and Stepping through Your Code

When you are trying to fix problems in your code, it is nice to be able to stop the code during execution to see what is going on. You can accomplish this in Xcode by using breakpoints.

You can place breakpoints in your code to stop execution at any point. Once you have stopped execution, you can view the values stored in your variables. When you understand the current state, you can then step through your code line-by-line using the debugger and watching as the values of your variables change.

The easiest way to place a breakpoint is by clicking in the Breakpoint gutter on the left side of the Editor area as you can see in Figure 2-4. After you have created a breakpoint, that breakpoint will be visible in the Breakpoint navigator. The Breakpoint navigator lists all of the breakpoints in your program.

To illustrate how to use the debugger, open Xcode and open the FirstProgram program that you created earlier in this chapter. Open the `ViewController.m` file and find the `viewDidLoad` method. Click in the left margin or Breakpoint gutter on the line that says `for (int i=0; i<100; i++)`. You should see a little blue icon appear in the Breakpoint gutter as you can see in Figure 2-13. This icon indicates that you have set a breakpoint on this line. If you open the Breakpoint navigator in the Navigator area, you will see the breakpoint listed in the navigator. The next time that you run your program, execution will stop on that line.

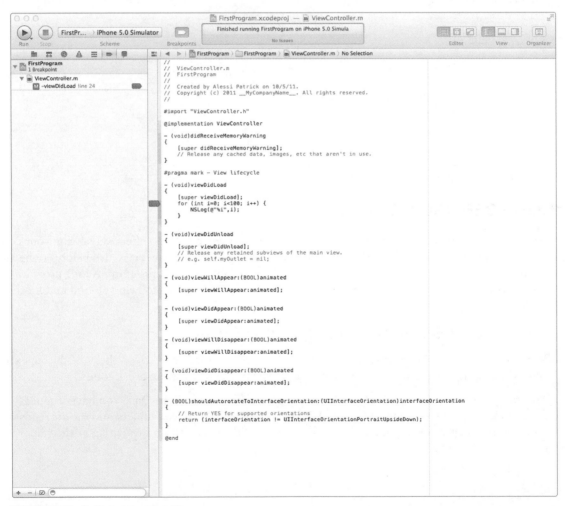

FIGURE 2-13: Setting a breakpoint

Now you are ready to re-run your program and see your breakpoint in action. Click the Run button at the top left corner of the Xcode window. When your code gets to the line on which you have placed a breakpoint, Xcode will pause execution. Xcode will also automatically reconfigure your environment to one that is more conducive to debugging. You can see the default debugging environment in Figure 2-14.

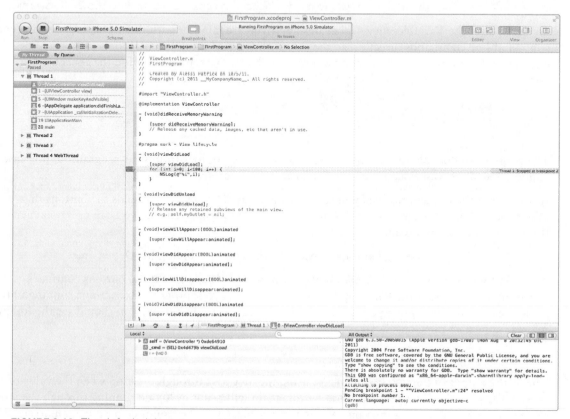

FIGURE 2-14: The default debugging environment

First, you will notice that Xcode has changed the Navigator area to the Debugging navigator. This navigator provides a list of the current threads in your application. Each thread shows its call stack. The *call stack* is the list of functions that you have called in your program, in reverse order. At the bottom of the stack in Figure 2-14, you can see the main method. This is the entry point for C and Objective-C programs, so it is the last method in the list. At the top of the call stack is the viewDidLoad method, which is where you have placed your breakpoint. Clicking on any method or function name in the call stack will take you to the source code for that method. If source code is not available, Xcode will show you the assembly code for the function.

At the bottom of the Debug navigator is a slider that you can use to control the amount of detail in the thread view. Sliding the slider to the left will show fewer methods, and hide the ones that Xcode thinks are less important. Sliding the slider to the right will show you all of the functions in the call stack.

Moving on to the Editor area, you will see a little green icon on top of your blue breakpoint icon. The green icon is the instruction pointer and it shows you the line of code that Xcode is about to execute. In the right-hand margin, you can see a tip that helps point this out.

Below the Editor area, you can see the Debug area. On the left side of the Debug area, you can see the Variables view. You can use the Variables view to inspect all of the variables in your program. By default, the Variables view shows only the variables that are local to the function where execution has stopped. You can use the pull down where it says, "Local" to change the view to show all variables.

To the right of the Variables view is the console. If you are familiar with the debugger, you can type command-line commands directly into the console instead of using the GUI tools in Xcode. For example, you can use the po command to print an object. Try typing **po self** in the console window to print out the self object. You should see something like this:

```
(gdb) po self
<ViewController: 0x7864370>
(gdb)
```

The console window also shows any command-line output or logs from your program. In this case, you will see all of your NSLog statements appear in the console.

At the top of the Debug area, you will see the Debug bar. The Debug bar holds the buttons that allow you to control the execution of your code as well as a jump bar that you can use to navigate through your code by thread.

The first button in the Debug bar toggles between showing and hiding the Debug area.

The next four buttons control execution of your program. The first of those buttons continues execution of your program. Clicking this button will cause your program to continue running until Xcode reaches the next breakpoint. Click the Continue execution button. You should see the following text appear in the Console area:

```
2011-08-01 19:54:37.879 FirstProgram[1479:ef03] 0
```

This is the output of the NSLog statement during the first pass through the loop when the value of i is zero. Clicking the Continue execution button again will result in Xcode running through the loop one more time and printing the value of 1 in the console. Click the Continue button again to see this. You should also notice that the value of the variable i is changing in the Variables area.

The next button in the Debug bar is the Step over button. This button allows you to step line-by-line through your code, stepping over calls to external functions. This means that Xcode will execute any function call and continue to the next line of code in the module that you are looking at. Contrast this with the next button, the Step into button, which will move Xcode into the function that is called to allow you to debug it. You will learn more about functions in the next chapter.

Click the Step over button. You should notice that Xcode has executed the line where you placed your breakpoint and has moved the instruction pointer to the next line. To verify this, you can check the Variables window and see that the value of i has been incremented to two. Click the Step over button again to have Xcode execute the NSLog statement. You should see the value of 2 printed out to the Console. Since the loop is finished, Xcode will move the instruction pointer back to the top of the loop for its next time through. Continue clicking the Step over button to iterate through the loop and see the variable i change in the variables area and the log statements printed to the Console. This is how you step thorough your code line-by-line to watch it work.

If you are finished using a breakpoint, you can delete it by grabbing the breakpoint icon and dragging it out of the Editor area. The breakpoint will disappear in a puff of smoke. If you think that you may want to break at that point in your code later, you can deactivate a breakpoint by clicking on the icon. You will see that the breakpoint icon becomes a hollow outline indicating that the breakpoint is disabled. Click on the breakpoint again to re-enable it.

Additional Breakpoint Features

As you learned in the last section, you use breakpoints to pause the execution of your program anywhere you want. There is a problem though. Imagine that you have a loop that runs millions of times, and the bug that you are trying to fix happens toward the end of the loop. You really do not want to sit there clicking the Step over button a million times. Fortunately, Xcode has some advanced features that you can use to modify when breakpoints pause your code and what they do once the code is paused.

Place a breakpoint on the NSLog statement in the viewDidLoad method of the ViewController.m file. Now, option-click on the breakpoint. You should see a popup appear as in Figure 2-15.

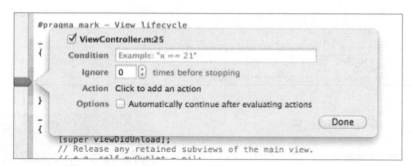

FIGURE 2-15: Edit Breakpoint popup

This popup allows you to edit the attributes of your breakpoint. At the top of the popup, you can add a condition that will cause the breakpoint to pause your code if the condition is true. To see this in action, type the condition i==90 into the condition box, click the Done button, and run your program. You should see the numbers from zero through 89 printed to the debug console. You should also notice that the value of i is 90 in the Variables view. Xcode has run your code until the condition that you specified in the breakpoint was true.

Below the Condition box in the Edit Breakpoint popup in Figure 2-15, you can see an Ignore option. Using this feature, you can tell Xcode to ignore the breakpoint the first n times that the debugger hits the breakpoint. To demonstrate this feature, remove the condition that you added in the previous demo and set the Ignore value to 30. Here, you are telling Xcode to break every time, by removing the condition, but to ignore the breakpoint 30 times. Run your program to see the effect of this change.

The next option in the edit breakpoint popup allows you to have Xcode execute an action when the debugger hits your breakpoint. You can tell Xcode to play a sound, run a debugger command, write a log entry, or even execute a shell script or AppleScript. This feature comes in very handy when you do not want to sprinkle NSLog statements throughout your code. To see this in action, reset the ignore count in the popup to zero. Then, select the Log Message action from the Action drop-down menu. Enter the text **The value of i: @i@** in the Message box. This will cause the debugger to print the text message and the actual value of the variable i each time that you hit the breakpoint. Run your program and step through execution several times and you should see output like this in the console window:

```
The value of i: 0
2011-08-01 19:42:50.386 FirstProgram[3167:ef03] 0
The value of i: 1
2011-08-01 19:42:52.354 FirstProgram[3167:ef03] 1
The value of i: 2
2011-08-01 19:42:55.047 FirstProgram[3167:ef03] 2
The value of i: 3
```

You can combine the Condition and Action in interesting ways too. Try adding a breakpoint to the NSLog statement with the condition i%10==0 and the log message "@i@ is divisible by 10." Run the application and you will see that every time that the value of i is divisible by 10, Xcode breaks and prints your message to the log. Here, you used the modulus operator (%) to determine if the variable was divisible by 10 and to break accordingly.

If you want to further speed things up, you can check the "Automatically continue after evaluating actions" checkbox. This will cause Xcode to evaluate your condition each time through the loop, print out the message if i is divisible by 10, and then just continue running without even stopping! If you run your program now, you will see that Xcode blows through your loop, telling you each time that i is divisible by 10 without ever stopping at the breakpoint.

BUILDING A SIMPLE INTERFACE

Besides providing tools for writing and debugging your code, Xcode gives you a graphical way to lay out your user interfaces. The tool that you use to build interfaces is called, logically, Interface Builder. In this section, you will learn how to use Interface Builder to build the very simple program that you see in Figure 2-16.

The label at the top of the application will display a number. When the user taps the button below, you will increment the number and move the slider below to the appropriate position. When the user moves the slider, you will update the number. It is not much to look at nor is it very exciting, but it will serve to teach you the basics of creating interfaces and tying the interface to your code.

Before you get starting building the sample program, you need to learn a little about how the interface that you create in Interface Builder communicates with your code. The two important concepts are actions and outlets.

In Xcode, *actions* represent what you want your code to do in response to user interaction with a control or widget. For example, when a user taps a button, you want to take the action of running a

FIGURE 2-16: Simple Interface Builder project

particular function or method. In the case of the example program in Figure 2-16, you will create an action to increment a counter and update the label with the new value.

The other way to tie your code to the interface is through *outlets*. Outlets connect your interface to the code by letting you refer to the items in your interface by name. When you create outlets, you create variables in your code that you can use to work with the UI widgets. In the case of the sample program, you will create an outlet for the label that will allow you to update its contents through your code.

You will use both an action and an outlet with the slider at the bottom of the program. You will need an action because you want to respond to the user sliding the slider by changing the value of the label. You will need an outlet because when the user taps the button to increment the value, you need to change the value of the slider in your code.

TRY IT OUT **Building a Simple Interface Application**

codefile SampleUI available for download at Wrox.com

In this example, you will build a simple application that uses interface widgets to change the value of a counter label. You will learn how to use Interface Builder to add the widgets to your application. Then, you will learn how to write the code that works with the widgets.

1. To begin, start up Xcode and select File ➪ New ➪ New Project. A dialog box appears that displays templates for the various types of applications that you can create for the iPhone and Mac OS X. For this sample project, you are going to use the Single View Application template. Select Single View Application from the dialog box, and click the Next button.

2. In the Product Name text box, type the name of your project, **SampleUI**. Uncheck the "Include Unit Tests" and "Use Storyboard" checkboxes, and select "iPhone" from the Device Family drop down. Click Next.

3. Click ViewController.xib to see the UI for the project. The .xib file contains the user interface for the view that displays your application.

4. Open the Utility area by clicking the third button in the View section of the toolbar in the top right side of Xcode. The utility area contains the Inspector pane at the top and the Library pane at the bottom. You use the Inspector pane to view information about the current file. The Library pane contains panels with code snippets, new file templates, media files, and most importantly for this example, UI Objects.

5. In the Library pane at the bottom of the Utility area, click on the third icon in the Library selector bar to display the Object library. The Object library is a set of objects that you can use in conjunction with Interface Builder to build your interfaces. You can see the Object library, with the controls that you need for this project highlighted, in Figure 2-17.

6. Drag a Label object out of the Object library and place it on the View at the top. You can see the label control in Figure 2-17.

7. Drag a Round Rect button object out of the Object library and place it on the View below the label. Double-click on the button and type the text **Press** to add a label to the button.

Label Control   Round Rect Button   Slider

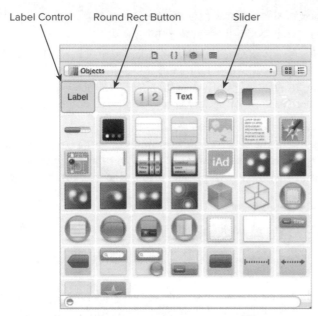

FIGURE 2-17: The Object library, showing the controls for this project

8. Drag a Slider object out of the Object library and place it on the View.

9. While the slider is still selected and active, switch the Inspector pane to the Attributes inspector by clicking the fourth button in the Inspector selector bar. At the top of the Attributes inspector, you will see the default values for the slider. Use the Attributes inspector to set the Maximum value for the slider to 100 and set the Current value to zero.

10. You are now finished adding all of the UI elements from the Object library to your program. You can close the Utility area if you need more room on your screen to continue working.

11. Open the Assistant editor by clicking the second button in the top right corner of the Xcode window. It looks like a little tuxedo. The Assistant window will allow you to look at your header file and your interface at the same time. This makes it very easy to add your outlets and actions to your code, as you will see in the next step.

12. As I mentioned before, to link the controls that you added to your user interface to your code, you use outlets and actions. Since you want to be able to update the label through your code, you have to add an outlet for the label. Hold down the Control key and drag the label from the Interface Builder into the interface header code in the assistant editor. You will see a line drawn from IB to the code and a popup will appear that says Insert Outlet or Outlet Collection as you can see in Figure 2-18. Let go of the mouse button under the line that says @interface, and you will see a popup that allows you to configure the outlet. Leave the connection as Outlet. Type the name **myLabel** in the Name field and click the Connect button.

13. You create actions in the same way by using Control-drag. Create the action for the button by control-dragging it into the @interface block. In the Popup that appears when you release the mouse button, select Action from the Connection type drop down box. Name the action **buttonPressed** and click Connect.

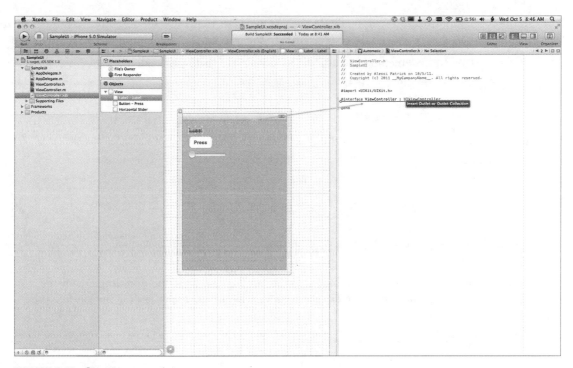

FIGURE 2-18: Creating an outlet

14. Add both an outlet and an action for the slider. Control-drag the slider into the @interface block to create the outlet. Call the outlet **mySlider**. Then, control-drag the slider below the closing brace of the @interface block to create the Action. Call the Action **sliderMoved**.

Now you are finished working with the interface. Your ViewController.h header file should look like this:

```
#import <UIKit/UIKit.h>

@interface ViewController : UIViewController
@property (weak, nonatomic) IBOutlet UILabel *myLabel;
- (IBAction)buttonPressed:(id)sender;
@property (weak, nonatomic) IBOutlet UISlider *mySlider;
- (IBAction)sliderMoved:(id)sender;

@end
```

15. Now you are ready to implement your code. Do not worry if the code is confusing or seems strange; you will learn all about the Objective-C syntax later on in the book. In the ViewController.h header file, add an int variable to hold your counter. Add the following code after the @interface line:

```
{
    int counter;
}
```

16. In the Navigator area, or by using the Jump bars, navigate to the `ViewController.m` implementation file. In this file, you will write the code to react to the user tapping the button or moving the slider.

17. Find the `viewDidLoad` method and add the following code below the call to `[super viewDidLoad];` to initialize the program:

```
counter = 0;
self.myLabel.text = [[NSNumber numberWithInt:counter] stringValue];
```

The complete `viewDidLoad` method should look like this:

```
- (void)viewDidLoad
{
    [super viewDidLoad];
    // Do any additional setup after loading the view, typically from a nib.

    counter = 0;
    self.myLabel.text = [[NSNumber numberWithInt:counter] stringValue];
}
```

18. Near the bottom of the file, you should find the `buttonPressed:` method. Implement the `buttonPressed` method to increment the counter when the user presses the button like this:

```
- (IBAction)buttonPressed:(id)sender {
    // Increment the counter
    counter++;

    // Update the label using the outlet
    self.myLabel.text = [[NSNumber numberWithInt:counter] stringValue];

    // Move the slider using the outlet
    mySlider.value = counter;

}
```

19. Implement the `sliderMoved` method to update the counter when the user moves the slider:

```
- (IBAction)sliderMoved:(id)sender {
    // Update the counter using the slider
    counter = mySlider.value;

    // Update the label using the outlet
    self.myLabel.text = [[NSNumber numberWithInt:counter] stringValue];


}
```

20. Build and run the program by clicking the Run button at the top left corner of the Xcode window. The iOS simulator should start and you should see your UI application. Tap the button and notice how the counter label goes up by one and how the slider ticks over a bit to the right. Keep tapping the button and watch the counter label change and the slider move. Grab the slider and scrub it back and forth. You should see the label change as you move the slider. Congratulations, you just built a UI based application!

How It Works

After you created your project, the first thing that you did was to open the `.xib` file that holds your user interface. Once you had the interface open, you dragged the controls that you wanted to use out of the Object library and placed them onto your interface.

Next, you connected the interface objects to your code by using Outlets and Actions. First, you created an Outlet for the label because you need to access the label in your code to change its value each time that the user pressed the button or slid the slider. Next, you added an Action for the button because you wanted to execute some code when the user tapped the button. Finally, you added an Outlet and Action for the slider. You needed the Outlet because you needed to modify the value of the slider in your code when the user tapped the button. You needed the Action because you wanted to run some code when the user interacted with the slider.

Next, you moved on to the code. While you still had the header file open, you added an `int` variable called `counter` to hold on to the value of your counter.

After that, you moved over into the implementation code. In the implementation, you first initialized your program in the `viewDidLoad` method. You initialized the value of your counter variable to zero:

```
counter = 0;
```

Then, you took that value, converted it into a string, and displayed it in your label by using the `text` property of the label:

```
self.myLabel.text = [[NSNumber numberWithInt:counter] stringValue];
```

Next, you implemented the `buttonPressed:` action method. This method runs any time that a user taps the button. You connected the button to this code when you created the Action by dragging the button from Interface Builder to the header code.

The `buttonPressed:` method first increments the counter by using the `++` operator:

```
// Increment the counter
counter++;
```

Then, you updated the label by using the same code as in the `viewDidLoad` method:

```
// Update the label using the outlet
self.myLabel.text = [[NSNumber numberWithInt:counter] stringValue];
```

Finally, you used the slider outlet to set its value to the new value of the `counter`:

```
// Move the slider using the outlet
mySlider.value = counter;
```

Next, you moved on to the `sliderMoved:` method. This method runs any time the user slides the slider. First, you set the value of your `counter` variable based on the `value` of the slider:

```
// Update the counter using the slider
counter = mySlider.value;
```

Then, you updated the label by using the same code as in the `viewDidLoad` method:

```
// Update the label using the outlet
self.myLabel.text = [[NSNumber numberWithInt:counter] stringValue];
```

This is only the tip of the iceberg for using Interface Builder. However, for the purposes of building simple games like the ones in this book, you now have enough knowledge to get you started. If you are interested in creating interfaces that are more complex or just learning more about how Interface Builder works, I recommend reading the Xcode 4 User Guide. You can get to the user guide very easily in Xcode by choosing Xcode User Guide from the Help menu in the menu bar.

SUMMARY

In this chapter, you learned how to use Xcode to create, modify, and debug your programs.

You learned about the templates that Xcode provides to get you started building your projects. Then, you learned about the coding environment and how to navigate the files in your project by using the Navigation area and the Jump bars.

Next, you learned about the features of the editor that help you to write your code, like code completion and Fix-it. You also learned that Xcode will help you to make your code more readable by using syntax coloring and indentation.

Then, you learned how to use the debugger to help you to find errors in your code. You learned how to step through your code line-by-line and inspect the values of your variables. You also learned a few different ways to pause the execution of your code by using breakpoints.

Finally, you learned how to use Interface Builder to build user interfaces. You learned about drawing the interface and connecting the interface elements to your code using Outlets and Actions.

Now you are ready to put your knowledge of Xcode to use as you learn the fundamental languages that you will use to write games on iOS: C and Objective-C.

EXERCISES

1. After creating a new Single View Application project, how would you find the `viewDidLoad` method?

2. After compiling your code, you are presented with a slew of errors. What is the easiest way to work through each of the errors, fixing them as you go along?

3. Suppose that you inherited this poorly formatted block of code:

```
for (int i=0;i<10;i++){
for (j=0; j<100; j++) {
for (k=100; k>0; k--) {
// Do something in your code

}
}
}
```

   This code is very difficult to read due to incorrect indentation. How would you use Xcode to re-indent it so that it is easier to see the structure of the nested loops?

4. Using the Quick Help inspector in Xcode, determine the header file that declares the `viewDidLoad` function in the SampleUI project.

5. Build a simple user interface application with three buttons labeled "one", "two", and "three." Add a label to the application. When the user taps one of the buttons, the text of the label should change to reflect the button that the user tapped.

Answers to the Exercises can be found in the Appendix.

▶ **WHAT YOU LEARNED IN THIS CHAPTER**

TOPIC	MAIN POINTS
Navigating your project	Navigate through the files in your project by using the Navigation area or the Jump bars. Use the Assistant view to display your code and header side-by-side.
Editing code	Use the Editor area to edit your code. Xcode automatically colors and indents your code for you. Fix-it helps you to correct problems with your code before they become bugs or compiler errors.
Breakpoints and debugging	You can pause execution of your program where you need to by using breakpoints. You can configure breakpoints in different ways based on when you need your program to pause.
Interface Builder	You use Interface Builder to draw the user interface for your programs. You drag controls from the Object library and drop them on to your user interface.
Outlet	The connection that you make from a UI element to your code when you need to be able to work with the UI element from code.
Action	The connection that you make from a UI element to your code when you need to respond to a user interacting with a UI element.

3

The C Programming Language

WHAT YOU WILL LEARN IN THIS CHAPTER:

➤ Holding data in variables and explaining variable scope and how it works in C

➤ Iterating through blocks of code using `for`, `while` and `do ... while` loops

➤ Controlling execution of your programs by using the `if` and `switch` statements

➤ Breaking your code into logical units by using functions

➤ Explaining what pointers are and how you use them to reference data

Before you can begin writing full-featured games for iOS with graphics, animation, and sound, you need to know the basics. The most fundamental level of programming for iOS starts with the C programming language. In this chapter, you will learn the fundamental concepts of C while building a simple, command-line game. When you have finished, you will be ready to move on to the more advanced concepts of Objective-C. After you are comfortable with both languages, you will be ready for graphics, animation, and sound.

INTRODUCING C

The C language is rooted in the PDP-7 assembler language that the creators of Unix used to write the first version of the operating system. Later, programmers developed a language called TMG to wrap PDP-7 assembler. TMG evolved into a higher-level language, B, which could accomplish tasks that required many lines of PDP-7 assembler in only a few lines. At Bell Labs, Dennis Ritchie enhanced the B language, which morphed into C. The developers of Unix then used C to write most of the components of the operating system.

C is a good language in which to implement an operating system because it combines the ease of use and terseness of a high-level language with the low-level power of assembler. Unlike Op Code-based languages like Java and .Net, C programs compile into native assembler code and therefore perform very quickly. Additionally, the C language allows direct access to memory thorough pointers, which you can also use to enhance the performance of your applications.

The C language became an ANSI standard in 1983. This resulted in programmers developing many libraries for the platform. This is a boon to programmers because much of the functionality that you would have to write yourself may already be available in a library. This modularity helps to make C easy to learn. The developers of C have left out a lot of functionality typically included in other languages because those features are available in libraries in C. For example, file I/O and console I/O are not part of the core language. The C standard library contains these functions. If you are writing embedded code that does not require I/O, there is no need to include those functions in your program.

You can find further information about the history of the development of the C language in an excellent online article by one of the original developers of the C language, "The Development of the C Language" by Dennis M. Ritchie. (http://cm.bell-labs.com/cm/cs/who/dmr/chist.html)

Since the implementers of Unix chose C, and Mac OS X is fundamentally a Unix platform, it made sense for Apple to use C as the base language for Mac OS X development. iOS is a minimal version of the OS X operating system, so the same reasons for using C to implement programs on the desktop OS apply to developing applications for the mobile platform. More so, probably because code designed for speed and small memory footprint is more important on a mobile platform than it is in a desktop environment.

Where C excels in its simplicity, it lacks in some features found in modern programming languages, namely, object orientation. C is a "structured" programming language, meaning that a program fundamentally runs from the top down with the programmer controlling program flow by calling functions. Most modern languages are "Object Oriented," meaning that the designer encapsulates the logic of the program in objects instead of functions. You will learn more about Object Oriented (OO) programming in the next chapter. This need for Object orientation in C led to the development of the Objective-C language, which you will cover in the next chapter. Developers implement programs on iOS in Objective-C (or Objective-C++), which is a superset of C. Therefore, before moving into the complexity of OO and the structure of Objective-C, you need to be rooted in its foundation, C.

VARIABLES AND EXPRESSIONS

The most fundamental abilities of a computer program are its capability to store, retrieve, and perform operations on data. You will also see how you can operate on that data. Next, you will learn about scope, which determines where the variables that you define are available in your code. Then, you will learn to create your own data types by using structures. Finally, you will learn how to store groups of data in arrays.

Data Types

The C language is *strongly typed*. This means that you must declare variables as being of a particular type before you can use them. In this section, you will learn about the base data types for variables in C.

Variables

You store data in a program by using variables. A variable is a location in memory that is set aside to hold some data. Since C is a strongly typed language, you must declare each variable that you will use in your program along with its type. You will learn more about the C data types in the next section.

You declare a variable by specifying its type and name. Then, you end the variable declaration with a semicolon. You would use this line to declare an integer type variable called var:

```
int var;
```

Variable names in C are case sensitive. Therefore, the variables MyVar, myVar, and MYVAR are all different. This goes for keywords and function names as well.

You can declare and initialize a variable in one statement by using an initializer like this:

```
int one = 1;
```

Base Data Types

There are four base data types in C: char, int, float, and double. The amount of memory used by each data type is dependent on the platform that is running the code.

You use the char data type to store a single character. A char variable has a size of one byte. You can use the char type to store any single character from the local character set.

In addition to storing single characters, you also use the char data type to work with strings. You use strings to store text. In C, a string is stored as an array of chars, ending with a null character \0. You will learn more about arrays later in this chapter. I will not cover using C strings thoroughly because you will not generally use C-style strings when programming for iOS. When you write iOS programs, you will typically use the Cocoa framework class NSString. This class greatly simplifies working with strings. You will use NSString to work with strings in the next chapter.

The int data type stores integer data; that is, data that does not contain a decimal point. The int type requires four bytes of storage in iOS. The int type has a range from –2,147,483,648 to 2,147,483,647.

The float and double types store *floating-point data* to various degrees of precision. A floating-point number is any number that has a fractional part separated from the whole part by a decimal point. The float type uses four bytes of memory where the double type uses eight bytes. The name double refers to the fact that variables of this type use double precision. This means that double variables retain more decimal places after the decimal point. You will rarely use double variables in game development for several reasons. First, they require more memory and the enhanced precision that they retain is rarely useful. Second, it takes the processor longer to deal with double precision numbers than it does to deal with floats.

Generating Output and Accepting Input

You generate output from your command-line programs using the printf function. printf prints formatted content to the console. You use this function by passing in a literal string along with formatting characters. You also pass in the values that you want to print. At run time, the function replaces the formatting characters with the values that you passed. You will see this in action in a moment. Table 3-1 lists the most common formatting characters and explains their use.

For more details, you should read the IEEE `printf` specification. (`www.opengroup.org/onlinepubs/009695399/functions/printf.html`)

TABLE 3-1: Format Specifiers

SPECIFIER	DESCRIPTION
%d, %D, %i	Signed 32-bit integer (int type)
%u, %U	Unsigned 32-bit integer (unsigned int type)
%lu	Unsigned long type (Platform dependent)
%hi	Signed 16-bit integer (short type)
%hu	Unsigned 16-bit integer (unsigned short type)
%qi	Signed 64-bit integer (long long type)
%qu	Unsigned 64-bit integer (unsigned long long type)
%f	64-bit floating-point number (double)
%c	8-bit unsigned character (unsigned char)
%s	Null-terminated array of 8-bit unsigned characters. Used to print strings.

You use the `printf` function to output text to the console. There is another I/O function called `scanf` that you can use to get user input from the console. To use `scanf`, you pass a format specifier like the ones you use with `printf`, along with the address of a variable that you will use to hold the value that the user typed. For example, to get an `int` value from a user, you would use this command:

```
scanf("Enter your age: %i", &age);
```

In this function, the `%i` is the format specifier for an integer value and `&age` is the address of an `int` variable called age. You will learn more about the `&` address-of operator in the section on pointers.

TRY IT OUT Identifying Data Type Sizes

codefile CSizes available for download at Wrox.com

To write a simple program to show the amount of memory used by each data type, follow these steps:

1. Start up Xcode and select File ⇨ New ⇨ New Project …. For this project, you will be developing a simple command-line tool for Mac OS X. This will ensure that you start from the most barebones of C programs. So, in the dialog, select, "Application" under the Mac OS X section on the left-hand side. Then, in the right pane, select, "Command Line Tool" and click Next. Come up with a clever name for your project and type it into the Product Name text box. I used CSizes. Make sure that you select "C" in the Type dropdown box because you want to create a C program. Click Next. Now, you will see a prompt for a location to save your program. Pick a location that you will remember. Also, uncheck the "Create local git repository for this project" checkbox. You will not need to use source control for this project. Finally, click Create and Xcode will create your new project.

2. Open the project navigator in the left-hand pane and click on `main.c`. You should see the following code (I've eliminated the header comments):

```
#include <stdio.h>

int main (int argc, const char * argv[])
{

    // insert code here...
    printf("Hello, World!\n");
    return 0;
}
```

3. You are going to modify this code to print the size of each basic C type. Delete the line that prints "Hello, World!" Then, insert the following code:

```
printf ("Size of int: %lu \n", sizeof(int));
printf ("Size of char: %lu \n", sizeof(char));
printf ("Size of float: %lu \n", sizeof(float));
printf ("Size of double: %lu \n", sizeof(double));
```

Your main function should look like this:

```
int main (int argc, const char * argv[])
{
    // insert code here...
    printf ("Size of int: %lu \n", sizeof(int));
    printf ("Size of char: %lu \n", sizeof(char));
    printf ("Size of float: %lu \n", sizeof(float));
    printf ("Size of double: %lu \n", sizeof(double));

    return 0;
}
```

4. Select Product ⇨ Run from the menu bar. To keep things clear in the debug output window, change its mode to Target Output by using the selection list at the top of the pane. You should see the following in the debug output window:

```
Size of int: 4
Size of char: 1
Size of float: 4
Size of double: 8
```

How It Works

Congratulations, you have just written your first C program! In your program, you included external functions in the I/O library and wrote data to the console. You also used the `sizeof` function with various data types to learn more about those data types.

The first line includes the C standard I/O library headers into your program:

```
#include <stdio.h>
```

Including this header tells the compiler that you will be calling functions from this library. You need to use this library to print text out to the debug output window.

The next line defines a *function* called `main`:

```
int main (int argc, const char * argv[])
```

You will learn more about functions later in this chapter. The `main` function is the entry point for a C program. Every C program has a `main` function, which is where execution begins.

The next line is a comment:

```
// insert code here...
```

You create single-line comments in C by using two slashes (`//`). You can place comments at any point on a line of code, but the compiler will ignore anything after the two slashes. You could add a comment to the next line of code like this:

```
printf ("Size of int: %lu \n", sizeof(int)); // Print out size
```

You can create multi-line comments using the `/*` and `*/` delimiters. Everything after the `/*` and before the `*/` will be considered a comment. You should be aware that there is a danger in using multi-line comments in that they do not nest. The `*/` in this code closes the comment and any code after it would not be considered a comment:

```
/*
comment
/*
*/
```

If you do make this mistake, Xcode will warn you that there is a `/*` delimeter within a comment.

The next lines use the I/O function `printf` to print the size of each type:

```
printf ("Size of int: %lu \n", sizeof(int));
```

As you learned above, you use the `printf` function to print formatted content to the console. The `sizeof` function returns the size of the type that you pass as a parameter. Therefore, you can see that combining the `printf` function with the return of the `sizeof` function prints the size of each type.

You may have noticed the semicolon at the end of the line. You end each statement in a C program with a semicolon. Also, remember that C is case sensitive. So, be careful with your variable names, keywords, and function names.

Finally, the last line returns 0. All C programs should return 0 on successful completion. Other return values indicate an error during the execution of the program. You will learn more about functions and return values later on in the section on functions.

Extending the Data Types

Sometimes the base data types do not provide enough room for the data that you need to hold. Other times, they may use more memory and hold a larger range than you need. You can use the qualifier `long` to use twice as much memory and increase the range of a variable. Conversely, you can use the qualifier `short` to use only half the memory at the cost of reduced range. For instance, where an `int` can hold values in the range of –2,147,483,648 to 2,147,483,647, a `short int` has a range from –32,768 to 32,767.

If you know that the value of a variable will never be negative, you can extend the range of the basic types by using the unsigned qualifier. This tells the system to use the bit that normally holds the sign to instead store more data. The unsigned version of a variable does not use any more memory than the signed version. For example, an unsigned int has a range from 0 to 4,294,967,295.

TRY IT OUT   Identifying Extended Data Type Sizes

codefile CSizes available for download at Wrox.com

You can extend the previous example to display the amount of memory used by the long and short versions of a couple of types. Follow these steps:

1. Start up Xcode and select File ⇨ Open. Navigate to the CSizes project that you created in the last section. Select the CSizes.xcodeproj file and click Open. Select the main.c code file in the project navigator to open the code for the main function.

2. Below the last printf statement in the main function, add the following code:

```
printf("Size of short int: %lu \n", sizeof(short int));
printf("Size of long double: %lu \n", sizeof(long double));
```

3. Build and run your program. The output should look like this:

```
Size of int: 4
Size of char: 1
Size of float: 4
Size of double: 8
Size of short int: 2
Size of long double: 16
```

How It Works

You can see that the amount of memory used by a short int is half of that used by an int and that a long double is twice the size of a double.

The int and long int types are the same. The ANSI C specification only stipulates that short ints are at least 2 bytes, longs are at least 4 bytes, and short is no longer than int, and int is no longer than long. In the case of iOS and Mac OS X, int and long int are synonymous in that they are both 4 bytes long. If you needed to use an 8-byte int, you would use the long long type.

When you write code for memory-constrained devices like the iPhone and iPad, you can save memory by using the smaller types. However, there is a tradeoff. The current generation of iOS devices uses a 32-bit ARM processor. Since the 32-bit processor handles 32-bit integers natively, you will see the best possible performance when using 32-bit ints. Therefore, using smaller types to save memory might result in a very slight performance loss due to the way that the CPU handles shorts. You should carefully consider which types to use based on testing your application.

Operators

Now that you are comfortable with variables and their types, you are ready to look at how you operate on those variables. The first operators that you will look at are Assignment operators. Then you will see the arithmetic, relational, and logical operators.

Assignment Operators

When you want to assign a value to a variable, you use an assignment operator. The most common assignment operator is =. It is very important to remember that = is the assignment operator and == is the equality operator. If you attempt to test for equality by using the assignment operator, your program will not work correctly and may exhibit strange behavior that is often difficult to debug. Fortunately, Xcode will generate a warning if you try to use an assignment as a conditional statement without enclosing it in parentheses.

The assignment operator assigns the value on the right-hand side of the expression to the variable on the left-hand side. For instance, to assign the value of 5 to the variable i, you would use the statement i=5;. To test to see if the variable i equaled the value 5, you would use the expression i==5.

You can prepend arithmetic operators to the assignment operator as a coding shortcut. For example, instead of adding 5 to the value in n and assigning it back to n by using a statement like this: n=n+5, you can prepend the addition (+) operator to the assignment operator and write the statement as n+=5. You can use the operators +, -, *, /, and % in this manner.

TRY IT OUT   **Using the Assignment Operators**

codefile CSizes available for download at Wrox.com

To get a better understanding of how this works, you will add on to the CSizes project. Follow these steps:

1. Start up Xcode and select File ⇨ Open. Navigate to the CSizes project that you created in the last section. Select the CSizes.xcodeproj file and click Open. Select the main.c code file in the project navigator to open the code for the main function.

2. Append the following code to the end of the main function in your CSizes project after the line printf ("Size of long double: %lu \n", sizeof(long double));

```
    int i = 0;
    printf("i: %i\n",i);
    printf("i++: %i\n",i++);
    printf("i: %i\n\n",i);

    i=0;
    printf("i: %i\n",i);
    printf("++i: %i\n",++i);
    printf("i: %i\n",i);
```

Your main function should now look like this:

```
int main (int argc, const char * argv[])
{

    printf ("Size of int: %lu \n", sizeof(int)); // Print out size
    printf ("Size of char: %lu \n", sizeof(char));
    printf ("Size of float: %lu \n", sizeof(float));
```

```
printf ("Size of double: %lu \n", sizeof(double));

printf ("Size of short int: %lu \n", sizeof(short int));
printf ("Size of long double: %lu \n", sizeof(long double));


int i = 0;
printf("i: %i\n",i);
printf("i++: %i\n",i++);
printf("i: %i\n\n",i);

i=0;
printf("i: %i\n",i);
printf("++i: %i\n",++i);
printf("i: %i\n",i);

return 0;
}
```

3. Run the program now. You will now see the following at the bottom of the output:

```
i: 0
i++: 0
i: 1

i: 0
++i: 1
i: 1
```

How It Works

First, the code declares a variable of type `int` called `i` and sets it to 0:

```
int i - 0;
```

Then, you print the value of `i`:

```
printf("i: %i\n",i);
```

Next, you use the postfix version of the `++` operator to increment and print `i`:

```
printf("i++: %i\n",i++);
```

You can see that the value of `i` is used and then `i` is incremented. Contrast this with the results that you get when you use the prefix version of the `++` operator:

```
i=0;
printf("i: %i\n",i);
printf("++i: %i\n",++i);
printf("i: %i\n",i);
```

The value of `i` in the print statement is incremented first, and then used. Finally, note that the final resulting value of `i`, after the operator is applied is the same in both cases.

Arithmetic Operators

Arithmetic operators are the operators that you use in arithmetic. These are shown in Table 3-2.

TABLE 3-2: Arithmetic Operators

OPERATOR	FUNCTION
+	Addition
–	Subtraction
/	Division
*	Multiplication
%	Modulus

All of these should be self-explanatory with the exception of the modulus operator. The modulus operator returns the remainder of a division. For example, 10 % 3 would return 1 because 10 divided by 3 is 3 with a remainder of 1. If there is no remainder, the modulus operator returns 0. The modulus operator works only for integers. You cannot use the modulus operator with floating point types. You will see the modulus operator in use in the game example at the end of this chapter.

Relational Operators

The relational and equality operators are listed in Table 3-3.

TABLE 3-3: Relational Operators

OPERTOR	FUNCTION
>	greater than
>=	greater than or equal to
<	less than
<=	less than or equal to
==	is equal to
!=	is not equal to

You will use relational operators when evaluating criteria for decisions. You will learn more about the decision structures in C later in this chapter.

Logical Operators

Next, you have the logical operators && (and) and || (or). You use the && operator to express that you need both parts of the statement to be true for the entire statement to be true. For example, the statement a<5 && b<5 would only evaluate as true if both a AND b were less than 5. If you wanted the statement to be true if a OR b was less than 5, you use the || operator like this: a<5 || b<5.

Evaluation of the logical operators stops as soon as a true or false result can be determined. Therefore, you cannot count on the execution of every logical operator in a statement. You will learn to use logical operators in the section on decisions later in this chapter.

The C language also includes increment and decrement operators. The increment operator is ++ and increments a value by one. Similarly, the decrement operator is -- and decrements a value by one. You use these operators by appending them either to the beginning or the end of the variable that you want to effect. By placing the operator before the variable, the variable is incremented before it is used. Placing the operator after the variable increments the variable after it is used.

Scope

A variable name has meaning only in certain locations in a program. This is the variable's *scope*. When you declare a variable at the beginning of a function, like the variable i in the main function in our example code, that variable is available from the point where you declare it onward, in that function. Once the function ends, the variable goes out of scope and no longer has any meaning. Other functions cannot refer to the value of a variable declared inside of another function. A variable declared inside of a function is a local variable.

Even inside of a function, you can specify variable scope by using the curly braces ({}). To see the effects of the curly brackets on variable scope, modify the code in the previous example like this:

```
{
    int i = 0;
    printf("i: %i\n",i);
    printf("i++: %i\n",i++);
    printf("i: %i\n\n",i);
}

i=0;
printf("i: %i\n",i);
printf("++i: %i\n",++i);
printf("i: %i\n",i);
```

If you try to build this code by choosing Product ⇨ Build from the menu bar, you will get compiler errors on the four lines after the braces as shown in Figure 3-1. This is because the scope of the variable i extends only to the closing brace. Once the code gets past the closing brace, the variable i is undefined. To get your code back in working order, remove the curly braces. You will see a more practical example of scoping with curly braces in the section on loops later in this chapter.

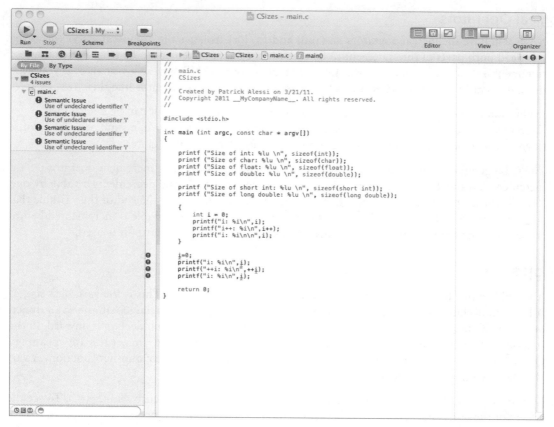

FIGURE 3-1: Flagged compiler errors

Declaring a variable outside of any function makes the variable available to all functions after the point at which the variable is declared.

Structures

Often times, the data that you need to use in your game will be more complicated than any of the basic data types: `char`, `int`, `float`, and `double`. Where a variable holds only one piece of data, for example an `int` or `float`, structures provide a way for you to group multiple variables, possibly of differing types, together in one place. This aspect of the C language will help you to better organize the data used for your games. By using structures, you can group all of the data that you need by using one name. A good example where this is convenient is in defining a `Point` structure.

Points are a very common data type that you will use when developing graphical-based applications, including games. Typically, you will define all of the shapes on the screen with points. For instance, you can define a rectangle by using two points as shown in Figure 3-2. You can also define circles by using a point and a radius, which you can see in Figure 3-2 as well. Since you will use points very frequently, it makes sense to group the x and y coordinates of a point into a single structure. Doing this lets you refer to the point as a unit as opposed to passing around separate x and y coordinates everywhere you need the point.

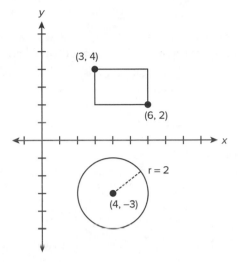

FIGURE 3-2: Defining shapes

You define a structure by using the keyword `struct` followed by the name of the structure. Then, you include all of the types and variables that you want to include in the structure between curly braces. Finally, you need to finish off the definition with a semicolon. Therefore, to define a point data structure, you would do it like this:

```
struct point {
    int x;
    int y;
};
```

TRY IT OUT   Defining the point Struct

codefile Shapes available for download at Wrox.com

To create a `point` struct to use in the following exercises, follow these steps:

1. Start up Xcode and from the File menu select New ➪ New Project .... Once again, you will be developing a simple command-line tool for Mac OS X. In the dialog, select, "Application" under the Mac OS X section on the left-hand side. Then, in the right pane, select, "Command Line Tool" and click Next. Call the project **Shapes** and type the name into the Product Name text box. Make sure that you select "C" in the Type dropdown box. Click Next. Xcode will prompt you for a location to save your program. Pick a location that you will remember. Also, uncheck the "Create local git repository for this project" checkbox. You will not need to use source control for this project. Finally, click Create, and Xcode will create your new project.

2. To make the point struct available to multiple functions in your code, you need to declare it outside of the `main` function. Add the following code below the `#include` but before the `main` function in the `main.c` file:

```
struct point {
    int x;
    int y;
};
```

How It Works

This code defines a new data structure called `point` that contains two members of type `int` with names `x` and `y`. Now that you have declared this structure, you can use your new `point` data type anywhere that you need to keep track of points.

Structures are not limited to containing only basic data types. You can nest structures within structures. To illustrate this, we will define a `rectangle` struct that contains two points, the top left coordinate and the bottom right coordinate, as shown in Figure 3-3:

```
struct rectangle {
    struct point upperLeft;
    struct point lowerRight;
};
```

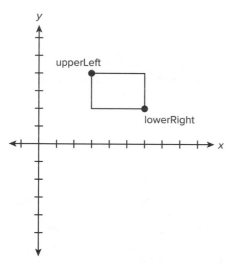

FIGURE 3-3: Defining a rectangle

Now, anywhere that you need to refer to a rectangle, you can use your new `rectangle` structure.

TRY IT OUT Moving a rectangle

codefile Shapes available for download at Wrox.com

To create a `rectangle` struct by using the `point` struct you already defined, follow these steps:

1. Add the definition of the `rectangle` structure to the Shapes project. Place the definition below the definition of the `point` structure. This is important because the compiler needs to know about the `point` structure before you use it to define the `rectangle` structure. Your main.c should look like this:

```
#include <stdio.h>
struct point {
    int x;
```

```
        int y;
};

struct rectangle {
    struct point upperLeft;
    struct point lowerRight;
};

int main (int argc, const char * argv[])
{

    // insert code here...
    printf("Hello, World!\n");
    return 0;
}
```

2. Next, you will add some code to the program to create a rectangle, print its coordinates, move it, and print the new coordinates. You can see this in Figure 3-4. Keep in mind that you are not moving a graphical rectangle; you are just moving the coordinates of a rectangle object. You will learn how to draw and animate graphics later in the book. You will be working in the main function for this part.

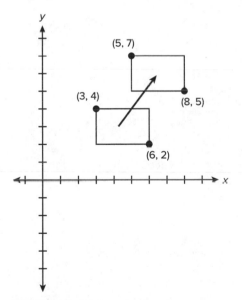

FIGURE 3-4: Moving a rectangle

Here is the completed main function:

```
int main (int argc, const char * argv[])
{

    // Declare points
    struct point ul;
    struct point lr;
```

```
// Specify the location of the ul point
ul.x = 3;
ul.y = 4;

// Specify the location of the lr point
lr.x = 6;
lr.y = 2;

// Declare the rectangle
struct rectangle theRectangle;

// Define the rectangle using the points
theRectangle.upperLeft = ul;
theRectangle.lowerRight = lr;

// Print the coordinates of the rectangle
printf("Upper Left -- x:%i y:%i  Lower Right -- x:%i y:%i\n",
       theRectangle.upperLeft.x,theRectangle.upperLeft.y,
       theRectangle.lowerRight.x,theRectangle.lowerRight.y);

// Move the rectangle right 2 units and up 3 units
theRectangle.upperLeft.x +=2;
theRectangle.upperLeft.y +=3;
theRectangle.lowerRight.x +=2;
theRectangle.lowerRight.y +=3;

// Print the new coordinates of the rectangle
printf("Upper Left -- x:%i y:%i  Lower Right -- x:%i y:%i\n",
       theRectangle.upperLeft.x,theRectangle.upperLeft.y,
       theRectangle.lowerRight.x,theRectangle.lowerRight.y);

    return 0;
}
```

3. Run the program and you should see the following output in the debug output window:

```
Upper Left -- x:3 y:4  Lower Right -- x:6 y:2
Upper Left -- x:5 y:7  Lower Right -- x:8 y:5
```

How It Works

The code first declares the two points that will determine the location of your rectangle:

```
struct point ul;
struct point lr;
```

You declare struct variables by using the keyword `struct` followed by the type name, the variable name, and then a semicolon.

I used the names `ul` and `lr` for the two points. You could call the points `upperLeft` and `lowerRight` if you wanted because the compiler knows the difference between local variables and structure members. I would not recommend doing this though because it makes your code more difficult to read.

The code uses the member operator to specify the locations of the two points by using the member operator to set the x and y coordinates:

```
        // Specify the location of the ul point
        ul.x = 3;
        ul.y = 4;

        // Specify the location of the lr point
        lr.x = 6;
        lr.y = 2;
```

After this, you declare and populate the `theRectangle` variable, once again by using the member operator, with the two points that you just created:

```
        // Declare the rectangle
        struct rectangle theRectangle;

        // Define the rectangle using the points
        theRectangle.upperLeft = ul;
        theRectangle.lowerRight = lr;
```

Now it is time to print out the coordinates of the rectangle by using the `printf` function. You can refer to the nested member variables x and y by using multiple member operators to drill down through the data structure:

```
        printf("Upper Left -- x:%i y:%i  Lower Right -- x:%i y:%i\n",
              theRectangle.upperLeft.x,theRectangle.upperLeft.y,
              theRectangle.lowerRight.x,theRectangle.lowerRight.y);
```

The statement `theRectangle.upperLeft.x` gets the `rectangle` struct, then the `upperLeft` point struct, and finally the `x` member from the point. This syntax allows navigation through complex nested structures.

After printing the coordinates, the code moves the rectangle:

```
        // Move the rectangle right 2 units and up 3 units
        theRectangle.upperLeft.x +=2;
        theRectangle.upperLeft.y +=3;
        theRectangle.lowerRight.x +=2;
        theRectangle.lowerRight.y +=3;
```

You can see that the code uses the += operator to increment the x positions of each point by two and the y positions of each point by three. Finally, you print the new position of the rectangle by using the same `printf` statement as before.

Arrays

In the last section, you learned how to group related pieces of data together by using structures. In this section, you will see another way to group data, arrays. You use arrays to group data of the same type. Arrays use an integer index, or subscript, to reference the stored data.

Suppose that you wanted to model a deck of cards. For simplicity, assume that each card has a number from 0 to 51 (a standard deck of playing cards contains 52 cards). You could declare an array of `int`s named `deck` with 52 slots like this:

```
    int deck[52];
```

This declaration allocates the memory to hold 52 integer values. Each of the places in the array has an index or subscript, starting with 0. Figure 3-5 shows the memory allocation for the deck array. You use a subscript to reference any particular card by its position in the array. For instance, deck[3] would refer to the fourth card in the deck. Remember that arrays are 0 based.

FIGURE 3-5: Memory allocation of an array

This is a decent way to store your deck of cards. However, how can you tell which card is which suit? What is the value of each card? You could come up with a look-up scheme that maps numbers to cards, but you should not have to. Beside the base data types, you can also store structures in an array. In the next example, you will define a card structure and then populate the deck array with cards.

TRY IT OUT   Modeling a Deck of Cards

codefile Cards available for download at Wrox.com

To create an array that models a deck of cards, for use in later examples, follow these steps:

1. Start up Xcode and from the File menu select New ⇨ New Project …. Once again, you will be developing a simple command-line tool for Mac OS X. In the dialog, select, "Application" under the Mac OS X section on the left-hand side. Then, in the right pane, select, "Command Line Tool" and click Next. Call the project **Cards** and type the name into the Product Name text box. Make sure that you have selected "C" in the Type dropdown box. Click Next. You Xcode will prompt you for a location to save your program. Pick a location that you will remember. Also, uncheck the "Create local git repository for this project" checkbox. You will not need to use source control for this project. Finally, click Create, and Xcode will create your new project.

2. Replace the code in the main.c file with this:

```c
#include <stdio.h>

struct card {
    char* name;
    char* suit;
    int value;
};

int main (int argc, const char * argv[])
{

    struct card deck[] =
    {
        {"ace", "spades",1}, {"two", "spades",2}, {"three", "spades",3},
        {"four", "spades",4}, {"five", "spades",5}, {"six", "spades",6},
        {"seven", "spades",7}, {"eight", "spades",8}, {"nine", "spades",9},
        {"ten", "spades",10}, {"jack", "spades",11}, {"queen", "spades",12},
        {"king", "spades",13},
        {"ace", "clubs",1}, {"two", "clubs",2}, {"three", "clubs",3},
        {"four", "clubs",4}, {"five", "clubs",5}, {"six", "clubs",6},
```

```
        {"seven", "clubs",7}, {"eight", "clubs",8}, {"nine", "clubs",9},
        {"ten", "clubs",10}, {"jack", "clubs",11}, {"queen", "clubs",12},
        {"king", "clubs",13},
        {"ace", "hearts",1}, {"two", "hearts",2}, {"three", "hearts",3},
        {"four", "hearts",4}, {"five", "hearts",5}, {"six", "hearts",6},
        {"seven", "hearts",7}, {"eight", "hearts",8}, {"nine", "hearts",9},
        {"ten", "hearts",10}, {"jack", "hearts",11}, {"queen", "hearts",12},
        {"king", "hearts",13},
        {"ace", "diamonds",1}, {"two", "diamonds",2}, {"three", "diamonds",3},
        {"four", "diamonds",4}, {"five", "diamonds",5}, {"six", "diamonds",6},
        {"seven", "diamonds",7}, {"eight", "diamonds",8},
        {"nine", "diamonds",9},{"ten", "diamonds",10}, {"jack", "diamonds",11},
        {"queen", "diamonds",12}, {"king", "diamonds",13}

    };

    printf("The first card is %s of %s\n", deck[0].value, deck[0].suit);

    return 0;
}
```

3. Build and run the program. The output should be:

```
The first card is ace of spades
```

How It Works

The first part of the code defines a `card` structure:

```
struct card {
    char* name;
    char* suit;
    int value;
};
```

To keep it simple, the card contains two strings, one for the name of the card and the other for the suit, and an `int` for the value of the card. The `main` function defines the array `deck` to be an array of `card` structures. Next, you used an *initializer* to initialize the values of the `deck` array:

```
struct card deck[] =
{
    {"ace", "spades",1}, {"two", "spades",2}, {"three", "spades",3},
    {"four", "spades",4}, {"five", "spades",5}, {"six", "spades",6},
    {"seven", "spades",7}, {"eight", "spades",8}, {"nine", "spades",9},
    {"ten", "spades",10}, {"jack", "spades",11}, {"queen", "spades",12},
    {"king", "spades",13},
    {"ace", "clubs",1}, {"two", "clubs",2}, {"three", "clubs",3},
    {"four", "clubs",4}, {"five", "clubs",5}, {"six", "clubs",6},
    {"seven", "clubs",7}, {"eight", "clubs",8}, {"nine", "clubs",9},
    {"ten", "clubs",10}, {"jack", "clubs",11}, {"queen", "clubs",12},
    {"king", "clubs",13},
    {"ace", "hearts",1}, {"two", "hearts",2}, {"three", "hearts",3},
    {"four", "hearts",4}, {"five", "hearts",5}, {"six", "hearts",6},
    {"seven", "hearts",7}, {"eight", "hearts",8}, {"nine", "hearts",9},
    {"ten", "hearts",10}, {"jack", "hearts",11}, {"queen", "hearts",12},
    {"king", "hearts",13},
    {"ace", "diamonds",1}, {"two", "diamonds",2}, {"three", "diamonds",3},
```

```
        {"four", "diamonds",4}, {"five", "diamonds",5}, {"six", "diamonds",6},
        {"seven", "diamonds",7}, {"eight", "diamonds",8},
        {"nine", "diamonds",9},{"ten", "diamonds",10}, {"jack", "diamonds",11},
        {"queen", "diamonds",12}, {"king", "diamonds",13}

    };
```

Notice that there is no subscript in the deck array declaration. The compiler is smart enough to know how many elements are in the array based on what you passed in the initializer. In this case, you initialized each card in the deck. Finally, you used the printf function to print out the contents of the first card in the deck, the ace of spades:

```
    printf("The first card is %s of %s\n", deck[0].value, deck[0].suit);
```

A nice feature of using arrays is that you can refer to the items contained in the array by index. You will see why this is useful in the next section where you will shuffle the deck!

LOOPS

One of the things that make computers useful is their ability to iterate, or repeat, the same thing over and over. Performing repetitive operations does not bore a computer. In this section, you will learn about the facilities in C to allow you to write loops.

for Loops

When you know the number of times that you want to execute a loop, a good approach is to use a for loop. When using a for loop, you will typically use a counter. You then specify an exit condition and an increment. The format of a for statement is:

```
    for (initializer; condition; incrementer)
```

You use the initializer to initialize your counter. You use the condition to check to see if the loop contents should execute, and you use the incrementer to increment the counter. Figure 3-6 shows a simple flowchart illustrating how a for loop works.

As an example, you could use the following block of code to print the numbers from 1 to 10:

```
    for (int i=1; i<=10; i++)
    {
        printf("%i ",i);
    }
```

The first part of the for statement declares an int variable called i and sets it to 1. You will use this variable for your counter. The next part says to

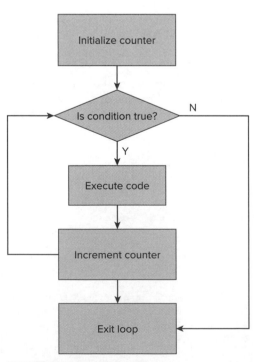

FIGURE 3-6: Loop flowchart

continue as long as i is less than or equal to 10. Finally, the last part increments the value of i. Remember that the postfix ++ operator returns the value of i and then increments it. So, the English translation of this for statement is, "start with i equal to one, continue looping while i is less than or equal to ten, and each time I come back to this for statement, increment i by one."

It is important to note that the statements contained in the braces may never be executed in a for loop. Suppose that you started out with a value of 11 for i. The i<=10 statement would evaluate to false and the contents of the loop would not be executed. You can contrast this behavior with do... while loops that you will learn about later on in this chapter. You should also be aware that the scope of the variable i is the for statement and its associated statements within the curly braces. The variable i is undefined after the loop ends.

In the next example, you will use a for loop to print out the contents of your deck of cards.

TRY IT OUT   Printing the Deck of Cards by Using a for Loop

codefile Cards available for download at Wrox.com

To use a for loop with an array, follow these steps:

1.   Open up the Cards project from the last section. Replace the following line of code:

```
printf("The first card is %s of %s\n", deck[0].value, deck[0].suit);
```

with this:

```
for (int i=0; i<52; i++) {
    printf("The card is %s of %s\n", deck[i].value, deck[i].suit);
}
```

2.   Run the program. Your output should look like this:

```
The card is ace of spades
The card is two of spades
The card is three of spades
The card is four of spades
The card is five of spades
The card is six of spades
The card is seven of spades
The card is eight of spades
The card is nine of spades
The card is ten of spades
The card is jack of spades
The card is queen of spades
The card is king of spades
The card is ace of clubs
The card is two of clubs
The card is three of clubs
The card is four of clubs
The card is five of clubs
The card is six of clubs
The card is seven of clubs
The card is eight of clubs
The card is nine of clubs
The card is ten of clubs
The card is jack of clubs
```

```
The card is queen of clubs
The card is king of clubs
The card is ace of hearts
The card is two of hearts
The card is three of hearts
The card is four of hearts
The card is five of hearts
The card is six of hearts
The card is seven of hearts
The card is eight of hearts
The card is nine of hearts
The card is ten of hearts
The card is jack of hearts
The card is queen of hearts
The card is king of hearts
The card is ace of diamonds
The card is two of diamonds
The card is three of diamonds
The card is four of diamonds
The card is five of diamonds
The card is six of diamonds
The card is seven of diamonds
The card is eight of diamonds
The card is nine of diamonds
The card is ten of diamonds
The card is jack of diamonds
The card is queen of diamonds
The card is king of diamonds
```

How It Works

You have written a simple `for` loop that uses an `int` variable `i` as a counter:

```
for (int i=0; i<52; i++)
```

First, the value of `i` is initialized to be 0. Then, you specified that the loop should run as long as `i` is less than 52. You use 52 here because there are 52 elements in the deck, numbered from 0 to 51. Remember that arrays are 0 based. Next, you say that you want to increment `i` by 1 each time through the loop. You could have also made the conditional run the loop as long as `i<=51` with the same result. Just be careful not to allow the loop to run past the end of the array. Since C does not have bounds checking, code that tried to index array element 100 would be okay with the compiler. The problem is that at runtime, the code thinks that it is still looking at cards when it is actually looking at undefined space in memory. This will certainly cause your program to operate incorrectly and will most likely cause it to crash.

In the body of the loop, you are printing out the contents of the array at location index `i`:

```
printf("The card is %s of %s\n", deck[i].value, deck[i].suit);
```

Therefore, the first time through the loop, `i` is 0 so you print out the value and suit of the 1st card in the array, `i[0]`, the ace of spades. `i` is then incremented. Then, you test `i` to see if the program should execute the loop again. Since `i` is now one, it is less than 52 so the loop runs again, printing out the element `i[1]` in the array, the two of spades. Execution continues until you have printed the 52nd element of the array, `i[51]`. After this point, `i` is incremented to 52. Now the condition `i<52` is false so the code drops out of the loop and execution ends.

while and do...while Loops

Another form of iteration structure is the `while` loop. The flowchart for a `while` loop looks identical to that of a `for` loop as shown in Figure 3-6. The difference is that `while` loops do not provide a method for you to initialize or increment the counter. You need to do these two things separately, rather than in a single statement as you did in the `for` loop.

The easiest way to see the difference is with an example. Here, you will change your Cards program to use a `while` loop instead of a `for` loop.

TRY IT OUT   Printing the Deck with a while Loop

codefile Cards available for download at Wrox.com

To use a `while` loop with the array, follow these steps:

1. Delete the `for` loop and its contents from the Cards program. Replace it with the following code:

```
int i=0;
while (i<52) {
    printf("The card is %s of %s\n", deck[i].value, deck[i].suit);
    i++;
}
```

2. When you run this code, the output should be the same as you saw in the example above.

How It Works

`while` loops are essentially the same as `for` loops. Their use when using a counter as in this example is typically a matter of preference. In the example, you declared a counter `i` and set it to 0:

```
int i=0;
```

Then you said that you wanted to execute the following code while `i` is less than 52:

```
while (i<52) {
```

In the loop block, you printed out the value of the card located in the deck array at index `i`:

```
printf("The card is %s of %s\n", deck[i].value, deck[i].suit);
```

Finally, you incremented `i`:

```
i++;
```

Where `while` loops differ from `for` loops is that they do not necessarily need a counter. Often times you will want to use a `while` loop when you want a factor other than a counter to cause the loop to exit. For instance, in a game, you might not want to count how many turns the players have taken before exiting the game. You may want to exit a game only when someone has won. The clearest way of expressing this case is with a while loop like this:

```
while (gameWon == false) {
    ...
    Game logic
```

```
    ...
}
// Game over
```

In this code, the game will continue to run as long as the `gameWon` variable is false. Since C does not have a Boolean data type, any non-zero value evaluates to true and the value of 0 is false. There is no explicit counter here, simply a test to see if a player has won the game or not.

Suppose that you have a block of code that you want to execute in a loop at least one time regardless of whether or not a condition is true. In this case, you would use a `do ... while` loop. Where the `for` and `while` loops check the condition at the top, before the loop contents are executed, the `do ... while` loop checks the condition at the bottom, after the loop contents have been executed. The syntax for a `do ... while` loop is as follows:

```
do {
    ...
}
while (condition);
```

You can see a flowchart for a `do ... while` loop in Figure 3-7.

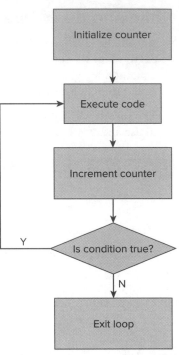

FIGURE 3-7: do...while flowchart

TRY IT OUT   **Shuffling the Deck of Cards**

codefile Cards available for download at Wrox.com

To use a `while` loop to shuffle the deck, follow these steps:

1. A simple way to shuffle a deck of cards is to randomly swap two cards many times. In this example, you will shuffle the deck by using this technique. Open up the Cards project in Xcode.

2. You will be using a couple of new functions in this example, so you will need to include two new header files to make these functions available to the compiler. Add the following code under the line `#include <stdio.h>`:

```
#include <stdlib.h>
#include <time.h>
```

3. In the `main` function, after the definition of the deck array but before the block of code that prints the contents of the deck out, add the following code:

```
// Seed the random number generator
srandom( time( NULL ) );

int randomA, randomB;
struct card tempCard;

int i=0;
do {
    // Generate 2 random numbers to determine which cards to swap
```

```
        randomA = random() % 52;
        randomB = random() % 52;

        if (randomA == randomB)
        {
            continue;
        }


        // Swap slots A and B
        tempCard = deck[randomA];
        deck[randomA] = deck[randomB];
        deck[randomB] = tempCard;

        // Increment the counter
        i++;
    }
    while (i<1000000);
```

How It Works

The first line *seeds* the random number generator:

```
    srandom( time( NULL ) );
```

The random numbers that a computer generates are not truly random; they are pseudo-random. You can think of the random numbers returned by the random function as a list. Every time you call random, the function returns the next number in the list.

Now, imagine each list of random numbers as the page of a book. Every time that you go to a given page, the list of numbers will be the same. The seeding function srandom tells the computer what page in the book the random number list should come from. If you don't seed the random number generator, you will get the same random numbers in the same order every time that you run your program. You can see this if you replace the call to time(NULL) in the srandom call with a constant like 1. This is great for testing a program because you can be sure that you will get the same random numbers every time you run, but it will not make for fun games if the random numbers are predictable.

This is where the time function comes in. The time function returns the number of seconds that have passed since January 1, 1970. Therefore, in this program, you are choosing the page of the random number book based on the number of seconds that have passed since January 1, 1970 at the instant that you run your program. Therefore, every time you run, the page from which the computer chooses the random numbers will be different. Keep in mind that using random numbers in this way is good enough for games, but generally, not good enough for advanced applications where more truly random numbers are needed like cryptography. Also, consider using a more robust way to generate random numbers if their lack of true randomness can cost money. A few years ago, I remember reading an article about some hackers that figured out how the software for an online poker site was generating the random numbers that controlled the shuffling. If you are playing poker and you know the order of the cards in the deck, you have a big advantage.

After seeding the random number generator, you declare two int variables to hold the random numbers that you are going to generate:

```
    int randomA, randomB;
```

Next, you need to declare a temporary `card` structure that you will use while swapping the two cards that you pick from the deck:

```
struct card tempCard;
```

Now comes the loop. First, you declare the variable `i` to use as a counter and set it to 0:

```
int i=0;
```

Next, you build the body of your loop:

```
do {
```

In the loop, you generate two random numbers between 0 and 51 that you will use as indexes into the deck array:

```
// Generate 2 random numbers to determine which cards to swap
randomA = random() % 52;
randomB = random() % 52;
```

The `random` function returns a random number between 0 and $2^{31}-1$. You do not really need a number that big, you only need a number between 0 and 51. You can use the modulus (`%`) operator to divide the number returned from the `random` function by 52. Remember that modulus returns the remainder of the division. Therefore, if the random number is evenly divisible by 52, `%` returns 0. You should see that dividing by 52 would return remainders from 0 to 51.

Next, you compared the two random numbers:

```
if (randomA == randomB)
{
        continue;
}
```

There is no sense in swapping a card with itself, so you just continued to the next iteration of the loop if the indices to swap were the same.

The next block of code swaps the cards chosen from the deck at index positions `randomA` and `randomB`:

```
// Swap slots A and B
tempCard = deck[randomA];
deck[randomA] = deck[randomB];
deck[randomB] = tempCard;
```

You need the `tempCard` variable to hold the card located at index `randomA`. If you did not use a temporary variable, you would overwrite the card at `deck[randomA]` with the card at `deck[randomB]` on the next line. Figure 3-8 should make the need for the `tempCard` a little bit clearer.

Next, you increment the counter:

```
// Increment the counter
i++;
```

After the loop body, you check to see if `i` is less than 1,000,000:

```
}
while (i<1000000);
```

If it is, the loop runs again. If not, the program drops out of the loop and prints out the contents of the deck. My run produced the following output. Yours will be different.

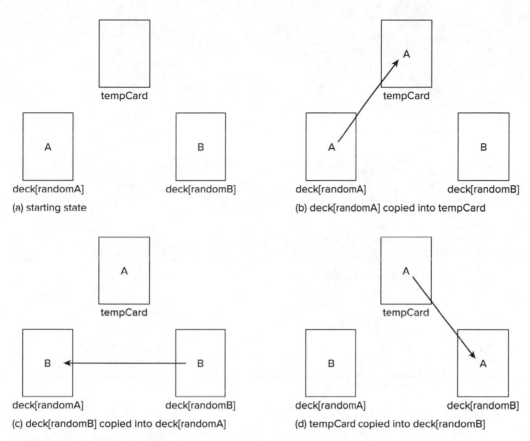

FIGURE 3-8: Swapping values with a temp variable

```
The card is three of hearts
The card is nine of clubs
The card is three of spades
The card is queen of diamonds
The card is five of diamonds
The card is king of diamonds
The card is ace of hearts
The card is seven of spades
The card is four of diamonds
The card is two of hearts
The card is three of diamonds
The card is nine of hearts
The card is queen of hearts
The card is two of spades
The card is jack of diamonds
The card is king of spades
The card is eight of clubs
The card is ace of spades
The card is six of spades
The card is jack of hearts
The card is five of hearts
```

```
The card is four of clubs
The card is seven of clubs
The card is eight of diamonds
The card is king of hearts
The card is four of spades
The card is ace of clubs
The card is two of clubs
The card is king of clubs
The card is seven of diamonds
The card is five of clubs
The card is queen of clubs
The card is seven of hearts
The card is jack of spades
The card is nine of spades
The card is eight of hearts
The card is jack of clubs
The card is three of clubs
The card is queen of spades
The card is ten of spades
The card is six of diamonds
The card is six of clubs
The card is six of hearts
The card is ace of diamonds
The card is two of diamonds
The card is four of hearts
The card is five of spades
The card is ten of diamonds
The card is ten of clubs
The card is ten of hearts
The card is eight of spades
The card is nine of diamonds
```

break and continue

There are two final keywords that you should know when dealing with loops: break and continue. You can use break to prematurely exit a loop regardless of the exit condition. You can use continue to end the current iteration of the loop code at any time and return to the top of the loop.

Break and continue are useful when you want to short circuit the execution of a loop. For example, if you were looping through a large array looking for a particular item, you would want to exit the loop as soon as you found the item. You could write something like this:

```
do
{
    theNumber = array[i];
    if (theNumber == myNumber)
        break;
}
while (i<arraySize);
```

Using break and continue may not always be elegant; however, sometimes using them can help with performance. If you do use break or continue, beware that they may make your code more difficult to debug because predicting when a loop will end becomes more difficult.

The keywords break and continue work in for loops as well as while and do ... while loops.

EXECUTION FLOW AND DECISIONS

In the last section, you learned about one thing that computers are very good at, loops. In this section, you will learn about another, decisions. Computers make decisions based on the logic that you provide. C has two decision structures, if ... else and switch.

The if Statement

Every program that you write will need to make decisions. The basic decision statement in C is if. This statement determines if a condition that you specify is true. If it is, the program executes the statements that are contained inside of a set of curly braces. If the condition is false, execution drops down below the closing brace.

The if statement can optionally be followed by an else block. If the condition in the if statement is false, the code in the else block is executed. If the condition is true, the program ignores the code in the else block.

The format of the if ... else block is:

```
if (condition) {
    Statements;
}
else {
    Statements;
}
```

You can test for multiple different cases within an if ... else block by using the else-if construct:

```
if (condition) {
    Statements;
}
else if (condition){
    Statements;
}
else if (condition){
    Statements;
}
else {
    Statements;
}
```

In this case, the program will run through each if statement until either a.) one of the conditions evaluates to true, or b.) execution reaches the final else block.

The else block is optional. So, if you only want to run a block of code based on some criteria and do not want to run any alternate code if the criteria is false, you can simply eliminate the else block.

You can include any code that you want to between the braces of an if statement. Therefore, nesting if statements like this is perfectly fine:

```
if (condition) {
    if (condition) {
```

```
        if (condition) {
            Statements;
        }


    }
}
```

TRY IT OUT Identifying Cards with if

codefile Cards available for download at Wrox.com

To update the Cards program to recognize your favorite card, follow this step:

1. Change the loop that prints out the deck of cards at the bottom of the program to this:

```
// Print out the shuffled deck
i=0;
while (i<52) {
    if (deck[i].value == 1){
        printf("The ace of %s is great!\n", deck[i].suit);
    }
    else {
        printf("The card is %s of %s\n", deck[i].name, deck[i].suit);
    }
    i++;
}
```

How It Works

You have added an if ... else block to print something special when the ace (card with a value of 1) is chosen from the deck:

```
if (deck[i].value == 1){
    printf("The ace of %s is great!\n", deck[i].suit);
}
else {
    printf("The card is %s of %s\n", deck[i].name, deck[i].suit);
}
```

Each time through the loop, the if statement checks to see if the value of the current card is 1. If it is, you will see the special output when the aces are printed. If the selected card is not an ace, you will see the normal output because the computer is executing the code in the else block.

The Conditional Operator

Some decisions are so common that the creators of C created a conditional operator ?:. This operator is a shorthand version of the if-else decision structure.

Look at this decision:

```
if (x>y)
    n=x;
else
    n=y;
```

This block of code assigns the value of x to the variable n if x is greater than y. If x is not greater than y, it assigns the value of y to n. You can express the same condition using the *conditional operator* like this:

```
n=(x>y)?x:y;
```

The conditional operator evaluates the conditional expression before the question mark (?). If the conditional evaluates to true, the conditional operator returns the value after the question mark. If the conditional evaluates to false, the conditional operator returns the value after the colon (.). Using this simple operator, you can reduce the amount of code that you must write to implement this decision from 4 lines to 1.

Choosing an Option with switch

Where the if statement allows you to test some criteria for truth and then execute a specific block of code, the switch statement allows you to determine program flow based on an integer value. Switch uses an integer to branch to a specific case that you label with that integer. Here is the syntax for switch:

```
switch (expression){
    case label:
    {
        Statements;
        break;
    }
    case label:
    {
        Statements;
        break;
    }
    default:
    {
        Statements;
        break;
    }
}
```

Depending on the value of the expression, the execution will jump to the specific case identified. If none of the cases is appropriate, execution will jump to the default label. The default case is optional. If you do not provide a default case, execution will just exit the switch and move on to the next statement. Each case label must be unique.

TRY IT OUT   Printing Messages with switch

codefile Cards available for download at Wrox.com

To add code to print out different messages for the face cards, follow this step:

1.   Modify the else block from the previous example like this:

```
else {
    switch (deck[i].value){
```

```
            case 11:
                printf("A jack of all trades (%s)\n", deck[i].suit);
                break;
            case 12:
                printf("A queen of the castle (%s)\n", deck[i].suit);
                break;
            case 13:
                printf("The king of the world (%s)\n", deck[i].suit);
                break;
            default:
                printf("The card is %s of %s\n", deck[i].name,
                    deck[i].suit);
                break;
        }
    }
```

How It Works

This code uses a `switch` statement to print out different things based on the chosen card:

```
switch (deck[i].value){
```

Each time through the `switch` statement, the computer evaluates the value of the chosen card. If the value is 11, the program executes the code in the `case 11:` section:

```
case 11:
    printf("A jack of all trades (%s)\n", deck[i].suit);
    break;
```

If the value is 12, the program executes the code in the `case 12:` section and so on. If none of the cases matches, the code in the `default` case runs and you will see the normal output:

```
default:
    printf("The card is %s of %s\n", deck[i].name,
        deck[i].suit);
    break;
```

Here is the output from when I ran the program:

```
The king of the world (spades)
The ace of diamonds is great!
The card is four of spades
The card is two of diamonds
The king of the world (clubs)
The card is ten of clubs
A jack of all trades (clubs)
The card is seven of diamonds
The card is ten of hearts
The card is nine of spades
The card is two of hearts
The card is six of diamonds
The card is four of clubs
A queen of the castle (diamonds)
The ace of clubs is great!
The ace of spades is great!
A queen of the castle (hearts)
The card is seven of clubs
The card is three of hearts
The card is eight of hearts
```

```
The card is eight of spades
The card is three of clubs
The card is eight of clubs
A jack of all trades (spades)
The card is four of diamonds
The card is ten of spades
The card is six of clubs
A jack of all trades (diamonds)
The card is five of hearts
The card is five of clubs
The card is three of diamonds
The king of the world (hearts)
The ace of hearts is great!
A jack of all trades (hearts)
The card is seven of hearts
The card is four of hearts
The card is six of hearts
The card is six of spades
The card is three of spades
The card is eight of diamonds
The card is nine of clubs
The card is nine of hearts
The card is five of spades
The card is ten of diamonds
The card is nine of diamonds
A queen of the castle (spades)
The card is two of clubs
A queen of the castle (clubs)
The card is seven of spades
The card is five of diamonds
The king of the world (diamonds)
The card is two of spades
```

BREAKING UP CODE WITH FUNCTIONS

For large programs, it gets very ugly to have all of your code for the entire program in one place. You can break up your program by writing *functions*. It is very important to break your program into smaller chunks of code because this makes the code easier to follow from a logical standpoint. In the end, this makes the program easier to read and easier to debug. Additionally, if there are many people working on a project, it is impossible to work on it if all of the code is in one file with one giant function.

In your Cards program, it makes sense to break out the shuffling of the cards into its own, separate function. Not only will this make the main function smaller and more readable, but also breaking out the function may allow you to reuse it in the future. Imagine that you were writing a game where you had to shuffle the deck many times. It is far easier and cleaner to call a function to shuffle the deck rather than re-writing the code to shuffle each time you needed it.

Functions can return values, but they do not have to. The syntax for a function definition is:

```
returnType functionName (parameters)
{
    Statements;
    return;
}
```

You use parameters to pass data into a function. You can use the return value to send a piece of data back to the function caller. The parameters and return value can be any types that you want. The parameters and return type are both optional. However, if a function will not return a value, it is common to specify the return type as void. By default, functions in C return an int type. Therefore, if you do not specify the return type, your function should return an int.

For example, you could write a function that adds two ints and returns their sum like this:

```
int addInts (int num1, int num2)
{
    return num1 + num2;
}
```

To call this function, a user would pass in the two numbers that they want to add and assign the return value to a variable like this:

```
sum = addInts(4,5);
```

This line would call the method addInts and pass in the values of 4 and 5 as parameters. Once inside the addInts function, the value of 4 is assigned to the parameter num1 and the 5 is assigned to num2. The return statement returns the sum of num1 and num2, which in this case is 9. Finally, the returned value of 9 is assigned to the variable sum.

Function parameters are passed *by value*. This means that the values are passed into the function, not the variable itself. In practice, this means that modifying the values of function parameters inside the function will not affect the values once the function exits.

The scope of function parameters is local to the function. Once the function exits, the parameters are undefined.

TRY IT OUT   Breaking Up Code with Functions

codefile Cards available for download at Wrox.com

To break out the code that shuffles the deck of cards and the code that prints the deck into their own functions, follow these steps:

1.   Under the definition of the card struct, define a new shuffle function like this:

```
void shuffle(struct card* deck) {
    //  Seed the random number generator
    srandom( time( NULL ) );
    int i=0;
    int randomA, randomB;
    struct card tempCard;

    do {
        // Generate 2 random numbers to determine which cards to swap
        randomA = random() % 52;
        randomB = random() % 52;

        // Swap slots A and B
        tempCard = deck[randomA];
```

```
        deck[randomA] = deck[randomB];
        deck[randomB] = tempCard;

        // Increment the counter
        i++;
    }
    while (i<1000000);

}
```

You can cut the body of the function from the main function and paste it into shuffle. In essence, you are moving the code from main into the shuffle function.

2. Under the shuffle function, define the printDeck function. Again, you can cut the code from the main function and paste it into printDeck. Here is the printDeck function.

3. Add calls to shuffle and printDeck to the main function like this:

```
// Run the function to shuffle the deck
shuffle(deck);

// Print the deck
printDeck(deck);
```

Here is the complete code for the Cards program:

```
#include <stdio.h>
#include <stdlib.h>
#include <time.h>

struct card {
    char* name;
    char* suit;
    int value;
};

void shuffle(struct card* deck) {
    // Seed the random number generator
    srandom( time( NULL ) );
    int i=0;
    int randomA, randomB;
    struct card tempCard;

    do {
        // Generate 2 random numbers to determine which cards to swap
        randomA = random() % 52;
        randomB = random() % 52;

        // Swap slots A and B
        tempCard = deck[randomA];
        deck[randomA] = deck[randomB];
        deck[randomB] = tempCard;

        // Increment the counter
        i++;
    }
```

```c
        while (i<1000000);

}


void printDeck(struct card* deck) {
    // Print out the shuffled deck
    int i=0;
    while (i<52) {
        if (deck[i].value == 1){
            printf("The ace of %s is great!\n", deck[i].suit);
        }
        else {
            switch (deck[i].value){
                case 11:
                    printf("A jack of all trades (%s)\n", deck[i].suit);
                    break;
                case 12:
                    printf("A queen of the castle (%s)\n", deck[i].suit);
                    break;
                case 13:
                    printf("The king of the world (%s)\n", deck[i].suit);
                    break;
                default:
                    printf("The card is %s of %s\n", deck[i].name,
                            deck[i].suit);
                    break;
            }
        }
        i++;
    }


}

int main (int argc, const char * argv[])
{

    struct card deck[] =
    {
        {"ace", "spades",1}, {"two", "spades",2}, {"three", "spades",3},
        {"four", "spades",4}, {"five", "spades",5}, {"six", "spades",6},
        {"seven", "spades",7}, {"eight", "spades",8}, {"nine", "spades",9},
        {"ten", "spades",10}, {"jack", "spades",11}, {"queen", "spades",12},
        {"king", "spades",13},
        {"ace", "clubs",1}, {"two", "clubs",2}, {"three", "clubs",3},
        {"four", "clubs",4}, {"five", "clubs",5}, {"six", "clubs",6},
        {"seven", "clubs",7}, {"eight", "clubs",8}, {"nine", "clubs",9},
        {"ten", "clubs",10}, {"jack", "clubs",11}, {"queen", "clubs",12},
        {"king", "clubs",13},
        {"ace", "hearts",1}, {"two", "hearts",2}, {"three", "hearts",3},
        {"four", "hearts",4}, {"five", "hearts",5}, {"six", "hearts",6},
        {"seven", "hearts",7}, {"eight", "hearts",8}, {"nine", "hearts",9},
        {"ten", "hearts",10}, {"jack", "hearts",11}, {"queen", "hearts",12},
        {"king", "hearts",13},
```

```
                 {"ace", "diamonds",1}, {"two", "diamonds",2}, {"three", "diamonds",3},
                 {"four", "diamonds",4}, {"five", "diamonds",5}, {"six", "diamonds",6},
                 {"seven", "diamonds",7}, {"eight", "diamonds",8},
                 {"nine", "diamonds",9},{"ten", "diamonds",10}, {"jack", "diamonds",11},
                 {"queen", "diamonds",12}, {"king", "diamonds",13}

         };

         // Run the function to shuffle the deck
         shuffle(deck);

         // Print the deck
         printDeck(deck);


         return 0;
    }
```

How It Works

The new `shuffle` function does not return a value and accepts a pointer to a `card` structure called `deck`:

```
    void shuffle(struct card* deck) {
```

You will learn about pointers in the next section. For now, you can think of this pointer as an arrow that tells the function the location of the first item in the `deck` array. Therefore, in effect, you are passing the `deck` array in to the `shuffle` function. The rest of the function is the same as the code was before, except it is now in its own function.

The same goes for the `printDeck` function:

```
    void printDeck(struct card* deck) {
```

It is also a void function and does not return a value. `printDeck` accepts a pointer to the `deck` as a parameter. The rest of the function is identical to the last example.

Finally, you will notice that the `main` function is quite a bit smaller now. All `main` does is define the `deck` and call the `shuffle` and `printDeck` functions:

```
    // Run the function to shuffle the deck
    shuffle(deck);

    // Print the deck
    printDeck(deck);
```

Can you see how using functions made the program simpler? You used functions to break down the logic of the program into bite-sized chunks. If you have a problem with the shuffling logic, you can go directly to the `shuffle` function to work on it. The same goes for the printing function. This has also greatly simplified the `main` function of the program. Additionally, the `printDeck` and `shuffle` functions are now reusable in your program. You can call them from anywhere you want, as long as you pass in the `deck` array.

POINTERS

For programmers coming from platforms like Java or .Net, pointers can be a foreign and scary topic. Do not be afraid. Although misusing pointers can cause difficult to debug problems, their correct use can be very powerful. Additionally, when dealing with objects in the next chapter, the only way to access those objects is through pointers.

A pointer is simply a variable that holds an address. This is typically the address of another variable or an object, as you will see in the next chapter. To explain further, let's take a step back. All variables that you create are stored somewhere in memory. This "somewhere" is the variable's address.

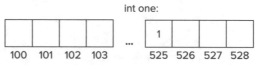

FIGURE 3-9: Storing an int in memory

Figure 3-9 shows how a variable named one of type int is stored in memory. In this case, the value of 1 is stored in memory location 525.

Now, look at a pointer to this variable. You declare pointers by using the type to which the pointer will point and the *, which is called the indirection or dereferencing operator. In this case, the declaration is int* pOne. You can read this as, "a pointer to an int called pOne." At this point, you have a pointer to an int type, that doesn't actually point to anything. To make your new pointer point to the value in memory address 525, also known by the variable one, you use the address of operator &. The syntax to assign the address of variable one to the pointer pOne is pOne=&one;. You can read this statement as, "set pOne equal to the address of one." Figure 3-10 illustrates the pointer that you have just created. Notice how the pointer variable pOne does not contain the value of 1. It contains the address of the memory location that holds the value.

You should also be aware that since the pointer is a variable, it has an address too. In Figure 3-10, pOne has the address 100. It is possible to create pointers to pointers like this: int** ppOne. So, ppOne is a pointer to a pointer to an int.

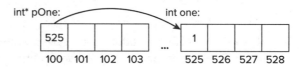

FIGURE 3-10: Pointer pointing to an int

In addition to using the * operator to declare pointer variables, it is also used to retrieve the value pointed to by the pointer. Say you wanted to assign the value in the variable one, which is 1, to another variable called temp. You could do it with the statement temp=one;. You could also do it by using the pointer to one like this, temp=*pOne;. You could read this as "set temp equal to the value pointed to by pOne."

The most important thing to remember about pointers is that they are addresses or references. You need to dereference the pointer to get the value stored in that memory address. Once you fully grasp this concept, the rest is easy.

You should now see how you used pointers in the Cards program in the shuffle and printDeck functions. Both of these functions require a reference to the deck that they will use. You provided this reference as a pointer to the deck. So, you did not pass the deck itself, you just passed a pointer to the memory location that holds the deck. In fact, you did not pass the location of the entire deck; you only passed the location of the first element in the array that holds the deck.

Pointers and arrays are closely related. You can use pointers instead of subscripts to work with arrays. Assigning an array to a pointer variable is the same as assigning the address of the first element of the array to the pointer. You can then use pointer arithmetic to move through the array. Adding one to the pointer will make the pointer point to the next item in the array and subtracting one will make the pointer point to the previous item in the array. Be careful though, because there is no bounds checking on pointers. If you try to point to elements that are outside of your array, the program may still run, but point to bad values. The program may also just crash in spectacular fashion.

TRY IT OUT   Using Pointers to Access an Array

codefile Cards available for download at Wrox.com

To change the `printDeck` function to move through the deck by using pointers instead of using the array subscript notation, follow these steps:

1. Since you will not be counting as you move through the array, you need to add a "sentinel" value to the deck array. You will use the sentinel to indicate that you are at the end of the deck. That way, you can test for the sentinel each time through the loop and stop printing cards when you reach the end of the deck. Add the sentinel to the deck array so that the definition looks like this:

```
struct card deck[] =
{
    {"ace", "spades",1}, {"two", "spades",2}, {"three", "spades",3},
    {"four", "spades",4}, {"five", "spades",5}, {"six", "spades",6},
    {"seven", "spades",7}, {"eight", "spades",8}, {"nine", "spades",9},
    {"ten", "spades",10}, {"jack", "spades",11}, {"queen", "spades",12},
    {"king", "spades",13},
    {"ace", "clubs",1}, {"two", "clubs",2}, {"three", "clubs",3},
    {"four", "clubs",4}, {"five", "clubs",5}, {"six", "clubs",6},
    {"seven", "clubs",7}, {"eight", "clubs",8}, {"nine", "clubs",9},
    {"ten", "clubs",10}, {"jack", "clubs",11}, {"queen", "clubs",12},
    {"king", "clubs",13},
    {"ace", "hearts",1}, {"two", "hearts",2}, {"three", "hearts",3},
    {"four", "hearts",4}, {"five", "hearts",5}, {"six", "hearts",6},
    {"seven", "hearts",7}, {"eight", "hearts",8}, {"nine", "hearts",9},
    {"ten", "hearts",10}, {"jack", "hearts",11}, {"queen", "hearts",12},
    {"king", "hearts",13},
    {"ace", "diamonds",1}, {"two", "diamonds",2}, {"three", "diamonds",3},
    {"four", "diamonds",4}, {"five", "diamonds",5}, {"six", "diamonds",6},
    {"seven", "diamonds",7}, {"eight", "diamonds",8},
    {"nine", "diamonds",9},{"ten", "diamonds",10}, {"jack", "diamonds",11},
    {"queen", "diamonds",12}, {"king", "diamonds",13},
    {"sentinel", "null", 0}
};
```

2. Now, change the `printDeck` function to:

```
void printDeck(struct card* deck) {
    // Print out the shuffled deck

    // Get the actual card
```

```
        struct card theCard = *deck;

    while (theCard.value!=0) {
        printf("The card is %s of %s\n", theCard.name,
                theCard.suit);


        // Move to the next card
        deck++;

        // Dereference the pointer so that the theCard variable holds
        // an actual card. Remember the variable deck points to the location
        // of theCard, not the card itself
        theCard = *deck;
    }
}
```

I have removed the code that illustrated the `if` and `switch` statements for clarity.

How It Works

As you learned, the `printDeck` function receives a pointer to the first element of the `deck` array, which is of type `struct card`, as its input parameter:

```
void printDeck(struct card* deck) {
```

The code first declares a temporary variable of type `struct card` called `theCard` that will hold the card that you are working with. You use the pointer dereferencing operator `*` to get the first card from the deck and assign it to `theCard`:

```
struct card theCard = *deck;
```

Next, you create a `while` loop that tests for the sentinel value:

```
while (theCard.value!=0) {
```

While the value of `theCard` is not 0, the loop will continue to run. Next, you print out the value of `theCard` by using the structure notation:

```
printf("The card is %s of %s\n", theCard.name,
        theCard.suit);
```

Note that you are using just a normal `struct` variable now and that the array notation is missing. Next, you move on to the next card in the deck by incrementing the pointer to the array, `deck`:

```
// Move to the next card
deck++;
```

Finally, you set the temporary variable `theCard` to the next card in the deck by dereferencing the pointer to the deck:

```
theCard = *deck;
```

Each time thorough the loop, you are moving the pointer to the next card in the deck. Only when the pointer reaches the sentinel will the loop end.

It is possible to simplify this code further and remove the temporary variable. Since using pointers to structures is so common, the creators of the C language came up with a shortcut, the arrow operator ->. This operator dereferences a pointer and returns the value of the structure element referenced at the same time. The usefulness of this operator should become clear with the next example.

TRY IT OUT   Using the Arrow Operator

codefile Cards available for download at Wrox.com

To use the arrow operator with the array, follow this step:

1. Replace the `printDeck` function with this:

```c
void printDeck(struct card* deck) {
    // Print out the shuffled deck

    while (deck->value!=0) {
        printf("The card is %s of %s\n", deck->name,
                deck->suit);

        // Move to the next card
        deck++;

    }
}
```

How It Works

Using the arrow operator, you have eliminated the need for a temporary variable to hold the card. In the `while` statement, the arrow operator dereferences the pointer to the deck and gets the `value` member from the structure all in one step:

```c
while (deck->value!=0) {
```

Likewise, in the `printf` statement, you use the arrow to dereference the `deck` pointer and obtain the `name` and `suit` values from the underlying structure:

```c
printf("The card is %s of %s\n", deck->name,
        deck->suit);
```

Then, you simply move to the next card in the deck by incrementing the pointer.

A GAME EXAMPLE

To sum up the concepts from this chapter, you will build a simple card game based on the classic game Acey-Deucy. In this game, the player starts with a bank of 100 credits. In each round, the player is dealt two cards and then asked to place a bet on whether the next card will fall in between the first two cards. If the next card is between the first two, the amount that the player bet is added to his bank. If not, the bet is deducted from the bank. The game ends when either the player's bank reaches 0 or there are not enough cards left in the deck to deal another hand.

To keep the example simple, aces are worth one point. In addition, if the third card is the same as either of the first two, the player loses.

TRY IT OUT **Creating a Simple Game**

codefile Acey available for download at Wrox.com

To update the Cards program to play Acey-Deucy, follow these steps:

1. Start up Xcode and select File ⇨ Open. Navigate to the Cards project that you worked on in the last section. Select the Cards.xcodeproj file and click Open. Select the main.c code file in the project navigator to open the code for the main function.

2. You will reuse the includes, card struct, and the shuffle function, so leave that area of the file alone. You will modify the main function in this section. In the main function, you can also leave the deck array alone. Delete all of the code in main after the deck array is declared and replace it with the following code:

```c
// Create the player's bank and start it off with 100 credits
int bank=100;

// Create a pointer to the deck
struct card* pDeck = deck;

// Create a variable to hold the bet
int bet=0;

// Run the function to shuffle the deck
shuffle(deck);

// Run the game in a loop. Continue as long as the bank is > and none of
// the next three cards are the sentinel
do {
    // Print the amount of credits in the bank
    printf("Your bank: %i\n", bank);

    // Print the cards
    printf("The cards: ");

    // First card
    printf("%s of %s ", pDeck->name, pDeck->suit);

    // Move to the next card
    pDeck++;

    // Second card
    printf("and %s of %s\n", pDeck->name, pDeck->suit);

    // Move the pointer to the next card
    pDeck++;

    // Ask for the bet
```

```
        // Do this in a loop because we cannot accept bets greater than the
        // amount that the player has in the bank and we cannot
        // accept a 0 bet
        do {
            printf("Enter your bet: ");
            scanf("%i", &bet);
        }
        while (bet <= 0 || bet > bank );

        // Draw the third card
        printf("The third card is %s of %s\n", pDeck->name, pDeck->suit);

        // Determine if the player won
        // The player is a winner if the third card falls between the first two
        // Ties go to the house
        if (((pDeck-2)->value < pDeck-> value &&
            (pDeck-1)->value > pDeck->value) ||
           ((pDeck-2)->value > pDeck-> value &&
            (pDeck-1)->value < pDeck->value)) {
               printf("We have a winner!\n\n");

               // Player won, add bet to the bank
               bank += bet;

        }
        else {
            printf("Sorry, you lose.\n\n");
            // Player lost, subsract bet from the bank
            bank -= bet;
        }

        // Move to the next card
        pDeck++;

    }
    while (bank > 0 &&
           pDeck->value!=0 &&
           (pDeck+1)->value!=0 &&
           (pDeck+2)->value!=0);

    // The game is over
    printf("The game is over. Your final score is %i\n", bank);

    return 0;
}
```

3. Run the program by selecting Product ⇨ Run from the menubar. Click in the debug console window to interact with the game. When you start the game, the output should look like this:

```
Your bank: 100
The cards: king of clubs and five of spades
Enter your bet:
```

4. Click in the debug output window next to where you see the prompt to enter your bet. Enter a bet and press return. You should see text indicating the next card, if you won or lost, the new amount in your bank, and the next hand of cards. Continue playing until you win, lose, or get sick of the game. Here is part of the output of my test run:

```
Your bank: 100
The cards: king of clubs and five of spades
Enter your bet: 20
The third card is seven of spades
We have a winner!

Your bank: 120
The cards: four of hearts and three of diamonds
Enter your bet: 5
The third card is six of diamonds
Sorry, you lose.

Your bank: 115
The cards: nine of spades and four of diamonds
Enter your bet: 55
The third card is jack of diamonds
Sorry, you lose.

Your bank: 60
The cards: king of diamonds and six of hearts
Enter your bet: 60
The third card is queen of hearts
We have a winner!

Your bank: 120
The cards: eight of spades and ace of hearts
Enter your bet: 120
The third card is three of spades
We have a winner!
```

How It Works

Everything from the top of the program down through the definition of the deck is the same as you have seen in the Cards examples that you worked through earlier in the chapter. Therefore, I will not rehash what you already know. If you have any questions about what is going on, I would refer you back to earlier sections of this chapter.

Let's pick up with the code after the definition of the deck. First, you create some variables to keep track of the player's bank, a pointer to the deck, and the amount that the player wants to bet. Next, you call the function to shuffle the deck:

```
// Create the player's bank and start it off with 100 credits
int bank=100;

// Create a pointer to the deck
struct card* pDeck = deck;

// Create a variable to hold the bet
int bet=0;

// Run the function to shuffle the deck
shuffle(deck);
```

Most of the rest of the program occurs in a loop. Running a game in a loop like this is so common that it has a name, the game loop. You will learn more about game loops later on in the book. The game loop contains all of the logic for running the game. The loop will continue running as long as the criteria in the `while` statement at the end are met. If you jump down to the end of the loop, you will see the `while` statement:

```
while (bank > 0 &&
       pDeck->value!=0 &&
       (pDeck+1)->value!=0 &&
       (pDeck+2)->value!=0);
```

The game loop will continue to run as long as the player's `bank` is greater than zero. Additionally, the `while` statement checks the next three cards to make sure that none of them are the sentinel. You need three cards to play a hand, so it would not make sense to start the loop again if there were not enough cards in the deck to finish a hand. You can see here that you are using pointer arithmetic to look forward in the deck. You look at the value of the current card (`pDeck->value`) the next card (`(pDeck+1)->value`) and the third card (`(pDeck+2)->value`). In this statement, you are taking advantage of the fact that the `&&` Boolean operator short circuits if any condition is true. Therefore, you do not have to worry about dereferencing a bad pointer at the end of the game in the case of `pDeck+2` because `pDeck+1` will return 0 for the sentinel card and end the conditional before the computer tries to get the value of `pDeck+2`, which may be invalid.

Now, jump back up into the `do` loop. Upon entering the loop, the code prints the number of credits in the player's `bank` and then prints the first card:

```
// Print the amount of credits in the bank
printf("Your bank: %i\n", bank);

// Print the cards
printf("The cards: ");

// First card
printf("%s of %s ", pDeck->name, pDeck->suit);
```

Next, the code increments the pointer to the deck, `pDeck`, to move to the next card. The code then prints the next card and once again increments the pointer:

```
// Move to the next card
pDeck++;

// Second card
printf("and %s of %s\n", pDeck->name, pDeck->suit);

// Move the pointer to the next card
pDeck++;
```

The next bit of code asks for the player's bet by using the `scanf` function:

```
do {
    printf("Enter your bet: ");
    scanf("%i", &bet);
}
while (bet <= 0 || bet > bank );
```

As you learned earlier, you use the scanf function to read input from the command line. There is not much input validation in this program, but we cannot allow bets of 0 (because 0 is not a bet!) or bets greater than the amount that the player has in the bank. Therefore, this loop will continually ask the player for a bet if the player put a value less than or equal to 0 as his bet or if he tried to bet an amount greater than his bank.

Once you have a valid bet, the code presents the third card:

```
printf("The third card is %s of %s\n", pDeck->name, pDeck->suit);
```

Once you have displayed the third card, you can determine if the player has won or not. That is exactly what the complicated looking if statement does:

```
if (((pDeck-2)->value < pDeck-> value &&
     (pDeck-1)->value > pDeck->value) ||
    ((pDeck-2)->value > pDeck-> value &&
     (pDeck-1)->value < pDeck->value)) {
        printf("We have a winner!\n\n");

        // Player won, add bet to the bank
        bank += bet;

    }
else {
    printf("Sorry, you lose.\n\n");
    // Player lost, subsract bet from the bank
    bank -= bet;
}
```

To determine if the player won, you need to decide if the value of the third card falls in between the first two. You have done this here with some pointer arithmetic. This is very similar to the code that you looked at in the while portion of the game loop above. This if statement checks whether:

➤ The first card (pDeck-2) has a value less than the current card (pDeck), and the second card (pDeck-1) has a value greater than the current card.

➤ The first card (pDeck-2) has a value greater than the current card (pDeck), and the second card (pDeck-1) has a value less than the current card.

This ensures that the current card is indeed between the two other cards regardless of the order of the first two cards. In other words, a five is between a seven and a two and also between a two and a seven. The order in which the first two cards are dealt is irrelevant to the game, but the code must check both ways.

If the player has won, the code prints out a congratulatory message and adds the amount that the player bet to the player's bank. If the player lost, the program prints its condolences and subtracts the bet from the bank. Finally, the program moves the pointer to the next card to prepare for the next hand:

```
pDeck++;
```

You already looked at the while condition above. As a brief refresher, the while statement will run the do loop again as long as the player has money in the bank and there are at least three more cards left in the deck.

When the game cannot continue, the program tells the player that the game is over and prints out the player's final bank:

```
printf("The game is over. Your final score is %i\n", bank);
```

SUMMARY

This chapter covered a lot of ground; however, it is not a definitive guide to the C programming language. To learn more about the C language, I would highly recommend that you pick up a copy of *The C Programming Language* by Brian W. Kernighan and Dennis M. Ritchie (Prentice Hall, 1988). This book has been the best way to learn C for about 25 years. Short of the more advanced and esoteric features of C, after reading this chapter, you should be well versed in the basic constructs of the C language and you are now ready to move on to Objective-C.

In this chapter, you learned about the basic constructs in the C language including variables, statements and expressions. You also looked at the two different looping structures for and while/ do ... while. Then, you moved on to the decision structures if and switch. After that, you learned how to make your code more modular by using functions. You finished up by conquering the often-feared topic of pointers.

To top all of that off, you wrote a fully functioning game. It may not be the best game, but perhaps it is your first!

EXERCISES

1. What are the four base data types in C?

2. What is the correct syntax for declaring an int variable called myInt and initializing it to 0?

3. Describe the difference between a while and a do...while loop.

4. How would you define a function doWork that accepts an int and a float as input parameters and returns a double?

5. If the function doWork that you wrote for the last exercise modifies the value of one of the input parameters, would the value that the main program passed to the function change?

6. Modify the code in the Acey project to crown the player a winner if the third card is between the first two cards or equal to either of the first two cards.

7. Rewrite the main function by using array subscript notation and a counter to work through the deck instead of using pointers and pointer arithmetic. Do you find this code easier or more difficult to write and understand?

Answers to the Exercises can be found in the Appendix.

▶ **WHAT YOU LEARNED IN THIS CHAPTER**

TOPIC	MAIN POINTS
Variables	You use variables in your code to store pieces of data.
Types	The base data types in C are `char`, `int`, `float`, and `double`.

`for` Loop	`for (initializer; condition; incrementer)`
	`{`
	
	`}`

`while` loop	`while (condition)`
	`{`
	
	`}`

`do…while` loop	`do`
	`{`
	
	`}`
	`while (condition)`

`if…then…else`	You control flow in C with the following structures:
	if…then…else:
	`if (condition) {`
	`    Statements;`
	`}`
	`else if (condition){`
	`    Statements;`
	`}`
	`else {`
	`    Statements;`
	`}`

switch	```c switch (expression){ case label: { Statements; break; } default: { Statements; break; } } ```
Functions	You use functions to break your code into logical groups. Using functions makes your code more readable, modular, and easier to maintain.
Pointers	Pointers are variables that hold addresses. You must de-reference a pointer to access the data to which the pointer points.

The Objective-C Programming Language

WHAT YOU WILL LEARN IN THIS CHAPTER:

➤ Understanding the relationship between C and Objective-C

➤ Learning basic object-oriented concepts like classes, objects, methods, and messages

➤ Building classes in Objective-C

➤ Managing memory

Objective-C is a superset of C. Everything that you can do in C, you can also do in Objective-C. The majority of features that Objective-C adds to C enable you to build your programs by using object-oriented (OO) programming techniques. In the last chapter, you learned that C is a structured programming language. Structured languages run in a top down manner and encourage a step-by-step, function-based approach to solving problems.

On the other hand, object-oriented languages encourage a more abstract approach, as you will learn in this chapter. In an object-oriented language like Objective-C, you model your software as a group of objects. Instead of writing functions that do a particular operation, you encapsulate your program logic into these objects. The objects have functions, or *methods*, that operate on the data contained in the objects. The objects can also contain their own data. Often, you will model the objects in your programs based on real-world objects. This can make object-oriented programs easier to understand. Object-oriented programs can also be easier to debug and modify because you encapsulate all of the functionality and data related to an object in the object itself.

CLASSES AND OBJECTS

The basic unit of functionality in an object-oriented program is the *object*. When your program runs, there may be hundreds, thousands, or perhaps millions of objects active at any given time. You create all of the objects in your program from classes.

A class is the blueprint for creating objects. Just as a builder uses a blueprint to create houses, you use classes to create objects. Each house may have a different color, but each follows the same blueprint. In Figure 4-1, you can see the blueprint for a house and three instances of that house: one red, one green, and one yellow. The builder made each house from the same blueprint, but changed the color. You can think of color as a property of a house. Each house has a color, but you can set the color for each instance of a house individually.

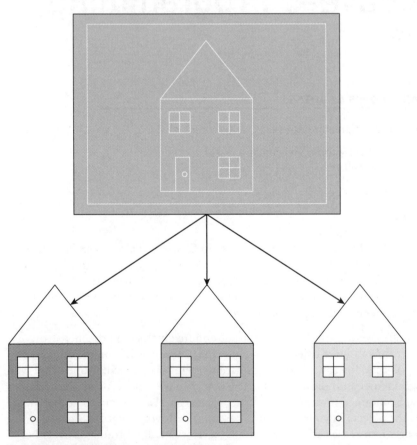

FIGURE 4-1: Building houses from a blueprint

In your code, you define classes that represent the kinds of objects that you will use in your program. Then, when you need to use an object, you create an *instance* of your class. The instance of the class that you have created is called an *object*. Once you have created an object, it stands alone in that, aside from being of the same type, it is not associated with any other objects that you have created from the class. To go back to the house analogy, each house is the same type, but you can independently change the color of any house without affecting any other house.

You could create a House class to represent houses in your code. To model the illustration in Figure 4-1, the House class would have a color member variable. Then, you could create as many instances of the House as you want, each with its own color. Changing the color of one house object has no effect on any other houses that you created.

Instance Variables

Member or instance variables maintain the state or current condition of your objects. The values that you place in member variables are stored independently for each instance of a class. As you will see, each object of type House that you create will have its own unique value stored in the color instance variable. You can access the member variables of your class in the implementation.

Instance variables have a different scope depending on how you define them. The three scope values that you will use most often are @private, @protected, and @public. Private instance variables are available only to the class in which they are declared. Protected variables are available to the class in which they are declared and any subclasses. You will learn more about subclasses later in this chapter. Public variables are available from any code. By default, instance variables have protected scope.

You can see this illustrated in Figure 4-2. The diagram depicts a variable declared in theClass at the various scope levels. The visibility of a private variable, shown in green, is only visible to theClass. Protected scope, illustrated in yellow, shows that the variable is available to both theClass and any class that inherits from theClass. Finally, public scope is shown in pink. Any code can access public instance variables.

One advantage of an object-oriented program is *encapsulation*. The concept of encapsulation is that you can contain all of the functionality of a class in the class itself without exposing the inner details to users of the class. That way, the class looks like a black box to the

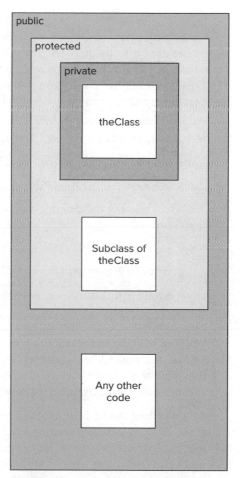

FIGURE 4-2: Member variable scope

outside world. Users of your class should not need to know nor should they care about how you implemented the class. You can hide the internal details of your class and achieve encapsulation by using private or protected member variables. That way, users of your class cannot access a class's members directly. All access should be through messages or properties. You will learn more about properties later in this chapter. By using this methodology, you can control how users get data from your class as opposed to users going directly to the internal data.

Methods and Messages

Besides maintaining state with member variables, classes also perform functionality. The functions that a class performs are called its *methods*. Methods are functions that you use to implement behavior in your class. A `House` class might have methods like `setColor:` to set the color of a house or `getColor` to get the color of the house.

You define methods by their name, return type, and parameters just like C functions. Methods do not necessarily need to return values. Just like C functions, you define methods that do not return values as returning `void`.

For someone new to Objective-C, the syntax for declaring methods often appears strange. Method names are typically quite lengthy with parameters specified by using a colon (:), the type, and the parameter name. This seems odd, but when you get used to it, you will miss it in other languages. This nomenclature allows you to specify functions that read well in code. You can tell what each parameter means without having to look up the function in the documentation. For example, consider the following C function to define a rectangle with two points, x1, y1 and x2, y2:

```
void defineRect (int x1, int y1, int x2, int y2)
```

Callers of this function would call it like this:

```
defineRect (20,30,60,120)
```

Without knowing the definition of the function, it is impossible to tell what the 20, 30, 60, and 120 represent.

Now, consider a similar Objective-C method:

```
-(void) defineRectWithx1: (int) x1 y1:(int) y1 x2:(int)x2 y2: (int)y2
```

Users would call this method like this:

```
defineRectWithx1:20 y1:30 x2:60 y2:120
```

Without looking at the definition of the method, it is clear that you are passing 20 as `x1`, 30 as `y1` and so on. In fact, the parameters and colons are included as part of the method name. Therefore, the name of this method is `defineRectWithx1:y1:x2:y2:`. I think that you will grow to enjoy the verbosity as you continue to work with Objective-C.

When calling methods on Objective-C objects, you are not really calling a method in the strictest sense. You are actually sending a message to the object. In other object-oriented languages like C++, methods are bound to a memory address within the class by the compiler using compile-time binding. Conversely, messages in Objective-C are bound at runtime by using a system called dynamic binding. The advantages and disadvantages of both binding schemes are beyond the scope of this book. Technically, a class has methods and you call them by sending messages. Many people often refer to sending the message as "calling the method" so I will use the terms *method* and *message* synonymously unless there is a specific need to address the messaging scheme at a lower level. For more detail, consult the, "The Objective-C Programming Language" document on Apple's website at `http://developer.apple.com/library/ios/#documentation/Cocoa/Conceptual/ObjectiveC/Chapters/ocObjectsClasses.html`.

TRY IT OUT   Methods and Messages

codefile Houses available for download at Wrox.com

In this section, you will write a program to model the houses in Figure 4-1. You will create a House class and create instances of that class with different colors. Then, you will print out the color of each house.

1. Start up Xcode and from the File menu select New ⇨ New Project …. Once again, you will be developing a simple command-line tool for Mac OS X. In the dialog, select, "Application" under the Mac OS X section on the left hand side. Then, in the right pane, select, "Command Line Tool" and click Next. Call the project **Houses** and type the name into the Product Name text box. Select "Foundation" in the Type dropdown box. Changing from a C project type to a Foundation project type tells Xcode that you will be working in Objective-C and that you want to use the Cocoa Foundation framework. You will learn more about Cocoa and Foundation in the next chapter. Make sure that the Use Automatic Reference Counting checkbox is checked and click Next.

2. Xcode prompts you for a location to save your program. Pick a location that you will remember. Also, uncheck the "Create local git repository for this project" checkbox. You will not need to use source control for this project. Finally, click Create, and Xcode will create your new project.

3. Now that you have created your project, it is time to create your House class. Select File ⇨ New ⇨ New File… from the menu bar. In the template chooser, under iOS on the left-hand side, select Cocoa Touch. In the right-hand pane, select Objective-C class and press Next. In the Class text box, name your class House. In the "Subclass of" dropdown, select NSObject and press Next. You will learn more about subclasses later in this chapter. In the next dialog box, click Create to create your class. You should see two new files in the Project Navigator under your Houses directory called House.h and House.m.

4. Erase everything from the House.h header file and replace it with the following:

```
#import <Foundation/Foundation.h>

@interface House : NSObject
{
    NSString* color;
}

-(void) setColor:(NSString*) theColor;
-(NSString*) getColor;
-(void) enterFrontDoor;

@end
```

5. Switch over to the implementation file, House.m, and replace the existing code with this:

```
#import "House.h"


@implementation House
```

```objc
-(void) setColor:(NSString*) theColor
{
    color = theColor;
}

-(NSString*) getColor
{
    return color;
}

-(void) enterFrontDoor
{
    NSLog(@"Entering front door");
}

@end
```

6. Switch to `main.m` and replace the existing code with this:

```objc
#import <Foundation/Foundation.h>
#import "House.h"

int main (int argc, const char * argv[])
{

    // Create houses
    House* redHouse;
    redHouse = [[House alloc] init];
    [redHouse setColor:@"Red"];

    House* greenHouse = [[House alloc] init];
    [greenHouse setColor:@"Green"];

    House* yellowHouse = [[House alloc] init];
    [yellowHouse setColor:@"Yellow"];

    // Print houses and enter
    NSLog(@"redHouse is %@", [redHouse getColor]);
    [redHouse enterFrontDoor];

    NSLog(@"greenHouse is %@", [greenHouse getColor]);
    [greenHouse enterFrontDoor];

    NSLog(@"yellowHouse is %@", [yellowHouse getColor]);
    [yellowHouse enterFrontDoor];
    return 0;
}
```

How It Works

The first thing that you did was to create your House class. You may find it strange that there were two new files created when you created the new class. The .h file is a *header file*. The header file holds the *declaration* of your class. The declaration includes the member variables and methods exposed by your class. You may remember from the last chapter that you needed to include header files in your Acey project so that the compiler would know about certain I/O functions. In this case, you will use the header file to declare the features of the House class. The .m file is the implementation file. You place the actual implementation of the functions in the implementation file.

First, you will look at the header file House.h. The first thing that the header does is import the Foundation.h header:

```
#import <Foundation/Foundation.h>
```

You may remember using the #include statement in the last chapter to inform the compiler about some of the functions that you would be using. The #import statement in Objective-C does almost the same thing. The difference is that in C, library developers need to include some safeguards to ensure that the same header is not mishandled if it is included multiple times. The #import statement improves upon #include, in that you do not have to add this extra code to your files. #import guarantees that the header will be included in your project only once, regardless of how many files #import the file. In this case, you are importing the functions found in the Foundation.h header.

The next line declares your House class:

```
@interface House : NSObject
```

The @interface directive tells the compiler that you are declaring a class. After the @interface you can see the name of your class, House followed by a colon and NSObject. This means that House inherits from NSObject. You will learn more about inheritance later in this chapter. Everything that you put between the @interface and the @end directive at the end of the file is part of the class.

The curly braces after the @interface contain all of the member variables for your class:

```
{
    NSString* color;
}
```

You use member variables to maintain the state of your objects. The values that you place in member variables are stored independently for each object. As you will see, each instance that you create of the House class will have its own unique value stored in the color member variable.

In this class, color is a member of type NSString*. You may remember from the last chapter that the * indicates that the variable is a pointer. Therefore, color is a pointer to an NSString. NSString is a class that is a part of the Foundation framework that you use to represent strings. You will learn more about NSString in the next chapter. In this example, you will just store the color in instances of your House as strings.

After the closing brace, you declare your instance methods:

```
-(void) setColor:(NSString*) theColor;
-(NSString*) getColor;
-(void) enterFrontDoor;
```

As you learned, methods are functions that you use to implement behavior in your class. This class will have three methods, setColor:, getColor, and enterFrontDoor. When a user of the class wants to set the color for an instance, he will call setColor:. Likewise, when the user wants to retrieve the color, he will call getColor. When the user wants to enter the house, he will call enterFrontDoor.

Methods can return values, but they do not have to. You can see that the `setColor:` and `enterFrontDoor` methods return `void` and the `getColor` method returns an `NSString*`. Additionally, the `setColor:` method accepts and `NSString*` parameter called `theColor`. Finally, you end the class declaration with the `@end` directive:

```
@end
```

Now, switch over to the implementation file, `House.m`. The first thing that you will notice is that you are #importing the `House.h` header file:

```
#import "House.h"
```

The implementation needs to know about the `@interface` for the class, so you need to import the header file.

Next, you can see that you are declaring the `@implementation` of the `House` class:

```
@implementation House
```

Everything between the `@implementation` and `@end` keywords are the implementation of the `House` class.

Below, you can see the implementation of the `setColor:` and `getColor` methods:

```
-(void) setColor:(NSString*) theColor
{
    color = theColor;
}

-(NSString*) getColor
{
    return color;
}
```

`setColor:` takes the values of the `theColor` parameter and assigns it to the `color` member variable. Similarly, the `getColor` method returns the value of the `color` member variable.

The `enterFrontDoor` method simply prints out a message that you are entering the front door:

```
-(void) enterFrontDoor
{
    NSLog(@"Entering front door");
}
```

That is all that you need to do to define and implement a class. Now, anywhere that you want to represent houses in your code, you can use the `House` class. Switch to the `main.m` file and you will see how to use your `House`.

Right below the #import for the Foundation header, you can see that you have added a #import for the `House.h` header:

```
#import "House.h"
```

This tells the compiler that you will be using the `House` class.

Below that, you will see the `main` function just as you did in the C programs in the previous chapter. Remember that Objective-C is just a superset of C. Objective-C programs run starting with the `main` function just like C programs.

In the first part of the program, you declare a `House*` pointer called `redHouse`:

```
// Create houses
House* redHouse;
```

You create instances of classes and reference them through pointers. The next line allocates the memory for a `House` instance by using the `alloc` method and then initializes the `House` by using the `init` method:

```
redHouse = [[House alloc] init];
```

You did not implement either of these methods in the `House` class. The class inherited these methods from the parent class `NSObject`. You will learn more about inheritance later on in the chapter. Inheritance allows children, or sub-classes, to inherit functionality implemented in their parent or super-class. Since `NSObject` implements the `alloc` and `init` methods, and `NSObject` is the superclass of `House`, those methods are available in `House`.

At this point, the variable `redHouse` points to an instance of the `House` class. Next, the code needs to set the color of the `redHouse` object to `Red`. You accomplish this by sending a `setColor:` message to the `redHouse` object:

```
[redHouse setColor:@"Red"];
```

The square brackets indicate that you are sending a message to an object, in effect, calling the `setColor:` method as discussed in the section on methods and messages above. You may be familiar with the dot notation for calling methods in other languages like Java, C#, and C++. In those languages, you use the syntax `redHouse.setColor` to call the setColor method on an object called `redHouse`. In Objective-C, you enclose the object, or receiver, and the message in brackets. You can read the code `[redHouse setColor]` as "send the setColor message to the redHouse object."

You may find the `@` sign in front of the string literal a bit strange. This is just shorthand to tell the compiler that `"Red"` is a string. You also could have created a new `NSString*` object and set its value to `Red`. However, since strings are so common, this shorthand is a lot easier.

The next part of the code goes on to declare and instantiate two more `House` objects: `greenHouse` and `yellowHouse`. It also sets the colors for each of these houses:

```
House* greenHouse = [[House alloc] init];
[greenHouse setColor:@"Green"];

House* yellowHouse = [[House alloc] init];
[yellowHouse setColor:@"Yellow"];
```

Now, you are ready to print the color of the houses and enter them:

```
// Print houses and enter
NSLog(@"redHouse is %@", [redHouse getColor]);
[redHouse enterFrontDoor];

NSLog(@"greenHouse is %@", [greenHouse getColor]);
[greenHouse enterFrontDoor];

NSLog(@"yellowHouse is %@", [yellowHouse getColor]);
[yellowHouse enterFrontDoor];
```

Since you are using `NSString` objects, you can use the `NSLog` function to print the strings. This function works almost identically to the `printf` function that you used in the last chapter to write strings to the console. NSLog just gives a bit of added output, including a timestamp and thread data. It is easier to use NSLog to print NSStrings than it is to use printf.

The first line calls the getColor method on the redHouse object, which returns Red. Then you called the enterFrontDoor method on the redHouse, which prints the enter message. The next four lines call the getColor and enterFrontDoor methods on the greenHouse and yellowHouse objects to print the colors from those objects and enter both houses. You should see the following output when you run the program (your timestamps will be different):

```
2011-04-12 18:18:10.559 Houses[17369:903] redHouse is Red
2011-04-12 18:18:10.560 Houses[17369:903] Entering front door
2011-04-12 18:18:10.561 Houses[17369:903] greenHouse is Green
2011-04-12 18:18:10.561 Houses[17369:903] Entering front door
2011-04-12 18:18:10.561 Houses[17369:903] yellowHouse is Yellow
2011-04-12 18:18:10.562 Houses[17369:903] Entering front door
```

You should notice that each instance of the House class, redHouse, greenHouse, and yellowHouse maintain their own, independent member variable for the color.

Managing Memory

Unlike garbage-collected languages like Java and C#, Objective-C does not offer garbage collection on the iOS platform. Therefore, when you allocate memory for an object that you create, you are responsible for releasing that memory when you are finished with it. If you fail to properly free the memory that you allocate, the total amount of memory consumed by your application will grow as the application runs. This failure to clean up unused memory results in a *memory leak*. Eventually, if your program consumes too much memory, the OS will terminate your application.

This may seem difficult and complicated, but as long as you have an understanding of how memory management works in Objective-C and remember a few simple rules, you will be fine. In iOS 5, Apple has introduced a new language feature to Objective-C called *Automatic Reference Counting*, or ARC. While ARC simplifies reference counting by eliminating most of the work for the developer, it is still important for you to have a basic understanding of how reference counting works in Objective-C. You will learn more about ARC in the next section.

All Objective-C classes that inherit from NSObject maintain a *retain count*. The retain count is a counter that indicates the number of bits of code that are interested in the object. When an object is allocated by using alloc or new, its retain count is set to 1. In Figure 4-3, your object is represented by the blue cube, and the retain count is in the pink circle.

When you are finished using the object, you should call the release method. Calling release reduces the retain count of the object by one. When the retain count reaches zero, the object is de-allocated and the Objective-C runtime calls its dealloc method. You can see this illustrated in Figure 4-3 (a). The gray cube represents the de-allocated object.

In addition to release, you can call the autorelease method. This indicates that the runtime should release the object at a point in the future, but not right away. Effectively, this reduces the retain count by 1 just like calling release. You can see this illustrated in Figure 4-3 (b).

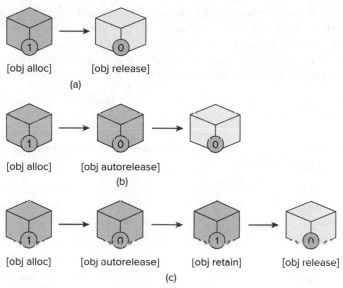

[obj alloc]   [obj release]

(a)

[obj alloc]   [obj autorelease]

(b)

[obj alloc]   [obj autorelease]   [obj retain]   [obj release]

(c)

FIGURE 4-3: Memory management

You use autorelease pools to keep track of all autoreleased objects. There is an application wide autorelease pool that most project templates create automatically when you begin building your application. You can create local pools yourself as well. You will see the autorelease pool in action in the game example at the end of this chapter.

Autorelease is particularly useful for returning objects from methods. You can allocate the object that you plan to return from the method, configure it, and then autorelease it before returning it to the caller. It is the caller's responsibility to retain the object. The Objective-C runtime will send an autoreleased object the release message one time for every time you call autorelease on it when the autorelease pool is drained or de-allocated.

When you need to hold on to a reference to an object, like an autoreleased object that you got back from a method call, you increment the retain count by calling the retain method on the object. Figure 4-3 (c) illustrates this situation. It is the responsibility of the caller of a method that returns an object to call retain. The default autorelease pool will de-allocate autoreleased objects each time through the application's run loop. So, if you get an autoreleased object from a function, use it right away, and you do not need it after the method call is complete, you do not need to worry about retaining it. However, if you plan to put an autoreleased object into an instance variable for access at a later time, you have to call retain on it or else it will be de-allocated at the end of the run loop and your application will crash when you try to send a message to the de-allocated object.

You should use release instead of autorelease whenever possible as there is less overhead in calling release. If you are going to be creating and autoreleasing many objects, in a loop perhaps, you should wrap the loop in its own autorelease pool. You do this by creating an instance of the NSAutoreleasePool object before you start looping. Then, you drain the autorelease pool by releasing it:

```
NSAutoreleasePool *pool = [[NSAutoreleasePool alloc] init];
loop a bunch of times
[pool release];
```

The key thing to remember about memory management in Objective-C is that you need to balance calls to new, `alloc`, or `retain` with calls to `release` or `autorelease`. If you have too few calls to `release`/`autorelease`, the retain count for the object will never drop to 0 and the object will never be de-allocated, resulting in a memory leak. If you call `release` or `autorelease` too many times, you will over-release the object, causing an application crash.

In general, adding an object to a Cocoa collection such as `NSMutableArray`, increments the retain count. Likewise, removing an object from a collection decrements the retain count. Simply obtaining an object from a collection typically returns an autoreleased object. If you need to hold on to the reference to an autoreleased object, you need to call `retain` on it. You will learn more about working with Cocoa collection classes in the next chapter.

When you create an object by calling a class helper method that has `alloc`, new, or `copy` in its name, it is your responsibility to release that object. Objects created in this way, by convention, have a retain count of 1. If you get an instance of an object using a class helper method that returns an object that does not have `alloc`, new, or `copy` in its name such as `stringWithString`, you should assume that the object is autoreleased.

You can send the `retainCount` message to any `NSObject` to obtain the current retain count of that object. You generally will not use this method in a production application, but it can be helpful to log the retain count of an object when you are trying to debug memory problems.

To summarize:

➤ If you create an object with `alloc`, new, or `copy`, the object will have a retain count of 1 and you are responsible for calling `release`.

➤ If you get a reference to an object in any other way, you can assume that it has a retain count of 1 and has been autoreleased. If you need to hold on to a reference to the object, `retain` it.

➤ If you call `retain` on an object, you have to balance the call to `retain` with a call to `release`.

For more information on memory management, I would recommend reading Apple's Memory Management Programming Guide (http://developer.apple.com/library/mac/#documentation/Cocoa/Conceptual/MemoryMgmt/MemoryMgmt.html).

Automatic Reference Counting

As I mentioned in the previous section, Apple introduced Automatic Reference Counting or ARC in iOS 5. ARC simplifies reference counting by having the compiler insert the `retains` and `releases` into your code for you automatically. The compiler does this by analyzing your code and determining the lifetime of your objects at compile time.

The impact of ARC on you as a developer is that you do not need to worry about typing `retain`, `release`, or `autorelease` in your code. The compiler will insert the correct memory management statements for you as it compiles. You do not need to worry about the lifetime of your objects because the compiler will take care of it for you. In fact, calling `retain`, `release`, or `autorelease` will result in compiler errors if you have ARC enabled for your project.

Xcode enables ARC by default for all new projects in version 4.2. You can turn ARC off on a file-by-file basis if you decide that you want complete control of memory management. In that case, you will need to revert to using `retain` and `release` as I explained previously. This feature enables you to use ARC in your new programs while you maintain compatibility with existing libraries that are not ARC enabled.

Because Xcode enables ARC by default for new projects, I will use it throughout the book. However, you need to be aware that if you disable ARC, you will need to manage memory yourself using `retain` and `release`.

INHERITANCE

Earlier in the chapter when you built your `House` class, you declared that the class *inherited* from another class `NSObject`. You did this by following the class name `House` with a colon and `NSObject` like this: `@interface House : NSObject`. Now you will learn what this means.

Inheritance is a basic concept in object-oriented programming. Inheritance allows you to build a hierarchy of related classes that exhibit an "is a" relationship. For example, you could use inheritance to model a `Dog` class that inherits from an `Animal` class because a `Dog` "is an" `Animal`. Using inheritance, you can build classes that inherit the instance members and methods from their parent. You can also exploit another object-oriented feature called *polymorphism* where you treat subclasses as their superclass.

Building Subclasses from a Base Class

To help you grasp the concept, we will expand on the house example from earlier in this chapter. Suppose that you needed to model two different kinds of houses, a two-story colonial and a huge mansion. Both a colonial and a mansion are houses, but they differ from each other. Since all houses share common characteristics, like color, a front door, etc., you could model a base class called `House` that contains these shared characteristics. This base class could have a `color` member variable and an `enterFrontDoor` method.

Since a colonial is a house, you would want a `Colonial` class to inherit all of the features of a house. Then, you could add the additional features that make a colonial unique. The colonial is a specialized type of house. Sometimes designers refer to inheritance relationships as specializations for just this reason. Suppose all colonials had only two floors. A `Colonial` may have a `goUpstairs` method that sends the user upstairs. Since other houses, like a ranch, might not have an upstairs, this method should go into the subclass `Colonial` and not the superclass `House`.

Now imagine a giant mansion with many floors. A mansion is also a house so it should inherit from the `House` base class. However, the `goUpstairs` method probably does not have much meaning because there could be many floors. Instead, a mansion might have a `useElevator` method. You can see a class diagram representing the `House`, `Colonial`, and `Mansion` classes in Figure 4-4.

Since the `Colonial` and `Mansion` classes inherit from `House`, they both inherit a `color` instance member and `getColor`, `setColor` and `enterFrontDoor` methods. However, the `Colonial` and `Mansion` are both specialized houses in that they also have their own methods.

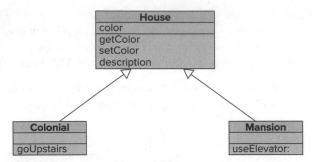

FIGURE 4-4: Class diagram for House, Colonial, and Mansion classes

TRY IT OUT Building a Subclass

codefile Houses available for download at Wrox.com

In this section, you will add two new classes to your Houses project: Colonial and Mansion.

1. Open the Houses project in Xcode.

2. Select File ⇨ New File… from the menu bar.

3. In the template chooser, under iOS on the left-hand side, select Cocoa Touch. In the right-hand pane, select Objective-C class, and click Next.

4. In the next dialog box, name your class Colonial. In the "Subclass of" dropdown, type **House** and click Next.

5. In the next dialog box, click Create. You should see two new files in the Project Navigator under your Houses directory called Colonial.h and Colonial.m.

6. Modify the code for Colonial.h to #import the House.h header file. Then, add the declaration for the goUpstairs method. The Colonial.h header should look like this:

```
#import <Foundation/Foundation.h>
#import "House.h"

@interface Colonial : House {

}

-(void) goUpstairs;

@end
```

7. Move over to the Colonial.m implementation file and add the goUpstairs method:

```
-(void) goUpstairs
{
    NSLog(@"Going upstairs");
}
```

8. Follow the same process to add a new class called Mansion that inherits from House. Do not forget to add the #import for the House.h header. Then, add the declaration for the useElevator: method. The Mansion.h header should look like this:

```
#import <Foundation/Foundation.h>
#import "House.h"

@interface Mansion : House {

}

-(void) useElevator:(int) floor;

@end
```

9. Switch over to the `Mansion.m` implementation file and add the `useElevator:` method:

```
-(void) useElevator:(int) floor
{

    NSLog(@"Going to floor: %i",floor);
}
```

10. Switch over to the `main.m` implementation file to use your new houses. You will need to add a couple of #import statements to import your two new header files. Below the #import for `House.h`, add the following two import statements:

```
#import "Mansion.h"
#import "Colonial.h"
```

11. In the main function, change the `greenHouse` to be a `Colonial` instead of a `House` like this:

```
Colonial* greenHouse = [[Colonial alloc] init];
```

12. Change the `yellowHouse` to a `Mansion` like this:

```
Mansion* yellowHouse = [[Mansion alloc] init];
```

13. To use your new subclass methods, you can add the following calls after the code that prints the houses:

```
// Call subclass methods
[greenHouse goUpstairs];
[yellowHouse useElevator:4];
```

14. Build and run your application. The output should look like this:

```
2011-04-12 18:24:50.367 Houses[17479:903] redHouse is Red
2011-04-12 18:24:50.369 Houses[17479:903] Entering front door
2011-04-12 18:24:50.369 Houses[17479:903] greenHouse is Green
2011-04-12 18:24:50.369 Houses[17479:903] Entering front door
2011-04-12 18:24:50.370 Houses[17479:903] yellowHouse is Yellow
2011-04-12 18:24:50.370 Houses[17479:903] Entering front door
2011-04-12 18:24:50.370 Houses[17479:903] Going upstairs
2011-04-12 18:24:50.370 Houses[17479:903] Going to floor: 4
```

How It Works

You just created two new classes, `Colonial` and `Mansion`, that both inherit from `House`:

```
@interface Colonial : House {

}
```

```
-(void) goUpstairs;

@end

@interface Mansion : House {

}
-(void) useElevator:(int) floor;

@end
```

You chose inheritance to build these new classes because both a colonial and a mansion exhibit an "is a" relationship to house (a colonial is a house and a mansion is a house).

In addition to the methods that it inherits from house, the `Colonial` class has an additional method called `goUpstairs`:

```
-(void) goUpstairs;
```

The `Mansion` class has an added `useElevator:` method:

```
-(void) useElevator:(int) floor;
```

You needed to `#import` the `House.h` header file in each subclass header or else the compiler would not have known about the `House` class when you declared that your subclasses would inherit from `House`:

```
#import "House.h"
```

Overriding Base Class Methods

When you are building classes by using inheritance, you inherit all of the public and protected member variables and all of the methods of the base class. Sometimes you may want to implement a method that exists in the base class differently in a subclass. This is called *overriding* the base class.

Sometimes when you override the functionality of a base class or superclass method, you need to execute the superclass method before you execute your own code. For example, when you override the superclass implementation of `init` to initialize your subclass, you need to make sure that the superclass is properly initialized by calling its version of `init`. You must do this to make sure that the object is ready for you to work with. You call the superclass version of a method using the keyword `super` like this:

```
self = [super init];
```

The `self` variable is a pointer to the instance of the class itself. This is identical to the `this` variable in Java or the `this` pointer in C++. Therefore, in this case you are saying that the `self` pointer should point to the value that superclass's `init` method returns.

TRY IT OUT   Overriding a Base Class Method

codefile Houses available for download at Wrox.com

In this section, you will implement different versions of the `enterFrontDoor` method in the `Colonial` and `Mansion` classes. For a generic `House`, this method prints, "Entering front door." However, for a colonial or a mansion you may want to print something different. You will override the `enterFrontDoor` method of the `Colonial` class to print, "You have entered the foyer."

1. Open the Houses project in Xcode.

2. Next, open the `Colonial.m` implementation file and add a new implementation of the `enterFrontDoor` method:

```
-(void) enterFrontDoor
{
    NSLog(@"You have entered the foyer");

}
```

3. Likewise, you will override the `enterFrontDoor` method of the `Mansion` class to print, "The butler awaits." Open the `Mansion.m` implementation file and add a new implementation of the `enterFrontDoor` method:

```
-(void) enterFrontDoor
{
    NSLog(@"The butler awaits.");

}
```

4. The `getColor` and `setColor` methods of the `House` base class will use the same implementation in the subclasses, so you do not have to modify them. You get the functionality of the `getColor` and `setColor` methods in your subclasses by inheriting from the `House` base class. Build and run the application. You should see output like this:

```
2011-04-12 18:36:56.263 Houses[17724:903] redHouse is Red
2011-04-12 18:36:56.266 Houses[17724:903] Entering front door
2011-04-12 18:36:56.266 Houses[17724:903] greenHouse is Green
2011-04-12 18:36:56.266 Houses[17724:903] You have entered the foyer
2011-04-12 18:36:56.267 Houses[17724:903] yellowHouse is Yellow
2011-04-12 18:36:56.267 Houses[17724:903] The butler awaits.
2011-04-12 18:36:56.267 Houses[17724:903] Going upstairs
2011-04-12 18:36:56.267 Houses[17724:903] Going to floor: 4
```

How It Works

You have added specialized implementations of the `enterFrontDoor` method to the `Colonial` and `Mansion` subclasses.

You should notice that you did not change the main function. You are still calling the `enterFrontDoor` method on each of your objects. However, now that you have new implementations of the `enterFrontDoor` method in the subclasses, you get different messages when you call the `enterFrontDoor` method on the `Mansion` and `Colonial` objects.

Polymorphism

The final object-oriented concept that I will cover in this chapter is *polymorphism*. Polymorphism allows you to treat instances of a subclass as if they were instances of the base class. This makes sense because you use inheritance to implement an "is a" relationship. Therefore, it follows that you can treat a subclass as if it is a base class.

For instance, if you wrote a function that expects a `House*` as an input parameter, you could pass in a `House*` or a `Colonial*` or a `Mansion*` because each type is also technically a `House*`.

Another thing that you can do with polymorphism is build a collection of objects of the base type, but have the method implementation of the subclass called. In the next example, you will build an array of `House` objects. However, you will populate it with one `House`, one `Colonial`, and one `Mansion`. Then, you will call the `enterFrontDoor` method on each object. Even though you have an array of `Houses`, the correct implementation of `enterFrontDoor` will run.

TRY IT OUT   Implementing Polymorphism

codefile Houses available for download at Wrox.com

In this example, you will use polymorphism to call the `enterFrontDoor` method of three objects. Even though you have an array of `House*` objects, you will see that the correct subclass version of `enterFrontDoor` is called.

1.   Open the Houses project in Xcode.

2.   Open the `main.m` implementation file and replace the `main` function with the following code:

```
int main (int argc, const char * argv[])
{

    // Declare an array of houses
    House* houses[3];

    // Create houses
    House* redHouse;
    redHouse = [[House alloc] init];
    [redHouse setColor:@"Red"];

    // put the red house into the array
    houses[0] = redHouse;

    Colonial* greenHouse = [[Colonial alloc] init];
    [greenHouse setColor:@"Green"];

    // put the green house into the array
    houses[1] = greenHouse;

    Mansion* yellowHouse = [[Mansion alloc] init];
    [yellowHouse setColor:@"Yellow"];

    // put the yellow house into the array
    houses[2] = yellowHouse;

    for (int i=0;i<=2;i++)
    {
        // Print houses and enter
        NSLog(@"house is %@", [houses[i] getColor]);
```

```
            [houses[i] enterFrontDoor];
        }
    return 0;
    }
```

3.   Build and run the application. You should see the following output:

```
2011-04-12 19:07:31.102 Houses[18135:903] house is Red
2011-04-12 19:07:31.104 Houses[18135:903] Entering front door
2011-04-12 19:07:31.104 Houses[18135:903] house is Green
2011-04-12 19:07:31.104 Houses[18135:903] You have entered the foyer
2011-04-12 19:07:31.105 Houses[18135:903] house is Yellow
2011-04-12 19:07:31.105 Houses[18135:903] The butler awaits.
```

How It Works

In the first part of the main function, you declared an array of House*s:

```
// Declare an array of houses
House* houses[3];
```

Next, you created a generic House object, set its color to red, and put it into the houses array:

```
// Create houses
House* redHouse;
redHouse = [[House alloc] init];
[redHouse setColor:@"Red"];

// put the red house into the array
houses[0] = redHouse;
```

The next block creates a Colonial, sets its color to green, and puts it into the houses array:

```
Colonial* greenHouse - [[Colonial alloc] init];
[greenHouse setColor:@"Green"];

// put the green house into the array
houses[1] = greenHouse;
```

Then, you created a Manion, set its color to yellow, and put it into the houses array:

```
Mansion* yellowHouse = [[Mansion alloc] init];
[yellowHouse setColor:@"Yellow"];

// put the yellow house into the array
houses[2] = yellowHouse;
```

Now, here is the interesting part. In the for loop, you iterate over each object in the houses array. Remember that these are declared as House* objects. For each House in the array, you print the color and call the enterFrontDoor method:

```
for (int i=0;i<=2;i++)
{
    // Print houses and enter
    NSLog(@"house is %@", [houses[i] getColor]);
    [houses[i] enterFrontDoor];
}
```

When you examine the output, you can see that the `enterFrontDoor` method that is specific to each class was called, not the generic method in the `House` object:

```
2011-04-12 19:07:31.102 Houses[18135:903] house is Red
2011-04-12 19:07:31.104 Houses[18135:903] Entering front door
2011-04-12 19:07:31.104 Houses[18135:903] house is Green
2011-04-12 19:07:31.104 Houses[18135:903] You have entered the foyer
2011-04-12 19:07:31.105 Houses[18135:903] house is Yellow
2011-04-12 19:07:31.105 Houses[18135:903] The butler awaits.
```

Finally, the `main` function ends by returning 0:

```
return 0;
```

BUILDING A GAME IN OBJECTIVE-C

Now that you are familiar with some object-oriented concepts and have successfully built an Objective-C program, it is time to move up and build another game. The game that you will be building in this chapter is a version of the classic board game Master Mind, but to avoid a lawsuit, we will call it MagicMind.

MagicMind is a two-player game. One player, I'll call him the MindPlayer, selects four colored pegs and hides them from the other player who I'll refer to as the player. There are six different-colored pegs. The MindPlayer can select any combination of the six colors with duplicate pegs allowed.

The player gets ten chances to guess the pegs that the MindPlayer has chosen. Each time the player guesses, the MindPlayer provides some information about the guess. The MindPlayer tells the player two things:

➤ How many pegs are the correct color and in the correct position

➤ How many pegs are the correct color, but not in the correct position

The MindPlayer needs to report only on each instance of the pegs that the player has guessed. For example, if the MindPlayer has selected four black pegs, and the player guesses Black, Red, Green, Black, the MindPlayer would report that the player has two pegs in the correct position.

Using the information that the MindPlayer has revealed, the player attempts to deduce the MindPlayer's pegs. The game is over when the player has either the correct sequence of pegs or has run out of guesses.

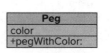
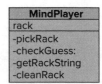

To implement the game, you will build two classes as you can see in Figure 4-5.

FIGURE 4-5: MagicMind class diagram

You will implement the game loop in the `main.m main` function just as you did in the last chapter.

Before you get started, you need to learn about how you can expose the data of your class by using properties.

Exposing Class Data with Properties

Earlier in this chapter, you built a House class. This class had an instance variable called color that you used to set the color of the House. If you recall, you did not set the color variable directly. You wrote a method called setColor: to set the color and getColor to get the color. In this way, you implemented the object-oriented concept of *encapsulation*. You encapsulated the instance variable color and exposed its value by using accessor methods. This prevented a user of the class from needing to know the inner details of how you implemented color in the class. You can also implement accessors as getter and setter methods. These methods provide a way for users of a class to get and set values.

Since encapsulation is such a key concept of object-oriented programming, the designers of Objective-C have implemented something called *properties*. Properties allow you to define instance variables and have the compiler create the setter and getter methods with very little code. Users of your class can then use dot (.) notation to access these properties as you will see in a moment.

Declaring a Property

To declare a property, you need to declare an instance variable just like you normally would in the @interface section of your class's header file. Then, anywhere in the method declaration of the header, you use the @property compiler directive to declare the property. Finally, you need to add an @synthesize compiler directive to the implementation file to instruct the compiler to build the accessor methods for you.

For example, in the MagicMind game that you will be building in the rest of this chapter, you will build a class called Peg. This class represents the pegs used to indicate your guess. Each peg has a color. Therefore, the Peg class should have a property called color. To keep the program simple, you will use the char type to store a one-character representation of the color. You will use the character-to-color mapping as indicated in the following table:

CHARACTER	COLOR
r	red
y	yellow
g	green
b	blue
o	orange
k	black

When you add @synthesize to the implementation file, you are instructing the compiler to build your accessor methods. The compiler creates two new methods for every read/write property that you synthesize. These methods are named by using your property name. Therefore, for the color property, the compiler will add two new methods to the implementation called color and setColor:.

TRY IT OUT Adding a Class with Properties

codefile MagicMind available for download at Wrox.com

Now it is time to get started building that game.

1. Start up Xcode and from the File menu select New ⇨ New Project …. Once again, you will be developing a simple command-line tool for Mac OS X.

2. In the dialog, select, "Application" under the Mac OS X section on the left-hand side. Then, in the right pane, select "Command Line Tool," and click Next.

3. Call the project **MagicMind**, and type the name into the Product Name text box. Select "Foundation" in the Type dropdown box. Click Next.

4. Xcode will prompt you for a location to save your program. Pick a location that you will remember. Also, uncheck the "Create local git repository for this project" checkbox. You will not need to use source control for this project. Finally, click Create, and Xcode will create your new project.

5. Next, you will create a new class called Peg that you will use to represent pegs in the game. Select File ⇨ New ⇨ New File… from the menu bar.

6. In the template chooser, under iOS on the left-hand side, select Cocoa Touch. In the right-hand pane, select Objective-C class, and press Next.

7. In the next dialog box, name your class Peg. In the "Subclass of" dropdown, select NSObject, and press Next.

8. In the next dialog box, click Create. You should see two new files in the Project Navigator under your MagicMind directory called Peg.h and Peg.m.

9. Open the Peg.h header file, and replace the contents with the following code:

```
#import <Foundation/Foundation.h>


@interface Peg : NSObject {
    char color;
}

@property char color;

@end
```

10. Switch over to the implementation file Peg.m. In the implementation, add a line to synthesize the color property so that the code looks like this:

```
#import "Peg.h"


@implementation Peg
@synthesize color;

@end
```

How It Works

In the header file `Peg.h`, you added a `char` member variable called `color`:

```
char color;
```

Then, you declared a `char` property called `color`:

```
@property char color;
```

Finally, you moved over to the implementation file `Peg.m` and added a synthesize directive for the color property:

```
@synthesize color;
```

The `synthesize` directive instructs the compiler to build the accessor methods for you automatically.

Accessing a Property

Now that you have declared a property, you need to be able to access it. In order to access a property, you use dot (.) notation. This means that you use the name of your object, followed by the dot, followed by the name of the property that you want to access.

For example, to get the `color` property from a `Peg` object that you have called `thePeg`, you would write `thePeg.color`. You can set a property by using the assignment operator (_) and the dot notation together. To set the `thePeg` object's `color` to 'r', which will represent red, you can write `thePeg.color = 'r';`.

It is important to note that when you use the dot notation, you are not accessing the member variable directly. The dot is a shortcut for calling the methods that the compiler creates for you automatically when you `@synthesize` the property. Therefore, the code `thePeg.color` is syntactically equivalent to `[thePeg color]`. Likewise, the assignment `thePeg.color = 'r';` is the same as `[thePeg setColor:'r'];`.

Class Methods

If you go back and look at Figure 4-5, you will notice that the `Peg` class contains a method called `pegWithColor:`. All of the methods that you have declared up until this point had a minus (-) sign in front of them. The minus indicates that the method is an instance method. Instance methods are methods that you call on an instance of the class. For example, you called the `setColor:` method on instances of the `House` class to set the color of a specific instance.

In the `Peg` class, the `pegWithColor:` method has a plus (+) sign in front of it. The plus sign indicates that you are declaring the method as a *class method*. Class methods do not require an instance of the class in order for you to call them. This concept is similar to static methods in other object-oriented languages. You call a class method by sending the message to the class, instead of sending it to an instance of the class. So, to call the `pegWithColor:` method, you would use the syntax `[Peg pegWithColor:'r'];`

Keep in mind that you will not be able to access instance variables in the implementation of a class method because class methods are called on a class, not an instance of the class. Most often, you will use class methods to provide convenience methods for creating instances of the class. Designers call these types of convenience methods *factory methods* because they are a factory for generating instances of the class.

The `pegWithColor:` method is a factory method. You will use `pegWithColor:` to quickly create `Peg` instances with the color set to whatever you send in the message.

TRY IT OUT   Adding a Class Method to the Peg Class

codefile MagicMind available for download at Wrox.com

In this section, you will add the `pegWithColor:` class method to your `Peg` class.

1. Open the MagicMind project in Xcode.

2. Open the `Peg.h` header file and add the `pegWithColor` method declaration below the `color` property declaration:

```
+(Peg*) pegWithColor: (char) theColor;
```

3. Switch over to the `Peg.m` implementation file and add the implementation of the `pegWithColor:` method below the compiler directive that synthesizes the `color` property:

```
+(Peg*) pegWithColor: (char) theColor
{
    // Create the peg
    Peg* thePeg = [[Peg alloc] init];

    // Set the peg's color
    thePeg.color = theColor;

    // Return the peg
    return thePeg;

}
```

How It Works

In the header file, you added a declaration for the `pegWithColor:` class method:

```
+(Peg*) pegWithColor: (char) theColor;
```

The important thing to notice is the plus sign in front of the method declaration. The plus indicates that the method is a class method.

Next, you implemented the `pegWithColor:` factory method. The purpose of this method is to create new `Peg` objects with the color that the caller specified.

The method first creates an instance of a `Peg`:

```
// Create the peg
Peg* thePeg = [[Peg alloc] init];
```

Next, you set the new `Peg` instance's `color` to the color that the caller specified:

```
// Set the peg's color
thePeg.color = theColor;
```

Last, you return the new `Peg` object to the caller:

```
// Return the peg
return thePeg;
```

Implementing the MindPlayer

In this section, you will implement the `MindPlayer` class. This class represents the computer player in the game.

When you design classes, you need to think about what the class will do. The main tasks that the computer player needs to perform are picking the pegs that the player will guess and providing feedback to the player on his guesses. Let's take a closer look at these tasks.

The computer player needs to pick the pegs for the rack. You should choose the color of each peg randomly so that the game is not predictable. For this, you will use the random number generation features of C that you learned about in the last chapter. Additionally, you will need to store the rack because the player will be submitting multiple guesses about the same rack. You will use an instance variable to store an array of `Peg` objects that represent the rack.

The other important feature that a computer player must be able to do is to provide feedback on the player's guesses. Each time a player submits a guess, the computer player must tell the player two things:

➤ How many pegs are the correct color and in the correct position.

➤ How many pegs are just the correct color, but not in the correct position.

In the code that follows, you will implement an algorithm that compares the player's guess to the rack and determines if the player has guessed correctly. If not, you will work through the guess to determine how many pegs are the correct color and in the correct position and how many pegs are only the correct color, but are not in the correct position.

TRY IT OUT   **Implementing the MindPlayer Class**

codefile MagicMind available for download at Wrox.com

In this section, you will implement the computer MindPlayer class.

1. Open the MagicMind project in Xcode.

2. Create a new class called `MindPlayer` that you will use to represent the computer player in the game. Select File ➪ New ➪ New File... from the menu bar.

3. In the template chooser, under iOS on the left-hand side, select Cocoa Touch. In the right-hand pane, select Objective-C class and press Next.

4. In the next dialog box, name your class MindPlayer. In the "Subclass of" dropdown, select NSObject and press Next.

5. In the next dialog box, click Create. You should see two new files in the Project Navigator under your MagicMind directory called `MindPlayer.h` and `MindPlayer.m`.

6. Open the `MindPlayer.h` header file and replace the contents with the following code:

```
#import <Foundation/Foundation.h>
#import "Peg.h"

@interface MindPlayer : NSObject {
    // An arrray to hold the rack
    Peg* rack[4];


}

// Pick the pegs for the rack
-(void) pickRack;

// Check the guess against the rack
-(NSString*) checkGuess:(NSString*) guess;

// Return rack string to print
-(NSString*) getRackString;

// Clean up the memory used by the rack
-(void) cleanRack;


@end
```

7. Open the `MindPlayer.m` implementation file and replace the contents with this code:

```
#import "MindPlayer.h"
#include <stdlib.h>
#include <time.h>

@implementation MindPlayer

// Pick the pegs for the rack
-(void) pickRack
{
    // Seed the random number generator
    srandom( time( NULL ) );
    int randomNum;

    // Declare a peg
    Peg* peg=nil;

    for (int i=0; i<=3; i++)
    {
        // Generate random number to determine peg color
        randomNum = (random() % 6);

        // Create a new peg object based on the random number
        switch (randomNum) {
            case 0:
                // Use peg convenience initializer
                peg=[Peg pegWithColor:'r'];
```

```objective-c
                break;
        case 1:
            peg=[Peg pegWithColor:'y'];
            break;
        case 2:
            peg=[Peg pegWithColor:'g'];
            break;
        case 3:
            peg=[Peg pegWithColor:'b'];
            break;
        case 4:
            peg=[Peg pegWithColor:'o'];
            break;
        case 5:
            peg=[Peg pegWithColor:'k'];
            break;
        default:
            break;
        }

        // Add the peg to the rack
        rack[i] = peg;

    }
}

// Check the guess against the rack
-(NSString*) checkGuess:(NSString*) guess
{
    // Declare two ints to keep track of response criteria
    int correctColorAndPosition = 0;
    int correctColorOnly = 0;

    // Declare a string to temporarily hold the guess peg letter
    char tempGuessPeg;

    // Build a temporary rack
    char tempRack[4];
    for (int i=0;i<=3; i++) {
        tempRack[i] = rack[i].color;
    }

    // Loop through each peg letter in the guess
    for (int i=0; i<=3; i++) {
        tempGuessPeg = [guess characterAtIndex:i];

        // If pegs are identical, increment correctColorAndPosition
        if (tempGuessPeg==tempRack[i])
        {
            correctColorAndPosition++;

            // Take the color out of the temp rack because you cannot have
            // more than one match
            // Use x because that is not a color
            tempRack[i]='x';
```

```objectivec
            }
        else
        {
            // Does a peg of this color exist in the rack?
            for (int j=0; j<=3; j++) {
                if (tempGuessPeg == tempRack[j]) {
                    correctColorOnly++;
                    // Take the color out of the temp rack
                    // Use x because that is not a color
                    tempRack[j]='x';

                    // You must exit the inner loop because
                    // you found a matching color peg
                    break;
                }
            }
        }

    }

    // Determine if the user won
    if (correctColorAndPosition == 4)
    {
        return @"win";
    }
    else
    {
        return [NSString stringWithFormat:
                @"\nCorrect Color And Position: %i \nCorrect Color Only: %i",
                correctColorAndPosition, correctColorOnly];

    }
}

// Return rack string to print
-(NSString*) getRackString
{
    NSString* returnString = [NSString stringWithFormat:@"%c%c%c%c",
                              rack[0].color,rack[1].color,rack[2].color,
                              rack[3].color];

    return returnString;

}

// Clean up the memory used by the rack
-(void) cleanRack
{
    for (int i=0; i<=3; i++)
    {
        rack[i]=nil;
    }
}


@end
```

How It Works

The first step in implementing the class is building the interface in the header file. In the `MindPlayer.h` header, you imported the header for the `Peg` class:

```
#import "Peg.h"
```

Since you will be using the `Peg` in this class, you need to import its header.

Next, you declared that the `MindPlayer` inherits from `NSObject` and you declared an instance variable array of 4 `Peg`s to hold the four pegs that will make up the MindPlayer's rack:

```
@interface MindPlayer : NSObject {
    // An arrray to hold the rack
    Peg* rack[4];


}
```

In the next section, you declared all of the methods that the `MindPlayer` class will implement:

```
// Pick the pegs for the rack
-(void) pickRack;

// Check the guess against the rack
-(NSString*) checkGuess:(NSString*) guess;

// Return rack string to print
-(NSString*) getRackString;

// Clean up the memory used by the rack
-(void) cleanRack;
```

Finally, you ended the class definition with the `@end` directive:

```
@end
```

After declaring the class in the header, you moved over to the implementation file. The first thing that you did there was to include all of the headers that you will use in building the class:

```
#import "MindPlayer.h"
#include <stdlib.h>
#include <time.h>
```

Next comes the `@implementation` directive that tells the compiler that what follows is the implementation of the class:

```
@implementation MindPlayer
```

After that come the interesting parts, the individual method implementations. The first method that you implemented is the `pickRack` method. This method is responsible for picking the four pegs that the computer player will have in his rack. This is accomplished by choosing four random numbers between 0 and 5 and then creating a corresponding `Peg` object to represent each individual peg. Then, you add these `Peg`s to the `rack` instance variable.

First, you define the method that you are implementing:

```
-(void) pickRack
{
```

Next, you seed the random number generator with the current time, declare an int variable that you will use to hold a random number, and declare a Peg* variable that will point to each instance of a Peg as you create it:

```
// Seed the random number generator
    srandom( time( NULL ) );
    int randomNum;

    // Declare a peg
    Peg* peg=nil;
```

The next block of code loops four times, once for each peg:

```
for (int i=0; i<=3; i++)
    {
```

In each iteration, you select a random number between 0 and 5:

```
// Generate random number to determine peg color
        randomNum = (random() % 6);
```

Then, you execute a switch statement to determine which color Peg object you will create:

```
// Create a new peg object based on the random number
        switch (randomNum) {
            case 0:
                // Use peg convenience initializer
                peg=[Peg pegWithColor:'r'];
                break;
            case 1:
                peg=[Peg pegWithColor:'y'];
                break;
            case 2:
                peg=[Peg pegWithColor:'g'];
                break;
            case 3:
                peg=[Peg pegWithColor:'b'];
                break;
            case 4:
                peg=[Peg pegWithColor:'o'];
                break;
            case 5:
                peg=[Peg pegWithColor:'k'];
                break;
            default:
                break;
        }
```

You will notice that we are specifying each peg color as a single character representing the color. I did this to try to keep the example as simple as possible. You will also notice that you are using the pegWithColor: class method to create the Peg objects. You are sending the pegWithColor: message to the class itself, and not a specific instance of the class.

Finally, the new Peg is added to the rack array, the for loop is closed, and the method is finished:

```
// Add the peg to the rack
rack[i] = peg;

    }
}
```

The next method, checkGuess:, checks the player's guess against the computer rack and returns the player feedback response. The response indicates if the player has any pegs of the correct color in the correct position and also if the player has any pegs that are the correct color only.

You start the method definition by stating that you will return an NSString* and that you accept an NSString* parameter called guess:

```
-(NSString*) checkGuess:(NSString*) guess
{
```

Next, you declared two int variables that you will use to keep track of the response criteria: correct color and position, and correct color only. You also declared a variable to hold a char that represents the current guess peg color that you will be working with:

```
// Declare two ints to keep track of response criteria
int correctColorAndPosition = 0;
int correctColorOnly = 0;

// Declare a string to temporarily hold the guess peg letter
char tempGuessPeg;
```

The next block builds a temporary rack that you will use in the algorithm to determine the feedback that you will give to the player:

```
// Build a temporary rack
char tempRack[4];
for (int i=0;i<=3; i++) {
    tempRack[i] = rack[i].color;
}
```

You need the temporary rack because each time you find a peg that the user guessed, you will mark that peg as "reported" to the player. You cannot change the actual rack because you need to maintain its original state from turn to turn.

The next block of code loops through each peg, or letter, in the player's guess and determines if the guess peg is in the rack. First, you start the loop:

```
// Loop through each peg letter in the guess
for (int i=0; i<=3; i++) {
```

Then, you populate the tempGuessPeg variable with the character in the string that the user submitted at the loop index. You can obtain any individual character in a string by calling the characterAtIndex method on the string:

```
tempGuessPeg = [guess characterAtIndex:i];
```

Next, you check to see if the guess peg color at index i is the same as the color of the peg in the rack at index i:

```
// If pegs are identical, increment correctColorAndPosition
if (tempGuessPeg==tempRack[i])
{
```

If it is, you increment the `correctColorAndPosition` variable:

```
correctColorAndPosition++;
```

Then, you take that peg out of the temporary rack because you do not want to check that peg again since it has already been matched. You replace the color representing character in the temporary rack with an 'x' because 'x' is not one of the characters that you are using to represent a color:

```
        // Take the color out of the temp rack because you cannot have
        // more than one match
        // Use x because that is not a color
        tempRack[i]='x';

    }
```

The `else` clause is executed if the guess peg at index `i` is not an exact match to the temporary rack peg at index `i`. In this case, you need to scan the rack for pegs that are the same color as the guessed peg:

```
    else
        {
            // Does a peg of this color exist in the rack?
            for (int j=0; j<=3; j++) {
                if (tempGuessPeg == tempRack[j]) {
```

If you find a peg that is the same color as the guess peg, increment the `correctColorOnly` counter:

```
            correctColorOnly++;
```

Then, you need to take the peg that you found out of the temporary rack because you need to report only that there is a correct color match on each individual peg that was submitted:

```
                // Take the color out of the temp rack
                // Use x because that is not a color
                tempRack[j]='x';
```

After this, you must exit the loop because you already found a colored peg that matched the guess:

```
                // You must exit the inner loop because
                // you found a matching color peg
                break;
                }
            }
        }

    }
```

The last bit of code in this method determines if the user won by having 4 pegs of the correct color in the correct position:

```
    // Determine if the user won
    if (correctColorAndPosition == 4)
    {
```

If the user won, you return the string "win":

```
        return @"win";
    }
```

If not, you return the feedback that you generated above:

```
        else
        {
            return [NSString stringWithFormat:
                    @"\nCorrect Color And Position: %i \nCorrect Color Only: %i",
                    correctColorAndPosition, correctColorOnly];

        }
    }
```

The next method, getRackString is straightforward. It returns a string representation of the rack. You will use this at the end of the game to display the rack if the player loses. First, you define the method:

```
// Return rack string to print
-(NSString*) getRackString
{
```

Then, you declare an NSString* variable that you will use to return the string. Instead of using the alloc init pattern to create the string, you use the convenience method stringWithFormat:

```
    NSString* returnString = [NSString stringWithFormat:@"%c%c%c%c",
                              rack[0].color,rack[1].color,rack[2].color,
                              rack[3].color];
```

Finally, you return the returnString:

```
    return returnString;

}
```

The final method in the class is cleanRack. You will call this from main after the game is over to clean up the memory used by the rack. The method loops through each element in the rack array, setting each object to nil:

```
// Clean up the memory used by the rack
-(void) cleanRack
{
    for (int i=0; i<=3; i++)
    {
        rack[i]=nil;
    }
}
```

Building the Game Loop

In this section, you will implement the MagicMind game loop. The game loop controls the flow of the game.

During the course of the game, you will tell the computer player that you implemented in the MindPlayer class to pick the rack. Then, you will ask the player for 10 guesses. Each time the player submits a guess, you will ask the computer player if the guess is correct. If the guess is not correct, you will report the status of the guess back to the player so that he can refine his next guess. Finally, if the user wins, you will tell him so, if not, you will display the rack.

You will do all of this in the main method in the main.m implementation file. The main function is the entry point to C and Objective-C programs. You can see a flowchart of the game loop in Figure 4-6.

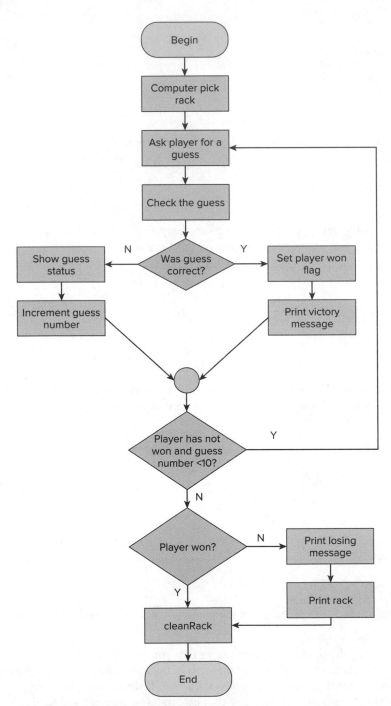

FIGURE 4-6: MagicMind game loop

TRY IT OUT Implementing the MagicMind Game Loop

codefile MagicMind available for download at Wrox.com

In this section, you will implement the game loop.

1. Open the MagicMind project in Xcode.

2. Open the main.m file and add an import statement to import the MindPlayer.h header file:

```
#import "MindPlayer.h"
```

3. Replace the main function with the following implementation:

```objc
int main (int argc, const char * argv[])
{

    MindPlayer* computerPlayer = [[MindPlayer alloc] init];

    // State of the game
    BOOL playerWon = NO;
    int guessNumber = 1;

    NSString* checkGuessStatus;
    char guess[5];

    // Pick the rack
    [computerPlayer pickRack];

    // Game loop
    do
    {
        // Tell the user which guess this is
        NSLog(@"You are on guess number %i",guessNumber);

        // Ask for a guess
        NSLog(@"Enter your guess: ");
        scanf("%s", &guess);
        NSString* guessString = [NSString stringWithCString:guess
                                    encoding:NSMacOSRomanStringEncoding];

        // Check the guess
        checkGuessStatus = [computerPlayer checkGuess:guessString];

        // Check to see if the player won
        if ([checkGuessStatus isEqualToString:@"win"])
        {
            playerWon = YES;

            // Tell the user that they won
            NSLog(@"You are a winner!");
        }
        else
        {
            // Show the guess status
```

```
            NSLog(@"%@",checkGuessStatus);

            // Increment the guess number
            guessNumber++;
        }

    }
    while (playerWon==NO && guessNumber<=10);

    // If the player didn't win
    if (playerWon == NO)
    {
        // Print a message and the rack
        NSLog(@"Sorry, you lost. The rack was: %@",
            [computerPlayer getRackString] );
    }

    // Clean up the rack
    [computerPlayer cleanRack];

    // Clean up the computer player
    computerPlayer=nil;
    return 0;
}
```

4. Build and run the program. Make sure that you type only 4 characters for each guess in the debug output window. Here is the output of my run:

```
2011-04-14 17:25:59.908 MagicMind[282:903] You are on guess number 1
2011-04-14 17:25:59.910 MagicMind[282:903] Enter your guess:
bbyy
2011-04-14 17:26:05.310 MagicMind[282:903]
Correct Color And Position: 1
Correct Color Only: 0
2011-04-14 17:26:05.311 MagicMind[282:903] You are on guess number 2
2011-04-14 17:26:05.312 MagicMind[282:903] Enter your guess:
rboo
2011-04-14 17:26:19.419 MagicMind[282:903]
Correct Color And Position: 1
Correct Color Only: 1
2011-04-14 17:26:19.419 MagicMind[282:903] You are on guess number 3
2011-04-14 17:26:19.420 MagicMind[282:903] Enter your guess:
bkyy
2011-04-14 17:26:32.557 MagicMind[282:903]
Correct Color And Position: 2
Correct Color Only: 0
2011-04-14 17:26:32.557 MagicMind[282:903] You are on guess number 4
2011-04-14 17:26:32.558 MagicMind[282:903] Enter your guess:
bkyo
2011-04-14 17:26:46.663 MagicMind[282:903]
Correct Color And Position: 3
Correct Color Only: 0
2011-04-14 17:26:46.664 MagicMind[282:903] You are on guess number 5
2011-04-14 17:26:46.664 MagicMind[282:903] Enter your guess:
ggrr
```

```
2011-04-14 17:27:23.301 MagicMind[282:903]
Correct Color And Position: 0
Correct Color Only: 1
2011-04-14 17:27:23.302 MagicMind[282:903] You are on guess number 6
2011-04-14 17:27:23.302 MagicMind[282:903] Enter your guess:
bkgo
2011-04-14 17:27:30.423 MagicMind[282:903]
Correct Color And Position: 2
Correct Color Only: 0
2011-04-14 17:27:30.423 MagicMind[282:903] You are on guess number 7
2011-04-14 17:27:30.424 MagicMind[282:903] Enter your guess:
bkro
2011-04-14 17:27:45.560 MagicMind[282:903]
Correct Color And Position: 2
Correct Color Only: 1
2011-04-14 17:27:45.561 MagicMind[282:903] You are on guess number 8
2011-04-14 17:27:45.561 MagicMind[282:903] Enter your guess:
gkyo
2011-04-14 17:28:03.020 MagicMind[282:903]
Correct Color And Position: 3
Correct Color Only: 0
2011-04-14 17:28:03.021 MagicMind[282:903] You are on guess number 9
2011-04-14 17:28:03.021 MagicMind[282:903] Enter your guess:
ggyo
2011-04-14 17:28:10.373 MagicMind[282:903]
Correct Color And Position: 2
Correct Color Only: 0
2011-04-14 17:28:10.374 MagicMind[282:903] You are on guess number 10
2011-04-14 17:28:10.374 MagicMind[282:903] Enter your guess:
gkoo
2011-04-14 17:28:21.455 MagicMind[282:903]
Correct Color And Position: 1
Correct Color Only: 1
2011-04-14 17:28:21.455 MagicMind[282:903] Sorry, you lost. The rack was: rkyo
Program ended with exit code: 0
```

How It Works

Before you implemented the main function, you added an import for the MindPlayer.h class:

```
#import "MindPlayer.h"
```

You must add this import because you will use the MindPlayer class in this file.

Next, you implemented the main function. This is the entry point for C and Objective-C programs:

```
int main (int argc, const char * argv[])
{
```

The next line allocates and initializes the computerPlayer, which is an instance of the MindPlayer class:

```
MindPlayer* computerPlayer = [[MindPlayer alloc] init];
```

Next, you declared and initialized some variables that you will use to maintain the state of the game:

```
// State of the game
BOOL playerWon = NO;
```

```
int guessNumber = 1;

NSString* checkGuessStatus;
char guess[5];
```

The BOOL type is unique to Objective-C. It is a Boolean data type where YES indicates a true value and NO indicates false. In this case, you are initializing the playerWon variable to NO. You will use the guessNumber variable to keep track of the player's guess number. The checkGuessStatus string will store the response from calls to checkGuess. You will display this string to the player each time he guesses incorrectly.

Finally, the guess array is a buffer that you will use with the scanf function to get the guess from the player on the command line. Even though a guess is only four characters, one for each peg, the buffer needs to be 5 characters long. That is because a C style string ends with a null terminator "\0". You don't need to be concerned with this because it doesn't play into building iOS-based games; just be aware that all C-style strings end with the null terminator.

The next line of code tells the computer player to pick the rack:

```
// Pick the rack
[computerPlayer pickRack];
```

Next, you enter the game loop:

```
// Game loop
do
{
```

Thanks to the objects that you built, the game loop is straightforward. First, you tell the player what guess number he is on:

```
// Tell the user which guess this is
NSLog(@"You are on guess number %i",guessNumber);
```

Next, you prompt the user for a guess. You use the scanf function to get the player's guess from the command line:

```
// Ask for a guess
NSLog(@"Enter your guess (valid letters r,y,g,b,o,k): ");

scanf("%s", &guess);
```

Notice that you are passing the address of your guess array. The scanf function will fill this buffer with anything that you type at the command line, so make sure that you type only four characters. If you type any more characters than that, you will see strange behavior and you may crash the game.

The next line converts the C-style string that you got from scanf to a Cocoa NSString:

```
NSString* guessString = [NSString stringWithCString:guess
                                   encoding:NSMacOSRomanStringEncoding];
```

Do not worry about this right now. You will learn about working with strings in the next chapter.

The next line asks the computer player to check the player's guess and assigns the response to the checkGuessStatus variable:

```
// Check the guess
checkGuessStatus = [computerPlayer checkGuess:guessString];
```

Next, the code checks to see if the checkGuessStatus is the string "win" by using the isEqualToString method of the NSString class:

```
// Check to see if the player won
if ([checkGuessStatus isEqualToString:@"win"])

{
```

Again, do not worry too much about this as you will learn about string comparison in the next chapter. If checkGuessStatus is the string "win", this will return YES.

If the player has won, you then set the playerWon flag to YES and tell the user that he won:

```
playerWon = YES;

// Tell the user that they won
NSLog(@"You are a winner!");
}
```

If the player did not win, you display the checkGuessStatus string to the player and increment the guessNumber:

```
else
{
    // Show the guess status
    NSLog(@"%@",checkGuessStatus);

    // Increment the guess number
    guessNumber++;
}
```

At the end of the do loop is the while condition that determines if you should run the loop again:

```
while (playerWon==NO && guessNumber<=10);
```

The loop will continue to run as long as the player has not yet won and the number of guesses that the player has made is less than or equal to 10.

After exiting the loop for either reason, you move on to test to see if the player won. If not, you print a condolence message and show the computer player's rack:

```
// If the player didn't win
if (playerWon == NO)
{
    // Print a message and the rack
    NSLog(@"Sorry, you lost. The rack was: %@",
        [computerPlayer getRackString] );
}
```

The rest of the code cleans up after completing the game. First, tell the computer player to clean the rack, freeing the memory used by the pegs:

```
// Clean up the rack
[computerPlayer cleanRack];
```

Then, clean up the computerPlayer:

```
// Clean up the computer player
computerPlayer=nil;
```

Finally, you return 0 to indicate that your program completed successfully:

```
return 0;
```

SUMMARY

Like the last chapter, this chapter moved quickly through many topics. You learned about basic object-oriented concepts like classes, objects, instance variables, and methods. You also looked at more-advanced topics like inheritance, encapsulation, and polymorphism. To learn more about object-oriented design, read Apple's "Object-Oriented Programming with Objective-C" at `http://developer.apple.com/library/mac/#documentation/Cocoa/Conceptual/OOP_ObjC/Introduction/Introduction.html`.

Then, you applied those concepts to actual programs by using Objective-C. You built classes with member variables and methods. You used inheritance to build a class hierarchy. Then, you used polymorphism to call methods on those classes. For more information on the Objective-C language, I would recommend reading Apple's, "The Objective-C Programming Language" at `http://developer.apple.com/library/ios/documentation/Cocoa/Conceptual/ObjectiveC/`.

Finally, you built another game. This time you used objects, object-oriented design principals, and Objective-C.

EXERCISES

1. Is it possible to use the C constructs that you learned in the previous chapter in Objective-C? Can you use C libraries in Objective-C?

2. What is the difference between a class and an object?

3. When you build a class hierarchy by using inheritance, what relationship are you expressing between the objects?

4. What is polymorphism and why is it useful?

5. Modify the Houses project to use a property called `color` instead of the `getColor` and `setColor` methods.

Answers to the Exercises can be found in the Appendix.

▶ WHAT YOU LEARNED IN THIS CHAPTER

TOPIC	MAIN POINTS
Objective-C and C	Objective-C is a superset of C. Anything that you can do in C, you can do in Objective-C.
Object-oriented design principals	Classes, Objects, Instance variables, methods and messages, inheritance, polymorphism.
Properties	Using properties is an easy way to make class data available.
Class methods	You can write class methods to make it easier for users of your class to create instances of the class.
Memory management	If you create an object with `alloc`, `new`, or `copy`, the object will have a retain count of 1 and you are responsible for calling `release`.
	If you get a reference to an object in any other way, you can assume that it has a retain count of 1 and has been autoreleased. If you need to hold on to a reference to the object, `retain` it.
	If you call `retain` on an object, you have to balance the call to `retain` with a call to `release`.
Automatic Reference Counting (ARC)	Using ARC simplifies your program's memory management by not requiring you to call retain and release on your objects. The compiler inserts the correct memory management code for you at compile time.

5

The Cocoa Foundation Framework

WHAT YOU WILL LEARN IN THIS CHAPTER:

➤ Building the interface for an iOS game by using Interface Builder

➤ Designing an iOS game by using the Model-View-Controller architecture

➤ Handling text with NSString

➤ Working with mutable and immutable types

➤ Using collections to store data

➤ Calling periodic methods with NSTimer

In the previous two chapters, you learned about the languages that you use to build games for iOS. You may remember using the #import statement in the programs in the last chapter to include classes from the Cocoa Foundation framework like NSString. In this chapter, you will take a closer look at some of the important classes that make up the Foundation framework. You will also begin developing games for iOS, leaving command-line games behind.

The Foundation framework provides many low-level classes that you will use in every iOS program, hence the name Foundation. Foundation includes object-oriented versions of base types like strings and dates, collections like arrays, dictionaries, and sets, along with utility classes for working with I/O, URLs, and timers. Foundation also includes the root class NSObject that you used to create your own classes in the last chapter.

MODEL-VIEW-CONTROLLER ARCHITECTURE

Before I move on with the sample, it is important that you understand the basic architecture used to build most iPhone applications: Model-View-Controller. There are three parts to the architecture, shown in Figure 5-1. As you can probably guess, they are the model, the view, and the controller.

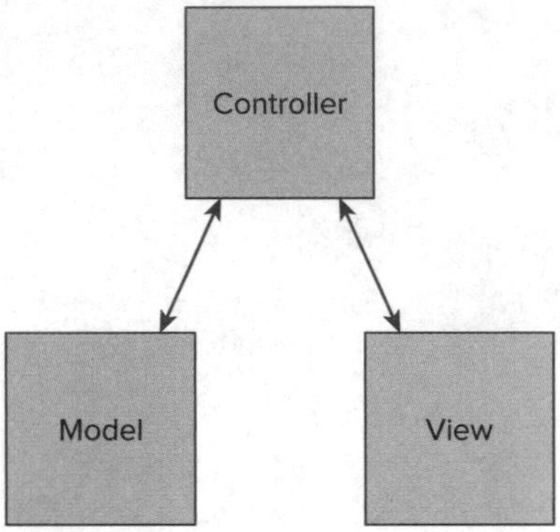

The *model* is the class or set of classes that represent your data. You should design your model classes to contain your data and the functions that operate on that data. Model classes should not need to know how to display the data that they contain. In fact, think of a model class as a class that does not know about anything else except its own data.

FIGURE 5-1: Model-View-Controller architecture

In general, model objects should *encapsulate* all of your data. Encapsulation is a very important object-oriented design principle. The idea of encapsulation is to prevent other objects from changing your object's data. To effectively encapsulate your data, you should implement interface methods or properties to expose the data of a model class. Classes should not make their data available through public variables.

You will develop a model class for the Scrambler game that you will call `ScramblerModel`. You will use the model to maintain the state of the game. The model will contain things such as the score, amount of time left on the clock, and the current word. You will implement methods in the model to get the scrambled word for display and check the player's guess.

The *view* portion of the MVC architecture is your user interface. The graphics, widgets, tables, and text boxes present the data in your model to the user. The user interacts with your model through the view. View classes typically contain only the code that is required to present the model data to the user. In many iOS applications like Scrambler, you will not need to write any code for your view. You will design and build it entirely within Xcode by using the Interface Builder tool.

The *controller* is the glue that binds your model to your view. The controller is responsible for telling the view what to display. It is also responsible for telling your model how to change based on input from the view. Most of the code in your games will be contained in controller classes. You will be implementing a controller in the Scrambler game in the `ViewController` class.

To quickly summarize, the model is your application data, the view is the user interface, and the controller is the logic code that binds the view to the model.

YOUR FIRST IOS GAME

All of the programs that you have built so far have worked only on the command line. In this chapter, you will build a simple word game for iOS that you will run in the iOS simulator. I called the game Scrambler.

The concept of Scrambler is simple. The computer player picks 10 words from a list. You have 60 seconds to unscramble all 10 words. To make the game a little more interesting, I decided that the player gets an additional 15 seconds on the game clock for each correct answer. However, the player will lose 10 seconds for each incorrect guess. The game ends when the player either runs out of time or has correctly guessed all 10 words. You can see a screen shot of the game running in the iOS simulator in Figure 5-2.

In the Scrambler game, you will create a class called `ScramblerModel` that acts as the model for the game. Xcode creates a default controller for the application when you start an application from the view-based application template. In the Scrambler game, the name of this controller is `ViewController`. You will write code in the controller to link the model and the view. Xcode also creates a default view for you in the `ViewController.xib` interface builder XIB file. You will add all of the controls that you need to build the game in this view.

FIGURE 5-2: Scrambler running in the iOS simulator

TRY IT OUT   Creating the Project

codefile Scrambler available for download at Wrox.com

In this section, you will create a new Xcode project from a template to start building your first iOS game.

1.   Start up Xcode and select File ⇨ New ⇨ New Project.

2.   A dialog box appears that displays templates for the various types of applications that you can create for the iPhone and Mac OS X, as shown in Figure 5-3. Each option presented provides you with the basic setup that you will need to start developing an application. For this game, you are going to use the Single View Application template. Select Single View Application from the dialog box and click the Next button.

3.   In the Product Name text box, type the name of your project, "Scrambler." Uncheck the "Include Unit Tests" and "Use Storyboard" checkboxes and select "iPhone" from the Device Family dropdown. Make sure that the "Use Automatic Reference Counting" checkbox is checked. Press the Next button.

4.   Select a location to save your project, and click the Create button. Xcode will create your project and present the project window. You are now ready to get started!

How It Works

You used the New Project feature of Xcode to start a new project. Using a project template for a View-based project, Xcode created a project for you. The template contains the files that you need to get started building your game. These include the view controller and the XIB file that contains your view.

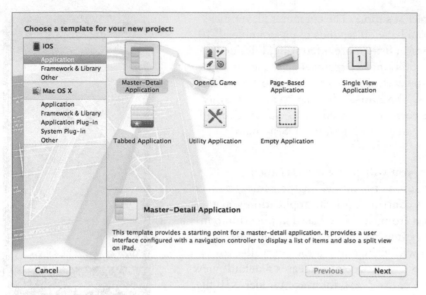

FIGURE 5-3: New Project dialog

BUILDING THE UI

In this section, you will build the UI for the Scrambler game as you saw in Figure 5-2. You will add labels to call out the current scrambled word, player time remaining, and player score.

In `ViewController.xib`, you will add labels for scrambled text, time, and score along with caption labels. You use labels to show text in the user interface that the user cannot change. You can control the text that you display in a label with your code. You will then add a text field where the player will enter his guess. Next, you will add a button that the player will use to submit his guess. Finally, you will connect all of the controls to your code with outlets and actions.

You learned the basics of using Interface Builder in Chapter 2. A full discussion of using Interface Builder to build user interfaces is beyond the scope of this book. For a complete introduction to using Interface Builder to build interfaces, take a look at Apple's article, "Designing User Interfaces in Xcode" located at `http://developer.apple.com/library/mac/#documentation/ ToolsLanguages/Conceptual/Xcode4UserGuide/InterfaceBuilder/InterfaceBuilder.html`.

OUTLETS AND ACTIONS

If you recall from Chapter 2, you build interfaces by graphically laying them out by using Interface Builder. Then, you connect the controls that you placed in Interface Builder to your code by creating outlets and actions. *Outlets* link the controls to your code by defining variables in your code that represent the controls. *Actions* link the controls to your code by defining methods that run when a user interacts with a control.

In Scrambler, you will create outlets for the guess text field along with the scrambled word, remaining time, and player score labels. You need to create outlets for these controls because you will either get data from them or write data to them in your view controller code. For example, you need to create an outlet for the guess text field because your code will read this text and submit it to the game model. Likewise, you need outlets for the labels because your code will need to write the current state of the game to the labels for display to the user.

You will create an action for the "Guess" button. When the user taps the button, you will want a method to run that will get the guess from the text box and submit it to the model.

TRY IT OUT   Building the Scrambler Interface

codefile Scrambler available for download at Wrox.com

In this section, you will build the user interface for the Scrambler game by using Interface Builder. You will add interface controls and connect them to your code by using Outlets and Actions.

1. Open the Scrambler project that you started in the last section in Xcode.

2. Select the `ViewController.xib` file in the Project Navigator to bring up the interface for the game.

3. If you do not already have it open, open the Utilities view by clicking the icon on the right side of the toolbar above the View label.

4. In the bottom pane of the Utilities view, show the Object Library by selecting the third icon at the top of the pane. Figure 5-4 shows you what your screen should look like to help you get started.

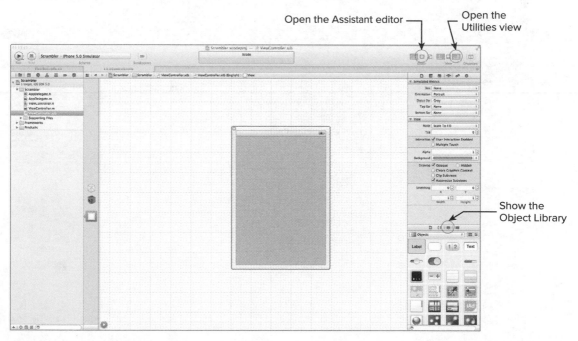

FIGURE 5-4: Interface Builder

5. The first control in the Object Library is a Label. Drag a Label control out from the Object Library and drop it on the interface.

6. Double-click on the label that you just created and type **Word:**. This is the caption label next to the scrambled word.

7. Drag another label out from the Object Library and drop it on the interface next to the "Word:" label. You do not need to change the text in this label because you will replace the text with the scrambled word in code.

8. Repeat the steps above to create the four remaining labels so that your interface looks like Figure 5-2.

9. The fourth control in the Object Library is a Text Field. Drag a Text Field control out from the Object Library and drop it on the interface. Position the text field below the labels as in Figure 5-2.

10. The second control in the Object Library is a Round Rect Button. Drag a Round Rect Button control out from the Object Library and drop it on the interface. Position the button below the text field as in Figure 5-2. Double-click the button and type "Guess" to give the button a label.

11. Now, you are ready to connect the controls that you just placed in Interface Builder to your code. Show the Assistant editor by clicking on the middle icon in the editor toolbar.

12. While holding down the control key, drag the Guess button into the `ViewController.h` in the assistant window. When you drag the button under the text `@interface`, the text, "Insert Outlet, Action or Outlet Collection" will appear in the header. Your screen should look like Figure 5-5.

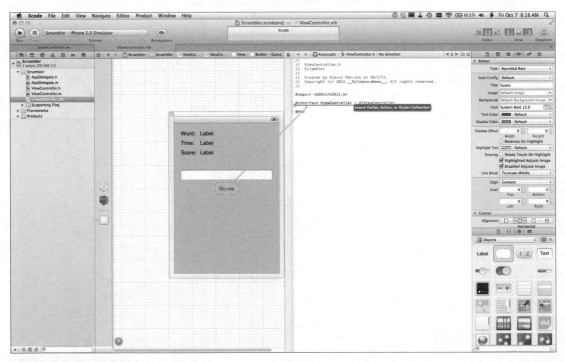

FIGURE 5-5: Wiring the Guess action

13. Let go of the mouse button to drop the control under the `@interface` directive. A popup will appear to the left of the `ViewController.h` code in the assistant window. You use this popup to configure the connection that you just made. In this case, you want to create an action that will run when the player taps the Guess button.

14. In the Connection dropdown in the popup box, select Action.

15. In the Name field, type **guessTap**. Click the Connect button to create the connection. You will notice that Xcode added a new method declaration to your header file:

```
- (IBAction)guessTap:(id)sender;
```

Interface Builder will also create an action method in the implementation `.m` file. Later on, you will implement this method to check the player's guess when he taps the Guess button.

16. Control-drag the text box to the header just like you did with the Guess button. This time, in the popup, leave the connection dropdown set to Outlet. Set the name to **guessText** and click Connect. This creates an outlet property for the outlet. You will use this outlet later on to obtain the text that the player input in the text box.

17. Follow this same process to create outlets for the scrambled word, time, and score labels. Control-drag the label to the right of the word caption label to the header and create an outlet called `scrambledWord`.

18. Control-drag the label to the right of the time caption label to the header and create an outlet called `remainingTime`.

19. Control-drag the label to the right of the score caption label to the header and create an outlet called `playerScore`.

When you are finished, your header should look like this:

```
#import <UIKit/UIKit.h>

@interface ViewController : UIViewController
- (IBAction)guessTap:(id)sender;

@property (weak, nonatomic) IBOutlet UITextField *guessText;
@property (weak, nonatomic) IBOutlet UILabel *scrambledWord;
@property (weak, nonatomic) IBOutlet UILabel *remainingTime;
@property (weak, nonatomic) IBOutlet UILabel *playerScore;

@end
```

How It Works

In this activity, you built the user interface for your application by using Interface Builder. By control-dragging controls from the interface picture to the code header, you linked the controls to your code.

You created Action methods by changing the Connection type in the popup window to Action. You created Outlets by selecting Outlet from the Connection dropdown in the popup window.

If you run the game by pressing Command-R or by selecting Product ⇨ Run from the menu bar, you should see your game start up in the iPhone simulator. The guess button will not do anything yet, but you can confirm that the application compiles successfully and that the interface looks like you expect.

HANDLING TEXT WITH NSSTRING

Now that your user interface is all set up and ready to go, you need to start building the game logic. Since this game will use strings, now is a good time to get more familiar with the classes that you use to work with strings in iOS applications: `NSString` and `NSMutableString`.

NSString Methods

You use the `NSString` class to work with immutable strings. If you are not aware, a string is an array of characters. Almost any place in your code where you work with text, you will use strings.

The two most basic methods implemented by the `NSString` class are `length` and `characterAtIndex:`. The `length` method returns an integer that tells you the number of characters in the string. The `characterAtIndex:` method accepts an integer parameter and returns the character at that position in the string. The index is 0 based, so the first character in a string is located at index 0. Passing in a number greater than or equal to the length of the string is an error.

The `NSString` class also implements many other methods for working with strings. Some of the tasks that you may want to do with strings include:

➤ Creating strings from other strings, files, or URLs by using methods like `initWithString:`, `initWithContentsOfFile:encoding:error:`, and `initWithContentsOfURL:encoding:error:`

➤ Combining and dividing strings with methods like `stringByAppendingString:`, `componentsSeparatedByString:`, `substringFromIndex:`, and `substringWithRange:`

➤ Finding and replacing substrings with methods like `rangeOfString:` and `stringByReplacingOccurrencesOfString:withString:`

➤ Comparing strings with methods like `compare:`, `hasPrefix:`, `hasSuffix:`, and `isEqualToString:`

➤ Changing the case of strings with methods like `capitalizedString`, `lowercaseString`, and `uppercaseString`

➤ Getting numeric values from strings with methods like `doubleValue`, `floatValue`, and `intValue`

Mutable and Immutable Types

`NSStrings` are immutable. That is, once you create an instance of `NSString`, you cannot change its value. Therefore, you should use the `NSString` class only when you are certain that you will not need to change the string.

When you do need to change a string on the fly, you should use the NSMutableString class. NSMutableString is a subclass of NSString, so you can use an NSMutableString anywhere that you can use an NSString.

In addition to the methods contained in NSString, NSMutableString has methods for modifying the string. These include:

➤   appendFormat: and appendString: to add to the end of a string

➤   deleteCharatersInRange: to delete characters from the string

➤   insertString:atIndex: to insert a string into the middle of the string

➤   replaceCharactersInRange:withString: and
    replaceOccurrencesOfString:withString:options:range: to replace
    characters or strings in the string

➤   setString: to replace the entire string with another string

There are many other types in the Cocoa frameworks that have both mutable and immutable variants. You will look at another in the section on collection classes: NSArray and NSMutableArray.

String Comparison

The first, and perhaps most important, thing to learn about string comparison is that you should not compare strings with the equality operator (==). Since you work with objects in Objective-C using pointers, comparing two strings using == does not compare the contents of the string, it compares the two pointers. If the two pointers are pointing to the same object as in Figure 5-6 (a), the == comparison will return true. If the two strings contain identical text, but are two different objects, as in Figure 5-6 (b), the == comparison will return

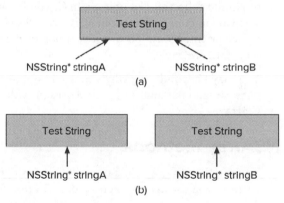

FIGURE 5-6: String Comparison

false. You may not expect this result because the two strings contain the same text, but it makes sense when you think about the fact that the two pointers are not pointing to the same object.

When you want to compare two strings for equality, you send the isEqualToString: message to one of the strings and pass the other string as the parameter. isEqualToString: returns a BOOL so you can test the return value of isEqualToString: against YES or NO using the == operator. Therefore, if you had two NSString objects called stringA and stringB, you could determine if they contained the same text with the statement if ([stringA isEqualToString: stringB] == YES).

You can determine the order of two strings by using the compare: method. The compare: method returns an NSComparisonResult. The NSComparisonResult can be one of the following values:

➤   NSOrderedAscending

➤   NSOrderedSame

➤   NSOrderedDescending

To demonstrate, suppose that you have two strings "alpha" and "omega" represented by NSString variables alpha and omega. If you call [alpha compare: omega] the method would return NSOrderedAscending because the strings are in ascending order. Calling [omega compare: omega] would return NSOrderedSame because the strings are the same. Finally, if you called [omega compare: alpha] the method would return NSOrderedDescending because the strings are in descending order.

In the Scrambler game, you will use length to determine the length of a string, characterAtIndex: to get individual characters from the string, appendFormat: to append to a mutable string, and isEqualToString: to compare the string that the user typed to the scrambled word.

To learn more about programming with strings, take a look at Apple's String Programming Guide for Cocoa at http://developer.apple.com/library/ios/#documentation/Cocoa/Conceptual/Strings/introStrings.html.

COLLECTING OBJECTS WITH NSARRAY

Now that you understand how to work with strings, the next thing that you need to learn is how to handle collections of objects. In C, you learned about using arrays to work with collections. The Cocoa Foundation framework provides classes that help you work with collections in an object-oriented way. The most common of these classes are NSArray and its mutable counterpart NSMutableArray.

You may be wondering why you would not just use C arrays to manage your collections. The NSArray and NSMutableArray classes provide a lot of functionality that you will not find in a basic C array.

NSArray Methods

You use the NSArray class to work with immutable arrays. If you do not remember from the C chapter, you use arrays to group data. In the example in this chapter, you will use an array to store the game's master word list. You will also use an array in the function that you will build to scramble words.

The two most basic methods implemented by the NSArray class are count and objectAtIndex:. The count method returns an integer that tells you the number of elements in the array. The objectAtIndex: method accepts an integer parameter and returns the object in the array at that position. This is like using the index [] in a C array. The index is 0 based, so the first element in an array is located at index 0. Passing in a number that is beyond the end of the array is an error.

The NSArray class also implements many other methods for working with arrays. Some of the tasks that you may want to do with arrays include:

➤   Creating arrays from other arrays, files, URLs, or lists of objects using methods like initWithArray:, initWithContentsOfFile:, initWithContentsOfURL:, initWithObjects:

➤   Querying arrays to determine if the array contains a particular object or getting a specific object by using methods like containsObject: and lastObject

➤ Finding specific objects by using methods like `indexOfObject:`

➤ Comparing arrays by using `isEqualToArray:`

➤ Sorting arrays with `sortedArrayUsingFunction:context:`, `sortedArrayUsingSelector:`, and `sortedArrayUsingComparator:`

Modifying Arrays by Using NSMutableArray

Like `NSString`, `NSArrays` are immutable. Once you create an instance of `NSArray`, you cannot change the array. You can modify the contents, but you cannot change the array itself by adding entries, removing entries, sorting, etc. Therefore, you should use the `NSArray` class only when you are certain that you will not need to modify the array.

In the Scrambler game, you will use an `NSArray` to maintain the list of words used by the game because the list will not change.

When you do need to change an array on the fly, you will use the `NSMutableArray` class. `NSMutableArray` is a subclass of `NSArray`, so you can use an `NSMutableArray` anywhere that you can use an `NSArray`.

In addition to the methods contained in `NSArray`, `NSMutableArray` has methods for modifying the array. These include:

➤ `addObject:` and `insertObject:atIndex:` to add objects to an array

➤ `removeAllObjects`, `removeLastObject`, and `removeObjectAtIndex:` to remove objects from an array

➤ `replaceObjectAtIndex:withObject:` to replace an object in an array

➤ `filterUsingPredicate:` to filter an array

➤ `exchangeObjectAtIndex:withObjectAtIndex:`, `sortUsingComparator:`, and `sortUsingFunction:context:` to rearrange the elements in an array

One thing that you have to keep in mind is that the array classes `NSArray` and `NSMutableArray` can contain only objects. Therefore, you cannot insert values of C scalar base types like `int`, `long`, or any other type that does not inherit from `NSObject`. To work around this, The Cocoa Foundation framework contains classes that you can use to wrap these scalar types.

Wrapping Numbers with NSNumber

You use the `NSNumber` class to wrap scalar C data types like `int`, `long`, etc. in an object wrapper. You can then use this object in collections like `NSArray` and `NSMutableArray`. `NSNumber` is immutable, and there is no mutable counterpart. If you need to modify a number, you must create a new `NSNumber` object to hold your new number.

You create `NSNumber` objects by using class helper methods like `numberWithInt:` and `numberWithLong:` or the familiar `[[object alloc] init]` pattern using initializers like `initWithInt:` and `initWithLong:`. You pass in the scalar C value, and you get back an `NSNumber` object that represents that value.

To get the number back out of the object, you use methods like `intValue` and `longValue` depending on the type of number you expect to get back. It is also possible to get a string representation of an `NSNumber` using the `stringValue` method.

You compare numbers by using `NSNumber` similar to the way that you compare strings by using `NSString`. You should not compare `NSNumbers` by using `==` because `==` compares the two pointers, not the numbers themselves. If the two pointers are pointing to the same object, the `==` comparison will be true. If the two numbers are mathematically equal but are two different objects, the comparison will return false. Just as with `NSString`, this result seems counterintuitive, but if you think about comparing the pointers, rather than the objects, it makes more sense.

When you want to compare two `NSNumbers` for equality, you use the `isEqualToNumber:` method. `isEqualToNumber:` returns a `BOOL` so you can test the return value against `YES` or `NO`. So, if you had two `NSNumber` objects called numA and numB, you could determine if they were equal with the statement `if ([numA isEqualToNumber: numB] == YES)`.

You can determine the order of two numbers by using the `compare:` method. The `compare:` method returns an `NSComparisonResult`. The `compare:` method works the same way for `NSNumbers` as it does for `NSStrings`.

In the Scrambler game, you will use `NSNumber` to put numbers into a mutable array.

Other Collection Classes

Besides `NSArray` there are a couple of other classes in the Cocoa Foundation framework that you can use to manage collections: `NSSet` and `NSDictionary`.

NSSet

When you need to maintain an ordered list, `NSArray` is the best choice. However, if order is not a concern and the objects are unique, you can use an `NSSet`. The advantage of using a set is that the test for membership in the set is significantly faster than the same test for an array. So, if testing for membership by using `containsObject:` is the prime reason for your collection, you should consider using the `NSSet` class.

Like `NSArray`, `NSSet` is immutable. If you need to add or remove items from a set, you must use the mutable version, `NSMutableSet`.

NSDictionary

The last collection class that you will look at is `NSDictionary`. You use a dictionary when you want to represent a key-value relationship.

`NSDictionary` allows you to create a unique key that relates to an object. You can use any object you want for the key, as long as the object responds to the `isEqual:` message. The dictionary uses the response from `isEqual:` to ensure that you do not insert two objects with the same key into the dictionary. It also uses `isEqual:` to determine which object to return to the caller when the `objectForKey:` method is called.

You can read the Apple article "Collections Programming Topics" located at `http://developer` `.apple.com/library/ios/#documentation/Cocoa/Conceptual/Collections/Collections` `.html%23//apple_ref/doc/uid/10000034i` to learn more about using the collection classes in the Cocoa Foundation framework.

TRY IT OUT Building the ScramblerPlayer Class

codefile Scrambler available for download at Wrox.com

Now that you know how to work with text strings and arrays, you are ready to start coding up the Scrambler game. The first thing that you will do is build the `ScramblerPlayer` class. This class represents the computer player and will be responsible for holding the word list, scrambling words, and providing words to the player.

1. Open the Scrambler project in Xcode.

2. Select File ➪ New ➪ New File... from the menu bar. In the template chooser, under iOS on the left-hand side, select Cocoa Touch. In the right-hand pane, select Objective-C class and press Next.

3. In the "Subclass of" dropdown, make sure that you select NSObject and press Next.

4. Name your class **ScramblerPlayer** and click Next. In the next dialog box, click Create. You should see two new files in the Project Navigator under your Scrambler directory called `ScramblerPlayer.h` and `ScramblerPlayer.m`.

5. Open the `ScramblerPlayer.h` header file. Inside the `@interface` block, add an `NSMutableArray*` member variable called `scrambledWords` like this:

```
@interface ScramblerPlayer : NSObject {

    // The chosen words for the game
    NSMutableArray* scrambledWords;


}

@end
```

Since you will not expose the `scrambledWords` array to external users of the class, you do not need to declare a property for the array.

6. Below the `@interface` block, add the following method declarations:

```
-(NSString*) getNextWord;
-(NSString*) scrambleWord:(NSString*) wordToScramble;
-(int) getRemainingWordCount;
-(void) initializeWordList;
```

The `getNextWord` method will return the next word from the list of 10 words that the computer player has chosen. `scrambleWord:` will accept a string and return that string scrambled. Finally, `getRemainingWordCount` will return a number indicating how many words remain in the list for the player to guess.

The first method that you will build is `scrambleWord:`.

7. Open the ScramblerPlayer.m implementation file. Type the following method implementation below the `@implementation` directive:

```
-(NSString*) scrambleWord:(NSString*) wordToScramble
{
    // This method scrambles a word

    // Allocate an array to hold the used numbers
    NSMutableSet *usedNumberSet= [[NSMutableSet alloc]init];

    // Allocate a string that you will use to build the output
    NSMutableString *outputString = [[NSMutableString alloc]init];

    // Loop the number of times that there are letters in the word
    for (int i=0; i<[wordToScramble length]; i++) {

        // Pick a number
        int randomNum = random() % [wordToScramble length];

        // Is the number in the set?
        while ([usedNumberSet containsObject:[NSNumber numberWithInt:randomNum]] ==YES)
        {

            // If the number is in the list, you need to pick a different number
            randomNum = random() % [wordToScramble length];
        }

        // The number is not in the list
        // Add it to the list of used numbers
        [usedNumberSet addObject:[NSNumber numberWithInt:randomNum]];

        // Append the character at the position chosen to the outputString
        [outputString appendFormat:@"%c",
         [wordToScramble characterAtIndex:randomNum]];


    }
    return outputString;


}
```

8. Write the code to implement the `initializeWordList` method. This method contains an `NSArray` that holds the master word list for the game. The method is responsible for initializing the `scrambledWords` array and choosing the 10 words that the computer will present to the player. Type the following method implementation below the `scrambleWord:` method:

```
-(void) initializeWordList
{
    // This method creates the chosen word list
    NSArray *masterWordList = [NSArray arrayWithObjects:
                                @"well", @"coin", @"address", @"novel",
                                @"mat", @"panther", @"chip", @"jump", @"scream",
```

```
                                @"spring", @"toothpick", @"shampoo", @"value",
                                @"buoy", @"skirt", @"general", @"ink",
                                @"engineer", @"epidemic", @"parasite", @"menu",
                                @"clay", @"sunglasses", @"ridge",@"noun",@"mill",
                                @"antique",@"gang",@"planet",@"headline",
                                @"ketchup",@"passion",@"queue",@"word",@"band",
                                @"thief",@"mustard",@"seat",@"sofa",
                                @"queue",@"flamenco",@"comet",@"pebble",
                                @"herald",@"factory",@"stew",@"loop",
                                @"volcro",@"thermostat",@"loaf",@"leaf",
                                @"salmon",@"curtain",
                                nil];

        // Initalize the scrambled word list
        scrambledWords = [[NSMutableArray alloc]
                        initWithCapacity:[masterWordList count]];

        // Seed the random number generator
        srandom( time( NULL ) );
        int randomNum;

        // Choose 10 words and them to the chosen words mutable array
        for (int i=0; i<10; i++) {
            // Generate random number to pick word
            randomNum = (random() % [masterWordList count]);

            // Add the word to the chosenWords mutable array
            [scrambledWords addObject:[masterWordList objectAtIndex:randomNum]];
        }


    }
```

9. Implement the getNextWord method. This method will return the next word from the word list. Add the following code below the initializeWordList method:

```
-(NSString*) getNextWord
{
    NSString* returnString = nil;

    if ([scrambledWords count] > 0)
    {
        // Get the string to return
        returnString = [scrambledWords objectAtIndex:0];

        // Remove the string from the array
        [scrambledWords removeObjectAtIndex:0];

    }


    return returnString;

}
```

10. Implement the `getRemainingWordCount` method. This method returns the number of words left in the scrambled word list. Add the following code below the `getNextWord` method:

```
-(int) getRemainingWordCount
{
    return [scrambledWords count];
}
```

11. Implement the `init` method. An initialized `ScramblerPlayer` should already have chosen its words. Therefore, you will override the `init` method from `NSObject` to do this. Add the following implementation of `init` under the `getRemainingWordCount` method:

```
- (id)init
{
    self = [super init];
    if (self) {
        // Initialize the word list
        [self initializeWordList];
    }
    return self;
}
```

How It Works

The first thing that you did was to add a member variable to your class to hold the list of words that the computer player will present to the player:

```
// The chosen words for the game
NSMutableArray* scrambledWords;
```

Next, you added the rest of the method declarations to the class:

```
-(NSString*) getNextWord;
-(NSString*) scrambleWord:(NSString*) wordToScramble;
-(int) getRemainingWordCount;
-(void) initializeWordList
```

Next, you moved on to building the methods themselves. The first method that you worked on was `scrambleWord:`. Instead of shuffling the word like you did with the cards in Chapter 3, this time you will implement a different algorithm. You will execute a loop for each letter in the word. Each time through the loop, you will choose a random number that you will use as an index into the word to get a letter from the word. You will store each index that you have chosen in a set. Then, you will check to make sure that you have not chosen that letter already by looking in the set. If you have not chosen the letter before, you will append the randomly chosen letter to an output string and add that index to the set. Then, you repeat until you have taken every letter from the original word and put it in the new word. Simply stated, you choose a letter randomly from the word, and append it to the output string and add the number to a set of already chosen numbers. Figure 5-7 shows a flowchart of the `scrambleWord:` method.

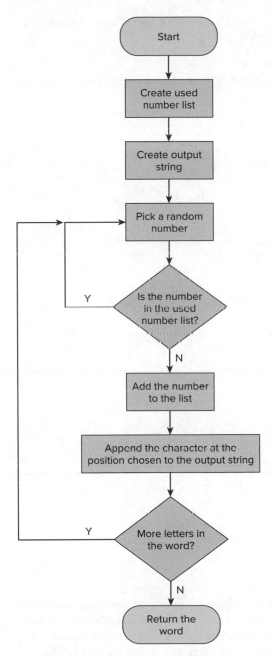

FIGURE 5-7: scrambleWord method flowchart

In Figure 5-8, you can see the state of the `usedNumberSet` and `outputString` variables at different times during the execution of the `scrambleWord:` method.

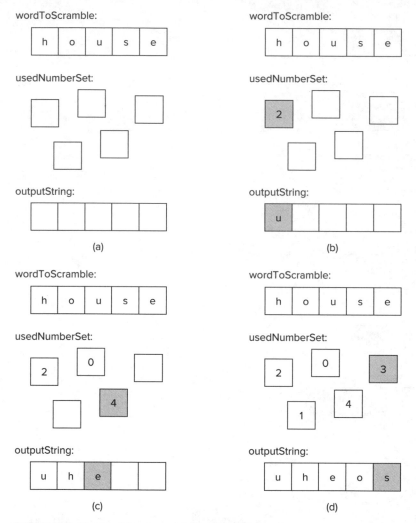

FIGURE 5-8: States of the scrambleWord method

The first thing that you did was to allocate and initialize two local variables: an `NSMutableSet` called `usedNumberSet` and an `NSMutableString` called `outputString`. You used the `usedNumberSet` to maintain a list of numbers that you have already chosen. You used the `outputString` to build the scrambled word character by character. Figure 5-8 (a) shows the starting state of these variables.

The next thing that you did was to build a loop. This loop needs to run once for each letter in the word that you are scrambling. Each time through the loop, you will pick a random number, identify the letter at that index in the `wordToScramble`, and place it into the `outputString`:

```
for (int i=0; i<[wordToScramble length]; i++) {
    int randomNum = random() % [wordToScramble length];
```

Next, you need to make sure that the number that you chose is not already in the usedNumberSet because you never want to choose the same index twice:

```
// Is the number in the set?
while ([usedNumberSet containsObject:[NSNumber numberWithInt:randomNum]] ==YES)
{

    // If the number is in the list, you need to pick a different number
    randomNum = random() % [wordToScramble length];
}
```

When you get a number that is not in the set already, you add the number to the set, indicating that you should not choose the character at that index again. Then, you add the actual character at the chosen index from the wordToScramble to the outputString.

Figure 5-8 (b) shows the state of the outputString and usedNumberSet after one pass through the loop. In this example, the wordToScramble is "house" and the first number chosen was 2.

You continue executing the loop until each letter from the wordToScramble is included in the outputString. Figure 5-8 (c) shows the state of the outputString and usedNumberSet after two more passes through the loop.

Finally, you return the scrambled outputString:

```
return outputString;
```

Figure 5-8 (d) shows the state after the loop ends.

In the next section, you built the initializeWordList method. First, you initialized the master word list with some words:

```
NSArray *masterWordList = [NSArray arrayWithObjects:
                            @"well", @"coin", @"address", @"novel",
                            @"mat", @"panther", @"chip", @"jump", @"scream",
                            @"spring", @"toothpick", @"shampoo", @"value",
                            @"buoy", @"skirt", @"general", @"ink",
                            @"engineer", @"epidemic", @"parasite", @"menu",
                            @"clay", @"sunglasses", @"ridge",@"noun",@"mill",
                            @"antique",@"gang",@"planet",@"headline",
                            @"ketchup",@"passion",@"queue",@"word",@"band",
                            @"thief",@"mustard",@"seat",@"sofa",
                            @"queue",@"flamenco",@"comet",@"pebble",
                            @"herald",@"factory",@"stew",@"loop",
                            @"velcro",@"thermostat",@"loaf",@"leaf",
                            @"salmon",@"curtain",
                            nil];
```

You used an NSArray here and not and NSMutableArray because the word list is static. Since you will not be modifying the word list during the game, there is no reason to make the list mutable. When you initialize an NSArray, the last element must always be nil. This tells the array that you are finished.

Next, you initialized the scrambledWords instance variable:

```
scrambledWords = [[NSMutableArray alloc]
          initWithCapacity:[masterWordList count]];
```

Then you seeded the random number generator and chose the ten words that you would present to the player. You added each word to the `scrambledWords` array:

```
//  Seed the random number generator
srandom( time( NULL ) );
int randomNum;

// Choose 10 words and them to the chosen words mutable array
for (int i=0; i<10; i++) {
    // Generate random number to pick word
    randomNum = (random() % [masterWordList count]);

    // Add the word to the chosenWords mutable array
    [scrambledWords addObject:[masterWordList objectAtIndex:randomNum]];
}
```

Next, you implemented the `getNextWord` method. This method returns the next word from the word list. First, you make sure that there are items in the list to return:

```
if ([scrambledWords count] > 0)
```

Then, you set a return variable to the first item in the list, item 0:

```
// Get the string to return
returnString = [scrambledWords objectAtIndex:0];
```

Next, you removed that string from the list:

```
// Remove the string from the array
[scrambledWords removeObjectAtIndex:0];
```

Finally, you return the string to the caller:

```
return returnString;
```

In this case, you are using the `scrambledWords` array as a queue. Each time a user of the class calls `getNextWord`, you pop the front element from the queue and return it to the caller. This reduces the size of the queue each time through. So, all you needed to do to implement the `getRemainingWordCount` method was to return the current size of the array:

```
return [scrambledWords count];
```

Next, you implemented your own version of the `init` method. Since it doesn't really make sense to have a `ScramblerPlayer` instance that doesn't have a word list already chosen, you are overriding the default implementation of `init` that comes from the superclass `NSObject` with a version that initializes the word list when called.

First, you have to call the superclass's version of `init`. You must do this to make sure that the object is ready for you to work with:

```
self = [super init];
```

If you remember from Chapter 4, the `self` variable is a pointer to the instance of the class itself. This is identical to the `this` variable in Java or the `this` pointer in C++. Therefore, in this case you are saying that the `self` pointer should point to the value that superclass's `init` method returns.

Next, you make sure that `[super init]` actually returned a valid object:

```
if (self) {
```

It is possible that `[super init]` could return nil if the application ran out of memory or the runtime was unable to allocate an instance of the superclass for some other reason. This is rare, but it could happen. In a production game, you would probably want to add an `else` clause to log some error message so that you could troubleshoot the issue.

After ensuring that you have a valid object, you call the `initializeWordList` method to initialize the word list:

```
[self initializeWordList];
```

Again, you are using the `self` pointer because you are calling the method on the instance that you have just created. Finally, you return the instance, once again, by using the `self` pointer:

```
return self;
```

BUILDING THE GAME MODEL

The model is the class or set of classes that you use to represent game data. In this example, the model will maintain the state of the game. The model will be responsible for keeping track of the player's score, the amount of time left on the clock, and the current word. The model will also hold a reference to the computer player. You will implement methods in the model to get the scrambled word for display and check the player's guess.

TRY IT OUT   Building the Game Model

codefile Scrambler available for download at Wrox.com

Earlier in this chapter, you learned about the MVC, Model-View-Controller architecture. You built the View portion of the Scrambler game by using interface builder. In this section, you will build the Model.

1. Open the Scrambler project in Xcode.

2. Select File ➪ New ➪ New File... from the menu bar. In the template chooser, under iOS on the left-hand side, select Cocoa Touch. In the right-hand pane, select Objective-C class and press Next.

3. In the "Subclass of" dropdown, make sure that NSObject is selected and press Next. Name your class **ScramblerModel** and click Next. In the next dialog box, click Create. You should see two new files in the Project Navigator under your Scrambler directory called `ScramblerModel.h` and `ScramblerModel.m`.

4. Open the `ScramblerModel.h` header file. At the top of the file, add a `#import` statement to import the ScramblerPlayer header:

```
#import "ScramblerPlayer.h"
```

5. Add the instance variables that you need to represent the state of the game. Inside the `@interface` block, add your member variables:

```
@interface ScramblerModel : NSObject {
    ScramblerPlayer* computerPlayer;
    int time;
    int score;
```

```
    NSString* currentWord;
}@end
```

6. The class will need to expose the time and score to the view controller, so you will use properties. Below the closing brace (}) in the @interface block, add property declarations for the time and score properties:

```
@property (readonly) int time;
@property (readonly) int score;
```

7. Declare the three methods that you will implement in the model:

```
-(NSString*) getScrambledWord;
-(BOOL) checkGuess:(NSString*) guess;
-(void) timerTick;
```

8. Switch over to the ScramblerModel.m implementation file. Below the @implementation directive, synthesize the properties that you declared in the header:

```
@synthesize time,score;
```

9. An initialized game model should automatically initialize its member variables. Therefore, you will override the init method to do this, just as you did in the ScramblerPlayer class. Add the implementation of the init method:

```
- (id)init
{
    self = [super init];
    if (self) {
        // Initialize the game model
        computerPlayer = [[ScramblerPlayer alloc] init];

        // Initialize time
        time = 60;

        // Initialize score
        score = 0;

        // Get the first word from the list
        currentWord = [computerPlayer getNextWord];
    }
    return self;
}
```

10. In the design of the game, I decided to make the model responsible for checking the player guess. Implement the checkGuess method like this:

```
-(BOOL) checkGuess:(NSString*) guess
{
    if ([guess isEqualToString:currentWord])
    {
        // Add one to the score
        score++;

        // Add 15 seconds to the timer
        time+=15;

        // If there are more words, pick the next word
```

```
            if ([computerPlayer getRemainingWordCount] > 0)
            {
                currentWord = [computerPlayer getNextWord];
            }
            else
            {
                // No more words, so clean up
                currentWord=nil;
            }

            return YES;
        }
        else
        {
            // Subtract 10 from the time
            time-=10;

            return NO;
        }
    }
```

11. Since the model holds an unscrambled version of the current word, it needs to provide a method for the view controller to obtain a scrambled version of the word to display to the player. Implement the getScrambledWord method to return a scrambled word to the caller:

```
-(NSString*) getScrambledWord
{
    return [computerPlayer scrambleWord:currentWord];
}
```

12. In the next section you will learn how to implement a timer to periodically call a function. Since the model class maintains the state of the game clock, you need to write a method that the view controller can call to tick a second off the game clock. Implement the timerTick method to decrement the game time by one:

```
-(void) timerTick
{
    time--;
}
```

How It Works

The first thing that you did was import the ScramblerPlayer.h header. You needed to do this because you are referencing the ScramblerPlayer class in your header. If you did not add this import, the ScramblerModel class would not know about the ScramblerPlayer class defined in that header. This would cause a compiler error when you tried to compile.

Next, you added the instance variables that you need to maintain the state of the game:

```
    ScramblerPlayer* computerPlayer;
int time;
int score;
NSString* currentWord;
}
```

The `computerPlayer` variable is an instance of the `ScramblerPlayer` class. This is the class that you implemented to represent the computer player. The model needs to ask this class for the current word. The model also uses the `computerPlayer` to scramble words. The `time` instance variable holds the amount of time remaining in the game. The `score` is the player's score. Finally, the `currentWord` is an unscrambled version of the word that the player is currently trying to unscramble.

Next, since the view controller will need to access the `time` and `score` members, you exposed them as properties:

```
@property (readonly) int time;
@property (readonly) int score;
```

The `readonly` modifier is new. Adding this modifier causes the compiler to treat the property as a read-only property in that the compiler will generate only the getter method and will not generate a setter method. You did this because no one should be modifying the `score` or the `time` directly.

You finished up in the header by declaring the methods that the class would implement:

```
-(NSString*) getScrambledWord;
-(BOOL) checkGuess:(NSString*) guess;
-(void) timerTick;
```

Next, you switched over to the implementation file and synthesized the properties that you declared in the header:

```
@synthesize time,score;
```

Remember that synthesizing properties tells the compiler to build the methods that implement the getters and setters for each property. You will not see these methods in your code, but the compiler builds them and makes them available to users of the class.

After synthesizing the properties, you overrode the default implementation of the `init` method from the `NSObject` class. You did this so that when a user initialized an instance of the class, the member variables would be set to the appropriate state.

First, you called the superclass implementation of the `init` method to ensure that you properly initialized the base class:

```
- (id)init
{
    self = [super init];
    if (self) {
```

Next, you initialized the computer player instance variable:

```
computerPlayer = [[ScramblerPlayer alloc] init];
```

Then, you initialized the game time to 60 seconds and set the player's score to 0:

```
// Initialize time
time = 60;

// Initialize score
score = 0;
```

Next, you got the first word from the word list:

```
        // Get the first word from the list
        currentWord = [computerPlayer getNextWord];
```

Finally, you returned a reference to the instance that you created:

```
        return self;
```

The model needs to be able to check guesses submitted from the view controller and report if the guess is correct or not. The model also updates the score and timer depending on the guess correctness. You implemented the checkGuess: method to do this.

First, you compared the guess to the currentWord:

```
        if ([guess isEqualToString:currentWord])
        {
```

If the guess is the same as the currentWord, you added one to the player's score:

```
            // Add one to the score
            score++;
```

Then, you gave the player a time bonus of 15 seconds:

```
            // Add 15 seconds to the timer
            time+=15;
```

Next, you checked to see if there were additional words left in the computerPlayers word list:

```
            // If there are more words, pick the next word
            if ([computerPlayer getRemainingWordCount] > 0)
```

If there were additional words, you got the next word:

```
        currentWord = [computerPlayer getNextWord];
```

If there were no words left, the game is over so you can set the currentWord variable to nil:

```
            else
        {
            // No more words, so clean up
            currentWord=nil;
        }
```

Finally, since the guess was equal to the currentWord the method returns the BOOL value of YES:

```
        return YES;
```

The else clause is executed if the guess was incorrect. In this case, you subtracted 10 seconds from the game timer as a penalty for submitting an incorrect guess. Then you returned the BOOL value of NO to indicate that the guess was incorrect:

```
        else
    {
        // Subtract 10 from the time
        time-=10;

        return NO;
    }
```

The final two methods are straightforward. The `getScrambledWord` method just calls the `scrambleWord:` method on the `computerPlayer` instance variable to get a scrambled version of the current word:

```
return [computerPlayer scrambleWord:currentWord];
```

The `timerTick` method just decrements the game time by one:

```
time--;
```

PERIODIC EVENTS AND TIMERS

When building games, you will often find the need to run code at certain time intervals. For example, in action games, you need to run code that will update the display every 33 milliseconds (or so) for a game to display at 30 frames per second. One way to implement this is by using timers.

Timers let you repeatedly call a method on an object at a time interval that you specify. You can specify that the timer calls the method once at a future time, or repeatedly at a fixed interval. In the Scrambler game, you will set up a timer to tick one second off the clock every second.

Timers do not work in real-time in that the run loop is responsible for calling the timer and will fire the timer only when it can. The working resolution for a timer is between 50 and 100 milliseconds. Therefore, you should not rely on timers for real-time critical applications.

It is possible that a timer will miss being called if the run loop is engaged in other long-running activities. In cases where a repeating timer's firing time elapses and another timer event occurs in the meantime, the timer will call the specified method only one time. So, if the timer in the game is supposed to fire once every second, but for some reason five seconds pass without the timer being called, the timer method will run only one time.

If you just want to delay sending a message once, you can use the method `performSelector:withObject:afterDelay:` instead of using a timer.

The steps for using a timer are: creating an instance, configuring it to call a specific message to a specific object, and associating the timer with a run loop. When you are finished using the timer, you need to invalidate it so that it stops sending the timed message.

When you specify the method to run from a timer, you use *selectors*. A selector is the name of a method. When you need to pass a method name to another method, as you do when configuring a timer, you use a compiled selector. Compiled selectors are of type SEL. The compiler assigns compiled selectors a unique id. You can then pass this ID around as a SEL object and use it to call the method. You create SEL objects from method names using the `@selector` compiler directive. In the Scrambler game, you will use the `@selector` directive to get a SEL compiled selector type that points to the `timerFired` method. Then, you will pass this selector to the NSTimer object to tell the timer that it should call the `timerFired` method when the timer fires.

In the example, you are creating the selector at compile time by using the `@selector` compiler directive. However, an interesting thing to note is that you can create selectors at runtime from strings by using the `NSSelectorFromString` function. In this way, you can call different methods based on user input at runtime. If you use this runtime functionality, you can use the `respondsToSelector:` method to determine if an object has an implementation of the selector that you are about to call. If you do not call this method to verify that the object implements the method and you try to call a method that the object does not implement, you will get a runtime error that will crash your application.

TRY IT OUT   Building the ViewController

codefile Scrambler available for download at Wrox.com

So far, you have built your model and view classes for the Scrambler game. You have also built a class to represent a computer player. In this section, you will build the controller that links the model to the view.

The `ViewController` is the glue between the `ScramblerModel` and the view that you built by using Interface Builder. The view controller configures the game model and updates the display when the game starts, accepts guesses from the UI, and submits them to the model, maintains the `NSTimer` that controls the game clock, and notifies the user when the game ends.

1. Open the Scrambler project in Xcode.

2. Open the `ViewController.h` header file. At the top of the file, add a `#import` statement to import the `ScramblerModel` header:

```
#import "ScramblerModel.h"
```

3. In the `@interface` block, add instance variables for the game model and the game timer. Your `@interface` block should look like this:

```
@interface ViewController : UIViewController {

    ScramblerModel* gameModel;
    NSTimer* gameTimer;

}
```

4. After the `@interface` block, add a method declaration for a new `endGameWithMessage:` function:

```
-(void) endGameWithMessage:(NSString*) message;
```

5. Switch over to the `ViewController.m` implementation file and implement the `viewDidLoad` method. In `viewDidLoad`, add code under `[super viewDidLoad]` to create and initialize the game model; display the time, score, and scrambled word in the view; and start the game timer. The code for `viewDidLoad` should look like this:

```
- (void)viewDidLoad
{
    [super viewDidLoad];
```

```
// Intialize the game model
gameModel = [[ScramblerModel alloc] init];

// Display the time, score and scrambled word in the view
remainingTime.text = [NSString stringWithFormat:@"%i",gameModel.time];
playerScore.text = [NSString stringWithFormat:@"%i",gameModel.score];
scrambledWord.text = [gameModel getScrambledWord];

// Start the game timer
gameTimer = [NSTimer scheduledTimerWithTimeInterval:1.0
                                             target:self
                                           selector:@selector(timerFired:)
                                           userInfo:nil
                                            repeats:YES];


}
```

6. It is a good idea to set variable values to nil when you are finished with them. In the
viewDidUnload method, add the following code before the call to [super viewDidUnload];:

```
gameModel=nil;
```

7. The viewDidUnload method should look like this:

```
- (void)viewDidUnload
{
    [self setGuessText:nil];
    [self setScrambledWord:nil];
    [self setRemainingTime:nil];
    [self setPlayerScore:nil];

    gameModel=nil;

    [super viewDidUnload];
    // Release any retained subviews of the main view.
    // e.g. self.myOutlet = nil;
}
```

8. Implement the guessTap: method. This method runs when the player taps the Guess button:

```
- (IBAction)guessTap:(id)sender {

    // Check the guess against the currentWord
    BOOL guessCorrect = [gameModel checkGuess:guessText.text];

    // Clear the guess text UI widget
    guessText.text=@"";

    if (guessCorrect)
    {
        if (gameModel.score==10)
        {
            // The game is over
```

```
            [self endGameWithMessage:@"You win!"];
        }
        else
        {
            // Update the view with the next scrambled word
            scrambledWord.text = [gameModel getScrambledWord];
        }
    }

    // Update the view
    remainingTime.text = [NSString stringWithFormat:@"%i",gameModel.time];
    playerScore.text = [NSString stringWithFormat:@"%i",gameModel.score];


}
```

9. After the `guessTap:` method, implement the `endGameWithMessage:` method. This method ends the game and displays a message to the player:

```
-(void) endGameWithMessage:(NSString*) message
{
    // Call this method to end the game
    // Invalidate the timer
    [gameTimer invalidate];

    // Show an alert with the results
    UIAlertView *alert = [[UIAlertView alloc] initWithTitle:@"Game Over"
                                            message:message
                                            delegate:self
                                  cancelButtonTitle:@"OK"
                                  otherButtonTitles: nil];
    [alert show];
}
```

10. In `viewDidLoad`, you configured your game timer to call the `timerFired:` method every second. Implement the `timerFired:` method like this:

```
- (void)timerFired:(NSTimer*)theTimer
{
    // The timer fires this method every second
    [gameModel timerTick];

    if (gameModel.time<=0) {
        remainingTime.text = 0;
        [self endGameWithMessage:@"You are out of time. You lose!"];
    }
    else
        remainingTime.text = [NSString stringWithFormat:@"%i", gameModel.time];
}
```

11. Build and run the game. Your screen should look something like Figure 5-9, with the possibility of a different scrambled word, of course.

FIGURE 5-9: Running Scrambler game

Test out the game. Try to unscramble the word correctly and verify that your score increases and you receive the time bonus that you earned. Try putting in bad guesses and verify that the game penalizes you by a reduction in time. At the end of the game, you should see a different message depending on whether you won or lost. Most of all, have fun!

How It Works

Earlier in the chapter, you built the model and view for your game. The last piece of the game is the controller that ties everything together. When you start a project from the Xcode template, the template includes a view controller in the project for you. This view controller works with the default view and is the main entry point for your application. You may have many view controllers in games that are more elaborate.

The first thing that you did was to import the `ScramblerModel` class header into the view controller:

```
#import "ScramblerModel.h"
```

You need to do this because you create an instance variable, `gameModel`, that is an instance of the `ScramblerModel` class. If you did not import the header, you would get an error when you compile because the compiler would not know about the `ScramblerModel` class in the view controller.

Next, you added instance variables for the game model and the game timer:

```
    ScramblerModel* gameModel;
    NSTimer* gameTimer;
}
```

Since the view controller is responsible for tying the model to the UI, it makes sense that the view controller will create the model instance and hold on to it in an instance variable.

After finishing in the header, you moved on to the `ViewController.m` implementation file. The first thing that you did there was to uncomment the `viewDidLoad` method. The Objective-C runtime calls the `viewDidLoad` method after the view is loaded. Implementing `viewDidLoad` allows you to do additional setup after the view is loaded. In this case, you initialized the game model:

```
// Intialize the game model
gameModel = [[ScramblerModel alloc] init];
```

Next, you told the view to display the time, score, and scrambled word:

```
// Display the time, score and scrambled word in the view
remainingTime.text = [NSString stringWithFormat:@"%i",gameModel.time];
playerScore.text = [NSString stringWithFormat:@"%i",gameModel.score];
scrambledWord.text = [gameModel getScrambledWord];
```

Finally, you configured and started the game timer:

```
// Start the game timer
gameTimer = [NSTimer scheduledTimerWithTimeInterval:1.0
                                             target:self
                                           selector:@selector(timerFired:)
                                           userInfo:nil
                                            repeats:YES];
```

When you configured the timer, you set the time interval to 1.0. This makes the timer send the message that you specify once every second. Next, you set the `target` to `self`. This means that the timer will call the method that you pass in the `selector` argument on the `self` object, in this case, the `ViewController`. Remember that `self` is a pointer to the instance of the object. You used the `@selector` compiler directive to get a `SEL` for the `timerFired:` method. You then set this as the selector, or method, to call when the timer fires. You did not pass any user info to the selector. The `userInfo` parameter allows you to pass an arbitrary object to the selector. Finally, you configured the timer to repeat by passing `YES` as the `repeats` parameter.

Next, you implemented the `guessTap:` method that runs when the player taps the Guess button. The first thing that the method does is call the `checkGuess` method of the `gameModel` to determine if the player has guessed correctly:

```
// Check the guess against the currentWord
BOOL guessCorrect = [gameModel checkGuess:guessText.text];
```

You obtained the player's guess by using the `text` property of the `guessText` object. Remember that `guessText` is the `UITextField` that you placed on the view using Interface Builder.

Next, you cleared out the text from the text field so that the UI was ready to accept the next player guess:

```
// Clear the guess text UI widget
guessText.text=@"";
```

Next, you did some processing if the player's guess was correct:

```
if (guessCorrect)
```

First, you checked the player's score in the game model. If it is 10, the game is over so you called `endGameWithMessage:` to show the user a message and end the game:

```
if (gameModel.score==10)
{
   // The game is over
   [self endGameWithMessage:@"You win!"];
}
```

If the game didn't end, you got the next scrambled word from the game model and updated the `scrambledWord` text field on the UI with the word:

```
else
{
   // Update the view with the next scrambled word
   scrambledWord.text = [gameModel getScrambledWord];
}
```

Finally, regardless of whether or not the user submitted the correct word, you updated the UI with the current time and player score from the game model:

```
// Update the view
remainingTime.text = [NSString stringWithFormat:@"%i",gameModel.time];
playerScore.text = [NSString stringWithFormat:@"%i",gameModel.score];
```

The next method that you worked on was `endGameWithMessage:`. This method ends the game and displays a message to the player. Since the game is over, you can stop the game timer. You do this by sending the timer the `invalidate` message:

```
// Call this method to end the game
// Invalidate the timer
[gameTimer invalidate];
```

Next, you created a `UIAlertView` object to display an alert message to the user. Then, you called the `show` method to show the alert:

```
// Show an alert with the results
UIAlertView *alert = [[UIAlertView alloc] initWithTitle:@"Game Over"
                                         message:message
                                         delegate:self
                                 cancelButtonTitle:@"OK"
                                 otherButtonTitles: nil];

[alert show];
```

The last method that you worked on was `timerFired:`. You configured the timer that you created in `viewDidLoad` to call this method every second. When this method runs, the first thing that it does is call the `timerTick` method in the model. If you recall, this method simply subtracts 1 from the game time:

```
// The timer fires this method every second
[gameModel timerTick];
```

Next, you updated the `remainingTime` label on the view by using the `time` property from the game model:

```
remainingTime.text = [NSString stringWithFormat:@"%i", gameModel.time];
```

Finally, you check to see if time has expired. If it has, you end the game:

```
// If time is up, end the game
if (gameModel.time<=0)
    [self endGameWithMessage:@"You are out of time. You lose!"];
```

SUMMARY

In this chapter, you learned about some of the most important classes in the Cocoa Foundation framework. Then, you applied these concepts and built your first iOS game, Scrambler.

You learned how to build a user interface with Interface Builder. Then, you learned about the iOS Model-View-Controller architecture. Next, you learned how to handle strings in iOS applications with NSString. You also learned about mutable and immutable types and when you should use each. After that, you explored the NSArray and NSSet collection classes. Finally, you learned how to call periodic methods using NSTimer.

Now that you are comfortable with the basic tools that you need to build iOS games: C, Objective-C, and the basic Cocoa Foundation classes, you are ready to move on to more advanced games. In the next section of the book, you will explore some exciting topics like graphics, sound, and animation.

EXERCISES

1. What is the root object from which all Cocoa objects inherit?

2. What are the roles of the Model, View, and Controller in the MVC architecture?

3. What is the difference between Outlets and Actions?

4. Is it possible to append text to an NSString? If not, how do you concatenate two strings?

5. Why do you need to wrap scalar C types like int with NSNumber before adding them to an NSArray?

6. Build a small program that initializes an NSArray with a list of words of your choice, prints the list, then, prints the list of words in reverse order.

7. What are the steps for creating an NSTimer to periodically call a method?

8. Build a simple application that counts the seconds since it started. Use Interface Builder to create a simple interface with a UILabel that you can use to display your counter. Use an NSTimer to update the counter each second.

Answers to the Exercises can be found in the Appendix.

▶ **WHAT YOU LEARNED IN THIS CHAPTER**

TOPIC	MAIN POINTS
Interface Builder	You use Interface Builder to design and implement the View portion of the Model-View-Controller architecture. You link the controls in the view to outlets and actions in your code.
Model-View-Controller architecture	The basic architecture used by my iOS applications. The Model represents your application data. The View is the application user interface, and the controller is the glue that binds the model to the view.
Strings	You use the `NSString` class to work with text strings in iOS. `NSString` is immutable; you need to use the mutable version `NSMutableString` or you need to work with a string that you can modify.
Collections	`NSArray` is the object-oriented version of the standard array. It provides more functionality than a simple array. You can only store objects, and not scalar types, in an array. If you need to store scalar types, you need to wrap them in an object like `NSNumber`. You can use `NSSet` to store unordered collections.
Timers	You use timers to call a specified method at a specified time interval.

PART II
Game Building Blocks

Drawing with UIKit and Core Graphics

WHAT YOU WILL LEARN IN THIS CHAPTER:

➤ Exploring the basics of the UIKit and Core Graphics drawing frameworks

➤ Learning about the iOS drawing environment

➤ Drawing shapes with `UIBezierPath`

➤ Specifying colors with `UIColor`

➤ Drawing shadows and gradients with Core Graphics

➤ Working with images

➤ Animating a game with `CADisplayLink`

➤ Building a complete, animated, graphical game

In the first section of the book, you learned about the tools that you needed to get started building games for iOS. These included the Xcode programming environment, the C and Objective-C languages, and the Cocoa Foundation framework. Now that you have a solid foundation in the basics, you are ready to move on to the next level of tools. In this chapter, you will learn about some of the APIs that iOS provides for drawing graphics.

INTRODUCING THE DRAWING FRAMEWORKS

There are two principal methods for drawing graphics in iOS. First, you can use the native drawing technologies in the UIKit and Core Graphics frameworks. These frameworks provide an object-oriented way to work with 2D graphics and images. You will be using these tools in this chapter to play with some samples and to build the example game, Blocker.

Blocker is a simple block-breaking game as you can see in Figure 6-1. The object of Blocker is to break all of the blocks at the top of the screen by hitting them with the ball. You must prevent the ball from going off the bottom of the screen by using the paddle. If you are as old as I am, you may have seen a similar game back in the arcades called Breakout. If you are a little younger, maybe you played Arkanoid. There are a lot of games in the "Block Breaking" genre, now, including Blocker!

The other drawing method is to use OpenGL ES. OpenGL is a C-based graphics library that you can use to build high-performance 2D and 3D graphics. The OpenGL ES library is very large and complicated, so it is beyond the scope of this book. However, I wanted to make you aware that you can use OpenGL on iOS. If you build a game by using the native drawing APIs and discover that the performance is not good enough to support the game, you can move the drawing code to OpenGL for a performance boost. If you design your game by using the MVC architecture, separating your drawing logic from your game logic, you should be able to move between drawing frameworks with minimal pain.

FIGURE 6-1: Blocker game

UIKit

As its name suggests, the UIKit framework contains classes that you use for building user interfaces. In the Scrambler example, you used the UIButton, UILabel, and UITextField classes from UIKit. You may not have realized that the canvas on which you drew the interface elements in Interface Builder was a UIView. That UIView was contained in a UIViewController and that view controller is contained in a UIWindow. You can see the UIKit user elements called out in Figure 6-2.

The most important class in UIKit for drawing graphics is the UIView. The UIView is the canvas on which you will draw. All of the drawings in iOS, regardless of which framework that you use, happens in a view. You can use views to define the area that you wish to draw on. In the example game in this chapter, you will define a custom subclass of UIView called BlockView. In that view, you will draw the blocks for the game.

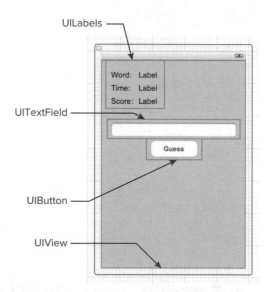

FIGURE 6-2: Annotated UIKit elements in Scrambler

UIKit also contains classes that you will use to draw images such as UIImage and UIImageView. These classes help you display pre-drawn images. You can use these images, also called *sprites*, to represent other objects in your games. In the Blocker game, you will use images for the ball and the paddle.

Core Graphics

Where UIKit provides the user interface elements and the canvas for your drawing, the Core Graphics framework provides the structures and functions that you will use to do your drawing. The base type in Core Graphics is the CGContext. The context is the drawing destination for all of your drawing calls. You will see in the sample that you can use the UIKit UIGraphicsGetCurrentContext function to get a reference to a graphic context. Then, you will use that context to do your drawing. You will learn more about contexts later in this chapter.

Besides the context, Core Graphics provides you with many structures that you will use in your drawing. The CGGeometry header defines the CGPoint struct, which represents points, and the CGRect struct, which represents rectangles. The CGColor header defines the CGColor struct that you use to represent colors. Finally, the CGGradient header defines CGGradient, which you can use to build gradients. You use a gradient to seamlessly blend two or more colors together.

There are also many useful utility functions that you can use to work with points and rectangles. You will use one of these, CGRectIntersectsRect to do the collision detection in the Blocker game. You can also use the helper function CGRectMake to make CGRect structs, CGPointMake to make points, and CGSizeMake to make CGSize structs.

I would encourage you to look through the headers in the Core Graphics frameworks. You may discover some very useful functions and structures.

THE DRAWING ENVIRONMENT

Now that you are aware of the frameworks available to you to do 2D drawing in iOS, you are ready to get started with some drawings. The first step is to learn about the drawing environment. As I mentioned in the last section, the basis for all drawing in iOS is the UIView. In this section, you will learn about views and how to draw in a view.

The Graphics Context

When you use any of the drawing features of UIKit or Core Graphics, you are drawing in a context. A context defines the features of the current drawing environment like the line width, line style, and color information. The context maintains the current state of your drawing, so some developers refer to it as a *state machine*.

The purpose of the context is to provide a device-independent canvas on which to draw. There are many different types of contexts. For instance, you can use a PDF context for drawing PDF files, a bitmap context for drawing to an off-screen bitmap, or a screen context for drawing to the screen. Since the context is device independent, you can use the same drawing code to draw in PDFs, bitmaps, or on screen. Specific contexts like PDF, screen context, and bitmap contain the device specific information to convert your drawing commands into the correct output for the device.

In the examples in this chapter, you will be working with a screen context; however, you could use all of the code that you develop to draw shapes, without modification, in any other context.

The UIView Coordinate System

When learning a drawing API, you need to understand how to specify where you want to draw your objects. That means learning the coordinate system.

When you are working with UIView objects as the container for your drawing, the origin is at the top left corner of the view. This coordinate system is called ULO for Upper Left Origin. The positive x-axis extends to the right and the positive y-axis extends down the view. You can see this in Figure 6-3.

There are times when the default coordinate system may not be convenient. For instance, if you needed to draw many objects at a specific angle, it may be helpful to transform the coordinate system by rotating the axes about the origin. You can do this using the CGContextRotateCTM function. Likewise, you may want to write a method that draws a certain object based at the origin. You can then translate the origin to any point by using the CGContextTranslateCTM function. You can save the state of the context by using the CGContextSaveGState function and restore the state by using the CGContextRestoreGState function.

FIGURE 6-3: UIView Coordinate system

You will see these functions in action later on in the activity in this section.

The drawRect: Method

When you want to develop your own custom drawing code, you typically place that code in a custom UIView subclass. Then, your view controller can work with your custom view just like any other view object.

Inside your custom subclass, you implement your drawing code in the drawRect: method. UIKit calls drawRect: when it needs the view to draw itself. drawRect: is defined in the UIView class. Its default implementation from UIView doesn't actually do anything. You are responsible for overriding drawRect: in your subclasses to perform the drawing that you need to do to display your view.

drawRect: receives a CGRect parameter. The CGRect represents the rectangle that you need to draw. To maximize drawing performance, you should draw only the portion of your view enclosed by this rectangle. Developing drawing code to draw only a portion of the view can complicate your drawing code, so for the sake of clarity we will not implement this feature in the examples in this chapter. Additionally, the drawing that you will see in this chapter will be very simple and would not benefit from doing partial rendering. You can see a diagram of the concept of partial rendering in Figure 6-4.

In Figure 6-4 (a) you see a complicated view with many boxes of different colors. Imagine that another view is covering this view in the bottom right corner of the screen. Now suppose that the overlapping view moves away and that portion of your view is now visible. UIKit will send your view the drawRect: message with a CGRect that represents the area that was covered but is now visible as in Figure 6-4 (b). Since this is a complicated view, you should not redraw every shape. You should redraw only the boxes that intersect with the CGRect that you received in the drawRect: message as in Figure 6-4 (c). You can see which rectangles intersect the CGRect by using the CGRectIntersectsRect function. You will use this function in the Blocker game to determine when the ball collides with a block or the player's paddle.

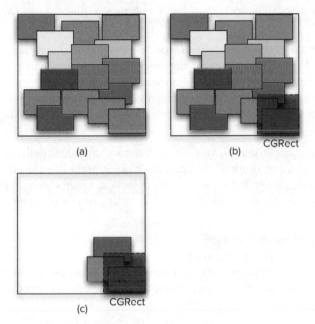

(a)   (b)   CGRect

(c)   CGRect

FIGURE 6-4: Partial rendering of a view

When you receive the drawRect: message, UIKit will provide you with a context that has its origin at the origin of the bounds of your view. You can create a pointer to this context with the UIGraphicsGetCurrentContext function.

You should never call drawRect: yourself. The method is reserved for use only by the UIKit framework. If you need to tell the view to redraw, you should call either setNeedsDisplay or setNeedsDisplayInRect: on your view. This invalidates the view, or part of the view, and causes UIKit to call drawRect:.

Drawing Shapes with UIBezierPath

The easiest way to draw shapes is by using the UIBezierPath class from the UIKit framework. A *Bezier path* is a mathematical definition of a shape that contains lines and curves. Using the UIBezierPath class, you can build paths from any number, and combination, of straight lines and curves.

In addition to providing the points that define a path, the UIBezierPath class has helper class methods that you can use to easily define simple shapes. For example, you can use the bezierPathWithRect: class method to create a rectangular path by passing in a CGRect struct. The bezierPathWithOvalInRect: method also accepts a CGRect and draws an oval inscribed in the rectangle.

Once you have defined the shape of a path, you can stroke it with solid or dashed lines. You can set properties on the UIBezierPath to define the stroke width, cap style (which sets the shape of the endpoints of the path), and join style (the shape of the joints of the path). Once you have set the stroke properties the way that you want them, you call the `stroke` method to draw the stroke or outline of the shape.

In addition to stroking your paths, you can also fill paths with color. To perform a fill, you call the `fill` method.

The `stroke` and `fill` methods use the current drawing properties from the context to determine the color with which to stroke or fill your shape. Remember that the context is a state machine. The `UIBezierPath` class is just a wrapper for some underlying Core Graphics functions that work to draw your path. Therefore, you need to set the context to the desired state before stroking or filling your path. You will see how to use the `UIColor` class in the next section to set the context to draw and fill with whatever colors you choose.

Aside from using the class methods to define simple shapes, you can also draw shapes manually. If you are going to work with paths this way, you can think of the current drawing point like the tip of a pen. You can move the pen, without drawing, using the `moveToPoint:` method. Once you have the pen where you want it, you can use the `addLineToPoint:` method to draw a line from the current point to a point that you specify.

You can add arcs and curves to the path by using the methods `addArcWithCenter:radius:startAngle:endAngle:clockwise:`, `addCurveToPoint:controlPoint1:controlPoint2:`, and `addQuadCurveToPoint:controlPoint:`. You specify arcs and curves in radians. In the default coordinate system, the angle of the arc is measured from the x-axis.

When you are ready to close your path, if you want to, you can call the `closePath` method.

Specifying Colors with UIColor

The UIKit framework provides the `UIColor` class to help you to work with colors. You can define colors in a few different ways. First, if you know the Hue, Saturation, and Brightness (HSB) values for your color, you can create a `UIColor` object with the `colorWithHue:saturation:brightness:alpha:` class method. If you know the Red, Green and Blue (RGB) values for your color, you can use the `colorWithRed:green:blue:alpha:` class method.

There is also a set of class methods for creating `UIColor` objects with preset color values. These include:

```
blackColor
darkGrayColor
lightGrayColor
whiteColor
grayColor
redColor
greenColor
blueColor
cyanColor
yellowColor
magentaColor
orangeColor
purpleColor
```

```
brownColor
clearColor
```

The alpha value of a color allows you to set the opacity of the color. The alpha value ranges from 0.0 to 1.0 where 0.0 is completely transparent and invisible to 1.0, which is completely opaque. Be aware that compositing alpha blended colors is a processor-intensive operation and takes a lot of CPU power. You should avoid using alpha blending, if possible, for the best performance.

Once you have initialized your UIColor object and set its color to whatever you want to use, you are ready to update the state of the context. You can use the setFill method to set the fill in the context to the current color. You use setStroke to set the current stroke color in the context.

TRY IT OUT   Creating Shapes with UIBezierPath

codefile GraphicsStart available for download at Wrox.com

In this section, you will learn how to use the UIBezierPath class to create some shapes. You will also use the UIColor class to stroke and fill those shapes with a variety of colors.

I would recommend that when you are finished working through this example, you play with the example project creating your own shapes to get a better feel for all of the drawing capabilities of the UIKit classes.

1. To get started, start up Xcode and select File ⇨ New ⇨ New Project.

2. A dialog box appears that displays templates for the various types of applications that you can create for the iPhone and Mac OS X. Each option presented provides you with the basic setup that you will need to start developing an application. For this sample project, you are going to use the Single View Application template. Select Single View Application from the dialog box, and click the Next button.

3. In the Product Name text box, type the name of your project, **GraphicsStart**. Uncheck the "Use Storyboard" and "Include Unit Tests" checkboxes. Make sure that the "Use Automatic Reference Counting" checkbox is checked. Select "iPhone" from the Device Family dropdown. Press the Next button.

4. Select a location to save your project, and click the Create button. Xcode will create your project and present the project window.

5. Add a new UIView subclass to the project. Select File ⇨ New ⇨ New File... from the menu bar. In the template chooser, under iOS on the left-hand side, select Cocoa Touch. In the right-hand pane, select Objective-C class, and press Next. In the "Subclass of" drop-down, make sure that UIView is selected. Name your class TestView and press Next. In the next window press Create to create your new files. You should see two new files in the Project Navigator under your GraphicStart directory called TestView.h and TestView.m.

6. Now, you will go into Interface Builder and configure the ViewController to use the new UIView subclass file, TestView that you just created. It is in this view that you will implement all of your custom drawing code. Open ViewController.xib in Xcode by clicking on it in the Project Navigator.

7. In the left-hand column, next to the grid in Interface Builder, click on the view. Click on the Show the Identity Inspector icon at the top of the right-hand pane. In the Class drop-down, under Custom Class, change the class to `TestView`. Now, the `TestView` class will be associated with the `ViewController`. Your screen should look like Figure 6-5.

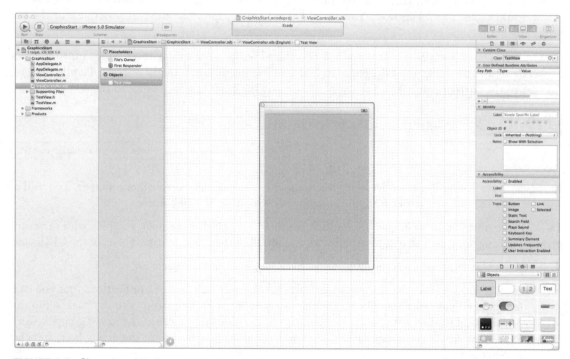

FIGURE 6-5: Changing the class in Interface Builder

8. In the `TestView.m` file, you will put your drawing code in the `drawRect:` method. When you run your app, your custom drawing code will run and you will be able to see it in the iPhone simulator. This is a good way to test out some basic drawing features. Implement the `drawRect:` function like this:

```
- (void)drawRect:(CGRect)rect
{
    // Make a 40 x 40 pixel square at 0,0
    CGRect aRectangle = CGRectMake(0.0, 0.0, 40.0, 40.0);

    // Make a path with the square
    UIBezierPath* path = [UIBezierPath bezierPathWithRect:aRectangle];

    // Stroke the square
    [path stroke];

    // Make a path for a circle with the same square
    path = [UIBezierPath bezierPathWithOvalInRect:aRectangle];

    // Fill the circle
    [path fill];
```

```objc
// Make a path for a star
UIBezierPath* starPath = [UIBezierPath bezierPath];

// Draw the path for a star
[starPath moveToPoint:CGPointMake(40.0, 0.0)];
[starPath addLineToPoint:CGPointMake(30.0, 30.0)];
[starPath addLineToPoint:CGPointMake(0.0, 30.0)];
[starPath addLineToPoint:CGPointMake(20.0, 50.0)];
[starPath addLineToPoint:CGPointMake(10.0, 80.0)];
[starPath addLineToPoint:CGPointMake(40.0, 60.0)];
[starPath addLineToPoint:CGPointMake(70.0, 80.0)];
[starPath addLineToPoint:CGPointMake(60.0, 50.0)];
[starPath addLineToPoint:CGPointMake(80.0, 30.0)];
[starPath addLineToPoint:CGPointMake(50.0, 30.0)];
[starPath closePath];

// Get the drawing context
CGContextRef context = UIGraphicsGetCurrentContext ();

// Save the context state
CGContextSaveGState (context);

// Translate the coordinate system origin
CGContextTranslateCTM(context, 100, 100);

// Set the fill color to yellow
UIColor* fillColor = [UIColor yellowColor];
[fillColor setFill];

// Fill the star
[starPath fill];

// Translate and rotate the coordinates
CGContextTranslateCTM(context, 100, 100);
CGContextRotateCTM(context, 3.14/4);

// Set the fill color to green
fillColor = [UIColor greenColor];
[fillColor setFill];

// Fill and stroke the star
[starPath fill];
[starPath stroke];

// Restore the context
CGContextRestoreGState(context);

// Save the context state
CGContextSaveGState (context);

// Translate the coordinate system origin
CGContextTranslateCTM(context, 50, 250);

// Fill the star
[starPath fill];
```

```
    // Restore the context
    CGContextRestoreGState(context);



}
```

9. When you build and run your program, the iPhone simulator should come up. Your output should look like Figure 6-6.

FIGURE 6-6: Output of GraphicsStart program

How It Works

In this example, you implemented the `drawRect:` method of a `UIView` subclass to provide custom drawing code for the view.

The first thing that you did was to define a `CGRect` struct by using the `CGRectMake` helper function. This function accepts the x and y coordinates of the top left corner of the rectangle along with the width and height of the rectangle. You created a square with the top left corner at the view origin with a size of 40 pixels by 40 pixels:

```
    // Make a 40 x 40 pixel square at 0,0
    CGRect aRectangle = CGRectMake(0.0, 0.0, 40.0, 40.0);
```

Next, you created a `UIBezierPath` object with the `CGRect` structure by using the `bezierPathWithRect:` class method. This method creates a rectangular path by using the `CGRect` that you pass in:

```
    // Make a path with the square
    UIBezierPath* path = [UIBezierPath bezierPathWithRect:aRectangle];
```

Next, you drew a line, or stroke, around the path by using the `stroke` method:

```
// Stroke the square
[path stroke];
```

Notice that the stroke is black because you did not do anything to change the current stroke color in the context.

The next step was to create the black circle inside of the square. You used the same `CGRect` to define the bounds of the circle. You also reused the `UIBezierPath` object. You called the `bezierPathWithOvalInRect:` method to draw the circle inscribed in the square:

```
// Make a path for a circle with the same rectangle
path = [UIBezierPath bezierPathWithOvalInRect:aRectangle];
```

Then, you filled the circle with the default color, black:

```
// Fill the circle
[path fill];
```

The next block of code defines a star shape as you can see in Figure 6-7. I drew the star on graph paper to determine the points to use for the vertices.

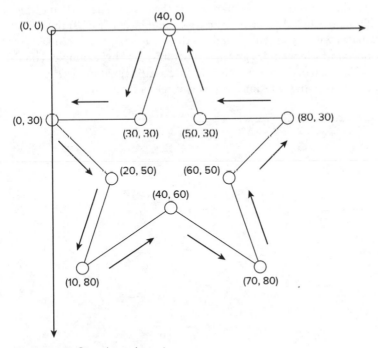

FIGURE 6-7: Star shape layout

First, you created a new `UIBezierPath` object:

```
// Make a path for a star
UIBezierPath* starPath = [UIBezierPath bezierPath];
```

You then moved the pen, without drawing, to the point (40,0) by using the moveToPoint: method. Also, notice that you used the helper method CGPointMake to create a CGPoint structure to pass into moveToPoint::

```
// Draw the path for a star
[starPath moveToPoint:CGPointMake(40.0, 0.0)];
```

Once you moved the pen into position, you drew all of the lines that make up the star, following the arrows in Figure 6-7. You used the addLineToPoint: method to connect the points with lines:

```
[starPath addLineToPoint:CGPointMake(30.0, 30.0)];
[starPath addLineToPoint:CGPointMake(0.0, 30.0)];
[starPath addLineToPoint:CGPointMake(20.0, 50.0)];
[starPath addLineToPoint:CGPointMake(10.0, 80.0)];
[starPath addLineToPoint:CGPointMake(40.0, 60.0)];
[starPath addLineToPoint:CGPointMake(70.0, 80.0)];
[starPath addLineToPoint:CGPointMake(60.0, 50.0)];
[starPath addLineToPoint:CGPointMake(80.0, 30.0)];
[starPath addLineToPoint:CGPointMake(50.0, 30.0)];
```

Once you got to the last point, you closed the path:

```
[starPath closePath];
```

In the next section of the code, you used some functions to manipulate the coordinate system of the context. It is generally easier to define shapes in a default coordinate system based at (0,0) then it is to define the shape based on the coordinates where you will ultimately draw the shape. Sometimes, you will not know where you want to draw your shape at design time. Therefore, in this example, you drew your star based at (0,0) as you saw in Figure 6-7. Then, you moved the coordinate system around to draw stars on the screen at different positions and rotations as you can see in Figure 6-8.

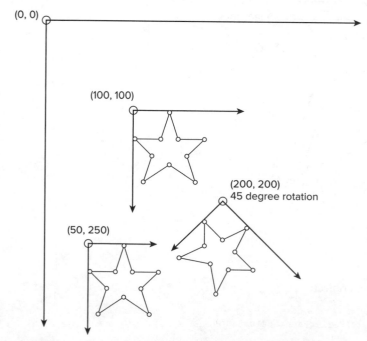

FIGURE 6-8: Translation and rotation of the coordinate system

First, you got a reference to the drawing context and saved the state of the context:

```
// Get the drawing context
CGContextRef context = UIGraphicsGetCurrentContext ();

// Save the context state
CGContextSaveGState (context);
```

Saving the state of the context at this point preserves the default coordinate system.

Next, you moved the coordinate system origin 100 pixels along the x-axis and 100 pixels along the y-axis:

```
// Translate the coordinate system origin
CGContextTranslateCTM(context, 100, 100);
```

Then, you initialized a UIColor object to the color yellow by using the yellowColor class method and set the context's fill color:

```
// Set the fill color to yellow
UIColor* fillColor = [UIColor yellowColor];
[fillColor setFill];
```

Now, you are ready to fill the star with yellow:

```
// Fill the star
[starPath fill];
```

Notice that the star was not drawn at the origin, but with its origin at (100,100).

Next, you moved the coordinate system origin another 100 pixels down the x-axis and 100 pixels down the y-axis. You also rotated the coordinate system 45 degrees (pi/4 radians) about the origin:

```
// Translate and rotate the coordinates
CGContextTranslateCTM(context, 100, 100);
CGContextRotateCTM(context, 3.14/4);
```

You should be aware that you provide delta values to the CGContextTranslateCTM and CGContextRotateCTM functions. So, by specifying that you want to translate the coordinate system with values 100,100, you are not moving the origin to point (100,100), you are moving the origin by 100 units on the x-axis and 100 units on the y-axis.

Next, you set the fill color to green, updated the context with the new fill color, and then stroked and filled another star:

```
// Set the fill color to green
fillColor = [UIColor greenColor];
[fillColor setFill];

// Fill and stroke the star
[starPath fill];
[starPath stroke];
```

For the final star, you want to place it with its origin at (50,250) with no rotation. However, at this point, you have configured the context such that the coordinate system origin is at (200,200) with a pi/4 radians rotation. This is why you saved the original coordinate system state. You can now restore the last saved state to move the coordinate system back to its default location and rotation and save the default state again:

```
// Restore the context
CGContextRestoreGState(context);

// Save the context state
CGContextSaveGState (context);
```

Now, you translate the coordinate system to its new position and fill the last star:

```
// Translate the coordinate system origin
CGContextTranslateCTM(context, 50, 250);

// Fill the star
[starPath fill];
```

Notice that you have filled this star with black. When you restored the context state, not only did you restore the coordinate system but also the colors that were set in the context at the point at which you saved it. In this case, the context was in its default state with black stroke and fill colors.

Finally, restore the context back to its original state:

```
// Restore the context
CGContextRestoreGState(context);
```

I hope that you can see why it is easier to define your shape by using one coordinate system and rendering it on screen by moving and rotating the context coordinate system. Especially in the case of the translated and rotated star, it would be difficult and time consuming to calculate all of the vertices, whereas it is simple to just move and rotate the coordinate system into the drawing position.

ADVANCED DRAWING WITH CORE GRAPHICS

The easiest way to draw to the screen is by using the object-oriented libraries included with the UIKit framework. In the previous section, you used the UIBezierPath class from UIKit to draw some shapes. The UIBezierPath class wraps some of the underlying features of the Core Graphics library in a nice, Objective-C package. The UIBezierPath class is great for what it can give you, but it does not wrap all of the features of Core Graphics. Sometimes, you have to drop a level deeper to use some of these advanced features.

In this section, you will explore a couple of the advanced features of Core Graphics that you can use to create drop shadows and gradients.

Shadows

Shadowing is a property of the context, so it is easy to set up. Typically, you would save the context state by using the CGContextSaveGState function. Then, you turn on shadowing in the context by using the CGContextSetShadow function. Finally, you fill the path that you would like to shadow, and the shadow is automatically applied.

The CGContextSetShadow function takes three parameters: the context, a CGSize that represents the shadow offset, and a float that represents the blur.

TRY IT OUT Building Drop Shadows

codefile GraphicsStart available for download at Wrox.com

In this section, you will add a new star to the GraphicsStart project. The new star will be orange and have a drop shadow.

1. If you do not already have it open, open up the GraphicsStart project.

2. Open the TestView.m implementation file and add the following code to the end of the drawRect: function:

```
// Save the context state
CGContextSaveGState (context);

// Translate the coordinate system origin
CGContextTranslateCTM(context, 220, 0);

// Create drop shadow
CGContextSetShadow(context, CGSizeMake(10, 10), 5);

// Set the fill color to green
fillColor = [UIColor orangeColor];
[fillColor setFill];

[starPath fill];

// Restore the context
CGContextRestoreGState(context);
```

3. Build and run the application. You should see an orange star with a drop shadow in the top right corner of the iOS simulator screen.

How It Works

The first thing that you did was save the default state of the context:

```
// Save the context state
CGContextSaveGState (context);
```

Remember that you set the shadow properties in the context. If you do not save the context before creating your shadow and then restore it when you are finished, all of your subsequent drawing will have shadows.

Next, you moved the coordinate system so that you could draw your star and shadow on the right-hand side of the screen:

```
// Translate the coordinate system origin
CGContextTranslateCTM(context, 220, 0);
```

Then, you enabled shadowing in the context:

```
// Create drop shadow
CGContextSetShadow(context, CGSizeMake(10, 10), 5);
```

I chose an offset of 10 in both the x and y direction and a blur of 5. Feel free to experiment to see the different results that you can get by changing these numbers.

Next, you set the fill color to orange and filled the path:

```
// Set the fill color to green
fillColor = [UIColor orangeColor];
[fillColor setFill];

[starPath fill];
```

Filling the path draws the shadow. If you stroked the path instead, you would see a shadow of the stroke, not the fill, which is not what you want.

Finally, you restored the context back to its default state:

```
// Restore the context
CGContextRestoreGState(context);
```

Gradients

Another advanced feature of Core Graphics that you can use to enhance your drawing is the gradient. You use gradients to smoothly blend two or more colors. There are two basic types of gradients: linear and radial. Linear gradients blend each color along a line. Radial gradients blend the colors in a circular pattern along the radius of the circle.

You can see examples of linear and radial gradients in Figure 6-9.

At the top of the figure, you can see the two colors that you are blending. Below is a linear gradient that smoothly blends the colors along a line. Below that is a radial gradient that blends the colors in a circular manner.

You can draw gradients by using CGGradient. You need to configure the gradient before you can use it to draw your gradient.

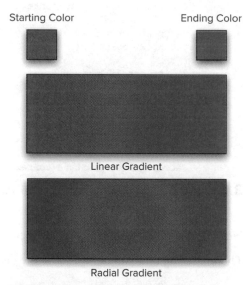

FIGURE 6-9: Linear and Radial gradients

First, you need to define the color space that you are working in. *Color spaces* map the numbers that you use to define colors to the actual colors that you see on the screen. Since you can use Core Graphics to draw in different contexts, you can use several different color spaces. Since you will be drawing only on the iOS device (in this book anyway) you can use the device dependent color space that you get from the CGColorSpaceCreateDeviceRGB function. Further discussion of color spaces is beyond the scope of this book. You can find more information on using different color spaces for different devices or color management in the CGColorSpace Reference in the Xcode help.

Next, you need to define the colors that you will use in your gradient. You can use an array of CGColor structs or define the colors in their own array by defining the red, green, blue, and alpha values of each color, assuming that you are working in the RGB color space.

Then, you need to define the location of each color component that you created in the previous step. You do this by defining an array of floats that range from 0 to 1. The starting position of the gradient is 0 and the ending position is 1. Therefore, if you want to create a two-color gradient where the solid colors are at the ends, you would create an array containing 0 and 1. If you wanted the solid colors to continue from the ends into the gradient, you could use values of 0.2 and 0.8. If you wanted a three-color gradient with the second color in the middle, you would use an array containing 0, 0.5, and 1.

Finally, you use the `CGGradientCreateWithColorComponents` function to create your gradient, passing in the color space, color components, locations, and number of locations as parameters.

Once you have created your gradient structure, you are ready to draw the gradient. You can draw a linear gradient by using the `CGContextDrawLinearGradient` function or a radial gradient by using the `CGContextDrawRadialGradient` function.

When you are finished working with the gradient you need to release the memory used by the color space and the gradient. You can free the color space by using the `CGColorSpaceRelease` function and the gradient by using the `CGGradientRelease` function.

TRY IT OUT   **Building Gradients**

codefile GraphicsStart available for download at Wrox.com

In this example, you will add a new star to the GraphicsStart project that you will fill with a gradient.

1.   If you do not already have it open, open up the GraphicsStart project.

2.   Open the `TestView.m` implementation file and add the following code to the end of the `drawRect:` function:

```
// Save the context state
CGContextSaveGState (context);

// Translate the coordinate system origin
CGContextTranslateCTM(context, 220, 320);

// Declare the gradient
CGGradientRef myGradient;

// Define the color space
CGColorSpaceRef colorSpace = CGColorSpaceCreateDeviceRGB();

// Define the color components of the gradient
CGFloat components[8] = { 1.0, 0.0, 0.0, 1.0,  // Start color
    0.0, 0.0, 1.0, 1.0 }; // End color

// Define the location of each component
int num_locations = 2;
CGFloat locations[2] = { 0.0, 1.0 };

// Create the gradient
myGradient = CGGradientCreateWithColorComponents (colorSpace, components,
                                    locations, num_locations);
```

```
// Use the star path as a clipping path for the gradient
[starPath addClip];

// Draw the gradient
CGContextDrawLinearGradient (context, myGradient, CGPointMake(0, 0),
                            CGPointMake(80, 0), 0);

//Clean up the color space & gradient
CGColorSpaceRelease(colorSpace);
CGGradientRelease(myGradient);

// Restore the context
CGContextRestoreGState(context);
```

3. Build and run the application. You should see a gradient filled star in the bottom right corner of the iOS simulator screen.

How It Works

The first thing that you need to do before you do any drawing is save the current state of the context:

```
// Save the context state
CGContextSaveGState (context);
```

Next, you translated the coordinate system so that you could position your star:

```
// Translate the coordinate system origin
CGContextTranslateCTM(context, 220, 320);
```

Now you are ready to start defining your gradient. First, you declared a reference to the gradient:

```
// Declare the gradient
CGGradientRef myGradient;
```

Then, you defined the color space:

```
// Define the color space
CGColorSpaceRef colorSpace = CGColorSpaceCreateDeviceRGB();
```

Next, you set the colors to use for the gradient. To make the gradient obvious, I used red and blue with an alpha of 1.0, indicating complete opacity:

```
// Define the color components of the gradient
CGFloat components[8] = { 1.0, 0.0, 0.0, 1.0,  // Start color
    0.0, 0.0, 1.0, 1.0 }; // End color
```

You specified the components as an array of red, green, blue, and alpha values. Therefore, the first color has a red of 1, a green of 0, a blue of 0, and an alpha of 1. The second color has a red of 0, a green of 0, a blue of 1, and an alpha of 1.

Now, you need to define the location along the gradient where you want to place each color. I decided to place the solid colors at either end of the gradient by specifying the values of 0 and 1:

```
// Define the location of each component
int num_locations = 2;
CGFloat locations[2] = { 0.0, 1.0 };
```

You can change these location values to move the point at which the solid color starts blending. Try using 0.2 and 0.8 for these values. You should notice that the solid red and solid blue colors extend farther into the gradient than when you started blending them from the very ends.

Next, you created the gradient by using the CGGradientCreateWithColorComponents function:

```
// Create the gradient
myGradient = CGGradientCreateWithColorComponents (colorSpace, components,
                                                  locations, num_locations);
```

If you were to draw the gradient now, it would fill the entire region from top to bottom of the screen along the points that you specify in the CGContextDrawLinearGradient function as you can see in Figure 6-10. The CGContextDrawLinearGradient function just paints a gradient with no regard for the current path. What you need to do is create a clipping path.

FIGURE 6-10: Unclipped gradient

Clipping paths allow you to constrain any drawing in a context to the fill area of the path that you specify. Therefore, in this case, you use the star path to clip the gradient so that it would apply the gradient only to the fill area of the star:

```
// Use the star path as a clipping path for the gradient
[starPath addClip];
```

It is important to note that the context holds onto the clipping path. Therefore, if you do not restore the default context after creating a clipping path, the clipping path will persist and clip all further drawing.

Now you are ready to draw the gradient, which you clipped inside of the star:

```
// Draw the gradient
CGContextDrawLinearGradient (context, myGradient, CGPointMake(0, 0),
                             CGPointMake(80, 0), 0);
```

Finally, you need to clean up the color space and gradient objects that you used and restore the graphics context to its default state:

```
//Clean up the color space & gradient
CGColorSpaceRelease(colorSpace);
CGGradientRelease(myGradient);

// Restore the context
CGContextRestoreGState(context);
```

Now you have a solid foundation in the basic drawing features that you need to build a game. You can draw anything that you can imagine with the drawing functions that you now know. Now it's time to move on to building a game.

STARTING THE BLOCKER GAME WITH THE BLOCKVIEW

At this point, you should be comfortable with the basic drawing features provided by UIKit and the Core Graphics frameworks. Now you are ready to begin working on the Blocker game illustrated in Figure 6-1 at the beginning of the chapter.

Blocker is a simple block breaking game. The game starts with three rows of blocks at the top of the screen, a ball that you will animate to bounce around the screen and break blocks, and a paddle that the player will move to keep the ball on the screen. To keep the game simple and to maintain focus on the drawing and animation code, you will not implement score keeping or a count of the number of balls that the player has remaining. If the player misses blocking the ball with his paddle and the ball travels beyond the bottom of the screen, it will simply reset. The game ends when all of the blocks are broken.

Like most iOS applications, you will build Blocker by using the Model-View-Controller (MVC) design pattern. You will build a model class called BlockerModel. The model will hold references to an array of blocks, the paddle and ball position, the velocity of the ball, and a couple of time values. You will implement methods to update the model based on the game time and to check for collisions with the screen edges, blocks, and the paddle.

You will build the game view as a collection of UIView objects. Each block will be a custom subclass of UIView called BlockView that you will develop. You will write the custom drawing code to draw the blocks in the drawRect: method of the view. You will use the UIImageView class to render the ball and paddle from image files. Sometimes it is easier to use images or sprites instead of drawing the view yourself in code.

The BlockerViewController will link the model to the view by maintaining references to the ball and paddle view objects. The view controller will also control the animation and timing of the game by using the `CADisplayLink` class. You will learn about `CADisplayLink` later in the example. Finally, the view controller will handle user input to control the position of the paddle.

TRY IT OUT Starting the Blocker Game

codefile Blocker available for download at Wrox.com

Now that you know the design of the Blocker game and how it will look, it is time to start building the game.

1. To begin, start up Xcode and select File ➪ New ➪ New Project.

2. The familiar dialog box appears that displays templates for the various types of applications that you can create for the iPhone and Mac OS X. Select Single View Application from the dialog box and click the Next button.

3. In the Product Name text box, type the name of your project, **Blocker**. Uncheck the "Use Storyboard" and "Include Unit Tests" checkboxes. Make sure that the "Use Automatic Reference Counting" checkbox is checked. Select "iPhone" from the Device Family dropdown. Press the Next button.

4. Select a location to save your project, and click the Create button. Xcode will create your project and present the project window.

5. Add a new `UIView` subclass to the project. Select File ➪ New ➪ New File… from the menu bar. In the template chooser, under iOS on the left-hand side, select Cocoa Touch. In the right-hand pane, select Objective-C class and press Next. In the "Subclass of" drop-down, make sure that `UIView` is selected. Name your class `BlockView` and press Next. In the next dialog, press Create. You should see two new files in the Project Navigator in your Blocker folder called `BlockView.h` and `BlockView.m`.

6. The template implementation file provides an initialization method called `initWithFrame:` Users of your class can call this method to initialize blocks with a given frame size. Since all of the blocks will have a color, you are going to change this method to accept an `int` parameter to represent the color of the block. In the `BlockView.h` header file, add the declaration for your new initializer method `initWithFrame:color:` after the `@interface` block:

```
- (id)initWithFrame:(CGRect)frame color:(int) inputColor;
```

7. While you are in the header file, below the `#import <UIKit/UIKit.h>` statement, add the following `#define` statements to define the constants that callers of your class will use to specify the color of the block:

```
#define RED_COLOR 0
#define GREEN_COLOR 1
#define BLUE_COLOR 2
```

8. Add a member variable to hold the color in the `@interface` definition:

```
int color;
```

9. Finally, add a property for the color:

```
@property int color;
```

Your header should look like this:

```
#import <UIKit/UIKit.h>

#define RED_COLOR 0
#define GREEN_COLOR 1
#define BLUE_COLOR 2


@interface BlockView : UIView {

    int color;
}


- (id)initWithFrame:(CGRect)frame color:(int) inputColor;

@property int color;

@end
```

10. Now, move over to the `BlockView.m` implementation file. Right below the `@implementation` directive, add an `@synthesize` directive to synthesize your `color` property:

```
@synthesize color;
```

11. Delete the default implementation of the `initWithFrame:` method and replace it with the following implementation of your new `initWithFrame:color:` method:

```
- (id)initWithFrame:(CGRect)frame color:(int) inputColor;
{
    self = [super initWithFrame:frame];
    if (self) {
        // Initialization code
        self.color = inputColor;
    }
    return self;
}
```

12. Next, you will override the superclass `drawRect:` method to draw the block. Replace the commented out (code inside the `/*` and `*/` block) `drawRect:` method and replace it with your new method:

```
- (void)drawRect:(CGRect)rect
{
    float viewWidth, viewHeight;
    viewWidth = self.bounds.size.width;
    viewHeight = self.bounds.size.height;

    // Get the drawing context
    CGContextRef context = UIGraphicsGetCurrentContext ();

    // Define a rect in the shape of the block
    CGRect blockRect = CGRectMake(0, 0, viewWidth, viewHeight);

    // Define a path using the rect
    UIBezierPath* path = [UIBezierPath bezierPathWithRect:blockRect];
```

```
    // Set the line width of the path
    path.lineWidth = 2.0;

    // Define a gradient to use to fill the blocks
    CGColorSpaceRef colorSpace = CGColorSpaceCreateDeviceRGB();
    CGGradientRef myGradient;
    int num_locations = 2;
    CGFloat locations[2] = { 0.0, 1.0 };

    CGFloat components[8] = { 0.0, 0.0, 0.0, 1.0,   // Start color
        1.0, 1.0, 1.0, 1.0 }; // End color

    // Determine gradient color based on color property
    switch (self.color) {
        case RED_COLOR:
            // Red Block
            components[0] = 1.0;
            break;
        case GREEN_COLOR:
            // Green Block
            components[1] = 1.0;
            break;
        case BLUE_COLOR:
            // Blue Block
            components[2] = 1.0;
            break;
        default:
            break;
    }

    myGradient = CGGradientCreateWithColorComponents (colorSpace, components,
                                          locations, num_locations);

    CGContextDrawLinearGradient (context, myGradient, CGPointMake(0, 0),
                            CGPointMake(viewWidth, 0), 0);

    // Clean up the color space & gradient
    CGColorSpaceRelease(colorSpace);
    CGGradientRelease(myGradient);

    // Stroke the path
    [path stroke];

}
```

13. Build the project. The project should compile and link without any errors.

How It Works

The first interesting bit of code in this example is the `initWithFrame:color:` method. Users of your class will pass you a frame size and a color to initialize blocks of a specified color. First, as you should always do when overriding or creating an `init` function, you called the superclass initializer:

```
    self = [super initWithFrame:frame];
```

Then, after ensuring that you got back an initialized instance, you added your code. In this case, you just set the `color` property of the class to whatever you received in the input parameter `inputColor`:

```
self.color = inputColor;
```

Next, you implemented the `drawRect:` method to draw the block in the view. First, you declared two variables to hold the width and the height of the view that you will be drawing. Then, you set those variables based on the bounds of the view itself:

```
float viewWidth, viewHeight;
viewWidth = self.bounds.size.width;
viewHeight = self.bounds.size.height;
```

Next, you obtained a reference to the context:

```
// Get the drawing context
CGContextRef context = UIGraphicsGetCurrentContext ();
```

The next step is to define the path that you will stroke and fill with a gradient to draw the block. First, you defined a `CGRect` structure that is the same size and shape as the view:

```
// Define a rect in the shape of the block
CGRect blockRect = CGRectMake(0, 0,  viewWidth, viewHeight);
```

Next, you defined a `UIBezierPath` by using the rectangle that you just defined:

```
// Define a path using the rect
UIBezierPath* path = [UIBezierPath bezierPathWithRect:blockRect];
```

After that, you set the line width of the line that you will use to stroke the path:

```
// Set the line width of the path
path.lineWidth = 2.0;
```

Then, you went to work building the gradient. You defined the color space, declared the gradient object, set the number of gradient locations, and set the gradient location positions:

```
// Define a gradient to use to fill the blocks
CGColorSpaceRef colorSpace = CGColorSpaceCreateDeviceRGB();
CGGradientRef myGradient;
int num_locations = 2;
CGFloat locations[2] = { 0.0, 1.0 };
```

Next, you set the start and end color for the gradient:

```
CGFloat components[8] = { 0.0, 0.0, 0.0, 1.0,  // Start color
    1.0, 1.0, 1.0, 1.0 }; // End color
```

If you just left the code like this, all of the blocks would contain a gradient that went from black (RGB color 0,0,0) to white (RGB color 1,1,1). To set the color of the block to the color that is set in the `color` property, you wrote a `switch` statement:

```
// Determine gradient color based on color property
switch (self.color) {
    case RED_COLOR:
        // Red Block
        components[0] = 1.0;
        break;
    case GREEN_COLOR:
```

```
        // Green Block
        components[1] = 1.0;
        break;
    case BLUE_COLOR:
        // Blue Block
        components[2] = 1.0;
        break;
    default:
        break;
}
```

Depending on the value of the `color` property, the red, green, or blue component of the gradient starting color is set to 1. That way, the block will contain a gradient from red, green, or blue to white.

Next, you created the gradient and drew it:

```
myGradient = CGGradientCreateWithColorComponents (colorSpace, components,
                                          locations, num_locations);
CGContextDrawLinearGradient (context, myGradient, CGPointMake(0, 0),
                        CGPointMake(viewWidth, 0), 0);
```

Notice how you did not need to create a clipping path. You did not need to because you want the gradient to fill the entire view.

After you finished with the gradient, you had to release the color space and the gradient itself:

```
//Clean up the color space & gradient
CGColorSpaceRelease(colorSpace);
CGGradientRelease(myGradient);
```

Finally, you stroked the path:

```
// Stroke the path
[path stroke];
```

You need to stroke the path after drawing the gradient because UIKit and Xcode use the *painter's model* for drawing. That means that each drawing command draws on top of any previous commands. There is no notion of z-order or layers, so you have to draw items in the order that you want them to be layered from the bottom, or the closest to the canvas, to the top, just as a painter would.

WORKING WITH IMAGES

While working with UIKit and Core Graphics to draw images for your games is a viable approach, sometimes it is easier to draw your game graphics by using external tools. You can export your graphics from these tools, like Adobe Illustrator or Photoshop, and use them in your games. Additionally, sometimes you will want artists to create the game assets for you. You will typically receive these assets as bitmap images. It is easy to use images as the graphics for your games. In this section, you will learn how to use the `UIImage` and `UIImageView` classes to work with images.

When you are thinking about how you want to draw the graphics for your game, you need to decide if you will draw the images with UIKit and Core Graphics or if you will use pre-drawn images. There are some advantages to both methods.

When you write custom drawing code, you have the flexibility to modify the graphics dynamically at runtime. Suppose that you wanted to make a star graphic that looked like it twinkled. You could do this by animating the vertices at the points of the star. Since you have complete control of every point that makes up the graphic, you could dynamically draw the star for each frame at runtime. This would be impossible with a pre-drawn image file. With the image, you do not have the same level of control over the points that make up the graphic.

On the other hand, an advantage of using images is that you can reduce the amount of code that you need to write because you will not be drawing the image in code. In addition, you can often draw more elaborate graphics with an image editor than you can with the Cocoa drawing APIs.

Since the graphics in the Blocker game were so simple and this chapter is about teaching you graphics techniques, I decided to write custom drawing code to draw the blocks, but to draw the paddle and ball in an external image editor. You will import these game elements into the Xcode project and load them from the application bundle at runtime. You will learn how to load images into your view in the upcoming sections.

The Image Classes

You use the UIImage class to work with images when you want to draw the image in a custom UIView subclass inside the drawRect: method.

You can create images by using a file with the imageWithContentsOfFile: class method. This method loads an image file from the specified path. You can also use raw data to create an image by using the imageWithData: method. Finally, you can use a Quartz image object to create a Cocoa UIImage with the imageWithCGImage: method.

The UIImage class supports the image file formats listed in Table 6-1.

TABLE 6-1: Image File Formats Supported by UIImage

FORMAT	EXTENSIONS
Tagged Image File Format (TIFF)	.tiff, .tif
Joint Photographic Experts Group (JPEG)	.jpg, .jpeg
Graphic Interchange Format (GIF)	.gif
Portable Network Graphic (PNG)	.png
Windows Bitmap Format (DIB)	.bmp, .BMPf
Windows Icon Format	.ico
Windows Cursor	.cur
XWindow bitmap	.xbm

Once you have created your image, you call one of the image drawing methods, typically `drawAtPoint:` or `drawInRect:` to draw the image into the current context.

Another option for working with images is the `UIImageView` class. You can use `UIImageView` if you do not need to build a `UIView` subclass to implement other features like additional drawing in the `drawRect:` method. The `UIImageView` is a `UIView` subclass designed specifically for showing an image or animating a series of images.

To use the `UIImageView`, you instantiate an instance of the class and initialize it with a `UIImage` by using the `initWithImage:` method. Then, you can use the `UIImageView` just like any other view. You can access the underlying image by using the `image` property.

The View Hierarchy

You have seen how to create your own views and how to create views with images. However, you may be wondering what you do with these views. In iOS applications, views are arranged in a view hierarchy. Each view can have many subviews, and each subview has a parent view. The root view typically resides in the view controller that you are working with. You can get a reference to this view by using the `view` property of the view controller.

In the Blocker game, you will build the view hierarchy shown in Figure 6-11. This is a simple, flat, hierarchy. You will add all of the blocks, the ball, and the paddle as subviews of the main view controller `view`.

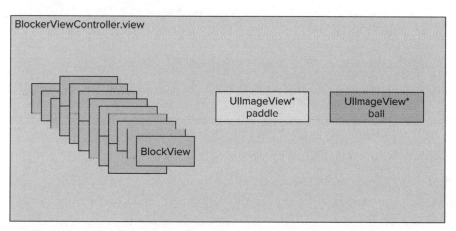

FIGURE 6-11: Blocker View Hierarchy

TRY IT OUT   Displaying Images

codefile Blocker available for download at Wrox.com

In this section, you will implement the `BlockerModel` and `ViewController` classes. You will learn how to load images from your application bundle and display them in your game. You will also learn how to load your views into the view hierarchy of the `ViewController`.

1. First, you will build the `BlockerModel` class. If you do not already have it open, open the Blocker project in Xcode.

2. Add a new class to the project called `BlockerModel`. Select File ➪ New ➪ New File… from the menu bar. In the template chooser, under iOS on the left-hand side, select Cocoa Touch. In the right-hand pane, select Objective-C class and press Next. In the "Subclass of" drop-down, select NSObject. Name your class **BlockerModel**, and press Next. In the next dialog, press Create. You should see two new files in the Project Navigator in your Blocker folder called `BlockerModel.h` and `BlockerModel.m`.

3. Add the following code to the `BlockerModel.h` header file:

```
#import "BlockView.h"


#define BLOCK_HEIGHT 20.0
#define BLOCK_WIDTH  64.0
#define BALL_SIZE 20.0
#define VIEW_WIDTH 320.0
#define VIEW_HEIGHT 460.0

@interface BlockerModel : NSObject {
    NSMutableArray* blocks;
    CGRect paddleRect;
    CGRect ballRect;
    CGPoint ballVelocity;
    CGFloat lastTime;
    CGFloat timeDelta;
}

@property (readonly) NSMutableArray* blocks;
@property (readonly) CGRect ballRect;
@property CGRect paddleRect;
@end
```

4. Switch over to the `BlockerModel.m` implementation file and add the following line below the `@implementation` directive to synthesize your properties:

```
@synthesize blocks,ballRect,paddleRect;
```

5. Override the default implementation of the `init` method to properly initialize the game model:

```
// Override superclass implementation of init so that we can provide a properly
// initialized game model
- (id)init {
    self = [super init];

    if (self) {
        // Init blocks
        // The array to hold the blocks
        blocks = [[NSMutableArray alloc] initWithCapacity:15];

        BlockView* bv;

        for (int row = 0; row<=2; row++)
        {
```

```
        for (int col = 0; col<5; col++)
        {
            bv = [[BlockView alloc ]
                    initWithFrame: CGRectMake(col * BLOCK_WIDTH ,
                                              row * BLOCK_HEIGHT,
                                              BLOCK_WIDTH, BLOCK_HEIGHT)
                    color:row];

            // Add the block to the array
            [blocks addObject:bv];

        }
    }

    // Set the paddle rect by using the size of the paddle image
    UIImage* paddleImage = [UIImage imageNamed:@"paddle.png"];
    CGSize paddleSize = [paddleImage size];
    paddleRect = CGRectMake(0.0, 420.0,
                            paddleSize.width, paddleSize.height);

    // Set the ball rect by using the size of the ball image
    UIImage* ballImage = [UIImage imageNamed:@"ball.png"];
    CGSize ballSize = [ballImage size];
    ballRect = CGRectMake(180.0, 220.0,
                          ballSize.width, ballSize.height);

    // Set the initial velocity for the ball
    ballVelocity = CGPointMake(200.0, -200.0);

    // Initialize the lastTime
    lastTime = 0.0;

    }

    return self;
}
```

6. Now you are ready to write code for the ViewController to display your graphics. Open the ViewController.h header file and add the following:

```
#import "BlockView.h"
#import "BlockerModel.h"

@interface ViewController : UIViewController {
    BlockerModel* gameModel;
    UIImageView* ball;
    UIImageView* paddle;

}
@end
```

7. Switch over to the ViewController.m implementation file and replace the viewDidLoad method with the following code:

```
- (void)viewDidLoad
{
```

```
        [super viewDidLoad];

        // initialize the game model
        gameModel = [[BlockerModel alloc] init];


        // Iterate over the blocks in the model, drawing them
        for (BlockView* bv in gameModel.blocks) {
            // Add the block to the view
            [self.view addSubview:bv];
        }


        // Draw the paddle
        paddle = [[UIImageView alloc] initWithImage:
                 [UIImage imageNamed:@"paddle.png"]];

        // Set the paddle position based on the model
        [paddle setFrame:gameModel.paddleRect];

        [self.view addSubview:paddle];

        // Draw the ball
        ball = [[UIImageView alloc] initWithImage:
                 [UIImage imageNamed:@"ball.png"]];

        [ball setFrame:gameModel.ballRect];

        [self.view addSubview:ball];


    }
```

8. Import the `paddle.png` and `ball.png` graphics into your project. You can download these graphics files from the book's website. In the File menu, select, "Add Files to Blocker…." Navigate to the location where you saved the image files, and select them. Check the box that says, "Copy items into destination group's folder (if needed)." Click "Add" to add the images to your project.

9. Build and run the project. You should see the blocks, ball, and paddle displayed in the iPhone simulator.

How It Works

The first thing that you did was to implement the `BlockerModel` class. This class is responsible for maintaining the state of the game. In the header, you declared that you were going to use the `BlockView` class by importing its header:

```
#import "BlockView.h"
```

Next, you defined a series of constants that you will use to build the model:

```
#define BLOCK_HEIGHT 20.0
#define BLOCK_WIDTH  64.0
#define BALL_SIZE 20.0
#define VIEW_WIDTH 320.0
#define VIEW_HEIGHT 460.0
```

You should always try to use constants instead of numbers in your code. Constants make your code much clearer than having apparently random numbers all over the place.

After defining the constants, you declared some instance variables that you will use in your implementation:

```
@interface BlockerModel : NSObject {
    NSMutableArray* blocks;
    CGRect paddleRect;
    CGRect ballRect;
    CGPoint ballVelocity;
    CGFloat lastTime;
    CGFloat timeDelta;
}
```

Finally, you declared the properties that you want to expose from your model class:

```
@property (readonly) NSMutableArray* blocks;
@property (readonly) CGRect ballRect;
@property CGRect paddleRect;
```

Upon completion of the header, you moved on to implement your model code. You started with the init method. The init method initializes the model to the starting state of the game. The first thing that it does is call the superclass init method:

```
self = [super init];
```

After ensuring that the superclass initialization was successful, you instantiated the blocks array to hold 15 blocks:

```
if (self) {
    // Init blocks
    // The array to hold the blocks
    blocks = [[NSMutableArray alloc] initWithCapacity:15];
```

The next section of code creates all of the instances of the BlockView class that you will use to show the blocks in the game. It uses two loops to create the grid of blocks. The outer loop creates each row, and the inner loop adds each block to a row:

```
BlockView* bv;

for (int row = 0; row<=2; row++)
{
    for (int col = 0; col<5; col++)
    {
```

Each time through the loop, you allocated a BlockView object. In the allocation, you pass a frame that defines the bounds of the block. You calculate this frame based on the row number and column number of the block that you are creating. You used the CGRectMake function to define the frame with the x coordinate as the column number times the BLOCK_WIDTH constant, the y coordinate as the row number times the BLOCK_HEIGHT constant, and the width and height as the BLOCK_WIDTH and BLOCK_HEIGHT constants. You also passed in the row number as the color parameter:

```
bv = [[BlockView alloc ]
        initWithFrame: CGRectMake(col * BLOCK_WIDTH ,
                                  row * BLOCK_HEIGHT,
```

```
                                                        BLOCK_WIDTH, BLOCK_HEIGHT)
                        color:row];
```

Once you had an initialized `BlockView`, you added it to the array of blocks:

```
// Add the block to the array
[blocks addObject:bv];
```

The next block of code initializes the `paddleRect` and `ballRect` variables. You use these variables to maintain the position of the ball and paddle in the model. You will use these positions when you implement the collision detection, and the view controller uses these positions to determine where to draw the paddle and ball images. You determined the rectangle that defines the paddle by loading the paddle image:

```
// Set the paddle rect by using the size of the paddle image
UIImage* paddleImage = [UIImage imageNamed:@"paddle.png"];
```

Then, you got the size of the image:

```
CGSize paddleSize = [paddleImage size];
```

Then you defined the rectangle using the `CGRectMake` function. You positioned the paddle at coordinates 0,420 and used the size of the image to determine the width and height of the rectangle:

```
paddleRect = CGRectMake(0.0, 420.0,
                        paddleSize.width, paddleSize.height);
```

You did the exact same thing to initialize the ball rectangle:

```
// Set the ball rect by using the size of the ball image
UIImage* ballImage = [UIImage imageNamed:@"ball.png"];
CGSize ballSize = [ballImage size];
ballRect = CGRectMake(180.0, 220.0,
                      ballSize.width, ballSize.height);
```

In order to animate the game, the ball needs to have a velocity. When you write the animation code, you will use this velocity to determine the position of the ball at any given time. I used a `CGPoint` struct to hold the velocity because it conveniently has x and y properties. Since the ball will be moving in two dimensions, you need to know its x and y velocity:

```
// Set the initial velocity for the ball
ballVelocity = CGPointMake(200.0, -200.0);
```

The velocity of 200 and –200 are not any particularly magical numbers. I just came up with them by trial and error while building the game.

Finally, you initialize the `lastTime` instance variable:

```
// Initialize the lastTime
lastTime = 0.0;
```

You will use this variable as a timestamp when you animate the game later in the chapter.

Once your model was complete, you moved on to the `ViewController` to connect the model to the view. First, you worked in the header. You imported the `BlockView` and `BlockerModel` header files because you will be using both of these classes in the view controller:

```
#import "BlockView.h"
#import "BlockerModel.h"
```

Next, you declared your instance variables for the model, ball and paddle:

```
@interface ViewController : UIViewController {
    BlockerModel* gameModel;
    UIImageView* ball;
    UIImageView* paddle;


}
```

After finishing with the header, you moved on to the implementation. First, you implemented the view controller's entry point, the `viewDidLoad` method. As usual, you needed to call the superclass implementation of `viewDidLoad` to ensure that the class was initialized before any of your code runs:

```
- (void)viewDidLoad
{
    [super viewDidLoad];
```

Next, you allocated and initialized the game model:

```
    // initialize the game model
    gameModel = [[BlockerModel alloc] init];
```

Then, you looped through all of the `BlockView` instances in the `blocks` array in the model, adding each one as a subview to the view controller's view:

```
    // Iterate over the blocks in the model, drawing them
    for (BlockView* bv in gameModel.blocks) {
        // Add the block to the view
        [self.view addSubview:bv];
    }
```

Next, you instantiated the `paddle` member variable. You allocated a new `UIImageView` object and initialized it with a `UIImage` that you loaded from the package bundle:

```
    // Draw the paddle
    paddle = [[UIImageView alloc] initWithImage:
            [UIImage imageNamed:@"paddle.png"]];
```

Then, you used the paddle's position as stored in the model to determine where to position the paddle on the screen:

```
    // Set the paddle position based on the model
    [paddle setFrame:gameModel.paddleRect];
```

Then, you added the paddle as a subview of the view controller's view and released the paddle:

```
    [self.view addSubview:paddle];
```

You then used almost identical code to load the ball image, set its position, and add it to the view:

```
    // Draw the ball
    ball = [[UIImageView alloc] initWithImage:
            [UIImage imageNamed:@"ball.png"]];

    [ball setFrame:gameModel.ballRect];

    [self.view addSubview:ball];
```

ANIMATION AND TIMING WITH CADISPLAYLINK

Back when you built the Scrambler game, you learned about using timers to run code at certain time intervals. In Scrambler, you used the NSTimer class to update the game clock every second. You may recall that I mentioned that timers do not work in real-time in that the run loop is responsible for calling the timer and will fire the timer only when it can. Because the timing of when a timer will actually fire is not guaranteed, timers are not very good for running game animation. Fortunately, Apple recognized this and included a class in the QuartzCore framework that you can use when working with animation, CADisplayLink.

The CADisplayLink is a timer that lets you synchronize your drawing code to the refresh rate of the view. You create an instance of CADisplayLink and specify an object and selector, just as you do when you set up a timer. Then, the OS will call the method that you specified when it is going to refresh the contents of the screen. The CADisplayLink provides a link between the refresh rate of the display and your code. Each time the screen refreshes, the OS will invoke the selector in your CADisplayLink.

The display link has a timestamp property that gives you the time when the previous frame was displayed. You can use this timestamp to determine how far to move your game objects. In the Blocker game, you will store the last timestamp in the lastTime variable. Then, when the next call to the updateModelWithTime: method comes in, you will use the lastTime and the timestamp to determine the amount of time that has elapsed since you last moved the ball. Using this delta time and the velocity of the ball, you can determine the new position of the ball.

When you are finished with the display link, you call invalidate to remove it from the run loop and stop it from calling the given selector. This works the same as it did for NSTimer.

TRY IT OUT   Animating the Blocker Game

codefile Blocker available for download at Wrox.com

In this example, you will enhance the Blocker game to include animating the ball. You will also add code to the BlockerModel to detect collisions with the sides of the screen, the paddle, and the blocks.

1. Open the Blocker project in Xcode and open the BlockerModel.h header file. Add the following method declarations to the header:

```
-(void) updateModelWithTime:(CFTimeInterval) timestamp;
- (void) checkCollisionWithScreenEdges;
- (void) checkCollisionWithBlocks;
- (void) checkCollisionWithPaddle;
```

The first method that you will implement is checkCollisionWithScreenEdges. This method will determine if the ball has reached the edge of the screen. If it has, it reverses the component of the velocity variable that corresponds with that screen edge. You can see this illustrated in Figure 6-12.

In Figure 6-12, the green line shows the path of the ball. The gray, dashed arrows represent the x and y components of the velocity of the ball. The black arrows represent the direction the ball is traveling. When the game starts, the ball has an x velocity of 200 and a y velocity of –200. Remember that in the view, the y-axis points down toward the bottom of the screen.

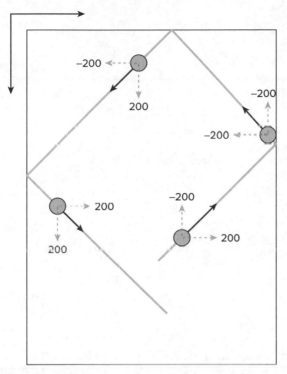

FIGURE 6-12: Ball velocity

After the ball hits the right side of the screen, you need to flip the sign of the x velocity component because the ball needs to move to the left instead of continuing to move to the right. When the ball hits the top of the screen, you need to flip the sign of the y velocity component because now the ball needs to move down.

2. Add the following code to the BlockerModel.m implementation file to check for collisions with the screen edges and change the velocity of the ball accordingly:

```
- (void) checkCollisionWithScreenEdges {
    // Change ball direction if it hit an edge of the screen
    // Left edge
    if (ballRect.origin.x <= 0)
    {
        // Flip the x velocity component
        ballVelocity.x = abs(ballVelocity.x);
    }

    // Right edge
    if (ballRect.origin.x >= VIEW_WIDTH - BALL_SIZE)
    {
        // Flip the x velocity component
        ballVelocity.x = -1 * abs(ballVelocity.x);
    }

    // Top edge
    if (ballRect.origin.y <=  0)
```

```
    {
        // Flip the x velocity component
        ballVelocity.y = abs(ballVelocity.y);
    }

    // Bottom edge
    if (ballRect.origin.y >=  VIEW_HEIGHT - BALL_SIZE)
    {
        // Ball went off the bottom of the screen
        // In a production game, you'd want to reduce the player's
        // ball count by one and reset the ball. To keep this example
        // simple, we are not keeping score or ball count. We'll
        // just reset the ball

        ballRect.origin.x = 180.0;
        ballRect.origin.y = 220.0;

        // Flip the y velocity component
        ballVelocity.y = -1*abs(ballVelocity.y);


    }

}
```

3. Next, you will implement similar logic for updating the ball's velocity when it collides with a block. You determine if the ball has hit a block by using the CGRectIntersectsRect function. This function returns true if the two rectangles that you pass in intersect each other. Add the following code to the BlockerModel.m file:

```
- (void) checkCollisionWithBlocks {
    // Iterate over the blocks to see if a collision has happened
    for (BlockView* bv in blocks) {
        if (CGRectIntersectsRect(bv.frame,ballRect)) {
            // Flip the y velocity component
            ballVelocity.y = -ballVelocity.y;

            // Remove the block from the collection
            [blocks removeObject:bv];

            // remove the block's view from the superview
            [bv removeFromSuperview];

            // In a production game, you'd want to add to the player's score
            // here, when a block is hit. To keep this example
            // simple, we are not keeping score.

            break;
        }

    }

}
```

4. Now, you need to add the code to check to see if the ball collided with the paddle:

```
- (void) checkCollisionWithPaddle {
    // Check to see if the paddle has blocked the ball
    if (CGRectIntersectsRect(ballRect,paddleRect)) {
        // Flip the y velocity component
        ballVelocity.y = -1 * abs( ballVelocity.y);

    }
}
```

5. Once you have the collision detection in place, you need to add some code to update the model based on the time. The view controller will call this method each time the display updates. Add the updateModelWithTime: method to the BlockerModel implementation:

```
-(void) updateModelWithTime:(CFTimeInterval) timestamp{
    if (lastTime == 0.0)
    {
        // First time through, initialize the lastTime
        lastTime = timestamp;
    }
    else
    {
        // Calculate time elapsed since last call
        timeDelta = timestamp - lastTime;

        // Update the lastTime
        lastTime = timestamp;

        // Calculate new position of the ball
        ballRect.origin.x += ballVelocity.x * timeDelta;
        ballRect.origin.y += ballVelocity.y * timeDelta;

        // Check for collision with screen edges
        [self checkCollisionWithScreenEdges];


        // Do collision detection with blocks
        [self checkCollisionWithBlocks];

        // Do collision detection with paddle
        [self checkCollisionWithPaddle];

    }

}
```

6. The model is now complete. Next, you will move over to the ViewController to tie the model to the view. At the top of the ViewController.h header file, add a #import statement to import the QuartzCore framework header:

```
#import <QuartzCore/QuartzCore.h>
```

7. Next, you need to add a reference to the QuartzCore framework to your Xcode project. Click on the Blocker project icon at the top of the Project Navigator view to bring up the project properties.

In the editor window, under the heading Targets, click on Blocker. Click on the tab at the top of the Editor window labeled Build Phases. Expand the item that says, "Link Binary With Libraries." Your screen should look like Figure 6-13.

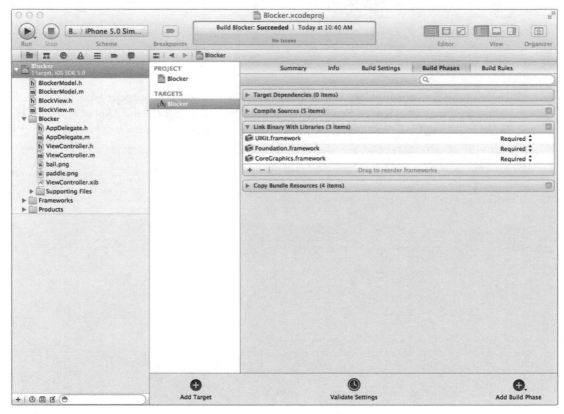

FIGURE 6-13: Adding a framework to the project

8. Click the plus sign at the bottom of the "Link Binary With Libraries." list. In the dialog box that comes up, select QuartzCore.framework and press the Add button.

9. Now that you have added the QuartzCore framework to your project, you are ready to set up the `CADisplayLink`. In the `ViewController.h` header file, add an instance variable to the `@interface` block for the display link timer:

```
CADisplayLink* gameTimer;
```

10. Add two new method declarations for the timer selector and the method to end the game:

```
-(void) updateDisplay:(CADisplayLink*)sender ;
-(void) endGameWithMessage:(NSString*) message;
```

11. The completed header file should look like this:

```
#import <UIKit/UIKit.h>
#import <QuartzCore/QuartzCore.h>

#import "BlockView.h"
```

```
#import "BlockerModel.h"

@interface ViewController : UIViewController {
    BlockerModel* gameModel;
    CADisplayLink* gameTimer;
    UIImageView* ball;
    UIImageView* paddle;

}

-(void) updateDisplay:(CADisplayLink*)sender ;
-(void) endGameWithMessage:(NSString*) message;

@end
```

12. Move over to the `ViewController.m` implementation file. At the end of the `viewDidLoad` method, add the following code to instantiate and configure the `CADisplayLink`:

```
// Set up the CADisplayLink for the animation
gameTimer = [CADisplayLink displayLinkWithTarget:self
                                        selector:@selector(updateDisplay:)];


// Add the display link to the current run loop
[gameTimer addToRunLoop:[NSRunLoop currentRunLoop]
           forMode:NSDefaultRunLoopMode];
```

13. Add the `updateDisplay` method that the `CADisplayLink` calls with each update of the display:

```
-(void) updateDisplay:(CADisplayLink*)sender
{
    // This method is called by the gameTimer each time the display should
    // update

    // Update the model
    [gameModel updateModelWithTime:sender.timestamp];

    // Update the display
    [ball setFrame:gameModel.ballRect];
    [paddle setFrame:gameModel.paddleRect];

    if ([gameModel.blocks count] == 0)
    {
        // No more blocks, end the game
        [self endGameWithMessage:@"You destroyed all of the blocks"];

    }


}
```

14. Add the `endGameWithMessage:` method that will run when the game ends:

```
-(void) endGameWithMessage:(NSString*) message
{
    // Call this method to end the game
    // Invalidate the timer
```

```
        [gameTimer invalidate];

        // Show an alert with the results
        UIAlertView *alert = [[UIAlertView alloc] initWithTitle:@"Game Over"
                                                         message:message
                                                        delegate:self
                                               cancelButtonTitle:@"OK"
                                               otherButtonTitles: nil];

        [alert show];
    }
```

15. Build and run the game. The ball should now be fully animated. When the ball hits a block, the paddle, or the sides or top of the screen, the ball should bounce off in the opposite direction. When the ball passes the paddle and goes off the bottom of the screen, it should reset to its starting position and velocity.

How It Works

The first thing that you did was implement the collision detection for the game. In the checkCollisionWithScreenEdges method, you determined if the ball was at the edge of the screen and, if it was, you reversed the appropriate component of the ball's velocity.

First, you checked the left side of the screen:

```
        // Change ball direction if it hit an edge of the screen
        // Left edge
        if (ballRect.origin.x <= 0)
        {
            // Flip the x velocity component
            ballVelocity.x = abs(ballVelocity.x);
        }
```

Then, you checked the right side:

```
        // Right edge
        if (ballRect.origin.x >= VIEW_WIDTH - BALL_SIZE)
        {
            // Flip the x velocity component
            ballVelocity.x = -1 * abs(ballVelocity.x);
        }
```

Next, you checked the top:

```
        // Top edge
        if (ballRect.origin.y <=  0)
        {
            // Flip the x velocity component
            ballVelocity.y = abs(ballVelocity.y);
        }
```

And finally, the bottom:

```
        // Bottom edge
        if (ballRect.origin.y >=  VIEW_HEIGHT - BALL_SIZE)
        {
            // Ball went off the bottom of the screen
            // In a production game, you'd want to reduce the player's
            // ball count by one and reset the ball. To keep this example
            // simple, we are not keeping score or ball count. We'll
```

```
        // just reset the ball

        ballRect.origin.x = 180.0;
        ballRect.origin.y = 220.0;

        // Flip the y velocity component
        ballVelocity.y = -1*abs(ballVelocity.y);



    }
```

In a finished game, you would probably want the player to have only a limited number of balls. However, to keep this example as simple as possible, I did not include that feature. If you wanted to include that as a feature, you would also decrement the number of balls that the player has remaining if you detected that the ball went off the bottom of the screen.

The next method you implemented, `checkCollisionWithBlocks`, checks to see if the ball collided with a block. You did this by looping through each block that is in the `blocks` array and comparing its frame with the `ballRect`:

```
        // Iterate over the blocks to see if a collision has happened
        for (BlockView* bv in blocks) {
            if (CGRectIntersectsRect(bv.frame,ballRect)) {
```

If you found a collision, you flipped the y velocity of the ball:

```
        // Flip the y velocity component
        ballVelocity.y = -ballVelocity.y;
```

Next, you updated the `blocks` array by removing the block that the ball hit:

```
        // Remove the block from the collection
        [blocks removeObject:bv];
```

Since you removed the block from the array, you need to also remove the block from the view. If you remember back, you added each block to the main view as a subview. Subclasses of `UIView`, like the `BlockView`, maintain a reference to their superview. In this method, you called the `removeFromSuperview` method to remove the block from the `ViewController`'s view:

```
        // remove the block's view from the superview
        [bv removeFromSuperview];
```

Once again for the sake of simplicity, I have omitted some code that you would probably want in a production game. Typically, you would want to add to the player's score when he eliminated a block. You could put that code in the `checkCollisionWithBlocks` method.

The next method that you implemented was `checkCollisionWithPaddle`. This method checks to see if the ball collided with the paddle. Just like the `checkCollisionWithBlocks` method, you first do the collision detection by using the `CGRectIntersectsRect` function:

```
        // Check to see if the paddle has blocked the ball
        if (CGRectIntersectsRect(ballRect,paddleRect)) {
```

If the `ballRect` and `paddleRect` intersect, you made the y component of the ball's velocity negative, so that the ball would always bounce up from the paddle:

```
        // Flip the y velocity component
        ballVelocity.y = -1 * abs( ballVelocity.y);
```

After you finished putting in the collision detection code, you added a method to update the game model based on the game time. The view controller calls this method when the CADisplayLink notifies it that the display is being refreshed.

When you initialized the class, you set the lastTime variable to 0. The first time this method runs, you will not have a timestamp value, so you cannot calculate a time delta between the current time reported by the display link and the previous timestamp. Therefore, the first time through, you just set the lastTime value:

```
if (lastTime == 0.0)
{
    // First time through, initialize the lastTime
    lastTime = timestamp;
}
```

Every other time through the method, you calculate the elapsed time since the last call to the method and update the lastTime timestamp:

```
else
{
    // Calculate time elapsed since last call
    timeDelta = timestamp - lastTime;

    // Update the lastTime
    lastTime = timestamp;
```

Next, you calculate the new position of the ball by using the velocity of the ball and the time that has elapsed between the last time that this method ran and the current time:

```
// Calculate new position of the ball
ballRect.origin.x += ballVelocity.x * timeDelta;
ballRect.origin.y += ballVelocity.y * timeDelta;
```

Lastly, you call all of the collision detection methods:

```
// Check for collision with screen edges
[self checkCollisionWithScreenEdges];


// Do collision detection with blocks
[self checkCollisionWithBlocks];

// Do collision detection with paddle
[self checkCollisionWithPaddle];

}
```

That finished the BlockerModel class. The next step was to add a CADisplayLink to the ViewController and configure it to call the appropriate method when the screen refreshes.

First, you updated the header to add an instance variable for the display link. Then, you added the updateDisplay: and endGameWithMessage: methods to the header.

Next, you instantiated the gameTimer and configured it to call the updateDisplay: method:

```
// Set up the CADisplayLink for the animation
gameTimer = [CADisplayLink displayLinkWithTarget:self
```

```
                                        selector:@selector(updateDisplay:)];
```

Just like an NSTimer, you then have to add the timer to the run loop:

```
// Add the display link to the current run loop
[gameTimer addToRunLoop:[NSRunLoop currentRunLoop]
             forMode:NSDefaultRunLoopMode];
```

After you configured the display link, you coded up the updateDisplay: method. First, you updated the model with the time reported by the display link:

```
// Update the model
[gameModel updateModelWithTime:sender.timestamp];
```

Next, you updated the display by setting the position of the ball and paddle based on the information stored in the model:

```
// Update the display
[ball setFrame:gameModel.ballRect];
[paddle setFrame:gameModel.paddleRect];
```

Finally, you added some code to display a message when there are no blocks left to smash:

```
if ([gameModel.blocks count] == 0)
{
    // No more blocks, end the game
    [self endGameWithMessage:@"You destroyed all of the blocks"];

}
```

The last thing that you did was implement the endGameWithMessage: method that you call when the game ends. First, you invalidated the gameTimer to stop the animation:

```
// Call this method to end the game
// Invalidate the timer
[gameTimer invalidate];
```

Then, you used the UIAlertView class to pop up an alert notifying the player that the game is over:

```
// Show an alert with the results
UIAlertView *alert = [[UIAlertView alloc] initWithTitle:@"Game Over"
                                          message:message
                                          delegate:self
                                   cancelButtonTitle:@"OK"
                                   otherButtonTitles: nil];

[alert show];
```

FINISHING THE BLOCKER GAME

You have just about everything in place to have a complete, animated, real time game. You have a model that maintains the game state including the blocks, the ball's position and velocity, and the paddle position. You have a view that displays all of the game elements, and you have a view controller that links the model to the view.

The only problem is that the player cannot move the paddle. The game is kind of boring if you just watch the ball bounce around the screen and you cannot try to block it! Therefore, in this last section, you will add some code to the `ViewController` to allow the player to move the paddle.

You will learn all about responding to user interaction in the next chapter, so I will be brief in the description of how this code works. The basic premise is that when the user drags his finger anywhere on the screen, you will move the paddle in the x direction of the drag.

TRY IT OUT   Adding User Interaction

codefile Blocker available for download at Wrox.com

In this section, you will learn how to add basic user interaction to the Blocker game. You will add code that will allow the user to move the paddle by moving a finger across the iOS device screen.

1. Open the `ViewController` implementation file. At the bottom of the file, before the `@end` directive, add the following code:

```
-(void)touchesMoved:(NSSet *)touches withEvent:(UIEvent *)event
{
    // Iterate over all touches
    for (UITouch* t in touches)
    {
        CGFloat delta = [t locationInView:self.view].x -
            [t previousLocationInView:self.view].x;

        CGRect newPaddleRect = gameModel.paddleRect;
        newPaddleRect.origin.x += delta;
        gameModel.paddleRect = newPaddleRect;

    }
}
```

2. Build and run the game. Try dragging the mouse inside the window of the iPhone simulator. The paddle should move in the direction that you drag. Try to block the ball from going off the screen. When you break all of the blocks, the game should display an alert telling you that you have broken all the blocks and the game is over. Congratulations, you just built your first, graphical, fully animated game!

How It Works

The `UIViewController` class, the superclass for `ViewController`, inherits from `UIResponder`. The `UIResponder` class contains the functionality for responding to user events. If the code does not make too much sense right now, do not worry too much about it because you will learn all about responding to user interaction in the next chapter.

The `UIResponder` class defines the methods that the framework calls when user interaction events occur. The framework calls one of these, `touchesMoved:withEvent:`, when it detects that a user touch has moved on the screen. When a touch moves, you will get a set of `UITouch` objects that represent each touch. The touch contains the current location that the user is touching as well as the previous location for the touch. From these two positions, you can determine which direction the touch is moving. Therefore, first, you iterate over all the touches that you receive in the method call:

```
// Iterate over all touches
for (UITouch* t in touches)
{
```

Then, you calculate the distance that the touch moved, in the x direction, from the previous touch:

```
CGFloat delta = [t locationInView:self.view].x -
    [t previousLocationInView:self.view].x;
```

Last, you move the `paddleRect` the distance that the user touch moved:

```
CGRect newPaddleRect = gameModel.paddleRect;
newPaddleRect.origin.x += delta;
gameModel.paddleRect = newPaddleRect;
```

SUMMARY

In this chapter, you learned how to display graphics in your iOS games. Then, you built an animated, graphics based game, Blocker.

You learned how to draw your own graphics dynamically at runtime by using the UIKit and Core Graphics frameworks. You also learned how to use sprites drawn in external programs by using the UIImage and UIImageView classes. Then, you learned how to animate your game by using CADisplayLink to drive your game loop. Finally, you got a little taste of handling user interactions while building the Blocker game.

Now you are ready to move on to learn all about the various ways users can interact with an iOS device and control your games.

EXERCISES

1. What is the difference between Core Graphics and UIKit? Why should I use one over the other?

2. Why would you ever want to transform the coordinate system when you are building custom drawing code?

3. Should I call `drawRect:` in my game loop when I want to execute my drawing code?

4. Why is it important to save the state of the context before you change it?

5. When would I want to do my own drawing in code as opposed to using sprite images?

6. Write a simple program that draws 10 randomly sized circles in random locations in a view. Use a custom view class like you did in the GraphicsStart program.

Answers to the Exercises can be found in the Appendix.

▶ **WHAT YOU LEARNED IN THIS CHAPTER**

TOPIC	MAIN POINTS
UIKit Framework	An Objective-C, object-oriented wrapper for Core Graphics. The easiest way to draw in iOS is by using the UIKit framework.
Core Graphics	Lower level drawing API. Compatible with UIKit. When you can't accomplish something that you want to do by using UIKit, like shadows and gradients, you can drop down into Core Graphics to get your work done.
context	The canvas for doing your drawing code.
drawRect method	The method in a `UIView` subclass where you place your custom drawing code. You should never call this method directly. The UIKit framework calls this method when it wants you to draw something.
CADisplayLink	Class that works as a timer but is called by the framework based on when the screen will be refreshed, not at a specific time.
UIBezierPath	Class used to draw lines and shapes.
UIImage and UIImageView	Classes used to work with images.

7

Responding to User Interaction

WHAT YOU WILL LEARN IN THIS CHAPTER:

➤ Learning the basics of the iOS event architecture

➤ Handling touch and multitouch events

➤ Building a game with touch event handling

➤ Responding to motion of the device

➤ Recognizing gestures

Probably the most important part of a game is user interaction. If the player cannot interact with the game, he has no role in the outcome. It is difficult to keep a player engaged in a game if he cannot interact with it. In this chapter, you will learn a few different ways that a player can interact with your games.

EVENTS IN IOS

The first thing that you need to understand is the basic concept of user interaction in iOS. That means understanding *events*. When a user touches a view, the iOS operating system generates events, represented by the UIEvent object. Multitouch events occur when a player touches a view in your program with one or more fingers. You work with multitouch events by using classes in the UIKit API.

Another type of event is the motion event. Motion events happen when the iOS device moves. You can detect these events by using the accelerometer available in the iPhone and iPad. In this chapter you will learn about handling both multitouch and motion events.

The Event Architecture

When a player touches the screen in an iOS game, the UIKit framework begins a process to determine which view should handle the event. Consider the view hierarchy in Figure 7-1. This game has its basic view, in yellow, configured in the standard way. It consists of a UIApplication that contains the application window. This window holds the default view controller, which has its own view. To this view, I have added a subview, in pink. Inside the pink subview, I have added three green circle subviews.

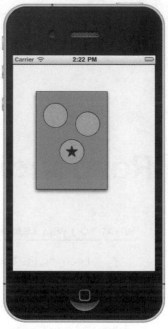

When the player of the game touches the screen, UIKit needs to determine which views should receive the touch event. It does this by first performing a hit test to determine the bounds of the object on which the user has touched. UIKit performs this hit test by calling the pointInside:withEvent: method recursively on each view in the view hierarchy that returns YES. In this way, UIKit can drill down to find the deepest object in the hierarchy that the player has touched.

In Figure 7-1, the black star represents the location that the player touched. When the player touches this location, the framework calls pointInside:withEvent: on the yellow view, the view controller's view, because it is at the top of the view hierarchy. This call would return YES because the black star is inside the yellow view.

FIGURE 7-1: View Hierarchy

Next, the framework calls pointInside:withEvent: on the pink rectangle because that is next in the view hierarchy. This call would return YES because the star is inside the pink rectangle.

Now the framework goes to work on the views inside the pink rectangle. A call to the pointInside:withEvent: method on the top left circle returns NO because the star is not inside that view. The same goes for the next circle. Finally, the framework calls pointInside:withEvent: on the last circle, which returns YES. At this point, the framework has reached the end of the view hierarchy, so the final green circle, the one that contains the black star, is the view that becomes the hit test view.

Once the framework has established the hit test view, it attempts to send the event to that view. If that view cannot handle the event, the event propagates up the responder chain. The responder chain is a sequence of objects that can respond to user events. In this case, the event would just work its way back up the view hierarchy. You can see the responder chain for this game illustrated in Figure 7-2.

First, the framework asks the green circle if it can handle the event. If not, the event passes to the pink view. If the pink view cannot handle the event, the event bubbles up to the yellow view. If the yellow view cannot handle the event, its view controller receives the event. If the view controller cannot handle it, the event is passed to the application window, and then, ultimately to the UIApplication object. If you have not configured any object to handle the event, the event is discarded.

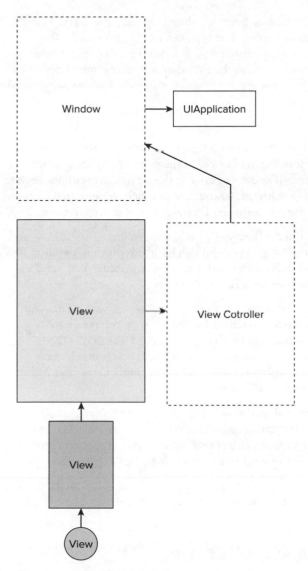

FIGURE 7-2: The Responder Chain

Event Objects

User interface events such as touches are represented by the UIEvent object. The UIEvent contains methods for getting the touches that correspond to the event. You can constrain the set of touches that you are interested in to a specific view by calling the touchesForView: method. You can do likewise for a window with touchesForWindow:.

You can determine the time that the event occurred by querying the `timestamp` property. The `type` property tells you what type of event has occurred. The type is a `UIEventType` of either `UIEventTypeTouches` for a touch event, `UIEventTypeMotion` for a motion event (like when the user shakes the device), or `UIEventTypeRemoteControl` when the user uses a remote control device to control multimedia playback.

Handling Multitouch Events

Most of the events that you will be interested in when developing a game are multitouch events. The system raises these events when the user touches the device. In the context of iOS, a touch occurs when one finger touches the device. Since iOS devices are capable of dealing with more than one touch at the same time, you will often work with sets of touches. A touch, represented by the `UITouch` class, primarily goes through three phases during its lifetime: begin, move, and end.

Objects that can handle and react to touches inherit from the `UIResponder` class. The `UIView` and `UIViewController` classes both inherit from `UIResponder` and can handle multitouch events. The `UIResponder` has methods that the framework calls when multitouch events occur. You handle these events by implementing the `UIResponder` methods in your code.

The first method that you will receive when UIKit detects a touch is `touchesBegan:withEvent:`. This tells you when one or more fingers have started touching the device. You receive an `NSSet` of `UITouch` objects that represent the touches. You also receive a `UIEvent` object that encapsulates other event attributes. In your custom view or view controller code, you override the `touchesBegan:withEvent:` method and add your own code to do something when a user begins touching a view. You will see this illustrated in the sample game.

If one or more of the fingers that the user has placed on the display move, you will receive a call to the `touchesMoved:withEvent:` method. Once again, you receive an `NSSet` of `UITouch` objects that represent the touches that moved. You also receive a `UIEvent` object that encapsulates other event attributes. You can override `touchesMoved:withEvent:` if you want to do something when touches move.

Finally, when the user lifts a finger from the display, the `touchesEnded:withEvent:` method runs. You can override this method if you want to write code that executes when the user lifts a finger from the display.

TRY IT OUT   Demonstrating How to Handle Touch Events

codefile MultiToucher available for download at Wrox.com

In this section, you will build a simple application to demonstrate the code that you will typically write to handle touch events.

1. To begin, start up Xcode and select File ⇨ New ⇨ New Project.

2. The familiar dialog box appears that displays templates for the various types of applications that you can create for the iPhone and Mac OS X. Select Single View Application from the dialog box and click the Next button.

3. In the Product Name text box, type the name of your project, **MultiToucher**. Uncheck the "Use Storyboard" and "Include Unit Tests" checkboxes. Make sure that the "Use Automatic

Reference Counting" checkbox is checked. Select "iPhone" from the Device Family dropdown. Click Next.

4. Select a location to save your project, and click the Create button. Xcode will create your project and present the project window.

5. Open the `ViewController.m` implementation file. At the bottom of the file, add the three multitouch event handler methods:

```objc
- (void)touchesBegan:(NSSet *)touches withEvent:(UIEvent *)event
{
    // Loop over each touch and log
    for (UITouch* t in touches)
    {
        CGPoint touchLocation;

        touchLocation = [t locationInView:self.view];

        NSLog(@"touchedBegan at: %f, %f",touchLocation.x, touchLocation.y);

    }
}

- (void)touchesMoved:(NSSet *)touches withEvent:(UIEvent *)event
{
    // Loop over each touch and log
    for (UITouch* t in touches)
    {
        CGPoint touchLocation;

        touchLocation = [t locationInView:self.view];

        NSLog(@"touchesMoved at: %f, %f",touchLocation.x, touchLocation.y);

    }
}

- (void)touchesEnded:(NSSet *)touches withEvent:(UIEvent *)event
{
    // Loop over each touch and log
    for (UITouch* t in touches)
    {
        CGPoint touchLocation;

        touchLocation = [t locationInView:self.view];

        NSLog(@"touchesEnded at: %f, %f",touchLocation.x, touchLocation.y);

    }
}
```

6. In the `viewDidLoad` method, add the following line of code to the end of the method to enable multitouch in the view:

```objc
self.view.multipleTouchEnabled = YES;
```

7. Build and run the application. You will get the best results if you run this application on a device, but it will still work in the simulator.

8. If it is not already visible, show the debug area in Xcode by selecting Show Debug Area from the View menu. Touch the screen and notice the line in the debug window:

```
2011-05-19 23:08:15.819 MultiToucher[1294:707] touchesBegan at: 79.000000, 270.000000
```

9. You will see the `touchesBegan` event logged each time a touch begins. Move your finger, or cursor if you are running in the simulator, around the screen. You will see a series of `touchesMoved` events logged like this:

```
2011-05-19 23:08:16.314 MultiToucher[1294:707] touchesMoved at: 81.000000, 272.000000
2011-05-19 23:08:16.331 MultiToucher[1294:707] touchesMoved at: 82.000000, 272.000000
2011-05-19 23:08:16.346 MultiToucher[1294:707] touchesMoved at: 82.000000, 271.000000
```

10. Finally, lift your finger. You will see a `touchesEnded` event logged:

```
2011-05-19 23:08:22.521 MultiToucher[1294:707] touchesEnded at: 266.000000, 353.000000
```

If you place multiple fingers on the screen at the same time, move them around, and then lift them; you should see a `touchesBegan` and `touchesEnded` event for each finger as well as a lot of `touchesMoved` events. Here is an abbreviated log from my test run. I placed three fingers on the display at different times, moved them around, and then lifted them off, one at a time. I have highlighted when each touch began and ended.

```
2011-05-19 23:08:15.819 MultiToucher[1294:707] touchesBegan at: 79.000000, 270.000000
2011-05-19 23:08:16.314 MultiToucher[1294:707] touchesMoved at: 81.000000, 272.000000
2011-05-19 23:08:16.602 MultiToucher[1294:707] touchesMoved at: 84.000000, 266.000000
2011-05-19 23:08:16.939 MultiToucher[1294:707] touchesBegan at: 166.000000, 117.000000
2011-05-19 23:08:17.003 MultiToucher[1294:707] touchesMoved at: 165.000000, 116.000000
2011-05-19 23:08:17.008 MultiToucher[1294:707] touchesMoved at: 83.000000, 266.000000
2011-05-19 23:08:18.298 MultiToucher[1294:707] touchesMoved at: 81.000000, 267.000000
2011-05-19 23:08:18.411 MultiToucher[1294:707] touchesMoved at: 80.000000, 267.000000
2011-05-19 23:08:18.588 MultiToucher[1294:707] touchesBegan at: 259.000000, 368.000000
2011-05-19 23:08:18.594 MultiToucher[1294:707] touchesMoved at: 79.000000, 267.000000
2011-05-19 23:08:18.619 MultiToucher[1294:707] touchesMoved at: 258.000000, 366.000000
2011-05-19 23:08:18.625 MultiToucher[1294:707] touchesMoved at: 165.000000, 109.000000
2011-05-19 23:08:18.628 MultiToucher[1294:707] touchesMoved at: 78.000000, 267.000000
2011-05-19 23:08:18.651 MultiToucher[1294:707] touchesMoved at: 256.000000, 365.000000
2011-05-19 23:08:21.066 MultiToucher[1294:707] touchesEnded at: 77.000000, 261.000000
2011-05-19 23:08:21.546 MultiToucher[1294:707] touchesMoved at: 164.000000, 99.000000
2011-05-19 23:08:21.833 MultiToucher[1294:707] touchesMoved at: 164.000000, 98.000000
2011-05-19 23:08:21.849 MultiToucher[1294:707] touchesEnded at: 164.000000, 98.000000
2011-05-19 23:08:21.881 MultiToucher[1294:707] touchesMoved at: 262.000000, 359.000000
2011-05-19 23:08:22.521 MultiToucher[1294:707] touchesEnded at: 266.000000, 353.000000
```

How It Works

This application is not very exciting, but playing with it should give you a good feel for how you will build code to handle multitouch events. The first thing that you did was to override the multitouch event methods that the `UIViewController` inherits from `UIResponder`. These methods are `touchesBegan:withEvent:`, `touchesMoved:withEvent:`, and `touchesEnded:withEvent:`. Since all three implementations are the same, except for the text that you log, I will detail only one of them, the `touchesBegan:withEvent:`.

As previously mentioned, a multitouch event begins with the user touching the screen. When this happens, the UIKit framework goes through the hit-testing process as described earlier to determine who it should call to handle the event. Once the hit test is complete, the framework begins working its way up the responder chain until the event is handled. In this application, the event is first sent to the `UIView` contained in the view controller. Since the view does not handle the event, it is propagated up the responder chain to the view controller. This is where you implemented the `touchesBegan:withEvent:`, so this is where the event is handled.

You handle the event in `touchesBegan:withEvent:` by iterating over all of the touches passed into the method in the `touches` set. Remember that the interface is designed to handle multiple concurrent touches so you have to think about handling sets of touches as opposed to handling touches individually. The code to loop over each touch in the set is:

```
// Loop over each touch and log
for (UITouch* t in touches)
{
```

Next, you created an instance variable to store the location of the touch, and you set that variable by using the `locationInView:` method of the `UITouch` object:

```
CGPoint touchLocation;

touchLocation = [t locationInView:self.view];
```

As you probably guessed, `locationInView:` returns the location of the touch in the coordinate system of the view that you pass in. In this case, you want the location in the view controller's view coordinate system.

Next, you log that you handled the event and the coordinates of the touch:

```
NSLog(@"touchedBegan at: %f, %f",touchLocation.x, touchLocation.y);
```

The other two event methods, `touchesMoved:withEvent:` and `touchesEnded:withEvent:` work exactly the same way.

The last thing that you did was to enable multitouch in the view:

```
self.view.multipleTouchEnabled = YES;
```

By default, views are only configured to handle one touch at a time.

BUILDING A SIMPLE TOUCH-BASED GAME: SIMON SAYS

Now that you understand how to handle user touch events, you are ready to build another game. In this case, you will build a version of the children's game, "Simon Says." You can see an illustration of the game in Figure 7-3.

The setup for the game is simple. At the top of the screen, you will create four views, each drawing a colored shape. Below the views, you will use a `UILabel` to give directions to the player.

The computer will randomly pick one of the shapes and randomly determine if "Simon says" or not. The goal of the game is to touch the shape that Simon says to touch, within a certain amount of time. The computer may direct you to touch something without saying, "Simon says." If Simon does not tell you to touch, don't touch!

Each time the player successfully touches a shape as directed by Simon, the length of time before the next command is reduced. This makes the game move quite frantically as the player continues to follow Simon's directions. If the player fails to touch a shape that Simon has directed him to touch within the allotted time, the game ends. If the player touches any shape without "Simon saying," the game is also over. Finally, if "Simon says," and the player touches the wrong shape, the game is over.

FIGURE 7-3: Simon Says game

TRY IT OUT Building a Simon Says Game

codefile SimonSays available for download at Wrox.com

In this section, you will build a simple touch-based game, **Simon Says**. Since this game is so simple, you will implement all of the game logic in the `ViewController`. You will also build a `ShapeView` class in which you will write code in the `drawRect:` method to draw the shapes.

1. To begin, start Xcode and select File ➪ New ➪ New Project.

2. The familiar dialog box appears that displays templates for the various types of applications that you can create for the iPhone and Mac OS X. Select Single View Application from the dialog box and click Next.

3. In the Product Name text box, type the name of your project, **SimonSays**. Uncheck the "Use Storyboard" and "Include Unit Tests" checkboxes. Make sure that the "Use Automatic Reference Counting" checkbox is checked. Select "iPhone" from the Device Family dropdown. Click Next.

4. In the next dialog, make sure that the "Create local git repository for this project" checkbox is not checked. Then, select a location to save your project, and click the Create button. Xcode will create your project and present the project window.

5. Add a new `UIView` subclass to the project. Select File ➪ New ➪ New File... from the menu bar. In the template chooser, under iOS on the left-hand side, select Cocoa Touch. In the right-hand pane, select Objective-C class and click Next. In the "Subclass of" drop-down, make sure that `UIView`

is selected. Name your class **ShapeView**, and click Next. In the next dialog, click Create to create your new class. You should see two new files in the Project Navigator under your SimonSays directory called `ShapeView.h` and `ShapeView.m`.

6. The first thing that you need to do is work on the `ShapeView` header file. Replace the `ShapeView.h` header file with the following code:

```
#import <UIKit/UIKit.h>
#define TRIANGLE        0
#define SQUARE          1
#define CIRCLE          2
#define PENTAGON        3


@interface ShapeView : UIView {
    int shape;
}

@property int shape;

- (id)initWithFrame:(CGRect)frame shape:(int) theShape;

@end
```

7. In the `ShapeView.m` implementation file, add an `@synthesize` directive to synthesize the `shape` property. Add the following code after the `@implementation` directive:

```
@synthesize shape;
```

8. Since you will want to create only certain shapes, you can delete the `initWithFrame:` initializer method. Replace it with the following code for a new `initWithFrame:shape:` initializer method:

```
- (id)initWithFrame:(CGRect)frame shape:(int) theShape
{
    self = [super initWithFrame:frame];
    if (self) {
        // Initialization code
        shape = theShape;

    }
    return self;
}
```

9. Add a `drawRect:` method to draw the shapes. Add the following code to the implementation file:

```
- (void)drawRect:(CGRect)rect
{
    // Declare the path
    UIBezierPath* path;
    UIColor* fillColor;

    // Draw the desired shape
    switch (shape) {
        case TRIANGLE:
            path = [UIBezierPath bezierPath];
            [path moveToPoint:CGPointMake(self.bounds.size.width/2, 0)];
            [path addLineToPoint:CGPointMake(0,self.bounds.size.height)];
```

```
        [path addLineToPoint:CGPointMake(self.bounds.size.width,
                                         self.bounds.size.height)];
        [path closePath];

        fillColor = [UIColor blueColor];
        break;
    case SQUARE:
        path = [UIBezierPath bezierPathWithRect:self.bounds];
        fillColor = [UIColor yellowColor];

        break;
    case CIRCLE:
        path = [UIBezierPath bezierPathWithOvalInRect:self.bounds];
        fillColor = [UIColor greenColor];
        break;
    case PENTAGON:
        path = [UIBezierPath bezierPath];
        [path moveToPoint:CGPointMake(self.bounds.size.width/2, 0)];
        [path addLineToPoint:CGPointMake(0,self.bounds.size.height/3)];
        [path addLineToPoint:CGPointMake(self.bounds.size.width/5
                                         ,self.bounds.size.height)];

        [path addLineToPoint:CGPointMake(4*self.bounds.size.width/5,
                                         self.bounds.size.height)];
        [path addLineToPoint:CGPointMake(self.bounds.size.width
                                         ,self.bounds.size.height/3)];
        [path closePath];
        fillColor = [UIColor redColor];
        break;
    default:
        path = [UIBezierPath bezierPathWithRect:self.bounds];
        fillColor = [UIColor yellowColor];
        break;
    }


    // Fill the path
    [fillColor setFill];
    [path fill];
}
```

10. Now, you are ready to move over to the ViewController and implement the game logic. First, you need to update the ViewController.h header file. Add an #import statement to import the ShapeView.h header:

```
#import "ShapeView.h"
```

11. Define the interface for the ViewController below the #import statement with the following code:

```
@interface ViewController : UIViewController {
    UILabel* simonLabel;
    NSTimer* gameTimer;

    // Track what simon said
    int shouldTouchShape;
    bool simonSaid;
```

```
    // Timer length
    float timerLength;
}
```

12. Below the `@interface` block, add the following method declarations:

```
-(void) getSimonString;
-(void)timerFired:(NSTimer*)theTimer;
-(void) endGameWithMessage:(NSString*) message;
```

13. Move over to the `ViewController.m` implementation file. Replace the `viewDidLoad` method with the following code:

```
- (void)viewDidLoad
{
    [super viewDidLoad];

    // Make the background black
    self.view.backgroundColor = [UIColor blackColor];

    // Add shape views to this view
    ShapeView* sv;
    sv = [[ShapeView alloc]
        initWithFrame:CGRectMake(10, 10, 140, 140) shape:SQUARE];
    [self.view addSubview:sv];

    sv = [[ShapeView alloc]
        initWithFrame:CGRectMake(170, 10, 140, 140) shape:CIRCLE];
    [self.view addSubview:sv];

    sv = [[ShapeView alloc]
        initWithFrame:CGRectMake(10, 170, 140, 140) shape:TRIANGLE];
    [self.view addSubview:sv];

    sv = [[ShapeView alloc]
        initWithFrame:CGRectMake(170, 170, 140, 140) shape:PENTAGON];
    [self.view addSubview:sv];

    // Configure and add Simon Label to the view
    simonLabel = [[UILabel alloc] initWithFrame:CGRectMake(10, 340, 260, 40)];
    simonLabel.backgroundColor=[UIColor blackColor];
    simonLabel.textColor = [UIColor whiteColor];
    [self.view addSubview:simonLabel];

    // Seed the random number generator
    srandom( time( NULL ) );

    // Initialize simonSaid
    simonSaid = NO;
    timerLength = 2.0;

    // Get the simon string and start the game
    [self getSimonString];

}
```

14. Next, you will write a method that determines what Simon will say. Add the following code for the getSimonString method:

```objc
-(void) getSimonString
{
    int simonSaysNum, shapeNum;
    simonSaysNum = (random() % 3);
    shapeNum = (random() % 4);

    NSMutableString* simonString = [[NSMutableString alloc] init];

    if (simonSaysNum == 0)
    {
        [simonString appendString:@"Simon says "];
        simonSaid = YES;
    }
    else
    {
        simonSaid = NO;
    }

    [simonString appendString:@"touch the "];

    switch (shapeNum) {
        case TRIANGLE:
            [simonString appendString:@"triangle"];
            break;
        case CIRCLE:
            [simonString appendString:@"circle"];
            break;
        case SQUARE:
            [simonString appendString:@"square"];
            break;
        case PENTAGON:
            [simonString appendString:@"pentagon"];
            break;
    }

    shouldTouchShape = shapeNum;


    gameTimer = [NSTimer scheduledTimerWithTimeInterval:timerLength
                                        target:self
                                    selector:@selector(timerFired:)
                                    userInfo:nil
                                     repeats:NO];
    simonLabel.text = simonString;
    return;

}
```

15. Add the method that is called each time that the timer fires:

```objc
- (void)timerFired:(NSTimer*)theTimer
{
```

```
    // If the timer fired and simon said, but the user didn't touch, end
    // the game
    if (simonSaid)
    {
        [self endGameWithMessage:@"Simon said, but you didn't!"];
    }
    else
    {
        // Reward the player
        simonLabel.text = @"Good job!";

        // Get the next simon string in 1 second
        [self performSelector:@selector(getSimonString) withObject:nil afterDelay:1];
    }
}
```

16. Add the code to handle touch events. You will be concerned only when touches begin in this example:

```
- (void)touchesBegan:(NSSet *)touches withEvent:(UIEvent *)event
{
    // Get any touch
    UITouch* t = [touches anyObject];

    // If the touch was on a ShapeView
    if ([t.view class] == [ShapeView class])
    {
        // Get the ShapeView
        ShapeView* sv = (ShapeView*)t.view;

        // Did simon say?  If not, end game
        if (!simonSaid)
        {
            // Simon didn't say!
            [self endGameWithMessage:@"Simon didn't say!"];
        }
        else
        {
            // Simon said, so make sure correct shape was touched
            if (sv.shape != shouldTouchShape) {
                [self endGameWithMessage:@"You touched the wrong shape!"];
            }
            else
            {
                // Player did the right thing.
                // Invalidate the timer because the player answered correctly
                [gameTimer invalidate];
                // Correct answer makes the timer shorter next time
                timerLength-=0.1;

                // Get the next simon string and start the timer
                // Reward the player
                simonLabel.text = @"Good job!";

                // Get the next simon string in 1 second
                [self performSelector:@selector(getSimonString)
```

```
withObject:nil afterDelay:1];
            }
        }

    }


}
```

17. Add a method to display an alert when the game ends:

```
-(void) endGameWithMessage:(NSString*) message
{
    // Call this method to end the game
    // Invalidate the timer
    [gameTimer invalidate];

    // Show an alert with the results
    UIAlertView *alert = [[UIAlertView alloc] initWithTitle:@"Game Over"
                                                    message:message
                                                   delegate:self
                                          cancelButtonTitle:@"OK"
                                          otherButtonTitles: nil];

    [alert show];


}
```

18. Add an alert view delegate method so that you can restart the game after the user acknowledges the end game alert box:

```
// Alert view delegate method
- (void)alertView:(UIAlertView *)alertView
    didDismissWithButtonIndex:(NSInteger)buttonIndex
{
    // User acknowledged the alert
    // Reset the game and start again
    simonSaid = NO;
    timerLength = 2.0;

    // Get the simon string and start the game
    [self getSimonString];

}
```

19. Build and run the game. You should be able to play the Simon Says game. I have found that it works better on a device than on the iOS simulator. Try all of the different rule cases. Try touching an object when "Simon doesn't say." Also, try touching the incorrect object when Simon says, and try not touching anything after Simon says. Most importantly, have fun!

How It Works

The first thing that you did was to declare the ShapeView class in the ShapeView.h header. You defined several constants to represent the different shapes that you will draw:

```
#define TRIANGLE        0
#define SQUARE          1
```

```
#define CIRCLE        2
#define PENTAGON      3
```

Remember, you should use constants instead of seemingly random numbers whenever possible.

Next, you declared the `shape` instance variable in the `@interface` block:

```
@interface ShapeView : UIView {
    int shape;
}
```

You use this variable to store the shape that the class will draw.

Next, you declared a property for the shape:

```
@property int shape;
```

Finally, you declared the `initWithFrame:shape:` method:

```
- (id)initWithFrame:(CGRect)frame shape:(int) theShape;
```

Users of your class will use this method to create instances of the class that are initialized to draw a specific shape.

Next, you moved on to the `ShapeView` implementation file. First, you synthesized the `shape` property:

```
@synthesize shape;
```

Then, you coded the `initWithFrame:shape:` method. In that method, you created an instance of the class calling the superclass' `initWithFrame:` method:

```
self = [super initWithFrame:frame];
```

Then, you set the `shape` instance variable with the value passed in the `theShape` parameter:

```
shape = theShape;
```

The last thing that you did was to implement the `drawRect:` method. If you recall, UIKit calls this method any time that it needs you to draw your custom view. I could have used sprites, or images, in this game. However, since the shapes were so simple, I chose to draw them at runtime by using the `UIBezierPath` class.

The first thing that the class does is declare variables for the path and the fill color:

```
UIBezierPath* path;
UIColor* fillColor;
```

Next, you used a `switch` statement to determine which drawing code to call. Depending on the value of the instance variable `shape`, the code draws different shapes:

```
switch (shape) {
```

The first shape to draw is the `TRIANGLE`. Notice how you used the constants that you defined in the header file to label the cases. This makes the code much more readable than using numbers:

```
case TRIANGLE:
```

The code to draw the triangle first creates a new instance of the `UIBezierPath` class:

```
path = [UIBezierPath bezierPath];
```

If you recall from the previous chapter, you can use the UIBezierPath class to stroke and fill shapes that you define.

After creating the path object, the code moves the "pen" to a point at the top of the view and half way across the width of the view:

```
[path moveToPoint:CGPointMake(self.bounds.size.width/2, 0)];
```

The pen is now located at the top point of the triangle. Next, the code draws a line to the bottom left corner of the view:

```
[path addLineToPoint:CGPointMake(0,self.bounds.size.height)];
```

Then, the code draws a line to the bottom right corner of the view:

```
[path addLineToPoint:CGPointMake(self.bounds.size.width,
self.bounds.size.height)];
```

Next, the code closes the path, forming the triangle:

```
[path closePath];
```

Finally, the code sets the color that it will use to fill the path:

```
fillColor = [UIColor blueColor];
```

The next case draws the square:

```
case SQUARE:
```

The square is easy to draw because the UIBezierPath class has a method to create a path from a rectangle. You used this feature to define a new path by using the bounds of the view as the rectangle:

```
path = [UIBezierPath bezierPathWithRect:self.bounds];
```

Then, the code sets the color that it will use to fill the path:

```
fillColor = [UIColor yellowColor];
```

Drawing the circle is easy as well. The UIBezierPath class has a method to create an oval path inscribed in a rectangle. Just like with the square, you defined a new path by using the bounds of the view as the rectangle. Then, you called bezierPathWithOvalInRect: to create the circular path:

```
path = [UIBezierPath bezierPathWithOvalInRect:self.bounds];
```

Then, the code sets the color that it will use to fill the path:

```
fillColor = [UIColor greenColor];
```

Finally, you had to draw the pentagon. There is a little bit more math involved in this code, but it is not difficult, or magic. I came up with the proportions for the pentagon by trial and error. Figure 7-4 shows the view and the coordinates that I came up with for the pentagon.

First, you instantiated the UIBezierPath:

```
path = [UIBezierPath bezierPath];
```

Next, you moved the pen to point 1 in Figure 7-4:

```
[path moveToPoint:CGPointMake(self.bounds.size.width/2, 0)];
```

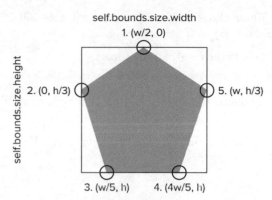

FIGURE 7-4: Drawing a pentagon

You continued drawing the pentagon by drawing lines to points 2, 3, 4, and 5 in Figure 7-4:

```
[path addLineToPoint:CGPointMake(0,self.bounds.size.height/3)];
        [path addLineToPoint:CGPointMake(self.bounds.size.width/5
                                ,self.bounds.size.height)];

        [path addLineToPoint:CGPointMake(4*self.bounds.size.width/5,
                                self.bounds.size.height)];
        [path addLineToPoint:CGPointMake(self.bounds.size.width
                                ,self.bounds.size.height/3)];
```

Then, you closed the path and set the fill color:

```
path closePath];
fillColor = [UIColor redColor];
```

Finally, you finished off the `drawRect:` method by filling the path:

```
[fillColor setFill];
[path fill];
```

Once you completed the drawing code, you moved over to the `ViewController` to implement the game logic. Since you will be using your `ShapeView` class, the first thing that you had to do was add an `#import` statement to the `ViewController.h` header file:

```
#import "ShapeView.h"
```

Next, you declared the interface for the `ViewController`. You declared an instance variable to hold a reference to the label that will give the user the instructions on what to touch, the `simonLabel`:

```
UILabel* simonLabel;
```

You also declared a variable to hold the timer that you used to determine if the player has touched the shape in time or to change the shape:

```
NSTimer* gameTimer;
```

Next, you declared variables to keep track of what Simon said:

```
int shouldTouchShape;
bool simonSaid;
```

The shouldTouchShape variable will hold the shape that Simon chooses. The simonSaid variable will hold YES if Simon said to touch a shape and NO if Simon did not say to touch anything.

Next, you declared a float variable called timerLength to hold the length of the timer:

```
float timerLength;
```

Remember that each time that the player touches the correct shape, the amount of time that he has to touch the next shape will decrease.

Once you finished with the @interface block, you declared the methods that you will implement. First was getSimonString:

```
-(void) getSimonString;
```

This method uses the random number generator to determine if "Simon says" and to pick the shape. It then creates an NSMutableString with the complete string for display to the user. This method also starts the timer.

Next, you declared the timerFired: method:

```
-(void)timerFired:(NSTimer*)theTimer;
```

This is the delegate method of the timer that will execute when the timer expires. In this method, you determined if Simon said to do something that the user did not do in time. The method also changes the simonLabel if the timer expired, and Simon did not tell the player to touch a shape.

Finally, you declared the endGameWithMessage: method that you used to display a message to the user when the game ends:

```
-(void) endGameWithMessage:(NSString*) message;
```

Once you finished working in the header, you switched over to the ViewController.m implementation file and went to work implementing the game.

First, you built the viewDidLoad method. The first thing that you needed to do here was to call the superclass viewDidLoad method:

```
[super viewDidLoad];
```

This ensures that the superclass gets a chance to do any initialization that it needs to do to get your class ready to go. After this, you set the background color to black by using the backgroundColor property of the view:

```
// Make the background black
self.view.backgroundColor = [UIColor blackColor];
```

Next, you created four instances of your ShapeView class and added them to the view. You first declared a ShapeView variable:

```
ShapeView* sv;
```

Then, you allocated and initialized the ShapeView by using the alloc class method and the initWithFrame:shape: instance method that you built in the ShapeView class:

```
sv = [[ShapeView alloc]
    initWithFrame:CGRectMake(10, 10, 140, 140) shape:SQUARE];
```

In the call, you made a CGRect struct by using the CGRectMake function, passing in the top left coordinate of the rectangle (10,10) and the height and width of the rectangle (140,140). You should also notice that you used the constant SQUARE to define the shape that you wanted to draw.

Next, you added the new ShapeView to the SimonSaysViewController's view:

```
[self.view addSubview:sv];
```

You followed that same process to create the circle, triangle, and pentagon shapes:

```
sv = [[ShapeView alloc]
      initWithFrame:CGRectMake(170, 10, 140, 140) shape:CIRCLE];
[self.view addSubview:sv];

sv = [[ShapeView alloc]
      initWithFrame:CGRectMake(10, 170, 140, 140) shape:TRIANGLE];
[self.view addSubview:sv];

sv = [[ShapeView alloc]
      initWithFrame:CGRectMake(170, 170, 140, 140) shape:PENTAGON];
[self.view addSubview:sv];
```

The next thing that you did was to create and configure the UILabel that you use to tell the player what to do. First, you allocated and initialized the UILabel:

```
simonLabel = [[UILabel alloc] initWithFrame:CGRectMake(10, 340, 260, 40)];
```

Then, you set its backgroundColor to black and set its textColor to white:

```
simonLabel.backgroundColor=[UIColor blackColor];
simonLabel.textColor = [UIColor whiteColor];
```

Finally, you added the simonLabel to the view:

```
[self.view addSubview:simonLabel];
```

Next, you seeded the random number generator:

```
srandom( time( NULL ) );
```

You used random numbers in the getSimonString method so you needed to seed the random number generator to ensure that the numbers were unpredictable.

Then, you initialized the simonSaid variable and set the starting length of the timer:

```
simonSaid = NO;
timerLength = 2.0;
```

Finally, you called the getSimonString method to set the text of the simonLabel and start the timer running:

```
[self getSimonString];
```

After completing the implementation of viewDidLoad, you built the getSimonString method. First, you declared two instance variables to hold two random numbers: simonSaysNum and shapeNum:

```
int simonSaysNum, shapeNum;
```

Then, you generated the random numbers:

```
simonSaysNum = (random() % 3);
shapeNum = (random() % 4);
```

The `simonSaysNum` is used to determine if "Simon Says" or not. The number 3 makes the random number range from 0 to 2, giving a 1/3 probability that "Simon Says." This number is not magic. I just tried a few different probabilities until I found something that felt right. Feel free to play with this number if you feel that "Simon says," too often or not often enough.

You used the `shapeNum` variable to determine which shape Simon chooses.

Next, you declared, allocated, and initialized an `NSMutableString` that you used to build what Simon will say:

```
NSMutableString* simonString = [[NSMutableString alloc] init];
```

Remember that the `NSString` class is immutable, so if you intend to build a string on the fly, you need to use `NSMutableString`.

Next, you determine if "Simon says" or not. If the `simonSaysNum` is 0, you append the string "Simon says" to the `simonString` and set the `simonSaid` instance variable to `YES`:

```
if (simonSaysNum == 0)
{
    [simonString appendString:@"Simon says "];
    simonSaid = YES;
}
```

If not, you set the `simonSaid` instance variable to `NO`:

```
else
{
    simonSaid = NO;
}
```

Since the `simonString` will always tell the player to touch something, whether "Simon says" or not, you next append the string "touch the" to the `simonString`:

```
[simonString appendString:@"touch the "];
```

Next, you decided what shape to tell the user to touch by using the `shapeNum` random number and a `switch` statement:

```
switch (shapeNum) {
    case TRIANGLE:
        [simonString appendString:@"triangle"];
        break;
    case CIRCLE:
        [simonString appendString:@"circle"];
        break;
    case SQUARE:
        [simonString appendString:@"square"];
        break;
    case PENTAGON:
        [simonString appendString:@"pentagon"];
        break;

}
```

Once again, notice that you are using the constants that you defined in the ShapeView header.

Next, you set the shouldTouchShape member variable so that you can keep track of the shape that the computer picked:

```
shouldTouchShape = shapeNum;
```

Next, you start the gameTimer by using the scheduledTimerWithTimeInterval:target:selector:userInfo:repeats: method:

```
gameTimer = [NSTimer scheduledTimerWithTimeInterval:timerLength
                                    target:self
                                  selector:@selector(timerFired:)
                                  userInfo:nil
                                   repeats:NO];
```

When scheduling the timer, you used the timerLength variable to determine how long the timer should wait before firing. You also configured the timer to call the timerFired: method when the timerLength expired. Finally, you configured the timer not to repeat by setting the repeats parameter to NO.

Finally, you set the text of the simonLabel to the simonString that you just built:

```
simonLabel.text = simonString;
```

After this, you implemented the timer method timerFired:. This method ends the game if the timer fires and Simon said to touch a shape:

```
// If the timer fired and simon said, but the user didn't touch, end
// the game
if (simonSaid)
{
    [self endGameWithMessage:@"Simon said, but you didn't!"];
}
```

If Simon did not say and the timer fires, that is ok. That means that the user correctly passed up on touching a shape that Simon did not tell the user to touch. Here, you reward the player with a message indicating that he correctly did not touch any shapes:

```
else
{
    simonLabel.text = @"Good job!";
```

Then, you waited one second to give the player a chance to read the reward message before selecting the next simon string by calling the getSimonString method:

```
    // Get the next simon string in 1 second
    [self performSelector:@selector(getSimonString) withObject:nil afterDelay:1];
}
```

Next, you implemented the code that handles the user interaction with the game. In this case, you implemented the touchesBegan:withEvent: method.

First, you got a UITouch object out of the touches set by using the anyObject method:

```
UITouch* t = [touches anyObject];
```

The anyObject method returns a UITouch object for any object that the player touched.

Next, you checked to see if the touch that you obtained was on a shape. You accomplished this by comparing the touch's view's `class` with the `ShapeView`'s `class`:

```
if ([t.view class] == [ShapeView class])
{
```

If the player did touch a shape, you get the `ShapeView` from the `view` property of the `UITouch` object:

```
ShapeView* sv = (ShapeView*)t.view;
```

Next, you check to see if "Simon said." If Simon did not tell the player to touch a shape and the player touched a shape anyway, the game is over:

```
// Did simon say?  If not, end game
if (!simonSaid)
{
    // Simon didn't say!
    [self endGameWithMessage:@"Simon didn't say!"];
}
```

If the player touched a shape and Simon did say to touch a shape, you needed to make sure that the player touched the correct shape:

```
else
{
    // Simon said, so make sure correct shape was touched
    if (sv.shape != shouldTouchShape) {
        [self endGameWithMessage:@"You touched the wrong shape!"];
    }
```

If Simon said to touch a shape and the player touched that shape, you needed to `invalidate` the timer because the player did everything correctly, and you do not want the timer to fire:

```
else
{
    // Player did the right thing.
    // Invalidate the timer because the player answered correctly
    [gameTimer invalidate];
```

Next, you reduced the `timerLength` by a tenth of a second:

```
// Correct answer makes the timer shorter next time
timerLength-=0.1;
```

Finally, you rewarded the player for performing the correct action and updated the label with a new string:

```
// Get the next simon string and start the timer
// Reward the player
simonLabel.text = @"Good job!";

// Get the next simon string in 1 second
[self performSelector:@selector(getSimonString) withObject:nil
afterDelay:1];
}
```

That completes the game logic. The last two methods that you implemented display an alert when the game ends and reset the game after the user acknowledges that the game has ended.

RESPONDING TO MOTION WITH THE ACCELEROMETER

In addition to the ability to handle events where the user touches the screen, iOS devices have a built in accelerometer. You can use the accelerometer to determine when the device moves, how much it has moved and in which direction it is oriented.

You can receive accelerometer data in your application by using the `UIAccelerometer` class. You get an instance of this class by using the class method `sharedAccelerometer`. Each application has a single accelerometer instance, so you just need to get a reference to it by using the `sharedAccelerometer`.

You use the accelerometer by setting its update interval and delegate. Then, each time the accelerometer updates, at your specified interval, you will receive a call to the delegate method `accelerometer:didAccelerate:`. The delegate method receives a pointer to the accelerometer and a pointer to a `UIAcceleration` object. This acceleration object contains the relevant information about the acceleration of the device.

The `UIAcceleration` object has four properties: x, y, z, and `timestamp`. The x, y, and z properties give you the acceleration of the device in each of these directions in terms of g, the acceleration due to gravity. You can see the coordinate system orientation in Figure 7-5.

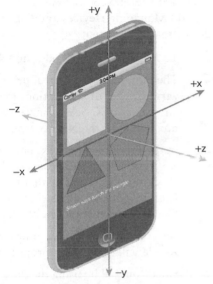

FIGURE 7-5: Accelerometer coordinate system

If the device is laying on a perfectly flat surface, the accelerometer should return an x value of 0, a y value of 0, and a z value of –1. This is because gravity is pulling down on the device, in the negative z direction, with 1g of force. If you stand the phone up on its bottom end, the accelerometer returns an x value of 0, a y value of –1, and a z value of 0. Keep in mind that the accelerometer positive y-axis goes in the opposite direction of the `UIView` y-axis. You will see this illustrated in the example code.

TRY IT OUT Using the Accelerometer

codefile Roller available for download at Wrox.com

In this section, you will build a simple test application to learn about using the accelerometer. The program will simulate a ball on a flat table. When you tilt the iPhone or iPad, the ball will accelerate in the direction that you tilt and roll in that direction. You can tilt the device any way and see the ball start rolling in that direction. Figure 7-6 shows a screenshot of this program. You could use something like this as a starting point for creating a game like Labyrinth where the player has to guide the ball through a maze.

To run this example, you will need a device such as an iPhone, iPod touch or iPad. You will also need to be a member of the iOS developer program as it is not possible to install your programs on a device without joining the program.

The process for getting your iOS applications running on a device is relatively simple, but there are many details surrounding the process. Since the process has changed substantially throughout the lifetime of iOS and will likely continue to change, it is not helpful to document the process in a book where it may become outdated. You can find all of the details of the process online on Apple's developer web site in the iOS development guide (http://developer.apple.com/library/ios/documentation/Xcode/Conceptual/iphone_development/index.html). Specifically, the section called "Managing Devices and Digital Identities" clearly explains how to configure your computer and device for development.

1. To begin, start up Xcode and select File ⇨ New ⇨ New Project.

2. The familiar dialog box appears that displays templates for the various types of applications that you can create for the iPhone and Mac OS X. Select Single View Application from the dialog box and click the Next button.

3. In the Product Name text box, type the name of your project, **Roller**. Uncheck the "Use Storyboard" and "Include Unit Tests" checkboxes. Make sure that the "Use Automatic Reference Counting" checkbox is checked. Select "iPhone" from the Device Family dropdown. Click Next.

4. Select a location to save your project, and click the Create button. Xcode will create your project and present the project window.

5. Since you will be using the CADisplayLink class to do your animation, you need to import the QuartzCore header and use the QuartzCore framework. At the top of the ViewController.h header file, add a #import statement to import the QuartzCore framework header:

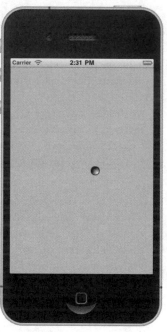

FIGURE 7-6: Roller program

```
#import <QuartzCore/QuartzCore.h>
```

6. Next, you need to add a reference to the QuartzCore framework to your Xcode project. Click on the Roller project icon at the top of the Project Navigator view to bring up the project properties. In the editor window, under the heading Targets, click on Roller. Click on the tab at the top of the Editor window labeled Build Phases. Expand the item that says, "Link Binary With Libraries."

7. Click the plus sign at the bottom of the "Link Binary With Libraries" table. In the dialog that comes up, select QuartzCore.framework and click the Add button.

8. Next, you need to import the ball.png graphic into your project. You can download the graphics file from the book's website. In the File menu, select, "Add Files to Roller...." Navigate to the location where you saved the image files, and select them. Check the box that says, "Copy items into destination group's folder (if needed)." Click "Add" to add the images to your project.

9. Next, you will need to update the @interface definition of the ViewController class in the ViewController.h header. You need to declare that you will implement the UIAccelerometerDelegate protocol. Change the @interface directive to this:

```
@interface ViewController : UIViewController <UIAccelerometerDelegate>
```

10. Add the following three member variables to the `@interface` block:

```
{
    CGPoint ballVelocity;

    CADisplayLink* gameTimer;

    UIImageView* ball;
}
```

11. The completed header should look like this:

```
#import <UIKit/UIKit.h>
#import <QuartzCore/QuartzCore.h>

@interface ViewController :
    UIViewController <UIAccelerometerDelegate>
{
    CGPoint ballVelocity;

    CADisplayLink* gameTimer;

    UIImageView* ball;


}

@end
```

12. Now, switch over to the `ViewController.m` implementation file. Implement the `viewDidLoad` method like this:

```
- (void)viewDidLoad
{
    [super viewDidLoad];

    // Configure the accelerometer
    UIAccelerometer* theAccelerometer = [UIAccelerometer sharedAccelerometer];
    // Use 30Hz update frequency
    theAccelerometer.updateInterval = 1 / 30;
    theAccelerometer.delegate = self;

    // Initialize the velocity vector
    ballVelocity.x=0;
    ballVelocity.y=0;

    // Draw the ball
    ball = [[UIImageView alloc] initWithImage:
            [UIImage imageNamed:@"ball.png"]];

    CGSize ballSize = [ball.image size];

    [ball setFrame:CGRectMake(180.0, 220.0,
                              ballSize.width, ballSize.height)];
```

```
    [self.view addSubview:ball];

    // Set up the CADisplayLink for the animation
    gameTimer = [CADisplayLink displayLinkWithTarget:self
                                      selector:@selector(updateDisplay:)];


    // Add the display link to the current run loop
    [gameTimer addToRunLoop:[NSRunLoop currentRunLoop]
               forMode:NSDefaultRunLoopMode];


}
```

13. Add the `accelerometer:didAccelerate:` method:

```
- (void)accelerometer:(UIAccelerometer *)accelerometer
       didAccelerate:(UIAcceleration *)acceleration
{

    ballVelocity.x += acceleration.x;
    ballVelocity.y -= acceleration.y;


}
```

14. Add the `updateDisplay` method:

```
-(void) updateDisplay:(CADisplayLink*)sender
{
    // This method is called by the gameTimer each time the display should
    // update

    CGPoint center = ball.center;

    // Stop the ball if it's reached a boundary
    if (center.x<0 || center.x > self.view.bounds.size.width) {
        ballVelocity.x= -1 * ballVelocity.x;
    }
    if (center.y<0 || center.y>self.view.bounds.size.height)
    {
        ballVelocity.y= -1 * ballVelocity.y;
    }

    // Move the ball

    center.x = center.x + ballVelocity.x;
    center.y = center.y + ballVelocity.y;

    ball.center = center;


}
```

15. Build and run the application on an iOS device. Running in the simulator will not work because you cannot simulate the accelerometer in the simulator. Once you have the program running on a device, tilt the device in different directions to see the ball roll in that direction.

How It Works

The first thing that you did was to modify the `@interface` directive to include the `UIAccelerometerDelegate` protocol:

```
@interface ViewController :
    UIViewController <UIAccelerometerDelegate>
```

Protocols in Objective-C are similar to interface definitions in other languages. The protocol defines a number of methods, but does not implement them. Then, when a class declares that it implements a protocol, it means that the class guarantees that it implements the methods in the protocol.

The `UIAccelerometerDelegate` protocol defines one method: `accelerometer:didAccelerate:`. This delegate method receives the acceleration information from the accelerometer. You implemented this method later on in the code to change the velocity of the ball based on the accelerometer data.

After that, you added three instance variables to your view controller: `ballVelocity`, `gameTimer`, and `ball`. You used the `ballVelocity` variable to keep track of the current velocity of the ball. Just like in the Blocker game, you used a `CGPoint` structure because it conveniently has `x` and `y` properties, just like the velocity vector that you are storing.

The `gameTimer` is a `CADisplayLink` that you used to update the position of the ball each time the display refreshes. If you do not remember how it works, you can refer back to the section, "Animation and timing with CADisplayLink," in the previous chapter.

Finally, `ball` is a `UIImageView` that holds the image of the ball.

Next, you switched over to the `ViewController.m` implementation file and started writing the code to run the program. First, you implemented the `viewDidLoad` method.

The first thing that you did in `viewDidLoad` is configure the accelerometer. You first got a reference to the accelerometer:

```
UIAccelerometer*  theAccelerometer = [UIAccelerometer sharedAccelerometer];
```

Then, you configured it to update 30 times per second. You specify the `updateInterval` in seconds so you set it to 1/30:

```
theAccelerometer.updateInterval = 1 / 30;
```

Next, you set the `delegate` of the accelerometer to `self`. This configures the accelerometer to call the `UIAccelerometerDelegate` protocol's `accelerometer:didAccelerate:` on this class:

```
theAccelerometer.delegate = self;
```

After that, you initialized the ball's velocity:

```
ballVelocity.x=0;
ballVelocity.y=0;
```

Then, you drew the ball:

```
// Draw the ball
ball = [[UIImageView alloc] initWithImage:
         [UIImage imageNamed:@"ball.png"]];

CGSize ballSize = [ball.image size];

[ball setFrame:CGRectMake(180.0, 220.0,
                          ballSize.width, ballSize.height)];

[self.view addSubview:ball];
```

Finally, you instantiated the CADisplayLink and started the animation:

```
gameTimer = [CADisplayLink displayLinkWithTarget:self
                                selector:@selector(updateDisplay:)];


// Add the display link to the current run loop
[gameTimer addToRunLoop:[NSRunLoop currentRunLoop]
            forMode:NSDefaultRunLoopMode];
```

When you were finished with viewDidLoad, you implemented the UIAccelerometerDelegate protocol's accelerometer:didAccelerate: method. The accelerometer calls this method each time an update occurs. In this method, you used the information from the accelerometer to update the velocity vector of the ball. First, you added the x acceleration from the accelerometer to the x component of the velocity of the ball:

```
ballVelocity.x += acceleration.x;
```

Then, you subtracted the y acceleration from the accelerometer from the y component of the velocity of the ball:

```
ballVelocity.y -= acceleration.y;
```

You needed to subtract the y acceleration because the positive y axis goes up in the coordinate system of the accelerometer, but down in the coordinate system of the view. Therefore, a positive acceleration would make the ball move down the screen, but it should actually move up. If you want to see this in action, change the -= to a += in the code and run the program. Do not forget to change it back when you are finished.

Next, you built the updateDisplay: method. This is the method that you configured the CADisplayLink to call in viewDidLoad. The display link will call this method each time the screen updates. The purpose of this method is to animate the motion of the ball on the screen.

To keep the example simple, I did not worry about ensuring that the ball did not partially go off the screen by using the bounds of the frame of the ball like you did in the Blocker game. I just used the center of the frame instead. Therefore, the first thing that you did was set a local CGPoint variable to the center of the ball:

```
CGPoint center = ball.center;
```

Then, you did bounds checking to stop the ball from going off the screen. First, you checked the x position:

```
if (center.x<0 || center.x > self.view.bounds.size.width) {
    ballVelocity.x= -1 * ballVelocity.x;
}
```

Then, you checked the y position:

```
if (center.y<0 || center.y>self.view.bounds.size.height)
{
    ballVelocity.y= -1 * ballVelocity.y;
}
```

In either case, if the ball was at a screen edge, you just flipped the velocity component of the ball for that edge.

After that, you calculated the new position of the ball based on the current position and the velocity:

```
center.x = center.x + ballVelocity.x;
center.y = center.y + ballVelocity.y;
```

Finally, you set center of the ball to its new, calculated, position:

```
ball.center = center;
```

The accelerometer is a unique piece of hardware in iOS devices. When you are designing the user interface for your games, think about how you can incorporate the accelerometer into your design. You may build a driving game where tilting the phone steers your car. Or maybe rotating the device rotates the world on the player's screen. Using your imagination, you may be able to come up with a new and innovative control system for your game.

RECOGNIZING GESTURES

Although not many games use them, I felt that it was necessary to include a brief word on gesture recognizers.

The basic UIKit controls, such as the UIButton, can detect simple user interactions like pressing down on the button and lifting a finger up. You can see these events in Interface Builder by selecting a UIButton and opening the Connections inspector. Additionally, you can write code to handle the underlying touch events that trigger these interactions, like touchesBegan:withEvent:, as you saw earlier in this chapter.

Before iPhone OS 3.2, if your application required a more complex behavior, like recognizing swipe or pinch gestures, you had to implement these features yourself. This would involve writing code to process user touches with the touchesMoved:withEvent: method and implementing heuristics algorithms to determine if the user was performing a gesture. To assist developers, Apple introduced the concept of Gesture Recognizers in iPhone OS 3.2.

The UIGestureRecognizer class is an abstract base class that defines what gesture recognizer classes must do and how they should operate. Apple has provided some concrete subclasses that you can use in your applications to recognize gestures as you can see in Table 7-1.

TABLE 7-1: Gestures Recognized as of iOS 3.2

GESTURE	CLASS
User taps the screen any number of times	UITapGestureRecognizer
User pinches the screen	UIPinchGestureRecognizer
User pans the screen	UIPanGestureRecognizer
User swipes across the screen	UISwipeGestureRecognizer
User twists or rotates fingers on the screen	UIRotationGestureRecognizer
User touches and holds the screen	UILongPressGestureRecognizer

This saves you from having to write the significant amount of code required to interpret a series of touches as one of these common gestures. However, if your game requires gestures that the framework does not support, you can implement your own custom gesture recognizer as a UIGestureRecognizer subclass to define any gesture that your game may need.

To use a gesture recognizer, you attach the gesture recognizer to a view. When you attach a gesture recognizer to a view, the framework routes touches in the application to the gesture recognizer before sending them to the view. This gives the gesture recognizer the chance to evaluate the touches to see if they qualify as a gesture. If the touches meet the requirements of a gesture, the framework cancels the touch messages and instead of sending the touches to the view, the framework sends a gesture message instead. If the touches do not qualify as a gesture, the framework sends the touches to the view.

There are two different types of gestures, discrete and continuous. A discrete gesture, like a tap, causes the gesture recognizer to send one action message when the action is complete. A continuous gesture, like a pinch, results in the gesture recognizer calling the action message multiple times until the continuous action is completed.

You implement a gesture recognizer in your code by instantiating one of the gesture recognizer concrete classes. Then, you assign a target and an action to the recognizer. The target is the class that will receive the action and the action is the method that the gesture recognizer will call when a gesture is recognized. Finally, you attach the gesture recognizer to the view in which you want gestures recognized.

SUMMARY

In this chapter, you learned how to handle user interaction events in iOS, how to use the accelerometer, and how to respond to user gestures.

You learned about the event architecture and how the operating system delivers user touch events to your application. You also learned about the responder chain and how these events are passed from one object to another until someone handles them. Then, you built a game with user interactions, Simon Says.

Next, you learned about another user input option, the accelerometer. You learned how to attach to the accelerometer, get acceleration readings, and incorporate those readings into your games. To demonstrate, you built the Roller program.

Finally, you learned about gesture recognizers and how to use them to easily recognize common gestures.

Now you are ready to move on to another fun topic, animation.

EXERCISES

1. How does UIKit determine the object that should handle touch events?

2. Which methods do you typically need to implement when you are writing custom code to handle touches?

3. How would you determine where a user was touching on the screen?

4. Build a simple program that draws a ball on the screen. Then, as the player touches and drags on the screen, move the ball along with the motion of the player's touches.

5. How do you enable the ability to detect multitouch events for a view?

6. How would you use a gesture recognizer to recognize when the user has performed a double tap?

Answers to the Exercises can be found in the Appendix.

▶ WHAT YOU LEARNED IN THIS CHAPTER

TOPIC	MAIN POINTS
The `UIEvent` object	Represents events that you may be interested in handling.
The responder chain	The sequence of objects that can respond to user events.

`touchesBegan:withEvent:`
`touchesMoved:withEvent:`
`touchesEnded:withEvent:`
	The event-handling methods that you can implement to respond to users touching the device.

`UIAccelerometer` class	The class that you use to get input from the device accelerometer.
Gesture recognizers	Classes that you can use to recognize common gestures in your games.

8

Animating Your Graphics

WHAT YOU WILL LEARN IN THIS CHAPTER:

- ➤ Animating a sequence of images with `UIImageView`
- ➤ Learning the basic uses for Core Animation
- ➤ Exploring the use of blocks in Objective-C
- ➤ Animating `UIViews`
- ➤ Using Core Animation layers
- ➤ Building a game by using property and transition animations

One of the most important things in just about any game is animation. Earlier in the book, you learned how to animate your games based on the display refresh rate using the `CADisplayLink` class. Using this class, you updated the position of the objects in your game based on the time since the previous update. In this chapter, you will explore two other animation methods.

First, you will look at animating individual sprites by using the `UIImageView` class. You may recall using `UIImageView` in the Blocker game to display the ball and paddle. Along with displaying static images, you can use the `UIImageView` to animate a series of images. You provide an array of images to the image view, set up the animation duration, and tell it to start animating. Then, the image view displays each of the images in the array for the total duration that you provide to perform animation.

After you finish with `UIImageView`, you will concentrate on learning Core Animation. Using this API, you can build very complex animations. You can use Core Animation to animate changes to many properties of your views and to animate the transition between views.

ANIMATING IMAGES WITH UIIMAGEVIEW

As you may recall from the Chapter 6, you can use the `UIImage` and `UIImageView` classes to display images, or sprites, in your games. You can also use the `UIImageView` in another way. You can load a sequence of images into a `UIImageView` and display them in sequence to perform animation. For the first example in this chapter, I have created 10 crude images of a clock face as you can see in Figure 8-1.

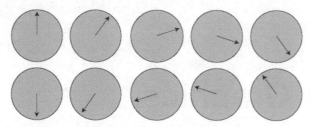

FIGURE 8-1: Individual clock images to animate

I created the original image with the clock hand pointed up to the 12 O'clock position. I decided to animate only 10 frames to keep the number of files small. To build the other images, I rotated the hand 36 degrees (360 degrees divided by 10 frames) and saved the new image. I continued this process until I had all of the images that I needed to complete the rotation of the hand around the dial.

To use the `UIImageView` for animation, you need to load your images into an array and set the image view's `animationImages` property to point to that array. You can set the duration of the animation, in seconds, by using the `animationDuration` property. You can also specify the number of times that you want to repeat the animation with the `animationRepeatCount` property. The `animationRepeatCount` defaults to zero, which indicates that the animation will repeat until you stop it.

Once you have configured the `UIImageView` with the images to display, you start the animation by sending it the `startAnimating` message. You can stop the animation by sending the image view the `stopAnimating` message. Finally, you can check to see if an image view is running an animation by using the `isAnimating` property.

TRY IT OUT   **Animating Images**

codefile ImageAnimation available for download at Wrox.com

In this example, you will use the `UIImageView` class to animate the hand on a clock rotating around the clock face.

1. To begin, start up Xcode and select File ➪ New ➪ New Project.

2. The familiar dialog box appears that displays templates for the various types of applications that you can create for the iPhone and Mac OS X. Select Single View Application from the dialog box, and click Next.

3. In the Product Name text box, type the name of your project, **ImageAnimation**. Uncheck the "Use Storyboard" and "Include Unit Tests" checkboxes. Make sure that the "Use Automatic

Reference Counting" checkbox is checked. Select "iPhone" from the Device Family dropdown. Click Next.

4. Select a location to save your project, and click the Create button. Xcode will create your project and present the project window.

5. Create a new File Group to hold the images that you want to animate by selecting File ➪ New ➪ New Group from the menu bar. Call the new group **Images**.

6. Select File ➪ Add files to ImageAnimation from the menu bar and add the image files to the Images folder. You can obtain the image files for this project from the book's website.

7. Open the `ViewController.m` implementation file. In the `viewDidLoad` method, below the line that calls the superview implementation of `viewDidLoad` (`[super viewDidLoad];`), add the following code:

```
// Set up the image view
UIImageView* animatedImages = [[UIImageView alloc] initWithFrame:CGRectMake(10, 10,
    100, 100)];
[self.view addSubview:animatedImages];

// Load the images into an array
NSMutableArray *imageArray = [[NSMutableArray alloc] initWithCapacity:10];
NSString* fileName;

// Build the file names dynamically
for (int i=1; i<=10; i++) {
    fileName = [NSString stringWithFormat: @"Clock%i.png",i];
    [imageArray addObject:[UIImage imageNamed:fileName]];

}

// Configure the animation
animatedImages.animationImages = imageArray;
animatedImages.animationDuration = 1;

// Start the animation
[animatedImages startAnimating];
```

8. Build and run the program. You should see the clock in the top left corner of the screen with the hand rotating around the clock face as in Figure 8-2.

How It Works

The first thing that you did was to create an instance of the `UIImageView` class and set its position. You used the `CGRectMake` function to create a rectangle to pass in as the image frame:

```
UIImageView* animatedImages = [[UIImageView alloc] initWithFrame:CGRectMake(10, 10,
    100, 100)];
```

The rectangle that you created had a top left position of (10,10) and a height and width of 100 pixels.

Next, you added the `UIImageView` that you just created as a subview of the view controller's view:

```
[self.view addSubview:animatedImages];
```

FIGURE 8-2: Running the
ImageAnimation application

After that, you went about configuring the image view for animation. The first step was to load the images that you wanted to animate into an array. Since you were loading the images into the array on-the-fly, you needed to use an NSMutableArray:

```
NSMutableArray *imageArray = [[NSMutableArray alloc] initWithCapacity:10];
```

Remember that NSArray is immutable, so once you have created the array, you cannot modify it. However, you can freely add and remove items from an NSMutableArray.

Next, you declared an NSString to hold the filename of the image that you are going to load into the array:

```
NSString* fileName;
```

I purposely named the files with sequential numbers so that they would be easy to load at runtime. The next block of code loops over each image, dynamically building its filename, creating a UIImage object, and adding it to the array. First, you start the loop:

```
for (int i=1; i<=10; i++) {
```

Next, you build the filename by using the stringWithFormat method. Here, you built the name Clock%i.png, inserting the loop counter in place of the %i in the string:

```
fileName = [NSString stringWithFormat: @"Clock%i.png",i];
```

Then, you called the addObject method of the NSMutableArray to add the image to the array. You created the image by using the filename that you generated above:

```
[imageArray addObject:[UIImage imageNamed:fileName]];
```

Once the array was loaded with your images, you went on to configure the animation parameters. First, you set the array to use for the animation:

```
animatedImages.animationImages = imageArray;
```

Then, you set the animation to run through all of the images in the array in one second:

```
animatedImages.animationDuration = 1;
```

Feel free to play with this duration number to make the animation run faster or more slowly.

Finally, you started the animation:

```
[animatedImages startAnimating];
```

INTRODUCING CORE ANIMATION

Core Animation, part of the Quartz Core framework, powers the animations that you see in the iPhone user interface. An example is the animation that you see when you are in an application and press the home button. The application seems to disappear in the distance and your home screen icons animate back on to the screen.

You can use Core Animation to easily create animations by changing various properties on animatable objects. These objects include the UIView and CALayer.

Core Animation delegates the work necessary to perform animations to a secondary thread. This means that the main thread of your program can continue to run and be responsive to user interaction as an animation runs. If you modify an animatable property while an animation is running, Core Animation starts that animation from the current point in the running animation.

It is easy to create very complex animations by using Core Animation. In the remainder of this chapter, you will explore using Core Animation. First, you will learn how to use Core Animation indirectly to animate some properties of the UIView. Then, you will build a game, Concentration, which uses Core Animation with UIViews. Then, you will dig deeper and learn how to use Core Animation Layers to do animations that you cannot achieve with the UIView animation methods.

A BRIEF INTRODUCTION TO BLOCKS

Before you get into looking at some animation code, you need to learn about blocks. Blocks are a (not yet standardized) feature of the C language that allows you to define a function inline in your code and pass it around like a variable. In other languages, blocks are sometimes called closures, lambda functions, or anonymous functions. Blocks are important in Core Animation because you use them to tell core animation what to do during an animation.

A block is an anonymous, or unnamed, block of code. In defining a block, you can specify a return type and arguments just as you do with any other function. Blocks run in the scope in which you define them, so they have access to all of your local variables.

You use the carat (^) operator to declare block variables and to declare the blocks themselves. The code for a block is contained within braces ({}) just like any other C or Objective-C function. In most cases, including the examples in this chapter, you do not need to explicitly create a block variable. You can just write blocks inline in your code as you will see in the upcoming example.

The important thing to remember about blocks is that they are anonymous snippets of code that you can pass around like variables.

ANIMATING UIVIEW PROPERTIES AND TRANSITIONS

If you remember the drawing discussion in Chapter 6, you should recall that there is a relationship between Core Graphics and UIKit. UIKit sits on top of Core Graphics and provides a simple API to do the most common operations. For example, you used the `UIBezierPath` UIKit class to draw paths instead of using Core Graphics directly. There is a similar relationship between Core Animation and UIKit.

There are certain types of animations that are very common in iOS programming. Instead of making you dig down into Core Animation to perform these animations, Apple has abstracted away the complexity and given you access to some of the features of Core Animation in UIKit classes. In particular, the `UIView` class has the ability to do some animation without you having to know anything about Core Animation. There are two types of animations that you can do with a `UIView`: property animations and transitions.

Property Animations

You can use property animations to animate changes to the following properties of a view:

➤   `frame`

➤   `bounds`

➤   `center`

➤   `transform`

➤   `alpha`

➤   `backgroundColor`

➤   `contentStretch`

To animate any of these properties, `UIView` provides block-based animation methods:

➤   `+animateWithDuration:delay:options:animations:completion:`

➤   `+animateWithDuration:animations:completion:`

➤   `+animateWithDuration:animations:`

Each method is a class method of `UIView` so you do not need an instance of a view to run the animation. Each method offers you various degrees of control of the animation.

The simplest method, + `animateWithDuration:animations:`, allows you to specify the duration of the animation and a block to execute that you write to perform the animation.

The +animateWithDuration:animations:completion: method builds on the previous method in that it allows you to specify a block to execute upon completion of the animation. Using the completion block, you can string together multiple animations in sequence.

Finally, the most complex method, +animateWithDuration:delay:options:animations:completion:, adds additional parameters that allow you to specify a delay before running the animation along with additional options for configuring the animation.

TRY IT OUT   Building a Game: Concentration

codefile Concentration available for download at Wrox.com

In this example, you will implement the classic card game Concentration. In the game, the player deals a set of cards face down on the playing surface. The player picks a card and flips it face up. Then, the player picks another card in an attempt to match it to the first card. If the cards match, the player removes the matching set from the board. If the cards do not match, they are both flipped face down. The object of the game is to remove all of the cards from the board.

Since there are so many cards in the game, you will be building this game as an iPad application. You can see a screenshot of a game in progress in Figure 8-3.

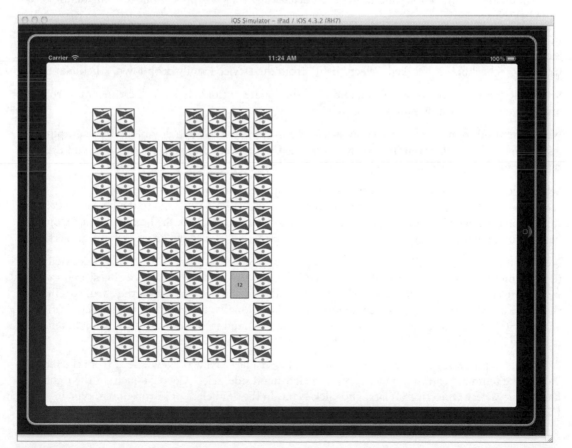

FIGURE 8-3: Concentration game in progress

At the point in the game shown in Figure 8-3, the player has successfully matched four pairs of cards and is currently searching for a match for the card with 12 on it. The challenge of the game is for the player to try to remember where he can find certain cards on the board.

The cards can have anything on them from words, to numbers, or even images. Due to my lack of graphic arts skills, I have constructed a simple deck with the numbers from 1 to 16 on them. You can see an example card in Figure 8-4. In addition, to keep the number of graphics down, you will create four instances of each card in the game, for a total of 64 cards. The player will be able to match any two cards with the same number on them.

FIGURE 8-4: Back and front of card

You will use `UIView` animation to do all of the animations for this project. In this section, you will start the project, build the `CardImageView` and use property animation to animate dealing the cards out on to the playing surface.

1. To begin, start up Xcode and select File ⇨ New ⇨ New Project.

2. The familiar dialog box appears that displays templates for the various types of applications that you can create for the iPhone and Mac OS X. Select Single View Application from the dialog box and click Next.

3. In the Product Name text box, type the name of your project, **Concentration**. Uncheck the "Use Storyboard" and "Include Unit Tests" checkboxes. Make sure that the "Use Automatic Reference Counting" checkbox is checked. Select "iPad" from the Device Family dropdown. Click Next.

4. Select a location to save your project, and click the Create button. Xcode will create your project and present the project window.

5. Next, you need to import the card graphics into your project. You can download these graphics files from the book's website. Create a new File Group to hold the images that you will use by selecting File ⇨ New ⇨ New Group from the menu bar. Call the new group **Images**.

6. Select File ⇨ Add files to Concentration from the menu bar and add the image files (`Card Front_#.png` where # is a number from 1 to 16 and `Card_Back.png`) to the Images folder. You can obtain the image files for this project from the book's website. Check the box that says, "Copy items into destination group's folder (if needed)." Click "Add" to add the images to your project.

    Now, you are ready to build the `CardImageView` class. Since the game is so simple, I decided not to implement it with the typical Model-View-Controller architecture. The model is stored in the views (the cards) and the view controller. So, I decided to store some data in the card, specifically, the value of the card and if it is face down or not. Additionally, the card has methods to initialize a card with a frame and value (`initWithFrame:value:`) and to flip the card (`flipCard`). Since the cards are just images, I decided to inherit from the `UIImageView` class.

7. Add a new `UIImageView` subclass to the project. Select File ⇨ New ⇨ New File... from the menu bar. In the template chooser, under iOS on the left-hand side, select Cocoa Touch. In the right-hand pane, select Objective-C class, and click Next. In the "Subclass of" drop-down, type in **UIImageView**. Name your class **CardImageView**, and click Next. In the next dialog, click Create.

You should see two new files in the Project Navigator under your Concentration directory called `CardImageView.h` and `CardImageView.m`.

8. Inside the `@interface` block, add instance variable declarations for the `faceDown` and `value` variables:

```
@interface CardImageView : UIImageView {
    BOOL faceDown;
    int value;
}
```

9. Outside of the `@interface` block, add the following method and property declarations:

```
- (id)initWithFrame:(CGRect)aRect value:(int) inValue;
-(void) flipCard;

@property BOOL faceDown;
@property int value;
```

10. Switch over to the `CardImageView` implementation file. Below the `@implementation` line, add the following `@synthesize` directive to synthesize the properties:

```
@synthesize faceDown,value;
```

11. Next, implement the `initWithFrame:value:` method:

```
- (id)initWithFrame:(CGRect)aRect value:(int) inValue
{
    self = [super initWithFrame:aRect];
    if (self) {
        self.value = inValue;
        self.faceDown = YES;
        self.image = [UIImage imageNamed:@"Card_Back.png"];
    }
    return self;

}
```

12. Implement the `flipCard` method:

```
-(void) flipCard
{
    if (self.faceDown)
    {
        NSString* frontFileName =
            [NSString stringWithFormat:@"Card Front_%i.png",self.value];

        self.image = [UIImage imageNamed:frontFileName];
        self.faceDown = NO;
    }
    else
    {
        self.image = [UIImage imageNamed:@"Card_Back.png"];
        self.faceDown = YES;
    }
}
```

13. Now, you are ready to work on the `ViewController`. Select the `ViewController.h` header file. Below the `#import` statement that imports UIKit, add the following `#import` directive to import the `CardImageView.h` header:

```
#import "CardImageView.h"
```

14. Outside of the `@interface` block, add the following method declarations:

```
-(void) createCards;
-(void) addCardsToView:(NSMutableArray*) cards;
```

15. Now, you are ready to switch over to the `ViewController.m` implementation file to implement the dealing of the cards. In the `viewDidLoad` method, add a call to the `createCards` method:

```
- (void)viewDidLoad
{
    [super viewDidLoad];

    [self createCards];

}
```

16. Add the `createCards` method:

```
-(void) createCards
{
    // 16 * 4 cards
    // Create cards
    NSMutableArray *cards = [[NSMutableArray alloc] initWithCapacity:64];

    for (int i=1; i<=16; i++) {
        for (int j=1; j<=4; j++) {
            [cards addObject:[NSNumber numberWithInt:i]];
        }
    }

    // Shuffle cards
    srandom( time( NULL ) );
    int swapA, swapB;

    for (int i=0; i<100000; i++) {

        swapA = (random() % 64);
        swapB = (random() % 64);

        NSNumber *tempNumber = [cards objectAtIndex:swapA];
        [cards replaceObjectAtIndex:swapA
                        withObject:[cards objectAtIndex:swapB]];
        [cards replaceObjectAtIndex:swapB
                        withObject:tempNumber];
    }

    [self addCardsToView:cards];

}
```

17. Add the `addCardsToView:` method:

```
-(void) addCardsToView:(NSMutableArray*) cards
{

    CardImageView* card;
    CGRect cardFrame;
    CGRect cardOrigin = CGRectMake(0,0, 40, 60);

    cardFrame.size = CGSizeMake(40, 60);
    CGPoint origin;
    int cardIndex = 0;

    NSTimeInterval timeDelay = 0.0;

    for (int i=0; i<8; i++) {
        for (int j=0; j<8; j++) {
            origin.y = i*70 + 100;
            origin.x = j * 50 + 100;
            cardFrame.origin = origin;

            // Create the card at the origin
            card = [[CardImageView alloc] initWithFrame:cardOrigin
                        value:[[cards objectAtIndex:cardIndex] intValue]];

            [self.view addSubview:card];

            // Animate moving the cards into position
            [UIView animateWithDuration:0.5
                            delay:timeDelay
                          options:UIViewAnimationOptionCurveLinear
                        animations: ^{
                            card.frame = cardFrame;
                        }
                        completion:NULL];

            timeDelay += 0.1;
            cardIndex++;
        }

    }
}
```

18. Build and run the project. You should see the program deal the cards. You used Core Animation, through the `UIView` methods, to animate dealing the cards from the deck at the top left corner of the screen to their final position on the game board.

How It Works

After you created the project, added the images to your project, and built the `CardImageView` header, you implemented the `CardImageView`. The first thing that you did was implement the `initWithFrame:value:` method. Users of the class will use this method to initialize cards with a given frame and value.

First, you called the superclass implementation of `initWithFrame:` to ensure that your class is ready for use:

```
self = [super initWithFrame:aRect];
if (self) {
```

Next, you set the initial property values for the class. You set the value of the object to the value that you received in the input parameter:

```
self.value = inValue;
```

Then, you set the state of the card to face down because the player deals the cards face down:

```
self.faceDown = YES;
```

After that, you set the image for the card to be the back of the card, because the card starts face down:

```
self.image = [UIImage imageNamed:@"Card_Back.png"];
```

Finally, you return the new instance of the class to the caller:

```
return self;
```

After you finished with `initWithFrame:value:`, you went on to implement the `flipCard` method. This method does not start the animation that flips the card; it changes the state of the card to its flipped state.

First, you checked the current state of the card to determine if you needed to flip the card face up or face down:

```
if (self.faceDown)
```

If the card was face down, you transitioned it to face up. You generated the name of the face up file at runtime based on the value of the card:

```
NSString* frontFileName =
    [NSString stringWithFormat:@"Card Front_%i.png",self.value];
```

Then, you set the `image` property to the image with the name that you just created:

```
self.image = [UIImage imageNamed:frontFileName];
```

Finally, you set the card state to face up (`faceDown=NO`):

```
self.faceDown = NO;
```

If the card was face up to begin with, you set the `image` property to the image of the back of the card:

```
self.image = [UIImage imageNamed:@"Card_Back.png"];
```

Then, you set the state of the card to face down:

```
self.faceDown = YES;
```

After you finished with the `CardImageView` you were ready to implement the shuffling and dealing of the cards in the `ViewController.m`. First, you added a call to the `viewDidLoad` method to call your `createCards` method:

```
[self createCards];
```

Then, you wrote the `createCards` method. The purpose of this method was to create and shuffle the deck of cards. First, you created an `NSMutableArray` to hold numbers representing the values of the cards:

```
NSMutableArray *cards = [[NSMutableArray alloc] initWithCapacity:64];
```

You needed to use an `NSMutableArray` because you needed to modify the array when you shuffled the cards. Next, you filled the array with four instances each of the numbers from 1 to 16. You used nested loops to do this:

```
for (int i=1; i<=16; i++) {
    for (int j=1; j<=4; j++) {
```

Since you cannot store `int`s in an `NSMutableArray`, you had to create an Objective-C object for each number. You represent numbers as objects by using the `NSNumber` class. Therefore, each time through the loop, you created an `NSNumber` object to represent the number:

```
        [cards addObject:[NSNumber numberWithInt:i]];
    }
}
```

When you finished creating the deck, you shuffled it. First, you seeded the random number generator:

```
srandom( time( NULL ) );
```

Next, you declared two `int` variables to hold the random numbers that you used to determine which cards to swap:

```
int swapA, swapB;
```

Then, you looped 100,000 times, swapping two random cards each time through the loop:

```
for (int i=0; i<100000; i++) {

    swapA = (random() % 64);
    swapB = (random() % 64);

    NSNumber *tempNumber = [cards objectAtIndex:swapA];
    [cards replaceObjectAtIndex:swapA
                    withObject:[cards objectAtIndex:swapB]];
    [cards replaceObjectAtIndex:swapB
                    withObject:tempNumber];
}
```

After shuffling the deck, you called your `addCardsToView:` method to add the cards to the view:

```
[self addCardsToView:cards];
```

The last thing that you did was to code the `addCardsToView:` method. You used this method to add the cards to the view controller's view and animate them being dealt from the deck to their position on the game board.

The first thing that you did was to create some local variables. You declared a `CardImageView` that you used throughout the rest of the method to work with each individual card:

```
CardImageView* card;
```

You also declared a `CGRect` for the `cardFrame`:

```
CGRect cardFrame;
```

This frame represents the frame at the destination position for the card. Next, you set the origin of all cards:

```
CGRect cardOrigin = CGRectMake(0,0, 40, 60);
```

Then, you set the size of the `cardFrame` because this is constant for every card:

```
cardFrame.size = CGSizeMake(40, 60);
```

Next, you declared a `CGPoint` variable to hold the `origin` or position of the `cardFrame`:

```
CGPoint origin;
```

Then, you declared a variable to keep track of the index in the array of the card that you are working on:

```
int cardIndex = 0;
```

Finally, you declared a variable to keep track of a time delay:

```
NSTimeInterval timeDelay = 0.0;
```

You used the time delay in the animation code to delay the dealing of each card to start a bit after the previous card so that all of the cards do not just shoot out of the deck at once.

After these declarations, you were ready to start positioning the cards. To keep things simple, I decided to lay out the cards in an 8-by-8 grid. This made it easy to use nested loops to determine the final frame position of each card. First, you set up the nested loops:

```
for (int i=0; i<8; i++) {
    for (int j=0; j<8; j++) {
```

The `i` loop corresponds with the y-axis or row and the `j` loop corresponds with the x axis or column. Therefore, the code starts at the first row (0) and moves along the x-axis placing cards in a row. The cards are placed by animating the change to the `origin` of the `cardFrame`. You set the `origin`'s x and y values based on the `i` and `j` indices:

```
origin.y = i*70 + 100;
origin.x = j * 50 + 100;
```

I decided that there should be a 10-pixel space around each card and that the cards should be offset by 100 pixels from the edge of the screen. The y position of each card is determined by using the height of the card (60) plus the extra 10-pixel spacing times the `i` index plus the 100-pixel offset. Likewise, you determined the x position by using the width of the card (40) plus the extra 10-pixel spacing times the `j` index plus the 100-pixel offset.

After you set the x and y components of the origin, you set the `origin` of the `cardFrame` to the `origin` variable:

```
cardFrame.origin = origin;
```

`cardFrame.origin` defines the final position of the card.

Once you calculated where the card needs to end up, you created an instance of the `CardImageView` class at the `cardOrigin`, set its value, and added it as a subview to the view controller's `view`:

```
// Create the card at the origin
card = [[CardImageView alloc] initWithFrame:cardOrigin
          value:[[cards objectAtIndex:cardIndex] intValue]];

self.view addSubview:card];
```

Then, you animated the card into position:

```
[UIView animateWithDuration:0.5
                delay:timeDelay
              options:UIViewAnimationOptionCurveLinear
           animations: ^{
              card.frame = cardFrame;
           }
           completion:NULL];
```

In order to animate dealing the card from the deck, you used the `UIView` class method `+animateWithDuration:delay:options:animations:completion:`. You specified that the animation should last 0.5 seconds and start with a delay based on the `timeDelay` variable. You deal the first card with a delay of zero, or no delay. However, you deal each subsequent card with a delay 0.1 seconds longer than the previous card because you increment the `timeDelay` variable by 0.1 each time through the loop in the code below. This delay is necessary to make it look like you are dealing each card one by one. If you did not add this incremental delay, all of the cards would shoot out of the deck at the same time. This is not the effect that you want. Feel free to change the code to use zero as the `delay` parameter to see this effect.

You set the `options` parameter to `UIViewAnimationOptionCurveLinear`. This specifies a linear timing curve to the animation. This means that the card appears to move with the same speed throughout the animation.

The `animations` parameter defines the block that Core Animation executes to animate your view. You use this block to specify the properties that you want to animate. In this case, you set the `frame` of the `card` object to the frame where you wanted the card to end up, namely `cardFrame`. Finally, you specified that you did not want any additional code to run after completion of the animation by passing `NULL` as the `completion` block. Figure 8-5 shows the card's position before and after animation.

Next, you incremented the `timeDelay` by 0.1:

```
timeDelay += 0.1;
```

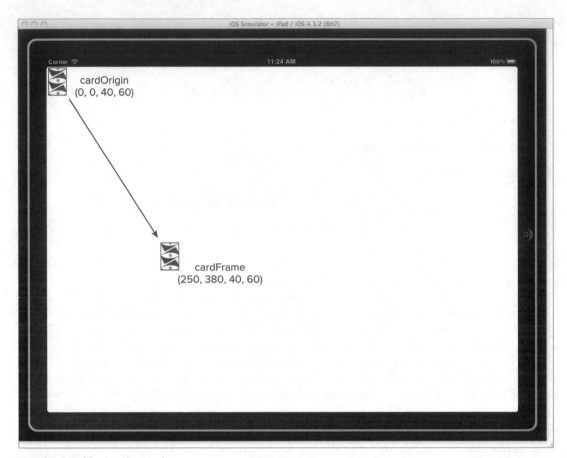

FIGURE 8-5: Moving the card

You saw in the code for the animation how you used this value. You need to increment it each time through the loop so that the animation waits 0.1 seconds longer to start the animation of each card. I have illustrated this in Figure 8-6.

Finally, you increment the index that you are using to look up the current card in the `cards` array:

```
cardIndex++;
```

Congratulations, you have just used Core Animation, behind the scenes, to animate the `frame` property of a `UIView`. You can use this same technique to animate changes to any of the properties listed in the table above.

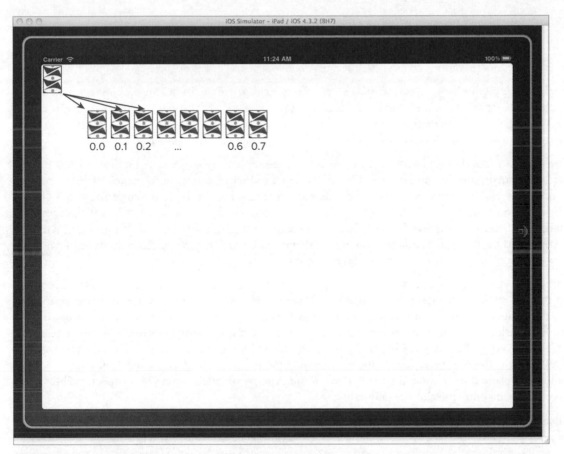

FIGURE 8-6: Time delaying the animation of the cards

Transition Animations

In addition to animating properties of a view, UIView supports animating transitions between views. You can also use the transition animations when you are making drastic changes to a view like switching from one image to another. You will use view transitions in this way in the upcoming example.

`UIView` provides two class methods to perform transition animation:

➤ `+transitionWithView:duration:options:animations:completion:`

➤ `+transitionFromView:toView:duration:options:completion:`

Again, both methods are class methods so you do not call them on an instance of a view; you call them on the `UIView` class. However, in these methods, you specify the view or views that you will be working with in the method call. These methods work only on the view(s) that you pass into the methods, so you should not try to modify other views in the `animations` or `completion` blocks.

The `+transitionWithView:duration:options:animations:completion:` method allows you to perform transitions on a single view. You use this method when you want to make a drastic change to one view and display that change to the user in an animation. In the example game, you will use this method to flip a card. You are not transitioning from one view to another; you are changing the image that the view displays from the back of the card to the front of the card. Without animation, there would be an abrupt change in the image displayed by the view, which may confuse players. It may not be readily apparent that the player had flipped the card.

Using the `+transitionWithView:duration:options:animations:completion:` method is similar to the `+animateWithDuration:delay:options:animations:completion:` property animation method. The major difference is that you need to pass in the view that you want to transition in the first parameter. The `duration` parameter specifies the duration of the animation. The `options` parameter lets you specify various transition parameters like the type of animation that you want to display during the transition. In the `animations` parameter, you specify a block of code that you want to execute during the animation. The `completion` parameter allows you to specify a block to execute upon completion of the animation.

The other view transition method, `+transitionFromView:toView:duration:options:completion:`, allows you to transition between two different views by using an animation. You provide the two views along with the `duration`, `options`, and a `completion` block to execute upon completion of the animation.

TRY IT OUT Finishing the Concentration Game

codefile Concentration available for download at Wrox.com

In this example, you will finish the Concentration game. You will implement a tap gesture recognizer so that you can react when a player taps on a card. You will also use a transition animation to animate flipping a card from face down to face up. In this transition, you will change the image used by the `CardImageView` by calling its `flipCard` method. You will also implement another property animation to fade two matching cards away.

1. First, you will need to enable user interaction in your `CardImageView` class. User interaction with `UIImageView` objects is disabled by default. In order to handle user events, like the tap, you need to enable it. Add the line `self.userInteractionEnabled = YES;` to the `initWithFrame:value:` method. The completed method should look like this:

```
- (id)initWithFrame:(CGRect)aRect value:(int) inValue
{
```

```
    self = [super initWithFrame:aRect];
    if (self) {
        self.value = inValue;
        self.faceDown = YES;
        self.userInteractionEnabled = YES;
        self.image = [UIImage imageNamed:@"Card_Back.png"];
    }
    return self;

}
```

2. Open the `ViewController.h` header file. You will need to add a few instance variables to the `ViewController` class. In the `@interface` block, add the following instance variables:

```
CardImageView *firstTappedView;
CardImageView *secondTappedView;
bool isAnimating;
```

3. After the declaration of the `addCardsToView:` method, add a declaration for the `flipCards` method:

```
-(void) flipCards;
```

4. Now, jump over to the `ViewController.m` implementation file. In the `viewDidLoad` method, add the following code to the end to initialize the `firstTappedView` and `isAnimating` instance variables:

```
firstTappedView = nil;
isAnimating = NO;
```

5. Next, you will need to modify the `addCardsToView` method to configure the `CardImageViews` to use a gesture recognizer. Below the line that creates the card instance
(`card = [[CardImageView alloc] initWithFrame:cardOrigin...`) add the following code:

```
        UITapGestureRecognizer *tap = [[UITapGestureRecognizer alloc]
                                    initWithTarget:self
                                    action:@selector(handletap:)];
        tap.numberOfTapsRequired = 1;

        [card addGestureRecognizer:tap];
```

6. The completed `addCardsToView` method should look like this:

```
-(void) addCardsToView:(NSMutableArray*) cards
{

    CardImageView* card;
    CGRect cardFrame;
    CGRect cardOrigin = CGRectMake(0,0, 40, 60);

    cardFrame.size = CGSizeMake(40, 60);
    CGPoint origin;
```

```
    int cardIndex = 0;

    NSTimeInterval timeDelay = 0.0;

    for (int i=0; i<8; i++) {
        for (int j=0; j<8; j++) {
            origin.y = i*70 + 100;
            origin.x = j * 50 + 100;
            cardFrame.origin = origin;

            // Create the card at the origin
            card = [[CardImageView alloc] initWithFrame:cardOrigin
                        value:[[cards objectAtIndex:cardIndex] intValue]];

            // Configure gesture recognizer
            UITapGestureRecognizer *tap = [[UITapGestureRecognizer alloc]
                                    initWithTarget:self
                                    action:@selector(handletap:)];
            tap.numberOfTapsRequired = 1;

            [card addGestureRecognizer:tap];


            [self.view addSubview:card];

            // Animate moving the cards into position
            // In iOS 4 and later, use the Block-based animation methods.
            [UIView animateWithDuration:0.5
                            delay:timeDelay
                          options:UIViewAnimationOptionCurveLinear
                       animations: ^{
                           card.frame = cardFrame;
                       }
                       completion:NULL];

            timeDelay += 0.1;
            cardIndex++;
        }

    }
}
```

7. Now that you have a gesture recognizer attached to each view, you need to implement the handletap: selector. Add the following code to ViewController.m:

```
- (void)handletap:(UIGestureRecognizer *)gestureRecognizer
{

    // If an animation is running, ignore taps
    if (isAnimating)
        return;

    CardImageView *tappedCard = (CardImageView*) gestureRecognizer.view;

    // Has a card already been tapped?
```

```objc
if (firstTappedView == nil)
{
    // Flip the tapped card
    [UIView transitionWithView:tappedCard
                      duration:0.5
                       options:UIViewAnimationOptionTransitionFlipFromLeft
                    animations:^{
                        [tappedCard flipCard];
                    }
                    completion:NULL];
    // This is the first card, so just set it
    firstTappedView = tappedCard;
}
else if (firstTappedView != tappedCard)
{
    // If the player didn't tap the same card again...

    // Ignore taps because we are animating
    isAnimating = YES;

    [UIView transitionWithView:tappedCard
                      duration:0.5
                       options:UIViewAnimationOptionTransitionFlipFromLeft
                    animations:^{
                        [tappedCard flipCard];
                    }
                    completion:NULL];
    // A card has already been tapped, so test for a match
    if (firstTappedView.value == tappedCard.value)
    {
        // Player found a match
        // Remove the cards
        [UIView animateWithDuration:1 delay:1
                    options:UIViewAnimationOptionTransitionNone
                 animations:^{
                     firstTappedView.alpha - 0;
                     tappedCard.alpha=0;
                 }
                 completion:^(BOOL finished) {
                     [firstTappedView removeFromSuperview];
                     [tappedCard removeFromSuperview];
                     // Stop ignoring taps because animation is done
                     isAnimating=NO;
                 }
        ];

        // Reset the first tapped card to nil
        firstTappedView = nil;
    }

    else
    {
        // Flip both cards back over
```

```objectivec
            secondTappedView = tappedCard;
            [self performSelector:@selector(flipCards) withObject:nil
                        afterDelay:2];

        }
    }
}
```

8. Finally, implement the `flipCards` method:

```objectivec
-(void) flipCards
{
    [UIView transitionWithView:firstTappedView
                    duration:1
                      options:UIViewAnimationOptionTransitionFlipFromRight
                    animations:^{
                        [firstTappedView flipCard];
                    }
                    completion:NULL
    ];
    [UIView transitionWithView:secondTappedView
                    duration:1
                      options:UIViewAnimationOptionTransitionFlipFromRight
                    animations:^{
                        [secondTappedView flipCard];
                    }
                    completion:^(BOOL finished) {
                        // Stop ignoring events because animation is done
                        isAnimating=NO;

                    }
    ];

    // Reset the first tapped cards to nil
    firstTappedView = nil;
    secondTappedView = nil;
}
```

9. Build and run the game. You should be able to play the game. Select a card and watch it flip. Select a second card. If the cards match, they should gradually fade out and disappear. If the cards do not match, they will stay face up for a moment so that you can remember both cards, then they will flip back over.

How It Works

The first thing that you needed to do was enable user interaction in your `UIImageView` subclass, `CardImageView`. After you did that, you moved into the `ViewController.m` file to implement the gameplay and animations.

The first thing that you did in the `ViewController` was to add gesture recognizers to the cards. Each card gets a gesture recognizer that you configure to call the `handletap:` method when the player taps it:

```objectivec
UITapGestureRecognizer *tap = [[UITapGestureRecognizer alloc]
                                initWithTarget:self
                                action:@selector(handletap:)];
```

Then, you configured the gesture recognizer to respond to a single tap:

```
tap.numberOfTapsRequired = 1;
```

Finally, you added the gesture recognizer to the view:

```
[card addGestureRecognizer:tap];
```

After you attached a gesture recognizer to each view, you implemented the `handletap:` selector. You configured each card's gesture recognizer to call this method when the player taps the card. The first thing that you did in the method is check the `isAnimating` flag:

```
// If an animation is running, ignore taps
if (isAnimating)
    return;
```

You set this flag to YES when you are running an animation and NO when you are done. Checking this flag allows you to ignore taps on cards while they are in the process of flipping or fading out. This prevents a lot of strange behavior in the application. So, if an animation is running, the `handletap:` method just returns, not performing any action. This is equivalent to just ignoring the tap.

Next, you create a local variable that points to the `view` passed in with the gesture recognizer parameter:

```
CardImageView *tappedCard = (CardImageView*) gestureRecognizer.view;
```

You cast this view to a `CardImageView*` because you know that every view handled by this method is a `CardImageView`.

Next, you checked to see if this was the first view that the player tapped:

```
// Has a card already been tapped?
if (firstTappedView == nil)
```

The start state of the game board is no cards turned over, and the `firstTappedView` variable is set to `nil` (in `viewDidLoad`). You use the `firstTappedView` variable to keep track of the first card that a user taps in any given turn. If `firstTappedView` is `nil`, this is the first card that the player has tapped in a turn. If it is not `nil`, the player has already flipped a card and you need to apply the logic to compare the `firstTappedView`, or first card, with the card that the player just tapped.

The first case that you coded was where `firstTappedView` is `nil`. In this case, you flip the card and set the `firstTappedView` to the card that the player tapped. To flip the card, you used a transition animation:

```
// Flip the tapped card
[UIView transitionWithView:tappedCard
            duration:0.5
              options:UIViewAnimationOptionTransitionFlipFromLeft
          animations:^{
              [tappedCard flipCard];
          }

          completion:NULL];
```

You configured the transition to work on the `tappedCard` view, to last for 0.5 seconds and to use the `options:UIViewAnimationOptionTransitionFlipFromLeft` animation. In the `animations` parameter, you passed a block that told Core Animation to call the `flipCard` method of the `tappedCard` object. If you recall, `flipCard` sets the image of the `CardImageView` to either the front or back card image depending on the value of the `faceDown` property. Feel free to look back at the code for `flipCard` if you do not remember how it works.

You are using a view transition in this case to change the image displayed in the view from the back of the card to the front of the card. Since you are using the flip from left animation, it looks like the player is flipping the card over to reveal the front. I think that it is amazing that you can do such a complex animation with only a couple of lines of code.

You set the `completion` parameter to `NULL` because you did not want to run any code after the animation is complete.

After you created the animation, you set the `fistTappedView` to the card that the user just tapped:

```
// This is the first card, so just set it
firstTappedView = tappedCard;
```

The next case that you coded was if the `firstTappedView` was not the `tappedCard`:

```
else if (firstTappedView != tappedCard)
```

You need to code the decision this way to prevent the user from tapping on the same card twice. If you just used an `else` block, the user could tap on the same card twice, resulting in a match because the check for a match tests each card's `value` to see if they are equal. If the player tapped the same card twice, the values would always be equal and the player would find a match every time. This is a major bug.

If the player did not tap the same card twice, you needed to implement the code for the case where the player was tapping the second card. Since there are a lot of animations and delays before the user can take another turn, you set the `isAnimating` flag to `YES`:

```
// Ignore taps because we are animating
isAnimating = YES;
```

Then, you flipped the second card by using the same code that you used to flip the first card:

```
[UIView transitionWithView:tappedCard
            duration:0.5
             options:UIViewAnimationOptionTransitionFlipFromLeft
         animations:^{
             [tappedCard flipCard];
         }

         completion:NULL];
```

After you flipped the card, you tested for a match between the first card and the second card by comparing their `values`:

```
// A card has already been tapped, so test for a match
if (firstTappedView.value == tappedCard.value)
```

If the values are equal, the cards match and should be removed from the board. You removed the cards by using a property animation:

```
// Player found a match
// Remove the cards
```

```
[UIView animateWithDuration:1 delay:1
            options:UIViewAnimationOptionTransitionNone
    animations:^{
        firstTappedView.alpha = 0;
        tappedCard.alpha=0;
    }
    completion:^(BOOL finished) {
        [firstTappedView removeFromSuperview];
        [tappedCard removeFromSuperview];
        // Stop ignoring taps because animation is done
        isAnimating=NO;
    }
];
```

You configured this animation to run for one second with a one-second delay. I decided to delay for one second to give the player some time to realize that he made a match. You are not using a transition for this animation so you set the option to UIViewAnimationOptionTransitionNone.

Next, you provided a block to tell Core Animation what to do during the animation. In this case, you animated the alpha property for both the firstTappedView and the tappedCard to zero. This makes each card slowly fade from complete opacity (alpha of 1) to complete transparency (alpha of 0).

Once the animation was complete, you needed to remove the cards from the superview. You did this by writing a block and passing it in the completion parameter. In the block, you removed both the firstTappedView and the tappedCard from the superview. Then, you set the isAnimating flag back to NO because all your animation is finished and you are once again ready to start accepting user input.

Before exiting the block, you reset the firstTappedCard variable to nil because the turn is over and you are ready to start a new turn:

```
// Reset the first tapped card to nil
firstTappedView = nil;
```

After implementing the case where there is a match, you implemented the else block, which executes in case that the two selected cards do not match. In this case, you need to flip the two cards back over:

```
else
{
    // Flip both cards back over
    secondTappedView = tappedCard;
    [self performSelector:@selector(flipCards) withObject:nil
            afterDelay:2];

}
```

Since there is no way, using the UIView animation methods, to execute a view transition animation with a delay, I decided to implement this by using the NSObject's performSelector:withObject:afterDelay: method. This method allows you to call another method after a delay that you specify. Therefore, you wrote a method called flipCards that flips two cards, the firstTappedView and the secondTappedView. You called this method after a delay of two seconds to give the player a moment to try to remember the location and value of the two unmatched cards.

Finally, you implemented the `flipCards` method that you used as the selector above to flip the two unmatched cards after a two-second delay. You did the flipping by using two transition animations. First, you flipped the `firstTappedView`:

```
[UIView transitionWithView:firstTappedView
            duration:1
             options:UIViewAnimationOptionTransitionFlipFromRight
          animations:^{
              [firstTappedView flipCard];
          }
          completion:NULL
    ];
```

Then, you flipped the `secondTappedView`:

```
[UIView transitionWithView:secondTappedView
            duration:1
             options:UIViewAnimationOptionTransitionFlipFromRight
          animations:^{
              [secondTappedView flipCard];
          }
          completion:^(BOOL finished) {
              // Stop ignoring events because animation is done
              isAnimating=NO;

          }
    ];
```

You called the `flipCard` method on each view in the `animation` block to swap the front of the card image with the back of the card image. In the `completion` block of the second transition, you set the `isAnimating` flag back to `NO` because your animation is complete at this point.

Finally, you set the instance variables that you use to keep track of your views back to `nil`:

```
firstTappedView = nil;
secondTappedView = nil;
```

I hope that you appreciate how easy it is to do some complex animations with the simple methods provided by `UIView`. In the upcoming sections, you will examine some of the features provided by Core Animation that let you do things that the `UIView` methods cannot.

CORE ANIMATION BASICS

Core Animation is organized by using a hierarchical layer schema similar to what you have seen used in the organization of views. The base of this schema is the `CALayer` class. In iOS, `UIView` instances have a `layer` property that returns a reference to that view's underlying Core Animation layer.

Unlike `UIView`, you do not need to create subclasses of `CALayer` to display your content. You can display an image in a layer by setting the `contents` property of the layer to a `CGImageRef`. You can also implement the `displayLayer:` delegate method to encapsulate the code responsible for setting a layer's image.

If you want to draw your own custom content at runtime, you can do that by implementing the `drawLayer:inContext:` delegate method. This method receives the layer that you are drawing for and a pointer to the context for that layer. Then, you can use this context just as you do with Core Graphics to draw whatever you need.

Layer Layout

In iOS, layers use the same coordinate system as views. The origin of a layer is at the top left corner. The positive x-axis extends to the right of the origin and the positive y-axis runs down the screen.

In addition, like views, each layer has its own coordinate system that is oriented the same way. Since every layer has its own coordinate system, you position the content of a layer by using the coordinates of the layer that contains it. To make it easier to move between the coordinate system of each layer, the `CALayer` class has helper methods that you can use to convert between systems. If you have a point in another layer that you want to convert to your layer, you can call `convertPoint:fromLayer:`. If you want to convert a point with coordinates in your layer to the coordinates of another layer, you can call `convertPoint:toLayer:`. Similar functions, `convertRect:fromLayer:` and `convertRect:toLayer:` are available for converting rectangles between coordinate systems.

Animatable Properties

You can animate most of the display attributes of a layer by changing their values. Core Animation implicitly animates changes to these properties by animating the change from the existing value to the new value. For example, if you move a layer by changing its `frame` property, Core Animation will animate the move from the old to the new position.

You can animate the following properties of a CALayer: `anchorPoint`, `backgroundColor`, `backgroundFilters`, `borderColor`, `borderWidth`, `bounds`, `compositingFilter`, `contents`, `contentsRect`, `cornerRadius`, `doubleSided`, `filters`, `frame`, `hidden`, `mask`, `masksToBounds`, `opacity`, `position`, `shadowColor`, `shadowOffset`, `shadowOpacity`, `shadowRadius`, `sublayers`, `sublayerTransform`, `transform`, and `zPosition`.

The list is much larger than the list of animatable properties of a `UIView`. If you are working with `UIView`s and need to animate a property of a layer that is not in the list of animatable properties for a view, you must drop down to the layer level and animate the property using the layer.

TRY IT OUT   Building a Core Animation Test Bed

codefile CoreAnimationPlay available for download at Wrox.com

In this example, you will build a little "test bed" application that you will use throughout the rest of the chapter to play with some of the different features of Core Animation. Once you are finished with this chapter, you can continue to use the test bed to play around with Core Animation. You will create three different space ships as you can see in Figure 8-7 to learn more about Core Animation.

1. To begin, start up Xcode and select File ⇨ New ⇨ New Project.

2. The familiar dialog box appears that displays templates for the various types of applications that you can create for the iPhone and Mac OS X. Select Single View Application from the dialog box and click Next.

3. In the Product Name text box, type the name of your project, **CoreAnimationPlay**. Uncheck the "Use Storyboard" and "Include Unit Tests" checkboxes. Make sure that the "Use Automatic Reference Counting" checkbox is checked. Select "iPhone" from the Device Family dropdown. Click Next.

4. Select a location to save your project, and click the Create button. Xcode will create your project and present the project window.

5. Next, you need to import the space ship and background graphics into your project. You can download these graphics files from the book's website. Create a new File Group to hold the images that you will use by selecting File ⇨ New ⇨ New Group from the menu bar. Call the new group Images.

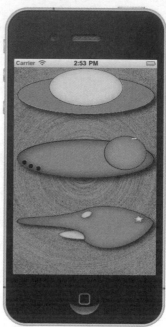

FIGURE 8-7: The space ships

6. Select File ⇨ Add files to CoreAnimationPlay from the menu bar and add the image files (`Background.png`, `SpaceShip_1.png`, `SpaceShip_2.png`, `SpaceShip_3.png`) to the Images folder. You can obtain the image files for this project from the book's website. Check the box that says, "Copy items into destination group's folder (if needed)." Click "Add" to add the images to your project.

7. Since Core Animation is contained in the Quartz Core framework, you need to add the framework to your project. Click on the CoreAnimationPlay project icon at the top of the Project Navigator view to bring up the project properties. In the editor window, under the heading Targets, click on CoreAnimationPlay. Click on the tab at the top of the Editor window labeled Build Phases. Expand the item that says, "Link Binary With Libraries." Click the plus sign at the bottom of the "Link Binary With Libraries" table. In the dialog that comes up, select QuartzCore.framework and click the Add button.

8. Open the `ViewController.h` header file and replace the contents with the following code:

```
#import <UIKit/UIKit.h>
#import <QuartzCore/QuartzCore.h>

// Constants defining image sizes for the ships
#define SHIP1_WIDTH    337
#define SHIP1_HEIGHT   125
#define SHIP2_WIDTH    337
#define SHIP2_HEIGHT   116
#define SHIP3_WIDTH    340
#define SHIP3_HEIGHT   169
```

```
@interface ViewController : UIViewController {
    CALayer *ship1;
    CALayer *ship2;
    CALayer *ship3;
    BOOL alternate;
}

-(void) addShipLayers;
-(void) returnShipsToDefaultState;
-(void) handletap:(UIGestureRecognizer *)gestureRecognizer;


@end
```

To keep the example simple and focused on the Core Animation concepts, all of your code will be in the
ViewController class. You will do the most basic configuration of the program in the viewDidLoad
method. Then, you will write an addShipLayers method to configure the Core Animation layers. When
you run the program, you will trigger all of the animations by tapping on the screen, so you will add a
gesture recognizer to the view controller's view and implement the handletap: method to run the animations. Finally, you will implement the returnShipsToDefaultState to return the ships to their default
positions. You will use the alternate variable to alternate between the animation and the default state
of the spaceships. That way, you can tap on the screen to run the animation and tap again to get the ships
back to their default state.

In this first example, you will animate the ships by changing their frame property.

9. Switch over to the ViewController.m implementation file. Replace the viewDidLoad method with
the following code:

```
- (void)viewDidLoad
{
    [super viewDidLoad];

    // Configure gesture recognizer
    UITapGestureRecognizer *tap = [[UITapGestureRecognizer alloc]
                                    initWithTarget:self
                                    action:@selector(handletap:)];
    tap.numberOfTapsRequired = 1;
    [self.view addGestureRecognizer:tap];

    // Set the background image by setting the contents of the view's layer
    UIImage *bg = [UIImage imageNamed:@"Background.png"];
    self.view.layer.contents = (id)[bg CGImage];

    // Set the alternate instance variable
    alternate = YES;

    // Add layers for the ships
    [self addShipLayers];

}
```

10. Add the `addShipLayers` method:

```
-(void) addShipLayers
{
    // Add layers for each space ship
    UIImage *shipImage = [UIImage imageNamed:@"SpaceShip_1.png"];
    ship1 = [[CALayer alloc] init];
    ship1.frame =
    CGRectMake(0, 0, SHIP1_WIDTH, SHIP1_HEIGHT);
    ship1.contents = (id)[shipImage CGImage];

    shipImage = [UIImage imageNamed:@"SpaceShip_2.png"];
    ship2 = [[CALayer alloc] init];
    ship2.frame =
    CGRectMake(0, 150, SHIP2_WIDTH, SHIP2_HEIGHT);
    ship2.contents = (id)[shipImage CGImage];

    shipImage = [UIImage imageNamed:@"SpaceShip_3.png"];
    ship3 = [[CALayer alloc] init];
    ship3.frame =
    CGRectMake(0, 300, SHIP2_WIDTH, SHIP2_HEIGHT);
    ship3.contents = (id)[shipImage CGImage];

    // Add each layer to the view's layer
    [self.view.layer addSublayer:ship1];
    [self.view.layer addSublayer:ship2];
    [self.view.layer addSublayer:ship3];

}
```

11. The `handleTap` method contains the code to perform your animation. Add the `handleTap` method:

```
- (void)handletap:(UIGestureRecognizer *)gestureRecognizer
{
    if(alternate)
    {
        // Move and shrink ships
        ship1.frame = CGRectMake(0, 0, 0,0);
        ship2.frame = CGRectMake(0, 0, 0,0);
        ship3.frame = CGRectMake(0, 0, 0,0);
    }
    else
    {
        [self returnShipsToDefaultState];
    }
    alternate = !alternate;

}
```

12. The `returnShipsToDefaultState` returns the ships to their default state. Add the following code to your implementation file:

```
-(void) returnShipsToDefaultState
{
```

```
ship1.frame =
CGRectMake(0, 0, SHIP1_WIDTH, SHIP1_HEIGHT);
ship2.frame =
CGRectMake(0, 150, SHIP2_WIDTH, SHIP2_HEIGHT);
ship3.frame =
CGRectMake(0, 300, SHIP2_WIDTH, SHIP2_HEIGHT);


}
```

13. Build and run the application. Tap on the screen. The first time you tap, you should see all three spaceships zoom away to the top left corner of the screen. Tap again and the ships return to their default position. You achieved this animation by manipulating the frame property of the CALayer objects. This is very similar to how you animated the card views in the Concentration game, except you did not have to use a method call to cause the animation to occur. Any time you change an animatable property of a CALayer, Core Animation automatically animates the change by using the default basic animation.

How It Works

The first thing that you did in the code was to implement the viewDidLoad method. Here, you set up a gesture recognizer so that you could animate the space ships when you tap the screen:

```
// Configure gesture recognizer
UITapGestureRecognizer *tap = [[UITapGestureRecognizer alloc]
                                initWithTarget:self
                                action:@selector(handletap:)];
tap.numberOfTapsRequired = 1;
[self.view addGestureRecognizer:tap];
```

Then, you set the background image for the application by setting the contents property of the view controller view's backing layer:

```
UIImage *bg = [UIImage imageNamed:@"Background.png"];
self.view.layer.contents = (id)[bg CGImage];
```

Next, you initialized the alternate instance variable to YES:

```
alternate = YES;
```

The purpose of the alternate variable is to allow you to toggle between two states by tapping the screen.

Finally, you called the addShipLayers method to add the ship layers to the view's layer:

```
[self addShipLayers];
```

Next, you implemented the addShipLayers method to instantiate the ship layers and add them to the view's layer. First, you created an instance of the UIImage class by using the SpaceShip_1.png image that you added to the project:

```
UIImage *shipImage = [UIImage imageNamed:@"SpaceShip_1.png"];
```

Then, you created an instance of the CALayer class:

```
ship1 = [[CALayer alloc] init];
```

Next, you defined the frame for the layer by using the SHIP1_WIDTH and SHIP1_HEIGHT constants that you defined in the header file:

```
ship1.frame =
CGRectMake(0, 0, SHIP1_WIDTH, SHIP1_HEIGHT);
```

Finally, you loaded the image into the layer by setting the contents property of the layer to a CGImage representation of the UIImage that you just created:

```
ship1.contents = (id)[shipImage CGImage];
```

After that, you repeated the process to load the SpaceShip_2.png and SpaceShip_3.png images into the ship2 and ship3 layers:

```
shipImage = [UIImage imageNamed:@"SpaceShip_2.png"];
ship2 = [[CALayer alloc] init];
ship2.frame =
CGRectMake(0, 150, SHIP2_WIDTH, SHIP2_HEIGHT);
ship2.contents = (id)[shipImage CGImage];

shipImage = [UIImage imageNamed:@"SpaceShip_3.png"];
ship3 = [[CALayer alloc] init];
ship3.frame =
CGRectMake(0, 300, SHIP2_WIDTH, SHIP2_HEIGHT);
ship3.contents = (id)[shipImage CGImage];
```

Finally, you added each layer to the view controller view's layer as a sublayer:

```
[self.view.layer addSublayer:ship1];
[self.view.layer addSublayer:ship2];
[self.view.layer addSublayer:ship3];
```

Next, you built the handleTap method. The handleTap method contains the code to perform your animation. The first thing that you did in handleTap was to check the state of the alternate variable:

```
if(alternate)
{
```

If alternate was set to YES, you moved and sized the ship layers by changing their frame property:

```
ship1.frame = CGRectMake(0, 0, 0,0);
ship2.frame = CGRectMake(0, 0, 0,0);
ship3.frame = CGRectMake(0, 0, 0,0);
```

If you have set alternate to NO, you called the returnShipsToDefaultState method to return the ships to their default state:

```
else
{
    [self returnShipsToDefaultState];
}
```

Then, you flipped the alternate variable's value so that the next time through, the user will see the opposite behavior:

```
alternate = !alternate;
```

Finally, you built the `returnShipsToDefaultState` method, which returns the ships to their default state. You did this by resetting the `frame` property on each layer to the configuration that you implemented in `addShipLayers`:

```
ship1.frame =
CGRectMake(0, 0, SHIP1_WIDTH, SHIP1_HEIGHT);
ship2.frame =
CGRectMake(0, 150, SHIP2_WIDTH, SHIP2_HEIGHT);
ship3.frame =
CGRectMake(0, 300, SHIP2_WIDTH, SHIP2_HEIGHT);
```

Layer Trees

Each `CALayer` can have a single `superlayer` and many `sublayers`. You can see an illustration of a generic layer hierarchy in Figure 8-8.

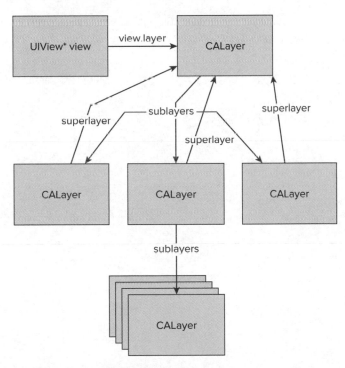

FIGURE 8-8: Generic CALayer hierarchy

The `CALayer` class provides methods for manipulating the layer hierarchy. You can add sublayers to a superlayer with the `addSublayer:` method. You can insert layers at specific positions in the hierarchy with the `insertSublayer:atIndex:`, `insertSublayer:below:`, and `insertSublayer:above:` methods. You can replace one layer with another by calling `replaceSublayer:with:`. Finally, you can remove a layer from its superlayer with the `removeFromSuperlayer` method.

When you manipulate a layer that has sublayers, all of the sublayers act as if they are part of the superlayer. In the next example, you will modify the CoreAnimationPlay application that you built in the last section to use layers. You will add the ship1 layer as a sublayer to the view controller view's layer. Then you will add ship2 and ship3 as sublayers to ship1. When you change the position of ship1, you will see ship2 and ship3 move as well.

TRY IT OUT   Using Layers in Core Animation

codefile CoreAnimationPlay available for download at Wrox.com

In this example, you will learn how to group layers together into a hierarchy. You can use this to group layers for easy manipulation.

1. Open the CoreAnimationPlay project that you created in the last example.

2. Replace the existing implementation of addShipLayers with the following code:

```
-(void) addShipLayers
{
    // Create ship layers
    UIImage *shipImage = [UIImage imageNamed:@"SpaceShip_1.png"];
    ship1 = [[CALayer alloc] init];
    ship1.frame =
    CGRectMake(0, 0, SHIP1_WIDTH/3, SHIP1_HEIGHT/3);
    ship1.contents = (id)[shipImage CGImage];

    shipImage = [UIImage imageNamed:@"SpaceShip_2.png"];
    ship2 = [[CALayer alloc] init];
    ship2.frame =
    CGRectMake(50,50, SHIP2_WIDTH/3, SHIP2_HEIGHT/3);
    ship2.contents = (id)[shipImage CGImage];

    shipImage = [UIImage imageNamed:@"SpaceShip_3.png"];
    ship3 = [[CALayer alloc] init];
    ship3.frame =
    CGRectMake(100, 100, SHIP3_WIDTH/3, SHIP3_HEIGHT/3);
    ship3.contents = (id)[shipImage CGImage];

    // Add ship1 layer to the view's layer
    [self.view.layer addSublayer:ship1];

    // Add ships 2 and 3 as sublayers of ship 1
    [ship1 addSublayer:ship2];
    [ship1 addSublayer:ship3];

}
```

3. Change the handletap: method to move only the ship1 layer:

```
- (void)handletap:(UIGestureRecognizer *)gestureRecognizer
{
    if(alternate)
    {
        // Set the anchor point of the ship to the top left of the frame
        ship1.anchorPoint = CGPointMake(0, 0);
```

```
    // Move ship1 and the other sublayers move too
    ship1.position = CGPointMake(150, 200);
}
else
{
    [self returnShipsToDefaultState];
}
alternate = !alternate;

}
```

4. Change the `returnShipsToDefaultState` method to set `ship1`'s position back to its default:

```
-(void) returnShipsToDefaultState
{
    // Move ship and sublayers back.
    ship1.position = CGPointMake(0, 0);

}
```

5. Build and run the program. You should see that when you tap the screen, all three ships move together, even though you changed only the position of `ship1`. This is because `ship2` and `ship3` are sublayers of `ship1`.

Feel free to continue to work with the CoreAnimationPlay project to explore some of the different options that are available to you when you are working with Core Animation.

How It Works

First, you modified the `addShipLayers` method to build a layer tree. You created the three layers then set their image and frame:

```
// Create ship layers
UIImage *shipImage = [UIImage imageNamed:@"SpaceShip_1.png"];
ship1 = [[CALayer alloc] init];
ship1.frame =
CGRectMake(0, 0, SHIP1_WIDTH/3, SHIP1_HEIGHT/3);
ship1.contents = (id)[shipImage CGImage];

shipImage = [UIImage imageNamed:@"SpaceShip_2.png"];
ship2 = [[CALayer alloc] init];
ship2.frame =
CGRectMake(50,50, SHIP2_WIDTH/3, SHIP2_HEIGHT/3);
ship2.contents = (id)[shipImage CGImage];

shipImage = [UIImage imageNamed:@"SpaceShip_3.png"];
ship3 = [[CALayer alloc] init];
ship3.frame =
CGRectMake(100, 100, SHIP3_WIDTH/3, SHIP3_HEIGHT/3);
ship3.contents = (id)[shipImage CGImage];
```

Next, you added the `ship1` layer as a sublayer to the view controller view's layer:

```
// Add ship1 layer to the view's layer
[self.view.layer addSublayer:ship1];
```

Then, you added `ship2` and `ship3` as sublayers to `ship1`. This effectively groups the layers together:

```
// Add ships 2 and 3 as sublayers of ship 1
[ship1 addSublayer:ship2];
[ship1 addSublayer:ship3];
```

Next, you changed the `handletap:` method to move only the `ship1` layer. First, you set the `anchorPoint` of the layer:

```
ship1.anchorPoint = CGPointMake(0, 0);
```

You use the `anchorPoint` property to define the anchor point for the layer. When you specify a position, as in the next line of code, you are telling Core Animation the position of the anchor point. The anchor point is not a coordinate; it is a percentage of the size of the frame. The default anchor point is the center of the frame: (0.5, 0.5). To specify the lower right-hand corner of the frame, you would set the `anchorPoint` to (1.0,1.0). In this example, you wanted the anchor point to be the top left corner of the frame, hence the coordinates (0,0).

Finally, you moved the ships by setting the `position` of `ship1`:

```
// Move ship1 and the other sublayers move too
ship1.position = CGPointMake(150, 200);
```

Setting the position moves the anchor point of the layer to the position defined by the `position` property.

To finish up, you changed the `returnShipsToDefaultState` method to set `ship1`'s position back to its default:

```
ship1.position = CGPointMake(0, 0);
```

SUMMARY

In this chapter, you learned some new techniques for performing animations. First, you learned how to animate your sprites by using image sequences and the `UIImageView` class. This is useful for animating the characters in a game. I may be dating myself here but, think of the animation of Mario running along a path in Super Mario Brothers. This animation is just a sequence of images that are played and simultaneously moved across the screen.

Next, you learned how to animate whole views by using property and transition animations. You used these animation types to build a card game. In the game, you animated changes to a view's properties to make it look like the program was dealing the deck of cards. You used transition animations to switch between the back and front side images on the card.

Finally, you looked a little deeper at the underlying structure in Core Animation, the `CALayer`. You examined how to animate properties of a layer and how to organize layers into a hierarchy.

Next step, noise!

EXERCISES

1. Build a program that implements a sprite animation that first animates one direction then animates back in reverse. Use the clock images provided in the first example in this chapter to make the clock run forward and then in reverse.

2. Which property of a `UIView` do you set to control the speed of a sprite animation?

3. When should you use `UIView` property animations and when should you use transition animations?

4. How can you organize your layers in Core Animation?

5. Build a simple program that displays a graphic on the screen. Then, using Core Animation and a Gesture Recognizer, animate moving the graphic to the location where the user touched the screen.

Answers to the Exercises can be found in the Appendix.

▶ **WHAT YOU LEARNED IN THIS CHAPTER**

TOPIC	MAIN POINTS
Animating images	Use the `animationImages` property of the `UIImageView` to provide a set of images to animate. Control the length of the animation with the `animationDuration` property. Start the animation by sending the `startAnimating` message.
Blocks	You use blocks to build small bits of anonymous code. You can pass this code around like a variable. You use blocks to tell Core Animation what to do during an animation.
`UIView` **Property animations**	You can animate changes to certain properties of a view. Call animate methods to animate changes to the property. Pass in a block of code to tell Core Animation what to do during the animation.
`UIView` **Transition animations**	You use transition animations to animate the change from one view to another or to animate a drastic change to a view. Call transition methods to animate changes to the view. Pass in a block of code to tell Core Animation what to do during the animation.
Core Animation Layers	Layers are the underlying structure in Core Animation. You can animate a lot more properties of a layer than for a view. You can arrange layers into a hierarchy to make manipulation easier.

Making Noise with iOS Audio APIs

➤ The important role of sound in your games

➤ How to play simple sounds with the System Sound Service

➤ How to develop more complex sound systems with AV Foundation

➤ How to use the MediaPlayer framework to play iPod music in your game

Your exploration of the basic building blocks that you can use to build games for iOS is almost complete. You have covered drawing graphics and displaying sprites, responding to user input for game control, and animation for enhancing visual impact. The last piece of the puzzle is sound.

Sound plays an important role in game design. You can create vastly different moods for your game by your choice of background music. Conversely, you could allow the player to play songs from his own iPod library during gameplay.

Sound effects also play a large part in game design. You can create atmosphere with sound effects as well as provide important audible feedback to the player. If you have ever played a first person shooter, you know how important it can be to hear the footsteps of another player creeping around a corner.

In this chapter, you will learn how to incorporate sounds into your games. You will explore the AV Foundation framework, which provides an Objective-C interface for playing audio. You will also examine the Media Player framework, which you can use to play music from the iPod library.

PLAYING SIMPLE SOUNDS WITH THE SYSTEM SOUND SERVICES

The easiest but least flexible way to play sounds in iOS is with the System Sound Services. System Sound Services is part of the AudioToolbox framework, which provides many tools for processing audio, including tools for audio conversion, parsing audio streams, and audio format querying, among other audio related tools. The System Sound Services is a C API, so it is a little less friendly than the Objective-C APIs that you will look at later in the chapter. However, if you can live with its limitations, System Sound Services is the easiest way to get sound out of an iOS device.

The purpose of the System Sound Services is to play notifications for UI events such as button clicks. As such, the API is designed to play sounds that are 30 seconds or shorter.

The System Sound Services API does not provide many of the features of the other audio APIs like AV Foundation. First, you have no control of audio levels so all of your sounds play at the system audio level. In addition, you are not able to loop the sound or position the sound by using stereo positioning. Additionally, System Sound Services does not support playing multiple sounds simultaneously so you can play only one sound at a time.

Due to these limitations, System Sound Services is not the most useful in games. However, if you need to play a sound only after a player moves or to indicate that the game is over, System Sound Services is very easy to use and may be the way to go.

To use System Sound Services, you need to include the AudioToolbox framework in your project. Then, in your header, you need to include the `AudioToolbox/AudioToolbox.h` header. The following code plays a sound called `1.aif` that has been included in an Xcode project:

```
- (void) playSound
{
    // Play the sound
    SystemSoundID ssid;
    NSString* sndpath = [[NSBundle mainBundle] pathForResource:@"1" ofType:@"aif"
inDirectory:@"/"];

    CFURLRef baseURL = (CFURLRef)[[NSURL alloc] initFileURLWithPath:sndpath];

    AudioServicesCreateSystemSoundID (baseURL, &ssid);

    AudioServicesPlaySystemSound (ssid);
}
```

Let's look at this function. First, you declare a `SystemSoundID`, which is an identifier for the sound that you want to play:

```
SystemSoundID ssid;
```

Then, you create a string that contains the path to the sound that you want to play in the application bundle:

```
NSString* sndpath = [[NSBundle mainBundle] pathForResource:@"1" ofType:@"aif"
inDirectory:@"/"];
```

Next, you create a URL from the path string because you will need to pass a URL to the function that creates the `SystemSoundID`:

```
CFURLRef baseURL = (CFURLRef)[[NSURL alloc] initFileURLWithPath:sndpath];
```

Now, you create the `SystemSoundID` by using the `AudioServicesCreateSystemSoundID` function and passing in the URL to the sound and a reference to the `SystemSoundID`. The function populates the `SystemSoundID`.

```
AudioServicesCreateSystemSoundID (baseURL, &ssid);
```

Finally, you call `AudioServicesPlaySystemSound` to play the sound.

PLAYING SOUNDS WITH THE AV FOUNDATION FRAMEWORK

When the audio needs of your game go beyond simply playing short sound effects in response to UI actions, you should move on to a more complete audio API, AV Foundation. The AV Foundation framework provides an extensive Objective-C interface for playing audio/visual media of many types including sounds, music and video.

In contrast to the System Sound Services, you can use AV Foundation to play audio of any length and in many different formats. You can also control other aspects of the playback through a configuration like the one letting the user's iPod audio play (or not) while your sound is playing. You can also play many sounds at once and vary the volume and stereo position of each sound.

The AVAudioPlayer Class

The easiest way to play sounds and music within the AV Foundation framework is with the `AVAudioPlayer` class. This class lets you play audio from a file or a memory buffer. You should use this class to play sounds unless you have very low latency requirements. In that case, you should use Audio Units or the OpenAL API. These two APIs are more advanced than AV Foundation and provide low-level access to the iOS device's hardware for processing sounds. An in-depth discussion of Audio Units and OpenAL is beyond the scope of this book.

You can use the `AVAudioPlayer` class to play sounds of any length and loop them as many times as you would like. You can also play multiple sounds simultaneously by creating multiple instances of the audio player. Finally, you can control the volume and stereo position of the sounds that you play by using `AVAudioPlayer`.

`AVAudioPlayer` plays your sounds and music asynchronously. Therefore, you can just start a sound playing and forget about it. If you are interested to know when the sound has finished playing, you can implement the `AVAudioPlayerDelegate` protocol. When certain events occur with your player, such as the sound finishing, a phone call interrupting the audio, or other OS event, the player will call the delegate methods. You will see this in action in the RepeatIt example later in the chapter.

Format and Performance Considerations

When you are designing the sound for your game, you should keep some things in mind. First is the format of your sound files. The first aspect of the format that you should think about is whether you want to use compressed sound files or not. Compression saves memory on the device at a cost of having to decompress the sounds to play them.

iOS devices have hardware capable of decompressing certain types of sound files. If you are going to use compressed sound formats, you should take advantage of the hardware decoder whenever possible. Using the hardware sound decoder frees the CPU to execute your game code instead of spending time decoding your audio. The disadvantage to using the hardware decoder is that it can play back only one sound at a time. The alternative is using software decoders, which consume CPU time that you could use for your game logic. However, using the software decoder allows you to play multiple sounds simultaneously.

This is not to say that using formats that the hardware decoder can decode prohibits you from playing multiple sounds at the same time, only that the decoder can only decode one at a time. Therefore, if you attempt to play two mp3-compressed sounds at the same time, the hardware would decode one and the software decoder would handle the other. Table 9-1 shows the audio formats that you can use in your games.

TABLE 9-1: Audio Formats Available for Use on iOS

AUDIO FORMAT	HARDWARE DECODING	SOFTWARE DECODING
AAC	Yes	Yes, starting in iOS 3.0
ALAC	Yes	Yes, starting in iOS 3.0
HE-AAC	Yes	—
iLBC	—	Yes
IMA4	—	Yes
Linear PCM	—	Yes
MP3	Yes	Yes, starting in iOS 3.0
μ-law and a-law	—	Yes

Alternatively, you could use uncompressed sound files. The advantage of uncompressed files is that they do not require decoding and you can play them without using the hardware or software decoder. The disadvantage is that uncompressed sound files can be quite large and take up quite a bit of precious memory.

As the game designer, you need to analyze the tradeoffs and decide if it is more important for game performance to use the hardware decoder or to minimize the size of your sound files. You can also change the audio files and formats that you use during the development cycle. Therefore, if you are using compressed audio and find that your game runs slowly, it is not too difficult to change over to an uncompressed format.

Configuring the Audio Session

Using the `AVAudioSession` class, you can configure various aspects of how you want to handle sound in your game.

You can set the `category` property of the `AVAudioSession` to define the category of your application. The default category is `AVAudioSessionCategorySoloAmbient`. This means that your game will mute the audio from other applications, for instance the iPod while your game is running. Additionally, a user locking the screen or flipping the silent switch on the device will mute your game audio.

If you want the user's iPod music to continue playing while your game plays, you can use the `AVAudioSessionCategoryAmbient` category.

If playback of your audio is essential to the operation of the program, you can use the `AVAudioSessionCategoryPlayback` category. You most likely will not use this for games as it allows playback to continue if the user locks the screen and even if the silent switch is set. However, it is good to know about if you are building a turn-based game and want to notify the player that it is his turn regardless of whether or not he has locked the screen or the device is muted.

You can also query the audio session object to determine the number of audio output channels that are available, determine the hardware sample rate, and determine if audio input is available.

TRY IT OUT   The RepeatIt Game

codefile RepeatIt available for download at Wrox.com

In this section, you will use the `AVAudioPlayer` class to implement a sound based game called RepeatIt. This is a clone of the 1980s era game, Simon, by Milton Bradley.

The game consists of an electronic device with four colored buttons. Each colored button is associated with a sound and lights up when the sound plays. The object of the game is for the player to repeat the sequence of lights and sounds played by the computer as many times as possible.

The game starts with the computer randomly playing a sound and lighting up the corresponding colored button. The player is then responsible for pressing the same button. Then, the computer adds another sound to the sequence and plays back the entire sequence. The player then attempts to match the sequence. Play continues until the player fails to correctly repeat the sequence.

In the real game, the player has only a limited time to press any particular button in the sequence. To keep things simple, you will not implement a timer or scoring, just the code to track and play a sequence and ensure that the player correctly plays back the sequence. Figure 9-1 shows the application in action.

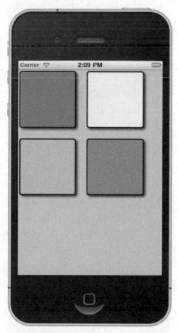

FIGURE 9-1: The RepeatIt game

I made the sounds for the game by using Garage Band, a part of the iLife suite that comes on each Mac computer. I edited the sound files that I exported from Garage Band by using the free sound editor, Audacity. Using Garage Band and Audacity is beyond the scope of this book, but I thought that it was worthwhile to mention that you can make the sounds for just about any game by using free tools available to all Mac users.

1. To begin, start up Xcode and select File ➪ New ➪ New Project.

2. The familiar dialog box appears that displays templates for the various types of applications that you can create for iOS and Mac OS X. Select Single View Application from the dialog box and click the Next button.

3. In the Product Name text box, type the name of your project, **RepeatIt**. Uncheck the "Use Storyboard" and "Include Unit Tests" checkboxes. Make sure that the "Use Automatic Reference Counting" checkbox is checked. Select "iPhone" from the Device Family dropdown. Press the Next button.

4. Select a location to save your project, and click Create. Xcode will create your project and present the project window.

5. Next, you need to import the sounds and images into your project. You can download these graphics and sound files from the book's website.

6. Create a new File Group to hold the images that you will use by selecting File ➪ New ➪ New Group from the menu bar. Call the new group Images.

7. Select File ➪ Add files to RepeatIt from the menu bar and add the image files (`0.png`, `0_light.png`, `1.png`, `1_light.png`, `2.png`, `2_light.png`, `3.png`, `3_light.png`) to the Images folder. You can obtain the image files for this project from the book's website. Check the box that says, "Copy items into destination group's folder (if needed)." Click Add to add the images to your project. Each image has a dark and a light version. You will use the light version as the standard image and the darker, more saturated version as the highlighted image. You will switch between the two images to display the highlighted image as a sound is playing.

8. Create a new File Group to hold the sounds by selecting File ➪ New ➪ New Group from the menu bar. Call the new group Sound.

9. Select File ➪ Add files to RepeatIt from the menu bar and add the sound files (`0.aiff`, `1.aiff`, `2.aiff`, `3.aiff`) to the Sound folder. You can obtain the sound files for this project from the book's website as well. Check the box that says, "Copy items into destination group's folder (if needed)." Click Add to add the images to your project.

10. Since you will be using the `AVAudioPlayer` class, which is contained in the AVFoundation framework, you need to add the framework to your project. Click RepeatIt project icon at the top of the Project Navigator view to bring up the project properties. In the editor window, under the heading Targets, click RepeatIt. Click on the tab at the top of the Editor window labeled Build Phases. Expand the item that says, "Link Binary With Libraries." Click the plus sign at the bottom of the "Link Binary With Libraries." table. In the dialog that comes up, select AVFoundation.framework and click Add.

11. To keep this program simple, you will not implement the MVC design pattern. For this simple game, you will implement all of the code in the `ViewController`. Open the `ViewController.h`

header file. Since you will be using the AVFoundation framework, you need to add a #import statement to import the AVFoundation header:

```
#import <AVFoundation/AVfoundation.h>
```

12. Add a couple of constants that you will use to lay out the buttons:

```
#define IMAGE_SIZE      140
#define SPACING         10
```

13. Since you will be implementing the AVAudioPlayerDelegate protocol in the ViewController, you need to add the protocol declaration to the class declaration. Change the @interface to add the protocol declaration like this:

```
@interface ViewController : UIViewController <AVAudioPlayerDelegate> {
```

14. Add the instance variables that you will be using in the game to the @interface block:

```
// The button images
UIImageView *image0;
UIImageView *image1;
UIImageView *image2;
UIImageView *image3;

// Track if a sequence is playing
BOOL playingSequence;

// The computer's button sequence
NSMutableArray* sequence;

// The audio players
AVAudioPlayer *audioPlayer0;
AVAudioPlayer *audioPlayer1;
AVAudioPlayer *audioPlayer2;
AVAudioPlayer *audioPlayer3;

int buttonCounter;
```

15. Outside of the @interface block, add the method declarations:

```
-(void) loadImages;
-(void) addToSequence;
-(void) playSequence;
-(void) playButton:(int) buttonNumber;
-(void) endGameWithMessage:(NSString*) message;
-(void) playerFinished;
```

16. Now you are ready to implement the game. Switch over to the ViewController.m implementation file. Implement the viewDidLoad method to initialize the game:

```
- (void)viewDidLoad
{
    [super viewDidLoad];

    // Load the images
    [self loadImages];
```

```objc
// Initialize the playingSequence flag
playingSequence = NO;

// Initialize the sequence
sequence = [[NSMutableArray alloc] initWithCapacity:100];

// Seed the random number generator
srandom( time( NULL ) );

// Init the audio players and load the sound files
NSURL *sound0URL = [NSURL fileURLWithPath:
                    [[NSBundle mainBundle] pathForResource: @"0"
                                             ofType: @"aiff"]];

audioPlayer0 = [[AVAudioPlayer alloc]
               initWithContentsOfURL:sound0URL error:nil];

NSURL *sound1URL = [NSURL fileURLWithPath:
                    [[NSBundle mainBundle] pathForResource: @"1"
                                             ofType: @"aiff"]];

audioPlayer1 = [[AVAudioPlayer alloc]
               initWithContentsOfURL:sound1URL error:nil];

NSURL *sound2URL = [NSURL fileURLWithPath:
                    [[NSBundle mainBundle] pathForResource: @"2"
                                             ofType: @"aiff"]];

audioPlayer2 = [[AVAudioPlayer alloc]
               initWithContentsOfURL:sound2URL error:nil];

NSURL *sound3URL = [NSURL fileURLWithPath:
                    [[NSBundle mainBundle] pathForResource: @"3"
                                             ofType: @"aiff"]];

audioPlayer3 = [[AVAudioPlayer alloc]
               initWithContentsOfURL:sound3URL error:nil];

// Set up the audio player delegates
[audioPlayer0 setDelegate: self];
[audioPlayer1 setDelegate: self];
[audioPlayer2 setDelegate: self];
[audioPlayer3 setDelegate: self];

// Prepare to play sounds
[audioPlayer0 prepareToPlay];
[audioPlayer1 prepareToPlay];
[audioPlayer2 prepareToPlay];
[audioPlayer3 prepareToPlay];

// Configure the audio session
NSError *setCategoryErr = nil;
[[AVAudioSession sharedInstance]
 setCategory: AVAudioSessionCategoryAmbient
 error: &setCategoryErr];
```

```objc
    // Start the game by adding the first note to the sequence
    [self addToSequence];

    // Play the sequence
    [self playSequence];

}
```

17. Implement the `loadImages` method, which loads the normal and highlight images and positions them in the view:

```objc
-(void) loadImages
{
    // Load the image views
    image0 = [[UIImageView alloc]
              initWithImage: [UIImage imageNamed:@"0_light.png"]
              highlightedImage: [UIImage imageNamed:@"0.png"]];
    image1 = [[UIImageView alloc]
              initWithImage: [UIImage imageNamed:@"1_light.png"]
              highlightedImage: [UIImage imageNamed:@"1.png"]];
    image2 = [[UIImageView alloc]
              initWithImage: [UIImage imageNamed:@"2_light.png"]
              highlightedImage: [UIImage imageNamed:@"2.png"]];
    image3 = [[UIImageView alloc]
              initWithImage: [UIImage imageNamed:@"3_light.png"]
              highlightedImage: [UIImage imageNamed:@"3.png"]];

    // Size and position the images
    CGRect position = CGRectMake(0, 0, IMAGE_SIZE, IMAGE_SIZE);
    image0.frame = position;
    [self.view addSubview:image0];

    position = CGRectMake(IMAGE_SIZE+SPACING, 0, IMAGE_SIZE, IMAGE_SIZE);
    image1.frame = position;
    [self.view addSubview:image1];

    position = CGRectMake(0, IMAGE_SIZE+SPACING,IMAGE_SIZE, IMAGE_SIZE);
    image2.frame = position;
    [self.view addSubview:image2];

    position = CGRectMake(IMAGE_SIZE+SPACING, IMAGE_SIZE+SPACING,
                          IMAGE_SIZE, IMAGE_SIZE);
    image3.frame = position;
    [self.view addSubview:image3];

    // Enable touch on images
    image0.userInteractionEnabled=YES;
    image1.userInteractionEnabled=YES;
    image2.userInteractionEnabled=YES;
    image3.userInteractionEnabled=YES;

    // Set view tags used to identify each view
    image0.tag=0;
    image1.tag=1;
    image2.tag=2;
```

```
    image3.tag=3;

}
```

18. Implement the `addToSequence` method, which you call when you want to add a new button press to the sound sequence:

```
-(void) addToSequence
{
    // Pick a random number from 0 to 3
    int randomNum = (random() % 4);

    // Add the number to the sequence
    [sequence addObject:[NSNumber numberWithInt:randomNum]];

}
```

19. Implement the `playSequence` method, which plays back the computer's sequence of sounds:

```
-(void) playSequence
{
    // Reset the button counter
    buttonCounter = 0;

    // Sequence is playing
    playingSequence=YES;

    // Play the first button
    [self playButton:
     [(NSNumber*)[sequence objectAtIndex:buttonCounter] intValue]];
}
```

20. Implement the `playButton:` method, which you call when you want to play the sound and switch to the highlight image for any of the buttons:

```
-(void) playButton:(int) buttonNumber
{


    // Highlight the image and play the sound
    switch (buttonNumber) {
        case 0:
            image0.highlighted = YES;
            audioPlayer0.currentTime = 0;
            [audioPlayer0 play];
            break;
        case 1:
            image1.highlighted = YES;
            audioPlayer1.currentTime = 0;
            [audioPlayer1 play];

            break;
        case 2:
            image2.highlighted = YES;
            audioPlayer2.currentTime = 0;
            [audioPlayer2 play];
```

```
                break;
        case 3:
            image3.highlighted = YES;
            audioPlayer3.currentTime = 0;
            [audioPlayer3 play];

            break;
        default:
            break;
    }


}
```

21. Implement the AVAudioPlayerDelegate delegate method
audioPlayerDidFinishPlaying:successfully:, which the AVAudioPlayer calls when it has
finished playing a sound:

```
- (void) audioPlayerDidFinishPlaying: (AVAudioPlayer *) player
                    successfully: (BOOL) completed {

    if (completed == YES) {

        // Finished playing a sound


        // Depending of the file that was played, un-highlight
        // the appropriate button
        NSString *urlString = [player.url lastPathComponent];
        if ([urlString isEqualToString:@"0.aiff"])
        {
            image0.highlighted = NO;
        }
        else if([urlString isEqualToString:@"1.aiff"])
        {
            image1.highlighted = NO;
        }
        else if([urlString isEqualToString:@"2.aiff"])
        {
            image2.highlighted = NO;
        }
        else if([urlString isEqualToString:@"3.aiff"])
        {
            image3.highlighted = NO;
        }

        // If we are playing the computer sequence
        if (playingSequence)
        {
            // Increment the button counter and see if we are finished
            if (++buttonCounter<[sequence count])
            {
                // Not finished the sequence
                // play the next button
                [self playButton:
                  [(NSNumber*)[sequence objectAtIndex:buttonCounter] intValue]];

            }
```

```
            else
            {
                // Finished the sequence
                // Reset the button counter
                buttonCounter=0;

                // Indicate that the sequence is finished playing
                playingSequence=NO;
            }
        }
    }

}
```

22. Implement the `touchesBegan:withEvent:` method to handle user interaction with the buttons:

```
- (void)touchesBegan:(NSSet *)touches withEvent:(UIEvent *)event
{
    // User needs to repeat the sequence

    // Ignore user input if playing the sequence or the player is finished

    if(!playingSequence && buttonCounter < [sequence count])     {

        // Get any touch
        UITouch* t = [touches anyObject];

        // If the touch was on a UIImageView
        if ([t.view class] == [UIImageView class])
        {
            // Get the tappedImageView
            UIImageView *tappedImageView = (UIImageView*) t.view;

            // Play the sound
            [self playButton:tappedImageView.tag];

            // Get the correct button for the location in the sequence
            int correctButton =
                [(NSNumber*)[sequence objectAtIndex:buttonCounter] intValue];

            // Did the user tap the correct button?
            if (tappedImageView.tag == correctButton)
            {
                // Player tapped correct button
                buttonCounter++;

                // Is the sequence complete?
                if ([sequence count]==buttonCounter)
                {
                    // Player played all sounds so wait 2 seconds then
                    // run the playerFinished routine
                    [self performSelector:@selector(playerFinished)
                            withObject:nil afterDelay:2.0];

                }

            }
```

```
            else
            {
                // Player tapped incorrect button
                [self endGameWithMessage:@"You missed."];
            }

        }
    }

}
```

23. Implement the `playerFinished` method, which you call when the player has successfully finished playing all of the sounds in the sound sequence:

```
-(void) playerFinished
{
    // The player correctly finished the sequence
    // Add a new note to the sequence
    [self addToSequence];

    // Play the sequence back
    [self playSequence];

}
```

24. Implement the `endGameWithMessage:` method to display an alert box when the player incorrectly attempts to repeat the sequence:

```
-(void) endGameWithMessage:(NSString*) message
{
    // Call this method to end the game
    // Show an alert with the results
    UIAlertView *alert = [[UIAlertView alloc] initWithTitle:@"Game Over"
                                            message:message
                                            delegate:self
                                  cancelButtonTitle:@"OK"
                                  otherButtonTitles: nil];
    [alert show];
}
```

25. Implement the `alertView:didDismissWithButtonIndex:` alert view delegate method to reset the game after the player acknowledges that he incorrectly played the sequence:

```
- (void)alertView:(UIAlertView *)alertView
didDismissWithButtonIndex:(NSInteger)buttonIndex
{
    // User acknowledged the alert
    // Reset the game and start again
    [sequence removeAllObjects];
    buttonCounter=0;
    [self addToSequence];

    // Play the sequence back
    [self playSequence];
```

26. Finally, implement the `viewDidUnload` method to clean up your instance variables:

```
- (void)viewDidUnload
{
    // Release any retained subviews of the main view.
    image0=nil;
    image1=nil;
    image2=nil;
    image3=nil;

    sequence=nil;

    audioPlayer0=nil;
    audioPlayer1=nil;
    audioPlayer2=nil;
    audioPlayer3=nil;

    [super viewDidUnload];


}
```

27. Build and run the game. The game starts with the computer playing a sound and highlighting the corresponding button. Tap the highlighted button. The computer will randomly select another button and then play back the sequence of the first button and the new, second, button. Tap the buttons in sequence. Keep playing until you cannot repeat the sequence correctly. When you fail, the computer should inform you that you have not played the sequence correctly with an alert. When you acknowledge the alert, the game will start over again.

How It Works

The first thing that you needed to do to start the project was work in the `RepeatItViewController.h` header file. First, you added a `#import` statement to import the AVFoundation header because you used classes from AVFoundation like `AVAudioPlayer`:

```
#import <AVFoundation/AVfoundation.h>
```

Next, you added a couple of constants for laying out the buttons in the application:

```
#define IMAGE_SIZE      140
#define SPACING         10
```

You could use Interface Builder to build the interface for this game, but since the interface was only a few buttons, I figured that it would be just as easy to do it in code. Since I was not sure what size and spacing would work the best, I set up these constants and then used the constants in the layout code. That way, I could tweak the size and spacing of the buttons by changing the values of these constants without messing with the code.

In addition, using constants makes the code easier to read. Instead of having the magic numbers of 140 and 10 in the code, you see the constants `IMAGE_SIZE` and `SPACING`.

Since you needed to take action when a sound finished playing, you had to declare the view controller as implementing the `AVAudioPlayerDelegate` protocol:

```
@interface RepeatItViewController : UIViewController <AVAudioPlayerDelegate> {
```

This allows you to set the view controller as a delegate for the `AVAudioPlayers` that you used to play the sounds for the game. Then, when an audio player finishes playing, it calls the `audioPlayerDidFinishPlaying:successfully:` delegate method.

Next, you added the instance variables that you needed for the game. First, you added image views to hold the game button images:

```
UIImageView *image0;
UIImageView *image1;
UIImageView *image2;
UIImageView *image3;
```

Next, you added a `BOOL` variables: to track if the computer is playing back its sequence:

```
// Track if a sequence is playing
BOOL playingSequence;

// Is a sound playing?
BOOL playingSound;
```

You also needed an instance variable to keep track of the computer's sequence of notes:

```
// The computer's button sequence
NSMutableArray* sequence;
```

You then added instance variables for players for each of the sounds:

```
// The audio players
AVAudioPlayer *audioPlayer0;
AVAudioPlayer *audioPlayer1;
AVAudioPlayer *audioPlayer2;
AVAudioPlayer *audioPlayer3;
```

I decided to use a separate audio player for each sound because I wanted to have the players ready to play their sound as quickly as possible. It takes some time to initialize a player and prepare it to play a sound. Therefore, by preloading the sound files into four individual players, you incur the overhead of loading and preparing to play each sound only once. The drawback to this approach is that you consume more memory because you have all four sounds loaded into memory at the same time.

On a side note, if you wanted to play multiple sounds simultaneously, you would need to follow this approach as well because an `AVAudioPlayer` can only play one sound at a time. However, multiple audio players can be playing different sounds simultaneously.

Finally, you added an `int` instance member to track which button in the sequence the computer is currently playing or which button the computer is waiting for the player to play:

```
int buttonCounter;
```

After you finished with the instance member declarations, you added method declarations for the methods that you would implement in the view controller:

```
-(void) loadImages;
-(void) addToSequence;
-(void) playSequence;
-(void) playButton:(int) buttonNumber;
-(void) endGameWithMessage:(NSString*) message;
-(void) playerFinished;
```

After you finished with the header, you started to implement the game. First, you implemented the viewDidLoad method to initialize the game. As usual, when you override a base class method, you always need to call the super version of the method:

```
- (void)viewDidLoad
{
    [super viewDidLoad];
```

Next, you called your implementation of the loadImages method to load the images and configure the user interface of the game:

```
    // Load the images
    [self loadImages];
```

Then, you initialized the playingSequence flag, initialized the computer sequence array, and seeded the random number generator:

```
    // Initialize the playingSequence flag
    playingSequence = NO;

    // Initialize the sequence
    sequence = [[NSMutableArray alloc] initWithCapacity:100];

    //  Seed the random number generator
    srandom( time( NULL ) );
```

After that, you initialized each of the audio players and loaded the appropriate sound file into each player. First, you created an NSURL that represented the location of the sound file that you wanted to play in the player:

```
    NSURL *sound0URL = [NSURL fileURLWithPath:
                        [[NSBundle mainBundle] pathForResource: @"0"
                                                         ofType: @"aiff"]];
```

Then, you allocated a player and initialized it with the sound URL that you just created:

```
    audioPlayer0 = [[AVAudioPlayer alloc]
                    initWithContentsOfURL:sound0URL error:nil];
```

You then repeated this process for the other three sound players by using the appropriate sound files:

```
    NSURL *sound1URL = [NSURL fileURLWithPath:
                        [[NSBundle mainBundle] pathForResource: @"1"
                                                         ofType: @"aiff"]];

    audioPlayer1 = [[AVAudioPlayer alloc]
                    initWithContentsOfURL:sound1URL error:nil];

    NSURL *sound2URL = [NSURL fileURLWithPath:
                        [[NSBundle mainBundle] pathForResource: @"2"
                                                         ofType: @"aiff"]];

    audioPlayer2 = [[AVAudioPlayer alloc]
                    initWithContentsOfURL:sound2URL error:nil];

    NSURL *sound3URL = [NSURL fileURLWithPath:
                        [[NSBundle mainBundle] pathForResource: @"3"
                                                         ofType: @"aiff"]];
```

```
audioPlayer3 = [[AVAudioPlayer alloc]
                 initWithContentsOfURL:sound3URL error:nil];
```

After you loaded the sounds, you set the delegate for each audio player to `self`:

```
// Set up the audio player delegates
[audioPlayer0 setDelegate: self];
[audioPlayer1 setDelegate: self];
[audioPlayer2 setDelegate: self];
[audioPlayer3 setDelegate: self];
```

This tells the audio players to call the `AVAudioPlayerDelegate` delegate methods on the view controller when appropriate. You needed to do this because you used the completion of the sound to trigger some actions like un-highlighting the button that was played and playing the next button in the sequence.

After you set the delegate for each player, you called the `prepareToPlay` method on each player:

```
// Prepare to play sounds
[audioPlayer0 prepareToPlay];
[audioPlayer1 prepareToPlay];
[audioPlayer2 prepareToPlay];
[audioPlayer3 prepareToPlay];
```

The `prepareToPlay` method preloads the buffers for the audio player allowing it to start more quickly when you ultimately call the `play` method to start audio playback. While you do not necessarily need to call `prepareToPlay`, calling the method reduces lag time from the time that you call the `play` method to the time that the sound actually starts playing.

After pre-loading the buffers and preparing for playback, you configured the audio session:

```
// Configure the audio session
NSError *setCategoryErr = nil;
[[AVAudioSession sharedInstance]
 setCategory: AVAudioSessionCategoryAmbient
 error: &setCategoryErr];
```

I thought that it would be interesting to allow the player to continue iTunes playback while playing the game, so I decided to set the audio session category to `AVAudioSessionCategoryAmbient`. If you wanted to stop other sounds while your game is playing, you can use the `AVAudioSessionCategorySoloAmbient` category that stops audio from any source other than your game.

Finally, you started the game by adding the first note to the computer sequence by calling the `addToSequence` method and then calling the `playSequence` method to play the sequence:

```
// Start the game by adding the first note to the sequence
[self addToSequence];

// Play the sequence
[self playSequence];
```

The next method that you implemented was `loadImages`. This method loads the images and configures the user interface of the game.

To make the buttons appear to light up, I created two images for each button, a normal, light colored image, and a darker, more saturated image. You can see the button images in Figure 9-2.

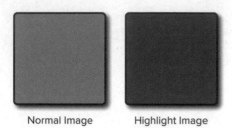

Normal Image   Highlight Image

FIGURE 9-2: Normal and Highlight button images

In the `loadImages` method, you loaded the light version of the button as the default image and the darker version as the `highlightedImage` for each of the four image views used as buttons:

```
// Load the image views
image0 = [[UIImageView alloc]
            initWithImage: [UIImage imageNamed:@"0_light.png"]
            highlightedImage: [UIImage imageNamed:@"0.png"]];
image1 = [[UIImageView alloc]
            initWithImage: [UIImage imageNamed:@"1_light.png"]
            highlightedImage: [UIImage imageNamed:@"1.png"]];
image2 = [[UIImageView alloc]
            initWithImage: [UIImage imageNamed:@"2_light.png"]
            highlightedImage: [UIImage imageNamed:@"2.png"]];
image3 = [[UIImageView alloc]
            initWithImage: [UIImage imageNamed:@"3_light.png"]
            highlightedImage: [UIImage imageNamed:@"3.png"]];
```

Loading the images in this way, with normal and highlighted images, allows you to easily switch between the two by toggling the `highlighted` property of the `UIImageView`. You will see this when you look at how the `playButton:` method works.

After loading the image files into the `UIImageViews`, you went on to size and position the images and add them as subviews to the view controller's view:

```
// Size and position the images
CGRect position = CGRectMake(0, 0, IMAGE_SIZE, IMAGE_SIZE);
image0.frame = position;
[self.view addSubview:image0];

position = CGRectMake(IMAGE_SIZE+SPACING, 0, IMAGE_SIZE, IMAGE_SIZE);
image1.frame = position;
[self.view addSubview:image1];

position = CGRectMake(0, IMAGE_SIZE+SPACING,IMAGE_SIZE, IMAGE_SIZE);
image2.frame = position;
[self.view addSubview:image2];

position = CGRectMake(IMAGE_SIZE+SPACING, IMAGE_SIZE+SPACING,
                      IMAGE_SIZE, IMAGE_SIZE);
image3.frame = position;
[self.view addSubview:image3];
```

You used the `IMAGE_SIZE` and `SPACING` constants to lay out the images. Using constants makes it easier for programmers unfamiliar with the code to understand what you are doing. Additionally, using constants allows you to easily tweak the layout by changing the constants in the header as opposed to changing numbers in many places in this method.

By default, the `UIImageView` class does not respond to user interaction. Since you are using these image views as buttons, you needed to enable user interaction so you could react when the player touches an image view. You did this by setting the `userInteractionEnabled` to `YES` for each image view:

```
// Enable touch on images
image0.userInteractionEnabled=YES;
image1.userInteractionEnabled=YES;
image2.userInteractionEnabled=YES;
image3.userInteractionEnabled=YES;
```

Finally, you used `tags` to identify each view. The `UIImageView` inherits that `tag` property from the `UIView` class. A `tag` is an integer value that you can use to identify the view. Later, in the `touchesBegan:withEvent:` method, you will use the `tag` to determine if the player touched the correct button and which sound to play.

The next method that you built was `addToSequence`. You call this method when you want to add a new button and sound to the computer's sequence of sounds. In this method, you first pick a random number from 0 to 3 to determine which button you will add to the sequence:

```
// Pick a random number from 0 to 3
int randomNum = (random() % 4);
```

Then, you add the number to the sequence array:

```
// Add the number to the sequence
[sequence addObject:[NSNumber numberWithInt:randomNum]];
```

If you recall, you cannot hold basic data types like `int` in an Objective-C array. Objective-C arrays can hold only Objective-C objects. Therefore, you converted the `int` into an Objective-C `NSNumber` using the `numberWithInt:` class method. Then, you added that object to the array.

Next, you implemented the `playSequence` method. This method starts the playback of the computer's sequence of sounds. You started the method by initializing the `buttonCounter` to zero and setting the `playingSequence` flag to `YES`:

```
// Reset the button counter
buttonCounter = 0;

// Sequence is playing
playingSequence=YES;
```

Then, you played the first button by calling the `playButton:` method:

```
// Play the first button
[self playButton:
  [(NSNumber*)[sequence objectAtIndex:buttonCounter] intValue]];
```

After the first button finished playing, the `audioPlayerDidFinishPlaying:successfully:` method plays each subsequent button in the sequence, as you will see shortly. Instead of looping through each button in this method, it made more sense to wait until each sound finished playing before playing the next sound. That way, it was not necessary to write any code to determine if the sound was finished before moving on to the next one.

Next, you implemented the code to play the sound and switch to the highlight image for any of the buttons in the `playButton:` method. This method accepts an integer number and plays the appropriate button.

In this method, you changed the image view to the highlighted version of the image and played the appropriate sound based on the `buttonNumber` that was passed in to the method by using a `switch` statement:

```
// Highlight the image and play the sound
switch (buttonNumber) {
    case 0:
        image0.highlighted = YES;
        audioPlayer0.currentTime = 0;
        [audioPlayer0 play];

        break;
    case 1:
        image1.highlighted = YES;
        audioPlayer1.currentTime = 0;
        [audioPlayer1 play];

        break;
    case 2:
        image2.highlighted = YES;
        audioPlayer2.currentTime = 0;
        [audioPlayer2 play];

        break;
    case 3:
        image3.highlighted = YES;
        audioPlayer3.currentTime = 0;
        [audioPlayer3 play];

        break;
    default:
        break;
}
```

You can see that switching from the default to the highlighted image is as simple as setting the `highlighted` property to YES.

Next, you set the playhead back to the beginning of the sound by setting the `currentTime` property to 0. This prevents the sound from playing only once even if the player pressed the button multiple times. To reproduce this problem, comment out each line that sets the `currentTime` to 0. Then, when you get a sequence in which the same button plays twice in a row, press that button rapidly two times. You should notice that you only hear the sound one time. Setting the current time to 0 prevents this by restarting the sound each time the player presses the button.

Finally, you played the sound by calling the `play` method on the correct `AVAudioPlayer`.

The next method that you implemented was `audioPlayerDidFinishPlaying:successfully:`. This is the `AVAudioPlayerDelegate` delegate method that the `AVAudioPlayer` calls when it has finished playing a sound.

First, you verified that the sound completed playing successfully:

```
if (completed == YES) {
```

In this simple example, there is no error handling. In a production game, you might want to add some code to handle the case where the sound could not complete playing successfully if playing the sound was important to the game.

Next, you set the `playingSound` flag to NO to indicate that a sound is no longer playing:

```
// Finished playing a sound
playingSound=NO;
```

Next, you un-highlighted the appropriate button image based on the sound that just finished playing. The AVAudioPlayer object `player` that this function receives contains information about the player that has just finished playing a sound. You got the `url` parameter from the player that contains the NSURL that points to the sound file that the player has played. From this URL, you determined the filename by calling the `lastPathComponent` of the NSURL:

```
// Depending of the file that was played, un-highlight
// the appropriate button
NSString *urlString = [player.url lastPathComponent];
```

Depending on the filename, you un-highlighted the appropriate button:

```
if ([urlString isEqualToString:@"0.aiff"])
{
    image0.highlighted = NO;
}
else if([urlString isEqualToString:@"1.aiff"])
{
    image1.highlighted = NO;
}
else if([urlString isEqualToString:@"2.aiff"])
{
    image2.highlighted = NO;
}
else if([urlString isEqualToString:@"3.aiff"])
{
    image3.highlighted = NO;
}
```

This was all that you needed to do if the player played the sound that was playing. However, if the computer sequence was playing, you needed to add code to continue the sequence or finish the sequence. So, you checked to see if you were playing the computer sequence:

```
// If we are playing the computer sequence
if (playingSequence)
```

If you were playing the computer sequence, you checked to see if you were finished playing the sequence by incrementing the `buttonCounter` and comparing the new value to the number of items in the sequence array:

```
// Increment the button counter and see if we are finished
if (++buttonCounter<[sequence count])
```

Notice how you used the prefix version of the ++ operator. In this case, you needed to increment the buttonCounter before you compared it to the count of the sequence array.

If the buttonCounter was less than the number of elements in the sequence, you were not finished playing the sequence, so you called the playButton: method to play the next button:

```
// Not finished the sequence
// play the next button
[self playButton:
  [(NSNumber*)[sequence objectAtIndex:buttonCounter] intValue]];
```

If you were finished, you reset the button counter and indicated that the sequence was finished by setting the playingSequence flag to NO:

```
else
{
    // Finished the sequence
    // Reset the button counter
    buttonCounter=0;

    // Indicate that the sequence is finished playing
    playingSequence=NO;
}
```

Next, you needed to add user interaction to the game. Therefore, you implemented the touchesBegan:withEvent: method to handle user touches.

First, you checked the playingSequence and buttonCounter variables to prevent user interaction while the sequence was playing:

```
// Ignore user input if playing the sequence or the player is finished
if(!playingSequence && buttonCounter < [sequence count])    {
```

If the sequence was not playing and if the player was not finished with the sequence, you would handle the touch. First, you needed to retrieve the touch by using the anyObject method of the touches collection that the method receives:

```
// Get any touch
UITouch* t = [touches anyObject];
```

Next, you added code to only handle touches when the player touches a UIImageView. You did this by comparing the class of the view that the player touched with the UIImageView class:

```
// If the touch was on a UIImageView
if ([t.view class] == [UIImageView class])
```

The class method returns a Class object that represents the class of any given object. You can compare class values to determine if an object is of a certain type.

Next, you retrieved a reference to the view that the player tapped:

```
// Get the tappedImageView
UIImageView *tappedImageView = (UIImageView*) t.view;
```

Then, you used the tag of that view to call the playButton method to play the appropriate sound and highlight the correct button:

```
// Play the sound
[self playButton:tappedImageView.tag];
```

Next, you retrieved the button in the sequence that the player was supposed to touch, to compare it with the button that the player actually touched:

```
// Get the correct button for the location in the sequence
int correctButton =
    [(NSNumber*)[sequence objectAtIndex:buttonCounter] intValue];
```

Then you compared the two buttons to see if the player did in fact touch the correct button:

```
// Did the user tap the correct button?
if (tappedImageView.tag == correctButton)
```

If the player tapped the correct button, you incremented the `buttonCounter` because the player should now touch the next button in the sequence:

```
// Player tapped correct button
buttonCounter++;
```

Next, you checked to see if the player completed the sequence:

```
// Is the sequence complete?
if ([sequence count]==buttonCounter)
```

If the player completed the sequence successfully, you waited two seconds and then called the `playerFinished` method by using the `performSelector:withObject:afterDelay:` method:

```
// Player played all sounds so wait 2 seconds then
// run the playerFinished routine
[self performSelector:@selector(playerFinished)
        withObject:nil afterDelay:2.0];
```

The `performSelector:withObject:afterDelay:` method is a method of `NSObject` that allows you to call methods by name after a delay. Using this method allowed you to give the player a short break before the computer added a new sound to the sequence and began playing back the sequence again.

In case you were wondering how I knew to put this delay in there, I will tell you. I determined that I needed this pause by play testing the game. Playing your game during development is an absolute necessity. Without this pause, the computer started playing the sequence back too quickly, which made it difficult to play the game.

Finally, if the player did not tap the correct button, you ended the game:

```
else
{
    // Player tapped incorrect button
    [self endGameWithMessage:@"You missed."];
}
```

Next, you built the `playerFinished` method, which you called by using the `performSelector` method when the player finished playing all of the sounds in the sound sequence. This method adds a new item to the sequence by using the `addToSequence` method and then plays back the sequence using the `playSequence` method:

```
// The player correctly finished the sequence
// Add a new note to the sequence
```

```
[self addToSequence];

// Play the sequence back
[self playSequence];
```

To finish the game, you had to write a few more methods to handle the end of the game. First, you built the `endGameWithMessage:` method to display an alert box when the player repeated the sequence incorrectly. In this method, you created a `UIAlertView` to display the message:

```
// Call this method to end the game
// Show an alert with the results
UIAlertView *alert = [[UIAlertView alloc] initWithTitle:@"Game Over"
                                         message:message
                                         delegate:self
                                 cancelButtonTitle:@"OK"
                                 otherButtonTitles: nil];
```

Then, you displayed the alert with the `show` method:

```
[alert show];
```

After the user acknowledged the alert, you wanted to start a new game. Therefore, you needed to implement the `alertView:didDismissWithButtonIndex:` alert view delegate method to reset the game.

First, the method resets the computer sequence by calling the `removeAllObjects` method on the sequence:

```
// User acknowledged the alert
// Reset the game and start again
[sequence removeAllObjects];
```

Calling the `removeAllObjects` method removes each object from the array.

Next, you reset the `buttonCounter`:

```
buttonCounter=0;
```

Finally, you restarted the game by calling `addToSequence` to add the first item to the computers sequence and by calling `playSequence` to play back the new sequence:

```
[self addToSequence];

// Play the sequence back
[self playSequence];
```

The last thing that you coded in this game was the `viewDidUnload` method. This method cleans up your instance variables.

First, you cleaned up your image views:

```
image0=nil;
image1=nil;
image2=nil;
image3=nil;
```

Then, you took care of the `sequence`:

```
sequence=nil;
```

Next, you cleaned up the audio players:

```
audioPlayer0=nil;
audioPlayer1=nil;
audioPlayer2=nil;
audioPlayer3=nil;
```

Finally, you called the superclass version of viewDidUnload:

```
[super viewDidUnload];
```

Playing Multiple Sounds Simultaneously

A major advantage of using the AVAudioPlayer class over System Sound Services in your games is that with the AVAudioPlayer, you can play multiple sounds simultaneously. To do this, you create multiple instances of the AVAudioPlayer class, configure, and play them as you saw in the last example. That is all there is to it.

One thing that you should note however is that the hardware decoder can decode only one audio stream at a time. Although decoding a single AAC, MP3, or ALAC formatted audio file can use hardware-assisted codecs, attempting to play a second file of one of these formats will result in software decoding. This has the potential to slow down your game because audio decoding takes some processor time.

To avoid this issue, you can store those sounds by using the IMA4 (compressed) or linear PCM (uncompressed) format. The IMA4 compressed format uses little CPU time for decompression, and uncompressed formats like PCM do not require decompression. As with most decisions in game development, there are tradeoffs. Sounds in IMA4 and especially PCM format have significantly larger file sizes than those compressed with other codecs. Therefore, you need to carefully consider the requirements of your game to determine the audio file formats for your game sounds.

Apple provides a command-line utility called afconvert that you can use to convert your audio files between various formats and codecs. The utility is located in /usr/bin/afconvert. A full discussion of using afconvert to convert between the various sound file formats is beyond the scope of this book. However, you can learn more about afconvert by launching the terminal in OS X and typing afconvert -h at the command prompt to get help about the utility. You can also type afconvert -hf to get more information about the sound formats that afconvert can work with.

Looping Sounds

One final advantage of using the AVAudioPlayer class over System Sound Services in your games is that with the AVAudioPlayer, you can loop your sounds. That is, you can configure that audio player to play the same sound multiple times in a loop. You can also configure the player to play a sound indefinitely until you stop it.

You use the numberOfLoops property to configure the number of times your sound will loop. By setting numberOfLoops to −1, you can tell the AVAudioPlayer to play your sound indefinitely. You will see this illustrated in the next example where you add sounds and music to the Blocker game that you built in Chapter 6.

TRY IT OUT **Adding Music and Sound to the Blocker Game**

codefile Blocker available for download at Wrox.com

In this section, you will add sound effects and music to the Blocker game that you built in Chapter 6. You will add a sound that you will play when the ball bounces off the paddle as well as a different sound that you will play when the ball collides with a brick. You will also add background music to the game.

This example will demonstrate playing multiple sounds simultaneously because you will play the background music the entire time that the game is running. As with the sounds from the RepeatIt game, I made the music for Blocker by using Garage Band. I used some of the pre-made loops that come with Garage Band and combined them to form a brief song. I edited the sound file that I exported from Garage Band by using the free sound editor, Audacity, to make sure that the song had no dead space at the end so that I could loop it seamlessly.

1. The first thing that you need to do is either open the existing Blocker project or make a copy of your existing Blocker project in a new location. Then, open the Blocker project.

2. Next, you need to import the sounds into your project. You can download these sound files from the book's website.

3. Create a new File Group to hold the sounds by selecting File ➪ New ➪ New Group from the menu bar. Call the new group **Sound**.

4. Select File ➪ Add files to Blocker from the menu bar and add the sound files (`0.aiff`, `2.aiff`, `BlockerMusic3.aiff`) to the Sound folder. To keep things simple, I reused two of the sounds from the RepeatIt game. You can obtain the sound files for this project from the book's website as well. Check the box that says, "Copy items into destination group's folder (if needed)." Click "Add" to add the images to your project.

5. Since you will be using the `AVAudioPlayer` class, which is contained in the AVFoundation framework, you need to add the framework to your project. Click on the Blocker project icon at the top of the Project Navigator view to bring up the project properties. In the editor window, under the heading Targets, click on Blocker. Click on the tab at the top of the Editor window labeled Build Phases. Expand the item that says, "Link Binary With Libraries." Click the plus sign at the bottom of the "Link Binary With Libraries." table. In the dialog that comes up, select AVFoundation .framework and click Add.

6. Open the `BlockerModel.h` header file. Since you will be using the AVFoundation framework, you need to add a `#import` statement to import the AVFoundation header:

```
#import <AVFoundation/AVfoundation.h>
```

7. Add two `AVAudioPlayer` instance members to the `@interface` block:

```
AVAudioPlayer *blockPlayer;
AVAudioPlayer *paddlePlayer;
```

8. You will use these players to play the sounds for when the ball collides with a block and when the ball collides with the paddle. The code for the `BlockerModel.h` header file should now look like this:

```
#import <Foundation/Foundation.h>
#import <AVFoundation/AVfoundation.h>
```

```
#import "BlockView.h"


#define BLOCK_HEIGHT 20.0
#define BLOCK_WIDTH  64.0
#define BALL_SIZE 20.0
#define VIEW_WIDTH 320.0
#define VIEW_HEIGHT 460.0

@interface BlockerModel : NSObject {
    NSMutableArray* blocks;
    CGRect paddleRect;
    CGRect ballRect;
    CGPoint ballVelocity;
    CGFloat lastTime;
    CGFloat timeDelta;

    AVAudioPlayer *blockPlayer;
    AVAudioPlayer *paddlePlayer;



}

@property (readonly) NSMutableArray* blocks;
@property (readonly) CGRect ballRect;
@property CGRect paddleRect;

-(void) updateModelWithTime:(CFTimeInterval) timestamp;
- (void) checkCollisionWithScreenEdges;
- (void) checkCollisionWithBlocks;
- (void) checkCollisionWithPaddle;

@end
```

9. Switch over to the `BlockerModel.m` implementation file. At the bottom of the init method, inside the `if (self)` block, add the following code to instantiate and prepare the audio players:

```
// Init audio players
NSURL *blockSoundURL = [NSURL fileURLWithPath: [[NSBundle mainBundle]
                                          pathForResource: @"0"
                                          ofType: @"aiff"]];

blockPlayer = [[AVAudioPlayer alloc] initWithContentsOfURL:blockSoundURL
                                          error:nil];

NSURL *paddleSoundURL = [NSURL fileURLWithPath: [[NSBundle mainBundle]
                                          pathForResource: @"2"
                                          ofType: @"aiff"]];

paddlePlayer = [[AVAudioPlayer alloc]
                initWithContentsOfURL:paddleSoundURL
                error:nil];

// Prepare to play sounds
```

```
[blockPlayer prepareToPlay];
[paddlePlayer prepareToPlay];
```

10. The complete `init` method should look like this:

```objc
- (id)init {
    self = [super init];

    if (self) {
        // Init blocks
        // The array to hold the blocks
        blocks = [[NSMutableArray alloc] initWithCapacity:15];

        BlockView* bv;

        for (int row = 0; row<=2; row++)
        {
            for (int col = 0; col<5; col++)
            {
                bv = [[BlockView alloc ]
                        initWithFrame: CGRectMake(col * BLOCK_WIDTH ,
                                                  row * BLOCK_HEIGHT,
                                                  BLOCK_WIDTH, BLOCK_HEIGHT)
                        color:row];

                // Add the tile to the view
                [blocks addObject:bv];

            }
        }

        // Set the paddle rect by using the size of the paddle image
        UIImage* paddleImage = [UIImage imageNamed:@"paddle.png"];
        CGSize paddleSize = [paddleImage size];
        paddleRect = CGRectMake(0.0, 420.0,
                                paddleSize.width, paddleSize.height);

        // Set the ball rect by using the size of the paddle image
        UIImage* ballImage = [UIImage imageNamed:@"ball.png"];
        CGSize ballSize = [ballImage size];
        ballRect = CGRectMake(180.0, 220.0,
                              ballSize.width, ballSize.height);

        // Set the initial velocity for the ball
        ballVelocity = CGPointMake(200.0, -200.0);

        // Initialize the lastTime
        lastTime = 0.0;

        // Init audio players
        NSURL *blockSoundURL = [NSURL fileURLWithPath: [[NSBundle mainBundle]
                                                        pathForResource: @"0"
                                                        ofType: @"aiff"]];

        blockPlayer = [[AVAudioPlayer alloc] initWithContentsOfURL:blockSoundURL
```

```
                                                      error:nil];

        NSURL *paddleSoundURL = [NSURL fileURLWithPath: [[NSBundle mainBundle]
                                                   pathForResource: @"2"
                                                   ofType: @"aiff"]];

        paddlePlayer = [[AVAudioPlayer alloc]
                      initWithContentsOfURL:paddleSoundURL
                      error:nil];

        // Prepare to play sounds
        [blockPlayer prepareToPlay];
        [paddlePlayer prepareToPlay];

    }

    return self;
}
```

11. To play the sound when the ball collides with a block, you will add code to the
    checkCollisionWithBlocks method. At the end of the if (CGRectIntersectsRect
    (bv.frame,ballRect)) block, before the break statement, add the following code to play the sound:

    ```
            // Play the block collision sound
            [blockPlayer play];
    ```

12. The revised checkCollisionWithBlocks method should look like this:

    ```
    - (void) checkCollisionWithBlocks {
        // Iterate over the blocks to see if a collision has happened
        for (BlockView* bv in blocks) {
            if (CGRectIntersectsRect(bv.frame,ballRect)) {
                // Flip the y velocity component
                ballVelocity.y = -ballVelocity.y;

                // Remove the block from the collection
                [blocks removeObject:bv];

                // remove the block's view from the superview
                [bv removeFromSuperview];

                // In a production game, you'd want to add to the player's score
                // here, when a block is hit. To keep this example
                // simple, we are not keeping score.

                // Play the block collision sound
                [blockPlayer play];

                break;
            }

        }

    }
    ```

13. To play the sound when the ball collides with the paddle, you will add code to the `checkCollisionWithPaddle` method. At the end of the `if (CGRectIntersectsRect(ballRect, paddleRect))` block, add the following code to play the sound:

```
// Play the paddle sound
paddlePlayer play];
```

14. The revised `checkCollisionWithPaddle` method should look like this:

```
- (void) checkCollisionWithPaddle {
    // Check to see if the paddle has blocked the ball
    if (CGRectIntersectsRect(ballRect,paddleRect)) {
        // Flip the y velocity component
        ballVelocity.y = -1 * abs( ballVelocity.y);

        // Play the paddle sound
        [paddlePlayer play];

    }
}
```

15. Next, you will add the music to the game. You will do this in the `ViewController`.

16. Open the `ViewController.h` header file. Since you will be using the AVFoundation framework, you need to add a `#import` statement to import the AVFoundation header:

```
#import <AVFoundation/AVfoundation.h>
```

17. Add an `AVAudioPlayer` instance member to the `@interface` block:

```
AVAudioPlayer *musicPlayer;
```

18. The updated `BlockerViewController.h` file should look like this:

```
#import <UIKit/UIKit.h>
#import <QuartzCore/QuartzCore.h>
#import <AVFoundation/AVfoundation.h>


#import "BlockView.h"
#import "BlockerModel.h"

@interface ViewController : UIViewController {
    BlockerModel* gameModel;
    CADisplayLink* gameTimer;
    UIImageView* ball;
    UIImageView* paddle;

    AVAudioPlayer *musicPlayer;


}

-(void) updateDisplay:(CADisplayLink*)sender ;
-(void) endGameWithMessage:(NSString*) message;

@end
```

19. In the `viewDidLoad` method under the line of code that adds that ball as a subview (`[self. view addSubview:ball];`) add the following code to initialize, configure, and start the music player:

```
// Init music player
NSURL *musicSoundURL = [NSURL fileURLWithPath: [[NSBundle mainBundle]
    pathForResource: @"BlockerMusic" ofType: @"aiff"]];

musicPlayer = [[AVAudioPlayer alloc] initWithContentsOfURL:musicSoundURL error:nil];

// Set to loop indefinitely
musicPlayer.numberOfLoops = -1;

// Set the volume
musicPlayer.volume = 0.3;

// Start the music
[musicPlayer play];
```

20. The modified `viewDidLoad` method should look like this:

```
- (void)viewDidLoad
{
    [super viewDidLoad];

    // initialize the game model
    gameModel = [[BlockerModel alloc] init];


    // Iterate over the blocks in the model, drawing them
    for (BlockView* bv in gameModel.blocks) {
        // Add the block to the array
        [self.view addSubview:bv];
    }


    // Draw the paddle
    paddle = [[UIImageView alloc] initWithImage:
                            [UIImage imageNamed:@"paddle.png"]];

    // Set the paddle position based on the model
    [paddle setFrame:gameModel.paddleRect];

    [self.view addSubview:paddle];

    // Draw the ball
    ball = [[UIImageView alloc] initWithImage:
            [UIImage imageNamed:@"ball.png"]];

    [ball setFrame:gameModel.ballRect];

    [self.view addSubview:ball];

    // Init music player
```

```
NSURL *musicSoundURL = [NSURL fileURLWithPath: [[NSBundle mainBundle]
    pathForResource: @"BlockerMusic" ofType: @"aiff"]];

musicPlayer = [[AVAudioPlayer alloc] initWithContentsOfURL:musicSoundURL error:nil];

// Set to loop indefinitely
musicPlayer.numberOfLoops = -1;

// Set the volume
musicPlayer.volume = 0.3;

// Start the music
[musicPlayer play];

// Set up the CADisplayLink for the animation
gameTimer = [CADisplayLink displayLinkWithTarget:self
                                        selector:@selector(updateDisplay:)];


// Add the display link to the current run loop
[gameTimer addToRunLoop:[NSRunLoop currentRunLoop]
            forMode:NSDefaultRunLoopMode];

}
```

21. Add the following code to the `endGameWithMessage:` method to stop the music when the game ends:

```
// Stop the music
[musicPlayer stop];
```

22. The `endGameWithMessage` method should now look like this:

```
-(void) endGameWithMessage:(NSString*) message
{
    // Call this method to end the game
    // Invalidate the timer
    [gameTimer invalidate];

    // Stop the music
    [musicPlayer stop];

    // Show an alert with the results
    UIAlertView *alert = [[UIAlertView alloc] initWithTitle:@"Game Over"
                                            message:message
                                            delegate:self
                                    cancelButtonTitle:@"OK"
                                    otherButtonTitles: nil];

    [alert show];
}
```

23. Build and run the game. You should hear the funky music playing as the game starts. Each time the ball hits either a block or the paddle, you should hear a sound. If you do not hear anything, make sure that you have the volume turned up on your computer or the device if you are running on a device.

How It Works

The first thing that you did was add sound effects to the `BlockerModel`. By using separate instances of the `AVAudioPlayer`, you enabled your application to play the music and sounds simultaneously. In the `BlockerModel` implementation file, you modified the `init` method to instantiate and prepare the audio players. First, you created an `NSURL` that pointed to the sound that you wanted to load into the `blockPlayer` audio player:

```
NSURL *blockSoundURL = [NSURL fileURLWithPath: [[NSBundle mainBundle]
                                     pathForResource: @"0"
                                     ofType: @"aiff"]];
```

Then, you initialized the audio player with that `NSURL`:

```
blockPlayer = [[AVAudioPlayer alloc] initWithContentsOfURL:blockSoundURL
                                     error:nil];
```

You did the same for the `paddlePlayer`.

```
NSURL *paddleSoundURL = [NSURL fileURLWithPath: [[NSBundle mainBundle]
                                      pathForResource: @"2"
                                      ofType: @"aiff"]];

paddlePlayer = [[AVAudioPlayer alloc]
                    initWithContentsOfURL:paddleSoundURL
                    error:nil];
```

Finally, you prepared each audio player to play by calling the `prepareToPlay` method:

```
// Prepare to play sounds
[blockPlayer prepareToPlay];
[paddlePlayer prepareToPlay];
```

If you recall from the previous example, the `prepareToPlay` method preloads the buffers for the audio player allowing it to start more quickly when you call the `play` method.

Next, you modified the collision detection methods to play the appropriate sound when you detected a collision. To play the sound, you called the `play` method on the appropriate audio player:

```
// Play the block collision sound
[blockPlayer play];
```

The other feature that you implemented in this example was adding music to the game. Since the music plays at the same time as the other sound effects, you needed to create a separate `AVAudioPlayer` to play the music. Since you wanted to play the music for the duration of the game, the logical place for the audio player was in the `BlockerViewController`. In the `viewDidLoad` method, you added the code to initialize, configure, and start the music player.

Just as above, you first created an `NSURL` to point to the music file:

```
NSURL *musicSoundURL = [NSURL fileURLWithPath: [[NSBundle mainBundle]
    pathForResource: @"BlockerMusic" ofType: @"aiff"]];
```

Next, you initialized the music player with that URL:

```
musicPlayer = [[AVAudioPlayer alloc] initWithContentsOfURL:musicSoundURL error:nil];
```

Then, you configured the music player to loop indefinitely by setting its `numberOfLoops` property to `-1`:

```
// Set to loop indefinitely
musicPlayer.numberOfLoops = -1;
```

Since the music should play in the background, you set the volume of the music player to `0.3`:

```
// Set the volume
musicPlayer.volume = 0.3;
```

Values for the `volume` property range from 0.0 to 1.0, so you can think of the volume as a percentage, from no volume to full volume. In this case, you set the volume to play at 30%.

Finally, you started the music by calling the `play` method:

```
// Start the music
[musicPlayer play];
```

The last thing that you did was stop the music in the `endGameWithMessage:` method by calling the stop method:

```
// Stop the music
[musicPlayer stop];
```

MEDIA PLAYER FRAMEWORK

In the last example, you learned how to add your own music to your games. Suppose however that you wanted to allow the player of your game to play his own music in the background. Well, you can do that by using the Media Player framework.

The Media Player framework includes classes that help you to play movies, music, podcasts, and audio book files. You can also use this framework to access the iPod library so that you can play audio files synced from iTunes on the desktop. Using the classes in this framework, you can allow your players to select their own music from their iPod library and play it in the background during your games.

You should be aware that you can only access the iPod library on devices. This will not work with the simulator because the simulator does not have access to an iPod library. Therefore, to build and test applications by using the iPod library, you need an iOS device.

iPod Library Access is a feature of the media player framework. There are classes in the framework that allow you to query a player's iPod library and select songs to play. There is also a media picker that you can use to allow the player to pick songs to play by using an interface that is practically identical to the native iPod application. Finally, you can use the `MPMusicPlayerController` class to play back the music that the player has selected.

You can configure a music player to provide change notifications when its state changes. The player can report an `MPMusicPlayerControllerPlaybackStateDidChangeNotification`, an `MPMusicPlayerControllerVolumeDidChangeNotification` or an `MPMusicPlayerControllerNowPlayingItemDidChangeNotification` to notify you of changes to the state of the player.

The easiest way to allow players of your game to pick their music is by using the media item picker. To do this, you create an instance of the `MPMediaPickerController` class, configure it as necessary, and display it to the user. The media item picker is a modal view controller that looks like the iPod application's, "On-the-go" interface. You can see an illustration of the media item picker in Figure 9-3.

When the user is finished with the media picker, you will receive a call to one of the media picker delegate methods. If the player picked a song, the media picker will call the `mediaPicker:didPickMediaItems:` delegate method. In this method, you should dismiss the picker as well as do something with the collection of items that the user has chosen. In the example that you will build, you will play the song that the user selected.

FIGURE 9-3: Media item picker

If the user cancels the media picker dialog, the media picker will call the `mediaPickerDidCancel:` delegate method. In this method, you will typically just dismiss the dialog.

If you want to select songs to play programmatically, instead of letting the user choose, you can use the `MPMediaQuery` class to query the iPod library. Using this class, you can generate complex queries based on iPod library criteria such as artist, album, or genre.

Once you have a song, or collection of songs, you use the `MPMusicPlayerController` to play the songs. You can set various properties of the music player to control playback features such as volume, repeat, and shuffle. When you are finished configuring the player, you can queue up a list of songs for the player by using the `setQueueWithItemCollection:` method. Finally, you start playback by using the `play` method. You can control the playback by using the `pause`, `stop`, `beginSeekingForward`, `beginSeekingBackward`, `endSeeking`, `skipToNextItem`, `skipToBeginning`, and `skipToPreviousItem` methods. Using these methods, you could build your own version of the iPod music player. You can also set the player to seek a specific point in a song by using the `currentPlaybackTime` property.

TRY IT OUT Playing iPod Music in Blocker

codefile Blocker available for download at Wrox.com

In this example, you will replace the music in the Blocker game with music from the player's iPod library. You will show the `MPMediaPickerController` and allow the player to choose a song to play during the game. Then, you will use the `MPMusicPlayerController` to play the song.

You will need to make some changes to the existing Blocker code to prepare to add iPod support to the game.

1. First, remove the `musicPlayer` variable from the `ViewController` header.

2. Then, remove this code from the `viewDidLoad` method:

```
// Init music player
NSURL *musicSoundURL = [NSURL fileURLWithPath: [[NSBundle mainBundle]
    pathForResource: @"BlockerMusic" ofType: @"aiff"]];
musicPlayer = [[AVAudioPlayer alloc] initWithContentsOfURL:musicSoundURL error:nil];

// Set to loop indefinitely
musicPlayer.numberOfLoops = -1;

// Set the volume
musicPlayer.volume = 0.3;

// Start the music
[musicPlayer play];
```

3. Remove this code from the `endGameWithMessage` method

```
// Stop the music
[musicPlayer stop];
```

4. Build and run the application and verify that it compiles without error and works correctly. The only difference that you should notice is that the music is gone.

5. Now, you need to refactor a bit of code to break the code that starts the game out of `viewDidLoad` into its own method. In the `ViewController.h` header, add a new method declaration:

```
-(void) startGame;
```

6. In the `ViewController.m` implementation file, cut the code that sets up and starts the game timer from the `viewDidLoad` method:

```
// Set up the CADisplayLink for the animation
gameTimer = [CADisplayLink displayLinkWithTarget:self
                                 selector:@selector(updateDisplay:)];


// Add the display link to the current run loop
[gameTimer addToRunLoop:[NSRunLoop currentRunLoop]
          forMode:NSDefaultRunLoopMode];
```

7. Create the new `startGame` method and paste the game timer code in there. The `startGame` method should look like this:

```
-(void) startGame
{
    // Set up the CADisplayLink for the animation
    gameTimer = [CADisplayLink displayLinkWithTarget:self
                                     selector:@selector(updateDisplay:)];


    // Add the display link to the current run loop
    [gameTimer addToRunLoop:[NSRunLoop currentRunLoop]
              forMode:NSDefaultRunLoopMode];
}
```

8. Now you are ready to implement the iPod functionality. In order to use the iPod library access and the media player, you need to add the MediaPlayer framework to your project. Click the Blocker project icon at the top of the Project Navigator view to bring up the project properties. In the editor window, under the heading Targets, click Blocker. Click the tab at the top of the Editor window labeled Build Phases. Expand the item that says, "Link Binary With Libraries." Click the plus sign at the bottom of the "Link Binary With Libraries." table. In the dialog that comes up, select MediaPlayer.framework and click Add.

9. In the `ViewController.h` header file, add a `#import` statement to import the MediaPlayer header:

```
#import <MediaPlayer/MediaPlayer.h>
```

10. Modify the `@interface` directive to make the `ViewController` support the `MPMediaPickerControllerDelegate` protocol:

```
@interface ViewController : UIViewController <MPMediaPickerControllerDelegate> {
```

11. In the `@interface` block, add a new bool instance variable to track if the player has selected a song:

```
bool selectedSong;
```

12. Move over to the `ViewController.m` implementation file. In the `viewDidLoad` method, below the line that initializes the game model, add the following code to initialize the `selectedSong` flag:

```
// Initialize the selectedSong flag
selectedSong=NO;
```

13. At the end of the `viewDidLoad` method, add the following code to configure the audio session to allow the game to play the music and sound effects simultaneously:

```
// Configure the audio session to allow the music and sound effects to play
NSError *setCategoryErr = nil;

[[AVAudioSession sharedInstance]
 setCategory: AVAudioSessionCategoryAmbient
 error: &setCategoryErr];
```

14. The `viewDidLoad` method should now look like this:

```
- (void)viewDidLoad
{
    [super viewDidLoad];

    // initialize the game model
    gameModel = [[BlockerModel alloc] init];

    // Initialize the selectedSong flag
    selectedSong=NO;

    // Iterate over the blocks in the model, drawing them
    for (BlockView* bv in gameModel.blocks) {
        // Add the block to the array
        [self.view addSubview:bv];
    }
```

```
        // Draw the paddle
        paddle = [[UIImageView alloc] initWithImage:
                [UIImage imageNamed:@"paddle.png"]];

        // Set the paddle position based on the model
        [paddle setFrame:gameModel.paddleRect];

        [self.view addSubview:paddle];

        // Draw the ball
        ball = [[UIImageView alloc] initWithImage:
                [UIImage imageNamed:@"ball.png"]];

        [ball setFrame:gameModel.ballRect];

        [self.view addSubview:ball];


        // Configure the audio session to allow the music and sound effects to play
        NSError *setCategoryErr = nil;

        [[AVAudioSession sharedInstance]
         setCategory: AVAudioSessionCategoryAmbient
         error: &setCategoryErr];

    }
```

15. Implement the `viewDidAppear:` method to show the music picker view to the player:

```
- (void)viewDidAppear:(BOOL)animated
{
    [super viewDidAppear:animated];

    if (!selectedSong)
    {
        // Instantiate the music picker to allow player to choose music
        MPMediaPickerController *musicPicker =
        [[MPMediaPickerController alloc] initWithMediaTypes: MPMediaTypeMusic];

        // Set the delegate
        [musicPicker setDelegate: self];

        // Limit the player to picking only one song
        [musicPicker setAllowsPickingMultipleItems: NO];

        // Show the music picker
        [self presentModalViewController: musicPicker animated: YES];


    }
}
```

16. Implement the two delegate methods from the `MPMediaPickerControllerDelegate` protocol:

```
- (void) mediaPicker: (MPMediaPickerController *) mediaPicker
   didPickMediaItems: (MPMediaItemCollection *) collection {
```

```
    // Finished with the picker, so dismiss it
    [self dismissModalViewControllerAnimated: YES];

    // Set the selectedSong flag
    selectedSong=YES;

    // Use the application music player and not the iPod player
    MPMusicPlayerController* appMusicPlayer =
    [MPMusicPlayerController applicationMusicPlayer];

    // Set to repeat the song
    [appMusicPlayer setRepeatMode: MPMusicRepeatModeOne];

    // Set the queue of songs to play based on what the player chose
    [appMusicPlayer setQueueWithItemCollection: collection];

    // Set the volume
    [appMusicPlayer setVolume:0.3];

    // Start the player
    [appMusicPlayer play];

    // Give music player a couple of seconds to start, then start game
    [self performSelector:@selector(startGame)
            withObject:nil afterDelay:2.0];

}


- (void) mediaPickerDidCancel: (MPMediaPickerController *) mediaPicker {

    // Finished with the picker, so dismiss it
    [self dismissModalViewControllerAnimated: YES];

    // Set the selectedSong flag
    selectedSong=YES;

    // Start the game
    [self  startGame];

}
```

17. Build and run the game. Remember that you have to run the game on an actual device or you will get a runtime error saying that the MPMediaPickerController is unable to access the iPod library. Instead of seeing the game, you will see the media picker. Choose a song from the library. After you select a song, the music and game should start.

How It Works

The first thing that you did was to remove the musicPlayer audio player from the code. You did not need it anymore because the goal of this project was to modify the code to use an MPMusicPlayerController instead.

After that, you moved some code from viewDidLoad into the new startGame method. You needed to do this because you no longer wanted to start the game in viewDidLoad. The code to start the game should run after the player chooses a song from the iPod library, so you needed to move the code to a different method.

Then you were ready to implement the new code. First, you added a new flag called `selectedSong` and initialized it in the `viewDidLoad` method:

```
// Initialize the selectedSong flag
selectedSong=NO;
```

At the end of `viewDidLoad`, you added code to configure the audio session to allow you to play music and sound effects simultaneously:

```
// Configure the audio session to allow the music and sound effects to play
NSError *setCategoryErr = nil;

[[AVAudioSession sharedInstance]
 setCategory: AVAudioSessionCategoryAmbient
 error: &setCategoryErr];
```

After that, you implemented the `viewDidAppear:` method to show the music picker view to the player. The view controller calls `viewDidAppear:` after the view has actually appeared to the player. Once the view appears, you wanted to show the modal media picker controller. The first thing that you did in `viewDidAppear:` was check the `selectedSong` flag:

```
if (!selectedSong)
```

You need the flag to prevent the media picker from showing up repeatedly. Since `viewDidAppear:` is called any time the view appears, the method will get called once when the view appears the first time, and then again when the media picker controller is dismissed, because the view has in fact appeared again. Therefore, you needed to use a flag to keep track of the fact that you have displayed the media picker and do not need to display it again. If you want to see the effect of not using the `selectedSong` flag, feel free to delete the `if` statement from the code and run the game. You will see that when you select a song, the code in `viewDidAppear` will run again displaying the media picker again.

After you confirmed that you have never shown the media picker, you instantiated it by using the `MPMediaTypeMusic` enumerator to indicate that you wanted music to be available only in the picker:

```
MPMediaPickerController *musicPicker =
[[MPMediaPickerController alloc] initWithMediaTypes: MPMediaTypeMusic];
```

Next, you set the view controller as the delegate of the media picker so that the media picker will call the delegate methods when the player has chosen a song or cancelled the dialog:

```
// Set the delegate
[musicPicker setDelegate: self];
```

Since the game is short, you then limited the player to picking only one song from the music picker:

```
// Limit the player to picking only one song
[musicPicker setAllowsPickingMultipleItems: NO];
```

Finally, you displayed the music picker to the player as a modal view controller:

```
// Show the music picker
[self presentModalViewController: musicPicker animated: YES];
```

Once you had the code to display the media picker in place, you implemented the media player delegate methods. First, you built `mediaPicker:didPickMediaItems:` to handle the case where the user chose a song. The first thing that you did in that method was to dismiss the modal view controller, which makes the picker go away:

```
// Finished with the picker, so dismiss it
[self dismissModalViewControllerAnimated: YES];
```

Next, you set the selectedSong flag to indicate that the dialog has been displayed and need not be displayed again when viewDidAppear ran again:

```
// Set the selectedSong flag
selectedSong=YES;
```

After that, you instantiated the MPMusicPlayerController by calling the applicationMusicPlayer class method:

```
// Use the application music player and not the iPod player
MPMusicPlayerController* appMusicPlayer =
[MPMusicPlayerController applicationMusicPlayer];
```

There are two different music players that you can use: the application player and the iPod player. The application player is unique to your application and its state is not maintained outside of your program. The iPod music player refers to the iPod music player on the device and uses its current state including the currently playing item, shuffle and repeat settings, and playback state. Therefore, you could use the iPod music player if you wanted to play the same song that the player was already listening to or if you wanted to pause the current iPod playback.

Next, you set the player to repeat the current song in case the game continues past the end of the song:

```
// Set to repeat the song
[appMusicPlayer setRepeatMode: MPMusicRepeatModeOne];
```

After that, you set the queue of songs to play in the media player to the song that the user had chosen in the media picker:

```
// Set the queue of songs to play based on what the player chose
[appMusicPlayer setQueueWithItemCollection: collection];
```

Next, you set the volume to 30% to make the music play softly in the background as you did to the AVAudioPlayer in the previous example:

```
// Set the volume
[appMusicPlayer setVolume:0.3];
```

Then, you started the music:

```
// Start the player
[appMusicPlayer play];
```

Finally, you called the new startGame method to start the game:

```
// Give music player a couple of seconds to start, then start game
[self performSelector:@selector(startGame)
         withObject:nil afterDelay:2.0];
```

I used the performSelector:withObject:afterDelay: method to give the music player a couple of seconds to start up before starting the game. I noticed in my testing that there was a slight delay in starting up the music on my iPhone and it was causing the game to misbehave. I solved the issue by waiting for two seconds after telling the music player to start before starting the game.

Finally, you built the `mediaPickerDidCancel:` delegate method to handle the case where the player cancelled out of the media picker, deciding not to choose a song. In this method, you first dismissed the view controller:

```
// Finished with the picker, so dismiss it
[self dismissModalViewControllerAnimated: YES];
```

Then, you set the `selectedSong` flag to indicate that the dialog has been displayed and need not be displayed again when `viewDidAppear` ran again:

```
// Set the selectedSong flag
selectedSong=YES;
```

Finally, you started the game:

```
// Start the game
[self  startGame];
```

There was no need to add the delay in this case as you are not playing music, so you can start the game right away.

SUMMARY

In this chapter, you learned the basics of playing sounds and music in iOS. First, you learned how to play simple user interface sounds by using System Sound Services. This is useful for playing short sounds, one at a time, in response to user actions in a game. If your game needs to play sounds only in response to user actions and does not need to be able to play multiple sounds simultaneously, using System Sound Services is the easiest was to play sounds in iOS.

Next, you learned how to build more complete soundscapes for your games by using the AVFoundation framework. You built a sample game RepeatIt, which used the AVAudioPlayer to play sounds. Then, you enhanced the Blocker game to include sounds and music playing simultaneously.

Finally, you learned how to use the MediaPlayer framework to let players choose music from their own iPod library to play in your game.

EXERCISES

1. When is it appropriate to use System Sound Services to provide sounds for your game?

2. What are the advantages of using AV Foundation over System Sound Services?

3. Why do you need to call `prepareToPlay` when using an AVAudioPlayer?

4. How can you determine if an `AVAudioPlayer` is currently playing a sound?

Answers to the Exercises can be found in the Appendix.

▶ **WHAT YOU LEARNED IN THIS CHAPTER**

TOPIC	MAIN POINTS
System Sound Service	Use the System Sound Service to play short sounds in response to user interface actions. System Sound Service is limited to playing short sounds and playing only one sound at a time
AVAudioPlayer	Use the `AVAudioPlayer` class to play multiple sounds simultaneously, when you need to play a sound longer than 30 seconds, when you need to loop a sound, or when you need more control over how a sound is played.
Media Player Framework	Use the Media Player Framework to integrate the native iPod application into your game. You can allow players to select songs to play using the media picker view controller. You can get music programmatically by querying the player's iPod library.

10

Building a Networked Game with GameKit

WHAT YOU WILL LEARN IN THIS CHAPTER:

➤ Creating a peer-to-peer network with GameKit

➤ Implementing the NSCoding protocol to enable serialization and deserialization of your objects

➤ Converting your classes to serialized data by using archivers

➤ Building a peer-to-peer networked game

INTRODUCING GAMEKIT

The final iOS framework that you will look at in this book is GameKit. As you may expect, you can use the GameKit framework to add some interesting functionality to your games. GameKit provides three somewhat distinct sets of functionality:

➤ **Game Center:** GameKit helps you to integrate Game Center features into your game. The Game Center application is part of the core iOS installation and is available on every phone running iOS 4 or greater. GameKit provides classes to let you authenticate a player with their Game Center account, add Achievements to your games, Auto-match players that want to play your game, and track and display game scores with Leaderboards.

➤ **Peer-to-peer connectivity:** GameKit provides APIs to allow you to easily set up peer-to-peer networked games using either Bluetooth or a local wireless network.

➤ **In-Game Voice:** GameKit contains classes that enable you to provide in-game voice chat to your game's players.

This chapter will focus on the peer-to-peer connectivity portion of the GameKit framework. In this chapter, you will build a tic-tac-toe game and then enable head-to-head play by using the peer-to-peer networking support in GameKit.

STARTING OUT

All of the games that you have built up to this point in the book either have been single-player games or games that you played against the computer. In this chapter, you will build a two-player game that you can play against another human opponent. The game will be Tic-Tac-Toe. It's not the most exciting game in the world, but it provides a well-known starting point for the exciting stuff in this chapter, peer-to-peer networking.

In the first part of the chapter, you will build the game in a way that works for "Pass and Play" competition. That is, you make a move and then pass the device to your opponent for him to play his turn. Once you have the game up and running, you will learn about the features of the GameKit framework that make it easy to add local network gameplay to your game. Once you are comfortable with the fundamentals, you will add network gameplay to your Tic-Tac-Toe game to allow two players to play against each other and different devices.

Unlike most of the rest of this book, this chapter requires you to have an iOS-capable device such as an iPhone, iPod Touch, or iPad. The reason is because, at this time, there is no way to run two instances of the iOS simulator at the same time. You need to be able to run two instances of the networked game to see it work. Additionally, you will need to be a paid member of the iOS developer program to run the networked example, because you cannot load your programs on to a device without being a paid member of the developer program.

With all that said, you should be ready to create the "Pass and Play" version of Tic-Tac-Toe.

TRY IT OUT   Starting the TicTac Game

codefile TicTac available for download at Wrox.com

In this section, you will build a simple version of Tic-Tac-Toe. You will build the game by using a "Pass and play" model where each player takes his turn and passes the device to the next player for her turn. Later in the chapter, after you learn how to implement peer-to-peer networking, you will enhance the game so that each player can play on his own device.

On the off chance that you have never played Tic-Tac-Toe, you play the game on a grid, as you can see in Figure 10-1. Each player is assigned a shape, either X or O. Each player takes turns placing her shape on an empty square in the grid. The player who gets three of her shapes in a row, horizontally, vertically, or diagonally, is the winner. In the game in Figure 10-1, both the X and O players have taken one turn.

1. To get started, begin Xcode and select File ⇨ New ⇨ New Project.

2. The familiar dialog box appears that displays templates for the various types of applications that you can create for iOS and Mac OS X. Select Single View Application from the dialog box and click Next.

3. In the Product Name text box, type the name of your project, **TicTac**. Select iPhone from the Device Family drop-down box. Uncheck the "Use Storyboard" and "Include Unit Tests" checkboxes. Make sure that you have selected the "Use Automatic Reference Counting" checkbox and then click Next.

4. Select a location to save your project, and click Create. Xcode will create your project and present the project window.

5. Next, you need to import the images into your project. You can download these graphics from the book's website.

6. Create a new File Group to hold the images that you will use by selecting File ⇨ New ⇨ New Group from the menu bar. Call the new group **Images**.

7. Select File ⇨ Add files to TicTac from the menu bar and add the image files (`Background.png`, `o.png`, and `x.png`) to the Images folder. You can obtain the image files for this project from the book's website. Check the box that says, "Copy items into destination group's folder (if needed)." Click Add to add the images to your project.

FIGURE 10-1: The Tic-Tac-Toe board

In this program, you will implement the MVC design pattern. You will build a class called `GameState` that will hold the state of the game. This will be the Model. You will build the View by using interface builder. Finally, you will use the default `ViewController` from the project template to implement the Controller.

The first thing that you will do is use Interface Builder to build the view, as seen in Figure 10-1. The view consists of an Image View for the grid and gradient background, nine buttons that the player will press to place his shape, and a label he will use to display the status of the game.

8. Open the `ViewController.xib` file. If you do not already have it open, open the Utilities panel. At the bottom, switch to the Object library so that you can see the objects available for you to place in the view. Drag a UIImageView object from the Object library and drop it in your view. Position it so that it covers the entire view. At the top of the Utilities panel, select the Attributes inspector. Click the Image drop-down in the Image View section and select `Background.png`. This sets the image in the image view to `Background.png`.

9. Now you are ready to add the buttons. Drag a UIButton from the Object library and drop it in your view. Position and size it so that it takes up most of the space in the first square in the grid. From the Type drop-down in the Attributes inspector, select Custom. Then, in the Image drop-down, select `x.png`. This will let you see the buttons so that you can lay them out. In the View section, use the Mode drop-down to select Aspect Fill.

10. Switch to the Size inspector and set the width and height of the button to 80. Make sure that you have placed the button as a subview of the main View in the view hierarchy by checking the Objects tree in interface builder.

11. Now, select the button by clicking Interface Builder and press CMD-C to copy it. You need to make eight more buttons, so the easiest way is by using Copy and Paste. Once you have copied the button, paste it by using CMD-V and move it into position to the right of the first button. Do the same for the third button. Place three more buttons below the first three and the final three below the second three. You should now have the grid filled with X buttons.

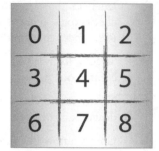

12. Next, you will set the Tag attribute for each button based on its position in the grid, as seen in Figure 10-2. In the View section of the Attributes inspector, under the Mode drop-down, you should see the Tag field. Each button that you pasted will have the tag set to 0. Pick the button in grid space one in Figure 10-2 and set its Tag to 1. Set the Tag for each of the other buttons to correspond with its position in the grid in Figure 10-2.

FIGURE 10-2: The tags for each space in the grid

13. Drag a UILabel from the Object library and drop it in your view. Position it near the top of the view and size it so that it stretches across the width of the view. Use the Attributes inspector to center-justify the text in the label.

14. Open the Assistant editor so that you can see the ViewController header file alongside your interface. Create an outlet for the UILabel in your header file by control-dragging the label into the header and dropping the label inside the `@interface` block. In the popover that appears, set the name of your UILabel to `statusLabel` and click the Connect button.

15. Next, you will create actions for each of the buttons. Ctrl-drag the first button to the ViewController header file and create an action method called `spaceButtonTapped`. Then, wire all the other buttons to the same method by Ctrl-dragging them and dropping them on to the new `spaceButtonTapped` method. When you drag over `spaceButtonTapped` in the header, you should see a blue box around the method signature, and the text, "Connect Action," should appear as a pop-up in the header. Now, anytime the player taps one of the spaces, this method will run.

16. To verify that you have correctly wired all of the buttons to the `spaceButtonTapped` action method, you will add an `NSLog` statement to the `spaceButtonTapped` method to log that the player tapped the button. Open the `ViewController.m` implementation file and locate the `-(IBAction)spaceButtonTapped:(id)sender` method. Add this code to the method:

```
NSLog(@"Player tapped: %i",[sender tag]);
```

17. Build and run the application. Tap each button and verify that you are logging the correct tag in the Output window. Your output should look like this:

```
2011-08-26 02:05:42.691 TicTac[35477:f203] Player tapped: 0
2011-08-26 02:05:43.377 TicTac[35477:f203] Player tapped: 1
2011-08-26 02:05:44.931 TicTac[35477:f203] Player tapped: 2
2011-08-26 02:05:45.815 TicTac[35477:f203] Player tapped: 3
2011-08-26 02:05:46.277 TicTac[35477:f203] Player tapped: 4
2011-08-26 02:05:46.907 TicTac[35477:f203] Player tapped: 5
2011-08-26 02:05:47.657 TicTac[35477:f203] Player tapped: 6
2011-08-26 02:05:48.119 TicTac[35477:f203] Player tapped: 7
2011-08-26 02:05:48.645 TicTac[35477:f203] Player tapped: 8
```

Next, you need to create outlets for the buttons because you will change the button image based on which player places his shape in that particular grid space. Since you will handle all of the buttons the same way, you will create an outlet collection.

18. Ctrl-drag the first button to the ViewController header file. In the Connection drop-down in the pop-up, select Outlet Collection. Set the name of the Outlet Collection to spaceButton, and click Connect. Then, wire all the other buttons to the same outlet collection by Ctrl-dragging them and dropping them on the spaceButton outlet collection property. When you drag over the spaceButton property in the header, you should see a blue box around the property, and the text, Connect Outlet Collection, should appear as a pop-up in the header. Now, all of the spaces should be part of the outlet collection.

19. Remove the image from each button by blanking out the Image field in the Attributes inspector for each button. When the game starts, you do not want all of the buttons pre-filled with the X shape.

20. Now you are ready to write the game code. First, you will build your model class. Select File ➪ New ➪ New File… from the menu bar. In the template chooser, under iOS on the left-hand side, select Cocoa Touch. In the right-hand pane, select Objective-C class, and press Next. Name your class **GameState**. In the "Subclass of" drop-down, select NSObject and click Next. In the next dialog, click Create. You should see two new files in the Project Navigator called GameState.h and GameState.m.

21. In the GameState.h header file, outside of the @interface block, add an enumeration to represent the player's turn:

```
typedef enum {
    TTxPlayerTurn - 1,      // The x player's turn
    TToPlayerTurn = 2       // The o player's turn
} TTPlayerTurn;
```

22. Inside the @interface block, add two member variables to track the player's turn and the board state like this:

```
TTPlayerTurn playersTurn;
NSMutableArray* boardState;
```

23. Below the @interface block, add two properties to expose the member variables that you just created:

```
@property TTPlayerTurn playersTurn;
@property (strong, nonatomic) NSMutableArray* boardState;
```

The header should look like this:

```
#import <Foundation/Foundation.h>

typedefenum {
    TTxPlayerTurn = 1,      // The x player's turn
    TToPlayerTurn = 2       // The o player's turn
} TTPlayerTurn;


@interface GameState : NSObject
{
    TTPlayerTurn playersTurn;
    NSMutableArray* boardState;
}


@property TTPlayerTurn playersTurn;
```

```
@property (strong, nonatomic) NSMutableArray* boardState;


@end
```

24. Now, switch over to the `GameState.m` implementation file. Below the `@implementation` line, synthesize your properties:

```
@synthesize playersTurn,boardState;
```

25. Next, add the `init` method:

```
-(id) init
{
    self = [super init];

    if (self) {
        // Alloc and init the board state
        boardState = [[NSMutableArray alloc] initWithCapacity:9];

        playersTurn=TTxPlayerTurn;

    }

    return self;

}
```

26. Switch over to the `ViewController.h` header file. Add a `#import` statement to import the `GameState.h` header:

```
#import "GameState.h"
```

27. Before the `@interface` block, create another enumeration. This one will represent the status of the game:

```
typedef enum {
    TTGameNotOver = 0,          // The game is not over
    TTGameOverxWins = 1,        // The x player won
    TTGameOveroWins = 2,        // The o player won
    TTGameOverTie = 3,          // The game is a tie
} TTGameOverStatus;
```

28. In the `@interface` block, add the following member variables:

```
{
    UIImage* xImage;
    UIImage* oImage;

    // The game state
    GameState* theGameState;
}
```

29. Below the closing brace of the `@interface` block, add properties for your new member variables:

```
@property (strong, nonatomic) UIImage* xImage;
@property (strong, nonatomic) UIImage* oImage;
@property (strong, nonatomic) GameState* theGameState;
```

30. Below the properties, add the following method declarations:

```
- (void) initGame;
- (void) updateBoard;
- (void) updateGameStatus;
- (TTGameOverStatus) checkGameOver;
- (BOOL) didPlayerWin: (NSString*) player;
- (void) endGameWithResult:(TTGameOverStatus) result;
```

The completed header should look like this:

```
#import <UIKit/UIKit.h>
#import "GameState.h"

typedefenum {
    TTGameNotOver = 0,              // The game is not over
    TTGameOverxWins = 1,           // The x player won
    TTGameOveroWins = 2,           // The o player won
    TTGameOverTie = 3,             // The game is a tie
} TTGameOverStatus;

@interface ViewController : UIViewController
{
    UIImage* xImage;
    UIImage* oImage;

    // The game state
    GameState* theGameState;
}
@property (strong, nonatomic) UIImage* xImage;
@property (strong, nonatomic) UIImage* oImage;
@property (strong, nonatomic) GameState* theGameState;

@property (strong, nonatomic) IBOutletCollection(UIButton) NSArray *spaceButton;
@property (strong, nonatomic) IBOutletUILabel *statusLabel;

- (IBAction)spaceButtonTapped:(id)sender;

- (void) initGame;
- (void) updateBoard;
- (void) updateGameStatus;
- (TTGameOverStatus) checkGameOver;
- (BOOL) didPlayerWin: (NSString*) player;
- (void) endGameWithResult:(TTGameOverStatus) result;

@end
```

31. Switch over to the `ViewController.m` implementation file. At the top of the `@implementation` block, synthesize your new properties:

```
@synthesize xImage,oImage,theGameState;
```

32. In the `viewDidLoad` method, add the following code below the line that calls `super viewDidLoad`:

```
// Load the images
xImage = [UIImage imageNamed:@"x.png"];
oImage = [UIImage imageNamed:@"o.png"];
```

```
// Create the game state
theGameState = [[GameState alloc] init];
```

33. In the `viewWillAppear` method, add the following code below the line that calls `super` `viewWillAppear`:

```
// Initialize the game
[self initGame];
```

34. Add the `initGame` method:

```
- (void) initGame
{
    // Initialize the game
    // Set player's turn to the x player because X always goes first
    self.theGameState.playersTurn=TTxPlayerTurn;

    // Set the status label
    self.statusLabel.text = @"X to move";

    // Clear the board state
    [self.theGameState.boardState removeAllObjects];
    for (int i=0;i<=8;i++)
    {
        // Insert a space to indicate a blank in the grid
        [self.theGameState.boardState insertObject:@" " atIndex:i];
    }
    [self updateBoard];

}
```

35. Add the `updateBoard` method:

```
- (void) updateBoard
{
// Given the state, update the board
for (int i=0;i<=8;i++)
    {
        if ([[self.theGameState.boardState objectAtIndex:i] isEqualToString:@"x"])
        {
            [[spaceButton objectAtIndex:i] setImage:self.xImage forState:UIControlStateNormal];
        }
        elseif ([[self.theGameState.boardState objectAtIndex:i] isEqualToString:@"o"])
        {
            [[spaceButton objectAtIndex:i] setImage:self.oImage forState:UIControlStateNormal];
        }
        else
        {
            [[spaceButton objectAtIndex:i] setImage:nil forState:UIControlStateNormal];
        }
    }

}
```

36. You need a method to determine if a player has won the game, so add the `didPlayerWin:` method:

```
- (BOOL) didPlayerWin: (NSString*) player
{
// This method determines if the given player has won

    if (((([self.theGameState.boardState objectAtIndex:0] isEqualToString:player] &&
          [[self.theGameState.boardState objectAtIndex:1] isEqualToString:player] &&
          [[self.theGameState.boardState objectAtIndex:2] isEqualToString:player]) ||
         ([[self.theGameState.boardState objectAtIndex:3] isEqualToString:player] &&
          [[self.theGameState.boardState objectAtIndex:4] isEqualToString:player] &&
          [[self.theGameState.boardState objectAtIndex:5] isEqualToString:player]) ||
         ([[self.theGameState.boardState objectAtIndex:6] isEqualToString:player] &&
          [[self.theGameState.boardState objectAtIndex:7] isEqualToString:player] &&
          [[self.theGameState.boardState objectAtIndex:8] isEqualToString:player]) ||

         ([[self.theGameState.boardState objectAtIndex:0] isEqualToString:player] &&
          [[self.theGameState.boardState objectAtIndex:3] isEqualToString:player] &&
          [[self.theGameState.boardState objectAtIndex:6] isEqualToString:player]) ||
         ([[self.theGameState.boardState objectAtIndex:1] isEqualToString:player] &&
          [[self.theGameState.boardState objectAtIndex:4] isEqualToString:player] &&
          [[self.theGameState.boardState objectAtIndex:7] isEqualToString:player]) ||
         ([[self.theGameState.boardState objectAtIndex:2] isEqualToString:player] &&
          [[self.theGameState.boardState objectAtIndex:5] isEqualToString:player] &&
          [[self.theGameState.boardState objectAtIndex:8] isEqualToString:player]) ||

         ([[self.theGameState.boardState objectAtIndex:0] isEqualToString:player] &&
          [[self.theGameState.boardState objectAtIndex:4] isEqualToString:player] &&
          [[self.theGameState.boardState objectAtIndex:8] isEqualToString:player]) ||
         ([[self.theGameState.boardState objectAtIndex:2] isEqualToString:player] &&
          [[self.theGameState.boardState objectAtIndex:4] isEqualToString:player] &&
          [[self.theGameState.boardState objectAtIndex:6] isEqualToString:player])
        )
    {
        return YES;
    }
    else
        return NO;
}
```

37. Add a method called `checkGameOver` to determine if the game is over:

```
- (TTGameOverStatus) checkGameOver
{
    // This method checks to see if the game is over

    // Did x win?
    if ([self didPlayerWin:@"x"])
    {
        return TTGameOverxWins;
    }
    // Did o win?
```

```
    elseif ([self didPlayerWin:@"o"])
    {
        return TTGameOveroWins    }

    // No winner. Check to see if there are open spaces left on the board
    // because if there are open spaces, the game is not over
    for (int i=0; i<=8; i++) {
        if ([[self.theGameState.boardState objectAtIndex:i] isEqualToString:@" "])
        {
            // Cannot be a tie because there is an open space
            return TTGameNotOver;
        }
    }

    // No open spaces and no winner, so the game is a tie
    return TTGameOverTie;

}
```

38. Add the `updateGameStatus` method, which updates the status label based on the status of the game:

```
- (void) updateGameStatus
{
    // Check for win or tie
    TTGameOverStatus gameOverStatus = [self checkGameOver];

    switch (gameOverStatus) {
        case TTGameNotOver:
            // The game is not over
            // Next player's turn
            if (self.theGameState.playersTurn == TTxPlayerTurn)
            {
                // Set the status label
                self.statusLabel.text = @"X to move";

            }
            else
            {
                // Set the status label
                self.statusLabel.text = @"O to move";

            }

            break;
        case TTGameOverxWins:
        case TTGameOveroWins:
        case TTGameOverTie:
            // Game is over
            [self endGameWithResult:gameOverStatus];
        break;
    }
}
```

39. Implement the `spaceButtonTapped` action method to place the player's shape in the space that he tapped:

```objc
- (IBAction)spaceButtonTapped:(id)sender {
    int spaceIndex = [sender tag];

    // If the space is blank let the player place the shape
    if ([[self.theGameState.boardState objectAtIndex:spaceIndex] isEqualToString:@" "])
    {
        // Update game state
        if (self.theGameState.playersTurn == TTxPlayerTurn)
        {
            [self.theGameState.boardState replaceObjectAtIndex:spaceIndex withObject: @"x"];

            // It is now o's turn
            self.theGameState.playersTurn = TToPlayerTurn;

        }
        else
        {
            [self.theGameState.boardState replaceObjectAtIndex:spaceIndex withObject: @"o"];

            // It is now x's turn
            self.theGameState.playersTurn = TTxPlayerTurn;

        }

        // Update the board
        [self updateBoard];

        // Update the game status
        [self updateGameStatus];
    }
}
```

40. Add the `endGameWithResult:` method to end the game:

```objc
-(void) endGameWithResult:(TTGameOverStatus) result
{
    NSString* gameOverMessage;

    switch (result) {
        case TTGameOverxWins:
            gameOverMessage = [NSString stringWithString:@"X wins"];
            break;
        case TTGameOveroWins:
            gameOverMessage = [NSString stringWithString:@"O wins"];
            break;
        case TTGameOverTie:
            gameOverMessage = [NSString stringWithString:@"The game is a tie"];
            break;
        default:
```

```
            break;
    }

    // Show an alert with the results
    UIAlertView *alert = [[UIAlertView alloc] initWithTitle:@"Game Over"
        message:gameOverMessage
        delegate:self
        cancelButtonTitle:@"OK"
        otherButtonTitles: nil];
    [alert show];
}
```

41. Add the `alertView:clickedButtonAtIndex:UIAlert` delegate method so that you can restart the game after the player has acknowledged that the game is over:

```
- (void)alertView:(UIAlertView *)alertView clickedButtonAtIndex:(NSInteger)buttonIndex
{
    // Reset the game
    [self initGame];

}
```

42. Build and run the game. You should be able to place shapes by adding the blank spaces in the grid. The game should display an alert when a player has won or if the game is a tie. After you acknowledge the alert, the game should restart. Play a few games with a friend and enjoy yourself!

How It Works

The first thing that you did in building TicTac was use Interface Builder to build the view for your game. Once you finished with that, you moved on to adding the `GameState` model class to your project.

In the `GameState` class header file, you created an enumeration to represent values that you used to keep track of which player should move next:

```
typedef enum {
    TTxPlayerTurn = 1,        // The x player's turn
    TToPlayerTurn = 2         // The o player's turn
} TTPlayerTurn;
```

An enumeration or `enum` is just a set of named integer constants. You can use the names in lieu of the numbers to make your code more readable. The `typedef` statement lets you define your own types based on other types. Therefore, in this case, you are saying that the type `TTPlayerTurn` is an enumeration with `TTxPlayerTurn` equal to 1 and `TToPlayerTurn` equal to 2.

Next, you added a member variable to keep track of the current player's turn by using your new enumeration type:

```
TTPlayerTurn playersTurn;
```

You also added an `NSMutableArray` member variable to keep track of the state of the board:

```
NSMutableArray* boardState;
```

Finally, you added two properties to expose the member variables that you previously created:

```
@property TTPlayerTurn playersTurn;
@property (strong, nonatomic) NSMutableArray* boardState;
```

After you finished with the header, you moved over to the GameState implementation. The only method that you implemented was init.

The first thing that you did in init was to call the superclass version of init:

```
self = [super init];
```

After verifying that you got a valid instance back from super init, you allocated and initialized the boardState array with an initial capacity of 9 since the board has nine spaces:

```
boardState = [[NSMutableArray alloc] initWithCapacity:9];
```

Since the player using the X shape always starts a game of Tic-Tac-Toe, you set the playersTurn member to the TTxPlayerTurn enumeration value:

```
playersTurn = TTxPlayerTurn;
```

Next, you needed to work on the view controller. First, you added an #import statement for the GameState.h header file because you used the GameState object in the view controller:

```
#import "GameState.h"
```

Next, you created another enumeration to represent the status of the game:

```
typedef enum {
    TTGameNotOver = 0,          // The game is not over
    TTGameOverxWins = 1,        // The x player won
    TTGameOveroWins = 2,        // The o player won
    TTGameOverTie = 3,          // The game is a tie
} TTGameOverStatus;
```

Then, you added member variables to hold instances of the images that you will place on the game board:

```
UIImage* xImage;
UIImage* oImage;
```

You also added an instance of the GameStateclass, which holds the state of the game:

```
GameState* theGameState;
```

Next, you added property declarations for your class properties:

```
@property (strong, nonatomic) UIImage* xImage;
@property (strong, nonatomic) UIImage* oImage;
@property (strong, nonatomic) GameState* theGameState;

@property (strong, nonatomic) IBOutletCollection(UIButton) NSArray *spaceButton;
@property (strong, nonatomic) IBOutlet UILabel *statusLabel;
```

Finally, you added your method declarations:

```
- (IBAction)spaceButtonTapped:(id)sender;

- (void) initGame;
- (void) updateBoard;
- (void) updateGameStatus;
- (TTGameOverStatus) checkGameOver;
- (BOOL) didPlayerWin: (NSString*) player;
- (void) endGameWithResult:(TTGameOverStatus) result;
```

After you finished with the header, you were ready to implement the game code. First, though, you needed to do some initial setup work in the `viewDidLoad` method. In `viewDidLoad`, you loaded the images for the player shapes:

```
xImage = [UIImage imageNamed:@"x.png"];
oImage = [UIImage imageNamed:@"o.png"];
```

Then, you created an instance of the `GameState`:

```
theGameState = [[GameState alloc] init];
```

After the initialization code, you moved on to add code to the `viewWillAppear` method. The framework calls this method after your view controller has loaded the elements in the XIB file but before the view actually appears on screen. In `viewWillAppear`, you added a line to call the `initGame` method:

```
[self initGame];
```

Next, you moved on to implement the `initGame` method. This method initializes the game. This code could have gone into `viewWillAppear`; however, I broke it out into a separate method because I knew that I would want to call it each time a game ended to prepare to start the next game.

The first thing that you did in `initGame` was to set the X player as the current player:

```
// Set player's turn to the x player because X always goes first
self.theGameState.playersTurn=TTxPlayerTurn;
```

Next, you set the text of the status label to reflect the current player's turn:

```
// Set the status label
self.statusLabel.text = @"X to move";
```

Then, you cleared the state of the board by inserting blank spaces into each slot in the array:

```
// Clear the board state
[self.theGameState.boardState removeAllObjects];
for (int i=0;i<=8;i++)
{
    // Insert a space to indicate a blank in the grid
    [self.theGameState.boardState insertObject:@" " atIndex:i];
}
```

Finally, you called the `updateBoard`method, which you will see shortly:

```
[self updateBoard];
```

Next, you implemented the `updateBoard`method, which updates the view of the board based on the contents of the board state array. To do this, you looped through each item in the array, indexed 0 through 8:

```
// Given the state, update the board
for (int i=0;i<=8;i++)
```

In the loop, you checked to see if the object at the current index was the string "x" which I used to indicate that an X shape was in a given square on the grid:

```
if ([[self.theGameState.boardState objectAtIndex:i] isEqualToString:@"x"])
{
```

If the array held an x in the grid space, you set the image of the button with the same index to the X image:

```
[[spaceButton objectAtIndex:i] setImage:self.xImage forState:UIControlStateNormal];
```

Then, you added an `else if` block to determine if you should place an o in the current grid square:

```
elseif ([[self.theGameState.boardState objectAtIndex:i] isEqualToString:@"o"])
{
    [[spaceButton objectAtIndex:i] setImage:self.oImage forState:UIControlStateNormal];
}
```

Finally, you added an `else` clause to handle the case where the grid square should be blank. You blanked out the square by setting the image for the button to `nil`:

```
else
{
    [[spaceButton objectAtIndex:i] setImage:nil forState:UIControlStateNormal];
}
```

Next, you built the method to determine if a player has won the game, `didPlayerWin:`. This method is just a large compound `if` statement that checks every possible winning combination. You used the `&&` operator to check consecutive grid squares and you used the `||` operator to link each test together. The `player` parameter is either x or o depending on which player you are testing for a win. If any of the conditions separated by the `||` operator are true, then the method returns YES indicating that the player won. If none of the conditions are true, the method returns NO.

The first part of the `if` statement checks the horizontal rows. First, you check the first row, board indices 0, 1, and 2:

```
if ((([[self.theGameState.boardState objectAtIndex:0] isEqualToString:player] &&
    [[self.theGameState.boardState objectAtIndex:1] isEqualToString:player] &&
    [[self.theGameState.boardState objectAtIndex:2] isEqualToString:player]) ||
```

Therefore, if indices 0, 1, and 2 all have the `player` shape then, this part will evaluate to true and the method will return YES. Next, you checked the next two rows, indices 3, 4, 5 and 6, 7, and 8:

```
([[self.theGameState.boardState objectAtIndex:3] isEqualToString:player] &&
    [[self.theGameState.boardState objectAtIndex:4] isEqualToString:player] &&
    [[self.theGameState.boardState objectAtIndex:5] isEqualToString:player]) ||
([[self.theGameState.boardState objectAtIndex:6] isEqualToString:player] &&
    [[self.theGameState.boardState objectAtIndex:7] isEqualToString:player] &&
    [[self.theGameState.boardState objectAtIndex:8] isEqualToString:player]) ||
```

After that, you moved on to check the vertical column with indices 0, 3, 6:

```
([[self.theGameState.boardState objectAtIndex:0] isEqualToString:player] &&
    [[self.theGameState.boardState objectAtIndex:3] isEqualToString:player] &&
    [[self.theGameState.boardState objectAtIndex:6] isEqualToString:player]) ||
```

Next, you checked the next two columns, indices 1, 4, 7 and 2, 5, and 8:

```
([[self.theGameState.boardState objectAtIndex:1] isEqualToString:player] &&
    [[self.theGameState.boardState objectAtIndex:4] isEqualToString:player] &&
    [[self.theGameState.boardState objectAtIndex:7] isEqualToString:player]) ||
([[self.theGameState.boardState objectAtIndex:2] isEqualToString:player] &&
```

```
[[self.theGameState.boardState objectAtIndex:5] isEqualToString:player] &&
[[self.theGameState.boardState objectAtIndex:8] isEqualToString:player]) ||
```

Finally, you checked the two diagonals with indices 0, 4, 8 and 2, 4, 6:

```
([[self.theGameState.boardState objectAtIndex:0] isEqualToString:player] &&
[[self.theGameState.boardState objectAtIndex:4] isEqualToString:player] &&
[[self.theGameState.boardState objectAtIndex:8] isEqualToString:player]) ||
([[self.theGameState.boardState objectAtIndex:2] isEqualToString:player] &&
[[self.theGameState.boardState objectAtIndex:4] isEqualToString:player] &&
[[self.theGameState.boardState objectAtIndex:6] isEqualToString:player])
)
```

If you are confused about which index represents which space in the grid, refer to Figure 10-2.

If any of the row, column, or diagonal tests were true, the submitted player won and you returned YES, or else, you returned NO:

```
    {
        return YES;
    }
    else
        return NO;
}
```

The next method that you built was checkGameOver. checkGameOver checks to see if the game is over and returns one of the members of the TTGameOverStatus enumeration that you built in the header. If you recall from the enumeration, there are four possible game states: X wins, O wins, Tie, and Game Not Over.

First, you checked to see if X won by using the didPlayerWin: method:

```
// Did x win?
if ([self didPlayerWin:@"x"])
```

If X did win, you returned the TTGameOverxWins enumeration value:

```
    return TTGameOverxWins;
}
```

Then, you checked to see if O won and, if so, returned the TTGameOveroWins enumeration value:

```
// Did o win?
elseif ([self didPlayerWin:@"o"])
{
    return TTGameOveroWins;
}
```

If you got past those two checks, then no one has won. At this point, you need to determine if the game is still going on or if it is a tie. The only way that you can have a tie is if all of the spaces of the grid are filled. Therefore, you looped through all of the elements in the boardState array checking to see if any grid space is empty:

```
// No winner. Check to see if there are open spaces left on the board
// because if there are open spaces, the game is not over
for (int i=0; i<=8; i++) {
    if ([[self.theGameState.boardState objectAtIndex:i] isEqualToString:@" "])
    {
```

If you did find an empty space, the game cannot be a tie so you returned `TTGameNotOver` to indicate that the game is not yet over:

```
    // Cannot be a tie because there is an open space
    return TTGameNotOver;
}
}
```

Finally, if the empty spaces check loop finishes without returning, then all spaces are full, so the game is a tie:

```
    // No open spaces and no winner, so the game is a tie
    return TTGameOverTie;
```

Next, you built the `updateGameStatus` method to update the status label based on the status of the game. This method also displays the Game Over message if the game is over.

First, you checked to see if the game is over:

```
// Check for win or tie
TTGameOverStatus gameOverStatus = [self checkGameOver];
```

Based on the `gameOverStatus`, you needed to do different things, so you used a `switch` statement to execute the correct block of code:

```
switch (gameOverStatus) {
```

If the game was not over, you updated the status label with appropriate text depending on which player was to move next:

```
case TTGameNotOver:
    // The game is not over
    // Next player's turn
    if (self.theGameState.playersTurn == TTxPlayerTurn)
    {
        // Set the status label
        self.statusLabel.text = @"X to move";

    }
    else
    {
        // Set the status label
        self.statusLabel.text = @"O to move";

    }

    break;
```

If the game was over, you called the `endGameWithResult:` method to end the game and display the results:

```
    case TTGameOverxWins:
    case TTGameOveroWins:
    case TTGameOverTie:
    // Game is over
    [self endGameWithResult:gameOverStatus];
    break;
}
```

After that, you were ready to build the UI interaction element of the game, the spaceButtonTapped action method. When you were working with Interface Builder, you wired up all of the space buttons to call this method when the player tapped them.

First, you stored the index of the button that the player tapped:

```
int spaceIndex = [sender tag];
```

You used the tag that you set in Interface Builder to differentiate between the buttons.

Next, you wrote an if statement to determine if the space that the player tapped is blank:

```
// If the space is blank let the player place the shape
if ([[self.theGameState.boardState objectAtIndex:spaceIndex] isEqualToString:@" "])
{
```

You needed this if statement to enforce the rule that a player can place his shape only in an unoccupied space on the grid.

After you verified that the player tapped into an open grid space, you updated the game state based on the player turn. You checked to see if it was X's turn:

```
// Update game state
if (self.theGameState.playersTurn == TTxPlayerTurn)
{
```

If it was in fact X's turn, you updated the boardState array by placing the string "x" in the index location corresponding with the space that the player touched:

```
[self.theGameState.boardState replaceObjectAtIndex:spaceIndex withObject: @"x"];
```

Then, you set the game state's playersTurn property to indicate that it is now o's turn:

```
// It is now o's turn
self.theGameState.playersTurn = TToPlayerTurn;
```

You did the same thing in the else clause if it was O's turn:

```
else
    {
        [self.theGameState.boardState replaceObjectAtIndex:spaceIndex withObject: @"o"];

        // It is now x's turn
        self.theGameState.playersTurn = TTxPlayerTurn;

    }
```

Here, you placed the string "o" in the array and set the playersTurn property to indicate that it is now X's turn.

Finally, you updated the board by calling updateBoard and updated the game status by calling updateGameStatus:

```
// Update the board
[self updateBoard];

// Update the game status
[self updateGameStatus];
```

To finish the game you wrote the endGameWithResult method to end the game. You needed to take different action based on the result parameter, so you used a switch statement:

```
switch (result) {
```

Based on the result, you set the game-over message appropriately:

```
case TTGameOverxWins:
    gameOverMessage = [NSString stringWithString:@"X wins"];
    break;
case TTGameOveroWins:
    gameOverMessage = [NSString stringWithString:@"O wins"];
    break;
case TTGameOverTie:
    gameOverMessage = [NSString stringWithString:@"The game is a tie"];
```

Then, you created and configured a UIAlertView to show an alert with your game over message:

```
// Show an alert with the results
UIAlertView *alert = [[UIAlertView alloc] initWithTitle:@"Game Over"
    message:gameOverMessage
    delegate:self
    cancelButtonTitle:@"OK"
    otherButtonTitles: nil];
```

You set the delegate method for the UIAlertView to self so that the framework will call the alertView:clickedButtonAtIndex: method when the player acknowledges the alert box.

Finally, you showed the alert:

```
[alert show];
```

The last thing that you did was implement the UIAlertView delegate method alertView:clickedButtonAtIndex:. In this method, you called initGame to reset the game:

```
[self initGame];
```

NETWORKING YOUR GAME

Now that you have the basic Tic-Tac-Toe game running correctly, you are ready to look at how to convert it into a two-player networked game. In this section, you will learn how to use the GameKit framework to add peer-to-peer connectivity to your games.

The peer-to-peer networking APIs in GameKit help you to create a network between the players of your game. This allows you to easily exchange data between instances of the game, which facilitates head-to-head play. Players do not even need to be connected to a network to play against each other, as GameKit can use Bluetooth to create a network between players.

The basic workflow for creating a network between players is straightforward. First, you present the players with a GKPeerPickerController, which presents a standard user interface for connecting two devices. In your code, you implement the GKPeerPickerControllerDelegate protocol to handle responses from the peer picker controller. Once the peer picker has established a connection between two devices, you can send data to peers by using the GKSession class. Finally, you code your classes to process data that they receive in the `receiveData:fromPeer:inSession:context:` method.

Do not worry if this seems confusing. You will see how easy it is to add peer-to-peer connectivity to your games in the upcoming example.

NSDATA AND NSCODING

Building a peer-to-peer game with GameKit is easy. The trickiest part is figuring out how to package your data for transfer between peers. Fortunately, this is not too difficult. Both of the methods that you use to send data to peers send the data in the form of an `NSData` object.

`NSData` is an object-oriented wrapper for a byte buffer. This means that all that you need to do to transfer arbitrary game data between peers is to convert your game data into an `NSData` object. Fortunately, there is an easy way to do this by implementing the `NSCoding` protocol.

The `NSCoding` protocol specifies two methods that must be implemented: `initWithCoder:` and `encodeWithCoder:`. The `initWithCoder:` method initializes a new object with a given state, otherwise known as *deserialization*. The `encodeWithCoder:` method takes an object with state and *serializes* it. You can think about `encodeWithCoder:` taking your object and packing it up for transfer, and `initWithCoder:` unpacking the received data back into a usable object.

Many common classes like `NSString`, `NSArray`, `NSNumber`, and many others already implement the `NSCoding` protocol. This means that objects of these types already know how to serialize themselves. In general, all you need to do is serialize your custom model classes in the `NSCoding` methods by calling the encoding methods on each of the member variables in your class.

TRY IT OUT   **Implementing the NSCoding Protocol**

codefile TicTac available for download at Wrox.com

In order to keep the two networked instances of a TicTac game coordinated, you will send the game state across the network each time a player makes a move. To do this, you will first update the `GameState` object to support the `NSCoding` protocol. The methods of `NSCoding` enable you to serialize your data objects for transfer or storage.

1. Open the `GameState.h` header file. Modify the `@interface` definition to indicate that the class implements the `NSCoding` protocol:

```
@interface GameState : NSObject<NSCoding>
```

2. Switch over to the `GameState.m` implementation file and add the `encodeWithCoder:` and `initWithCoder:` methods required to implement the `NSCoding` protocol:

```
- (void)encodeWithCoder:(NSCoder *)aCoder
{

    [aCoder encodeObject: boardState forKey:@"BoardState"];
    [aCoder encodeInt:playersTurn forKey:@"PlayersTurn"];
}
```

```
- (id)initWithCoder:(NSCoder *)aDecoder
{
    boardState = [aDecoder decodeObjectForKey:@"BoardState"];
    playersTurn = [aDecoder decodeIntForKey:@"PlayersTurn"];

    return self;

}
```

How It Works

The first thing that you did was update the GameState object to support the NSCoding protocol:

```
@interface GameState : NSObject<NSCoding>
```

The methods of NSCoding enable you to serialize your data objects for transfer or storage.

Next, you added the encodeWithCoder: and initWithCoder: methods required to implement the NSCoding protocol.

The encodeWithCoder: method is responsible for serializing your object. You are responsible for encoding all of your instance variables. In encodeWithCoder:, you used the encodeObject: method to encode the mutable array that holds the board state:

```
[aCoder encodeObject: boardState forKey:@"BoardState"];
```

Then, you called encodeInt: to encode the player turn indicator:

```
[aCoder encodeInt:playersTurn forKey:@"PlayersTurn"];
```

TheinitWithCoder: method is responsible for deserializing your object. You are responsible for decoding all of your instance variables. In initWithCoder:, you used the decodeObjectForKey: method to decode the mutable array that holds the board state:

```
boardState = [aDecoder decodeObjectForKey:@"BoardState"];
```

Then, you called decodeIntForKey: to decode the player turn indicator:

```
playersTurn = [aDecoder decodeIntForKey:@"PlayersTurn"];
```

Now you have a GameState object that implements the NSCoding protocol. Later, you will use the NSKeyedArchiver class to encode your GameState object into an NSData object.

CONVERTING CLASSES TO DATA WITH ARCHIVES

Once you have implemented the NSCoding protocol, you can encode and decode your class by using another helper class such as NSCoder. Well, you do not actually use NSCoder because NSCoder is an abstract class. However, you can use one of NSCoder's concrete subclasses: NSArchiver, NSUnarchiver, NSKeyedArchiver, NSKeyedUnarchiver, or NSPortCoder depending on your particular application. The most common combination is NSKeyedArchiver and NSKeyedUnarchiver, so that is what you will use.

You use the NSKeyedArchiver class to archive objects that implement the NSCoding protocol. You can archive an object to several formats, but the most important for this application is

NSData. Likewise, you use the NSKeyedUnarchiver to convert an NSData object back into your custom class.

The combination of sending NSData objects, implementing the NSCoding protocol, and using an archiver to serialize and de-serialize your objects fits well with a typical Model-View-Controller design. In a game, which you will see in the example, you can create a model class that holds the state of your game. Then, you implement the NSCoding protocol in your model class so it knows how to encode itself. Then, you use an archiver to convert the object into NSData for transfer across a network connection.

For more information on the NSCoding protocol, archivers, and how to use them to pack and unpack data, take a look at Apple's Archives and Serializations Programming Guide available at http://developer.apple.com/library/mac/#documentation/Cocoa/Conceptual/Archiving/Archiving.html.

The most important thing to know is that you transfer data between peers by using NSData, and you can package your custom classes into an NSData by implementing the NSCoding protocol and using an NSKeyedArchiver.

CONNECTING AND SENDING DATA

As you saw earlier, the first step in creating a peer-to-peer network between players is presenting the players with a GKPeerPickerController. You use the GKPeerPickerController to present a standard user interface for connecting two devices. While you can build your own interface for creating the connection between players, the peer picker works perfectly well and provides a common user experience for your players. When finished, the peer picker returns a configured GKSession object that you can use to transfer data between the peers.

In addition to displaying the view, the peer picker will call methods of the GKPeerPickerControllerDelegate protocol to let you handle responses from the peer picker controller.

The most important delegate method is peerPickerController:didConnectPeer:toSession:. The controller calls this method when the controller connects a peer to the session. In this method, you will typically write code to store a reference to the session and dismiss the peer picker. You will use the session later to send data to peers.

Another interesting delegate method is peerPickerControllerDidCancel:. The controller calls this method when the user cancels the connection process. Although I did not implement this method in the example, you would want to handle this case in a production quality game.

Once the peer picker has established a connection between two devices, you can send data to peers by using the GKSession class. The method that you will use in the example is sendDataToAllPeers:withDataMode:error:. This method sends the specified data to all of the peers connected to the session.

You can send data to any specific peer by using the sendData:toPeers:withDataMode:error: method. Here, you specify an array of peers to whom you wish to send the data.

The `withDataMode:` parameter of each send method allows you to specify a reliability level of the data transmission. The two options for this parameter are `GKSendDataReliable` and `GKSendDataUnreliable`.

Specifying `GKSendDataReliable` instructs the session to send the same data continuously until the intended peer receives it. Using this value ensures that the peer receives the sent data in the order that it was sent. However, this comes at a price in that you may waste time sending the same data many times until the peer receives it.

The other data mode is `GKSendDataUnreliable`. In this mode, the session sends the data one time with no regard for the fact that the peer may not receive the data. In this mode, the recipient may receive the data out of order. The advantage of using `GKSendDataUnreliable` is that it is faster. So, when transmission speed is crucial, use `GKSendDataUnreliable`. The drawback is that the data may be received out of order so you will have to write additional code to ensure that either you process the data in the correct order or you ignore messages that are out of order.

To receive data, you write your own implementation of the `receiveData.fromPeer.inSession :context:` method. The class that implements this function is called the data receive handler. By default, sessions are configured such that the session delegate is the data receive handler. In this method, you add code to do something with the data that you received from a peer. You will see this implemented in the example that follows.

TRY IT OUT Adding Networking to TicTac

codefile TicTac available for download at Wrox.com

In this section, you will finish the TicTac game by adding the peer-to-peer networking functionality.

1. Open the `ViewController.xib` interface file. Drag a UILabel from the Object library and drop it in your view. Position it near the top of the view above the status label and size it so that it stretches across the width of the view. Use the Attributes inspector to center-justify the text in the label.

2. Open the Assistant editor so that you can see the ViewController header file alongside your interface. Create an outlet for the UILabel in your header file by control-dragging the label into the header and dropping the label inside the `@interface` block. In the popover that appears, set the name of your UILabel to `playerLabel` and press the Connect button.

3. Set the text of the label to "Determining Player…".

4. Since you will be using the GameKit framework to implement the peer-to-peer networking, you need to add the framework to your project. Click on the TicTac project icon at the top of the Project Navigator view to bring up the project properties. In the editor window, under the heading Targets, click TicTac. Click the tab at the top of the Editor window labeled Build Phases. Expand the item that says, "Link Binary With Libraries." Click the plus sign at the bottom of the "Link Binary With Libraries" table. In the dialog that comes up, select GameKit.framework and click Add.

5. Open the `ViewController.h` header file. Since you will be using the GameKit framework, you need to add a `#import` statement to import the GameKit header:

```
#import <GameKit/GameKit.h>
```

6. With the players each playing on their own devices, you now need to keep track of the shape for each device. Add the following enumeration that defines the shapes:

```
typedef enum {
    TTMyShapeUndetermined = 0,
    TTMyShapeX = 1,
    TTMyShapeO= 2
} TTMyShape;
```

7. You will use the `GKPeerPickerController` to enable the player to find peers playing the game. Since you will handle delegate method calls from the `GKPeerPickerController`, you need to implement the `GKPeerPickerControllerDelegate` protocol in the `ViewController` class. Modify the `@interface` declaration to indicate that you are implementing the `GKPeerPickerControllerDelegate` protocol:

```
@interface ViewController : UIViewController <GKPeerPickerControllerDelegate>
```

8. Add the following instance members to the `ViewController@interface` block:

```
// Which player am I
TTMyShape myShape;

// Store my UUID
NSString* myUUID;

// Gamekit variables
GKSession* theSession;
NSString* myPeerID;
```

9. Below the `@interface` block, add these new properties to your class:

```
@property TTMyShape myShape;
@property (strong, nonatomic) NSString* myUUID;

// Gamekit properties
@property (strong, nonatomic) IBOutletGKSession* theSession;
@property (strong, nonatomic) IBOutletNSString* myPeerID;
```

10. Add a new method declaration for the `getUUIDString` method:

```
- (NSString *)getUUIDString;
```

The completed header should look like this:

```
#import <UIKit/UIKit.h>
#import "GameState.h"
#import <GameKit/GameKit.h>

typedef enum {
    TTGameNotOver = 0,       // The game is not over
    TTGameOverxWins = 1,     // The x player won
    TTGameOveroWins = 2,     // The o player won
    TTGameOverTie = 3,       // The game is a tie
```

```objc
} TTGameOverStatus;

typedef enum {
    TTMyShapeUndetermined = 0,
    TTMyShapeX = 1,
    TTMyShapeO= 2
} TTMyShape;

@interface ViewController : UIViewController<GKPeerPickerControllerDelegate>
{
    UIImage* xImage;
    UIImage* oImage;

    // The game state
    GameState* theGameState;

    // Which player am I
    TTMyShape myShape;

    // Store my UUID
    NSString* myUUID;

    // Gamekit variables
    GKSession* theSession;
    NSString* myPeerID;
}
@property (strong, nonatomic) UIImage* xImage;
@property (strong, nonatomic) UIImage* oImage;
@property (strong, nonatomic) GameState* theGameState;

@property (strong, nonatomic) IBOutletCollection(UIButton) NSArray *spaceButton;
@property (strong, nonatomic) IBOutletUILabel *statusLabel;
@property (strong, nonatomic) IBOutletUILabel *playerLabel;

@property TTMyShape myShape;
@property (strong, nonatomic) NSString* myUUID;

// Gamekit properties
@property (strong, nonatomic) IBOutletGKSession* theSession;
@property (strong, nonatomic) IBOutletNSString* myPeerID;

- (IBAction)spaceButtonTapped:(id)sender;

- (void) initGame;
- (void) updateBoard;
- (void) updateGameStatus;
- (TTGameOverStatus) checkGameOver;
- (BOOL) didPlayerWin: (NSString*) player;
- (void) endGameWithResult:(TTGameOverStatus) result;
- (NSString *)getUUIDString;

@end
```

11. Now, switch over to the `ViewController.m` implementation file. Below the current `@synthesize` lines, add the following code to synthesize your new properties:

```
@synthesize myShape,myUUID;

// Synthesize gamekit properties
@synthesize theSession,myPeerID;
```

12. Add the following additional initialization code to the end of the `viewDidLoad` method:

```
// Initialize my shape to undetermined
myShape = TTMyShapeUndetermined;

// Generate my UUID
myUUID = [self getUUIDString];
```

13. After the game is loaded and the main view appears, you want to show the `GKPeerPickerController`. Add the following code to the `viewDidAppear:` method after the line that calls the superclass `super viewDidAppear:` method:

```
// Show the peer picker
GKPeerPickerController* picker = [[GKPeerPickerController alloc] init];
picker.delegate = self;

[picker show];
```

14. Implement the new `getUUIDString` method:

```
- (NSString *)getUUIDString
{
    NSString *  result;
    CFUUIDRef   uuid;
    CFStringRef uuidStr;

    uuid = CFUUIDCreate(NULL);

    uuidStr = CFUUIDCreateString(NULL, uuid);

    result = [NSString stringWithFormat:@"%@", uuidStr];

    CFRelease(uuidStr);
    CFRelease(uuid);

    return result;
}
```

15. Next you need to update the `spaceButtonTapped:` method. First, modify the first `if` statement so that the code lets the player move only if it is his turn like this:

```
// If the space is blank and if it is my turn go, if not, ignore
if ([[self.theGameState.boardState objectAtIndex:spaceIndex] isEqualToString:@" "]
&& self.myShape == self.theGameState.playersTurn)
```

16. After the method updates the board and game status, you need to send out the new game state to the other player. Add the following code after the line that updates the game status:

```
// Send the new game state out to peers
NSData* theData = [NSKeyedArchiver archivedDataWithRootObject:self.theGameState];
```

```
NSError* error;

[self.theSession sendDataToAllPeers:theData withDataMode:GKSendDataReliable error:&error];
```

The `spaceButtonTapped:` method should now look like this:

```
- (IBAction)spaceButtonTapped:(id)sender {
    int spaceIndex = [sender tag];

    // If the space is blank and if it is my turn go, if not, ignore
    if ([[self.theGameState.boardState objectAtIndex:spaceIndex] isEqualToString:@" "]
    &&self.myShape == self.theGameState.playersTurn)
    {

        // Update game state
        if (self.theGameState.playersTurn == TTxPlayerTurn)
        {
            [self.theGameState.boardState replaceObjectAtIndex:spaceIndex withObject: @"x"];

            // It is now o's turn
            self.theGameState.playersTurn = TToPlayerTurn;

        }
        else
        {
            [self.theGameState.boardState replaceObjectAtIndex:spaceIndex withObject: @"o"];

            // It is now x's turn
            self.theGameState.playersTurn = TTxPlayerTurn;

        }

        // Update the board
        [self updateBoard];

        // Update the game status
        [self updateGameStatus];

        // Send the new game state out to peers
        NSData* theData = [NSKeyedArchiver archivedDataWithRootObject:self.theGameState];
        NSError* error;

        [self.theSession sendDataToAllPeers:theData withDataMode:GKSendDataReliable error:&error];

    }
}
```

17. The last thing that you will do is implement the `GKPeerPickerControllerDelegate` delegate methods. First, implement `peerPickerController:didConnectPeer:toSession:` like this:

```
- (void)peerPickerController:(GKPeerPickerController *)picker
            didConnectPeer:(NSString *)peerID
                toSession:(GKSession *)session
{
    // Tells the delegate that the controller connected a peer to the session.
    // Once a peer is connected to the session, your application should take
```

```
    // ownership of the session, dismiss the peer picker, and then use the
    // session to communicate with the other peer.

    // Store off the session
    self.theSession= session;

    // Store the Peer ID
    self.myPeerID = peerID;

    // Set the receive data handler
    [session setDataReceiveHandler:self withContext:nil];

    // Dismiss the picker
    [picker dismiss];

    // Session is connected so negotiate shapes
    // Send out UUID
    NSData* theData = [NSKeyedArchiver archivedDataWithRootObject:self.myUUID];
    NSError* error;

    [self.theSession sendDataToAllPeers:theData withDataMode:GKSendDataReliable error:&error];

}
```

18. Implement `receiveData:fromPeer:inSession:context:` like this:

```
- (void) receiveData:(NSData *)data fromPeer:(NSString *)peer
        inSession: (GKSession *)session context:(void *)context
{
    // The receive data handler
    NSLog(@"Received data");

    // If myShape == TTMyShapeUndetermined we should get shape negotiation data
    if (myShape == TTMyShapeUndetermined)
    {
        NSString* peerUUID = [NSKeyedUnarchiverunarchiveObjectWithData:data];
        if ([myUUID compare:peerUUID] == NSOrderedAscending)
        {
            myShape = TTMyShapeX;
            self.playerLabel.text = @"You are X";
        }
        else
        {
            myShape = TTMyShapeO;
            self.playerLabel.text = @"You are O";
        }
    }
    else
    {
        // Update the board state with the received data
        self.theGameState = [NSKeyedUnarchiver unarchiveObjectWithData:data] ;

        // Received data so update the board and the game status
        [self updateBoard];
        [self updateGameStatus];
```

```
    }

}
```

How It Works

First, you updated the user interface of the game. You added a new label to the view controller to let the player know which shape he was controlling, X or O.

You then added a new enumeration to the view controller, `TTMyShape`, to indicate the shape that the player was playing:

```
typedef enum {
    TTMyShapeUndetermined = 0,
    TTMyShapeX = 1,
    TTMyShapeO= 2
} TTMyShape;
```

You used the `GKPeerPickerController` to enable the player to find peers playing the game. You needed to implement the `GKPeerPickerControllerDelegate` protocol in the `ViewController` class to handle the peer picker callback methods so you modified the `@interface` declaration in the view controller:

```
@interface ViewController : UIViewController <GKPeerPickerControllerDelegate>
```

Next, you added some new instance members to the view controller:

```
// Which player am I
TTMyShape myShape;

// Store my UUID
NSString* myUUID;

// Gamekit variables
GKSession* theSession;
NSString* myPeerID;
```

You used the `myShape` variable to keep track of the shape that the current player was playing. The `myUUID` variable stored a unique identifier that you used to determine which player would play which shape.

Then, you moved on to the implementation of the new features of the view controller. You first updated the `viewDidLoad` method to initialize the new `myShape` and `myUUID` variables:

```
// Initialize my shape to undetermined
myShape = TTMyShapeUndetermined;

// Generate my UUID
myUUID = [self getUUIDString];
```

Next, you added code to the `viewDidAppear:` method to show the peer picker. First, you allocated and initialized a new instance of the `GKPeerPickerController`:

```
GKPeerPickerController* picker = [[GKPeerPickerController alloc] init];
```

Then, you set the view controller as the delegate of the peer picker:

```
picker.delegate = self;
```

Finally, you displayed the peer picker to the player to allow him to find someone to play the game with:

```
[picker show];
```

After this, you implemented the `getUUIDString` method. The purpose of this method is to get a unique string to identify each player. You used some Core Foundation functions to generate this unique identifier. You used this string to determine the shape that each player would play.

First, you created a UUID by using the `CFUUIDCreate` function:

```
uuid = CFUUIDCreate(NULL);
```

Next, you converted the UUID into a `CFStringRef` with the `CFUUIDCreateString` function:

```
uuidStr = CFUUIDCreateString(NULL, uuid);
```

Then you converted the `CFStringRef` into an `NSString` by calling the `stringWithFormat:` method:

```
result = [NSString stringWithFormat:@"%@", uuidStr];
```

Finally, you cleaned up your Core Foundation objects and returned the UUID string:

```
CFRelease(uuidStr);
CFRelease(uuid);

return result;
```

Next, you moved on to update the `spaceButtonTapped:` method. You needed to modify this method to send the game data out to the other player after the player made a move. First, though, you added code to let the player move only if it was his turn:

```
// If the space is blank and if it is my turn go, if not, ignore
if ([[self.theGameState.boardState objectAtIndex:spaceIndex] isEqualToString:@" "]
&& self.myShape == self.theGameState.playersTurn)
```

After the method updated the board and game status, you sent out the new game state to the other player. First, you used an `NSKeyedArchiver` to archive your game state object. This converts the object into an `NSData` object that you can send out to the peer:

```
// Send the new game state out to peers
NSData* theData = [NSKeyedArchiver archivedDataWithRootObject:self.theGameState];
NSError* error;
```

Then, you sent the data out to the peer by using the `sendDataToAllPeers:withDataMode:error:` method of the `GKSession` object:

```
[self.theSession sendDataToAllPeers:theData withDataMode:GKSendDataReliable error:&error];
```

Notice that you used the `GKSendDataReliable` data mode. This ensures that peers will receive the data in the order that you send it. In this case, you are sending the data only one time, when a player makes a move. Therefore, it is crucial that the peer receives the data. Speed of transfer is not as important in this case as is the guarantee that the peer has received the move. In an action game, like Blocker, you could use the unreliable data transfer method if you needed to send out the position of the ball for every frame.

That is all the code required to send data. First, you serialize the data, then, you send it out.

The last thing that you did was implement the `GKPeerPickerControllerDelegate` delegate methods. These are the methods that the peer picker uses to call back into your code when something interesting happens.

First, you built the `peerPickerController:didConnectPeer:toSession:` method. The peer picker calls this method when you first connect to a peer. The first thing that you did in this method was to store the session and peer ID information that the peer picker sent into the method:

```
// Store off the session
self.theSession- session;

// Store the Peer ID
self.myPeerID = peerID;
```

Then, you set the view controller as the class that would handle receiving data from the peer:

```
// Set the receive data handler
[session setDataReceiveHandler:self withContext:nil];
```

Setting the DataReceiveHandler tells the session which class implements the `receiveData:fromPeer:inSession:context:` method. Remember that the session calls this method in response to receiving data from a peer.

Since you have established a connection with the peer at this point, you dismissed the peer picker controller:

```
// Dismiss the picker
[picker dismiss];
```

Next, you needed to negotiate which player would play which shape. This is where the UUID comes in. Once you established the connection, you sent out your UUID to the peer by first encoding it and then sending it out:

```
// Session is connected so negotiate shapes
// Send out UUID
NSData* theData = [NSKeyedArchiver archivedDataWithRootObject:self.myUUID];
NSError* error;

[self.theSession sendDataToAllPeers:theData withDataMode:GKSendDataReliable error:&error];
```

Again, you used the `GKSendDataReliable` method because you are going to send the negotiation data only one time. It is important that the peer receives the information because you will never send it again.

Finally, you built the `receiveData:fromPeer:inSession:context:` method, which is called any time your game receives data from a peer. First, you logged that you received some data. This is helpful when you first start working with networking to verify that some data is coming across the peer-to-peer connection:

```
NSLog(@"Received data");
```

Next, if the player's shape is undetermined, that means that the first bit of data from the peer should be shape negotiation data. Therefore, you tested to see if the player's shape was undetermined:

```
if (myShape == TTMyShapeUndetermined)
```

If the player's shape was undetermined, you handled the incoming negotiation data. First, you unarchived the data as an `NSString`:

```
NSString* peerUUID = [NSKeyedUnarchiver unarchiveObjectWithData:data];
```

Then, you compared the UUID that the peer sent in with your own, using this comparison to determine the shape that you would play:

```
if ([myUUID compare:peerUUID] == NSOrderedAscending)
{
    myShape = TTMyShapeX;
    self.playerLabel.text = @"You are X";
}
else
{
    myShape = TTMyShapeO;
    self.playerLabel.text = @"You are O";
}
```

Then you coded the `else` statement to handle any data sent by the peer after the negotiation phase ended. Here, you unarchive the data that the peer sent in:

```
else
{
    // Update the board state with the received data
    self.theGameState = [NSKeyedUnarchiver unarchiveObjectWithData:data] ;
```

Since you just received new game state information, you needed to update the board and the game status. You did this by calling the `updateBoard` and `updateGameStatus` methods.

RUNNING THE GAME

You are now finished with the coding and are ready to test the game. To test the game, you will need a device such as an iPhone, iPod Touch, or iPad. You will also need to be a member of the iOS developer program as it is not possible to install your programs on a device without joining the program.

To test the application, you will start one instance of the game in the iOS simulator and pair up with another instance running on the device.

The process for getting your iOS applications running on a device is relatively simple, but there are many details surrounding the process. Since the process has changed substantially throughout the lifetime of iOS and will likely continue to change, it is not beneficial to document the process in a book where it may become outdated. You can find all of the details of the process online on Apple's developer website in the iOS development guide (`http://developer.apple.com/library/ios/documentation/Xcode/Conceptual/iphone_development/index.html`). Specifically, the section called "Managing Devices and Digital Identities" clearly explains how to configure your computer and device for development.

Ensure that you have the iPhone simulator selected in the scheme section of the Xcode toolbar as in Figure 10-3.

Start the debugger running with the simulator by clicking the Run button in Xcode.

Once the application starts up, you may see an OS X dialog like Figure 10-4. This dialog is asking if you want to allow TicTac to accept incoming connections. Click Allow.

FIGURE 10-3: The active scheme

FIGURE 10-4: OS X asking to accept incoming connections

At this point, the iOS simulator should begin looking for another device to connect to, as you can see in Figure 10-5.

Now, plug your device into your computer. Click on the right side of the scheme button at the top of the Xcode window. If you have correctly configured your device for debugging, you should see your device in the pop-up list. Choose your device. The scheme should now say something like TicTac ➪ {your device} (mine says TicTac ➪ Patrick Alessi's iPad). Click Run to start another instance of the debugger. This debugger will run by using your device. If you do not have Bluetooth enabled on the device, you will see a dialog asking you to enable it, which you should do.

Once the game is running on the device, you should see a screen that looks like Figure 10-5. However if you look at the simulator, you should see that the peer picker has found a device, as seen in Figure 10-6. Click the device name in the simulator to indicate that you want to connect to the device. The simulator will then indicate that it is waiting for a reply from the device.

Look at the device and you should notice that the searching display has changed to a request display, as seen in Figure 10-7. The peer picker is asking if you would like to accept a connection from the simulator. Tap the Accept button.

FIGURE 10-5: Looking for a connection

Once you tap Accept, all of the peer picker views should go away, the connection between the simulator and device should be established, and you should now be able to play the game. Try tapping grid spaces when it is not your turn, and you should notice that nothing happens. Now, try selecting a space when it is your turn. You should see both displays update with the new game state. Additionally, you should notice that the status label updates to indicate that it is now the other player's turn.

Congratulations, you have successfully created your own peer-to-peer game session!

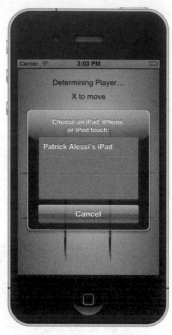

FIGURE 10-6: The peer picker has found a device

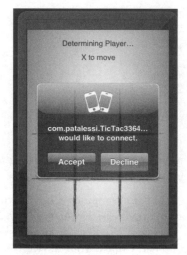

FIGURE 10-7: Asking to accept a connection

SUMMARY

In this chapter, you learned about the basic features of GameKit and then dove into peer-to-peer networking. First, you built a simple version of Tic-Tac-Toe. Then you looked at the basics of creating a networked game.

Next, you learned about the NSData object and the NSCoding protocol and how these combined to enable you to package your classes into data objects. Then, you enhanced the TicTac game to implement serialization and deserialization by using the NSCoding protocol. Then, you learned how to do the actual data serialization by using archivers.

Then, you learned how to use the GKPeerPickerController to allow players to set up a network between them. You also looked at how you use the GKSession class to send data between pairs and how to handle receiving data from peers.

Finally, you finished the TicTac game by adding peer-to-peer networking between two instances of the game.

EXERCISES

1. In the Scrambler game from Chapter 5, you built a model class with the following interface:

```
@interfaceScramblerModel : NSObject {
    ScramblerPlayer* computerPlayer;
    int time;
    int score;
    NSString* currentWord;
}
```

Assuming that the `ScramblerPlayer` class implements the `NSCoding` protocol, how would you modify this class so that you could serialize it for transfer to a peer?

2. Write a simple program that uses peer-to-peer networking to send a fixed string between peers. Log the received string to the debug log.

3. How do the `NSData` class, `NSCoding` protocol, and Archivers work together to help you send data between peers?

Answers to the Exercises can be found in the Appendix.

▶ **WHAT YOU LEARNED IN THIS CHAPTER**

TOPIC	MAIN POINTS
GameKit features	Game center integration including achievements, leaderboards, and auto matching.
	Peer-to-peer connectivity for creating local head-to-head games.
	In-Game Voice for enabling voice chat between your game players.
`NSData`	An object-oriented wrapper for a byte buffer.
`NSCoding` **protocol**	Specifies two methods that must be implemented to enable a class to serialize and de-serialize itself: `initWithCoder:` and `encodeWithCoder:`
Archivers	Used with classes to implement the `NSCoding` protocol to serialize and de-serialize the class.
`GKPeerPickerController`	Used to present a standard user interface for connecting two devices.
`GKSession` **class**	Used to send data to peers and handle receiving data from peers.

APPENDIX

Answers to Exercises

This appendix contains the answers to the exercises that are found at the end of each chapter.

CHAPTER 2

1. The easiest way to find anything in your code is by using the Search navigator in the Navigation area. Simply bring up the Search navigator by clicking the magnifying glass icon at the top of the Navigation area. Then, type **viewDidLoad** in the search box. The Navigation area will show the search results. Click on one of the results to move into the code file where you found the `viewDidLoad` method.

2. You can use the Issue navigator to see a list of the errors that the compiler found. You can click on any issue to navigate to the source of the error in your code. Fixing issues will cause the old issue to disappear from the Issue navigator.

3. You can easily re-indent blocks of code by highlighting them in the editor and choosing Editor ⇨ Structure ⇨ Re-indent from the menu bar. Executing the Re-indent command on the given code results in the following indentation:

```
for (int i=0;i<10;i++){
    for (j=0; j<100; j++) {
        for (k=100; k>0; k--) {
            // Do something in your code

        }
    }
}
```

    Notice how it is now easy to see the structure of the nested loops.

4. Open the Quick Help inspector and put the cursor on the `viewDidLoad` method in the `SampleUIViewController.m` code file. In the Quick Help inspector, you will see that `viewDidLoad` is declared in `UIViewController.h`.

5. Start a new Single View Application. I called mine, "Exercise." Open the XIB file in Interface builder and drag three buttons and a label into the view. Drag a label into the view. Double-click on each button and set their labels. Using the Assistant editor, control-drag each button into the View Controller header file to create Actions for each button. Control-drag the label into the header file to create an outlet for the label. The header file should look like this:

```
#import <UIKit/UIKit.h>

@interface ExerciseViewController : UIViewController {
    UILabel *textLabel;
}

@property (strong, nonatomic) IBOutlet UILabel *textLabel;

- (IBAction)tappedOne:(id)sender;
- (IBAction)tappedTwo:(id)sender;
- (IBAction)tappedThree:(id)sender;

@end
```

In the View Controller implementation file, write code for each of the action methods to update the label like this:

```
- (IBAction)tappedOne:(id)sender {
    textLabel.text = @"One";
}

- (IBAction)tappedTwo:(id)sender {
    textLabel.text = @"Two";
}

- (IBAction)tappedThree:(id)sender {
    textLabel.text = @"Three";
}
```

Build and run the program. Tapping each button should change the text appropriately.

CHAPTER 3

1. There are four base data types in C: char, int, float, and double.

2. The correct syntax for declaring an int variable and initializing it to zero is as follows:

```
int myInt=0;
```

3. A while loop checks the condition for executing the loop at the top, before an iteration of the loop is executed. A do...while loop checks the condition at the bottom after the code in the loop has run.

4. Define the function like this:

```
double doWork (int theInt, float, theFloat)
{

}
```

5. No, function parameters are passed by value in C. Modifying the parameters inside of the function has no effect outside of the function. The scope of function parameters is limited to the function.

6. The `if` statement should be changed to this:

```
if (((pDeck-2)->value <= pDeck-> value &&
     (pDeck-1)->value >= pDeck->value) ||
    ((pDeck-2)->value >= pDeck->value &&
     (pDeck-1)->value <= pDeck->value))
```

7. Here is the `main` function rewritten using just the array and subscript notation instead of pointers:

```
int main (int argc, const char * argv[])
{

    struct card deck[] =
    {
        {"ace", "spades",1}, {"two", "spades",2}, {"three", "spades",3},
        {"four", "spades",4}, {"five", "spades",5}, {"six", "spades",6},
        {"seven", "spades",7}, {"eight", "spades",8}, {"nine", "spades",9},
        {"ten", "spades",10}, {"jack", "spades",11}, {"queen", "spades",12},
        {"king", "spades",13},
        {"ace", "clubs",1}, {"two", "clubs",2}, {"three", "clubs",3},
        {"four", "clubs",4}, {"five", "clubs",5}, {"six", "clubs",6},
        {"seven", "clubs",7}, {"eight", "clubs",8}, {"nine", "clubs",9},
        {"ten", "clubs",10}, {"jack", "clubs",11}, {"queen", "clubs",12},
        {"king", "clubs",13},
        {"ace", "hearts",1}, {"two", "hearts",2}, {"three", "hearts",3},
        {"four", "hearts",4}, {"five", "hearts",5}, {"six", "hearts",6},
        {"seven", "hearts",7}, {"eight", "hearts",8}, {"nine", "hearts",9},
        {"ten", "hearts",10}, {"jack", "hearts",11}, {"queen", "hearts",12},
        {"king", "hearts",13},
        {"ace", "diamonds",1}, {"two", "diamonds",2}, {"three", "diamonds",3},
        {"four", "diamonds",4}, {"five", "diamonds",5}, {"six", "diamonds",6},
        {"seven", "diamonds",7}, {"eight", "diamonds",8},
        {"nine", "diamonds",9},{"ten", "diamonds",10}, {"jack", "diamonds",11},
        {"queen", "diamonds",12}, {"king", "diamonds",13},
        {"sentinel", "null", 0}
    };

    // Create the player's bank and start it off with 100 credits
    int bank=100;

    // Create a variable to hold the bet
    int bet=0;

    // Create a counter for the card index
    int index = 0;

    // Run the function to shuffle the deck
    shuffle(deck);

    // Run the game in a loop. Continue as long as the bank is > and none of
    // the next three cards are the sentinel
```

```
do {
    // Print the amount of credits in the bank
    printf("Your bank: %i\n", bank);

    // Print the cards
    printf("The cards: ");

    // First card
    printf("%s of %s ", deck[index].name, deck[index].suit);

    // Move to the next card
    index++;

    // Second card
    printf("and %s of %s\n", deck[index].name, deck[index].suit);

    // Move the pointer to the next card
    index++;

    // Ask for the bet
    // Do this in a loop because we cannot accept bets greater than the
    // amount that the player has in the bank and we cannot
    // accept a 0 bet
    do {
        printf("Enter your bet: ");
        scanf("%i", &bet);
    }
    while (bet <= 0 || bet > bank );

    // Draw the third card
    printf("The third card is %s of %s\n", deck[index].name, deck[index].suit);

    // Determine if the player won
    // The player is a winner if the third card falls between the first two
    // Ties go to the house
    if ((deck[index-2].value < deck[index].value &&
         deck[index-1].value > deck[index].value) ||
        (deck[index-2].value > deck[index].value &&
         deck[index-1].value < deck[index].value)) {
            printf("We have a winner!\n\n");

            // Player won, add bet to the bank
            bank += bet;

    }
    else {
        printf("Sorry, you lose.\n\n");
        // Player lost, subtract bet from the bank
        bank -= bet;
    }

    // Move to the next card
    index++;
```

```
    }
    while (bank > 0 &&
            52-index > 3);

    // The game is over
    printf("The game is over. Your final score is %i\n", bank);


    return 0;
}
```

CHAPTER 4

1. Yes, in fact C is the basis for Objective-C. Objective-C is a superset of C. Everything that you can do in C, you can also do in Objective-C.

An advantage to using C as the basis for Objective-C is that you can leverage the vast number of C libraries in your Objective-C programs.

2. A class is the blueprint for creating objects. Objects are instances of a class. You can create many object instances from a single class. Think of a class as a custom type, like `int` or `char`. You can create many `int` variables and you can create many variables that have the type of your class.

3. When you use inheritance, you are expressing an "is a" relationship between the objects. In the example in the chapter, you built a `House` class and inherited from `House` to build a `Colonial`. You used inheritance because a `Colonial` is a `House`.

4. Polymorphism is a feature of object-oriented languages that allows you to treat objects of a subclass as if they were the base class. This is useful because treating many objects the same way can simplify your code.

5. Change the `House.h` header to:

```
#import <Foundation/Foundation.h>

@interface House : NSObject {
    NSString* color;
}

@property (stong, nonatomic) NSString* color;

-(void) enterFrontDoor;


@end
```

Add the line:

```
@synthesize color;
```

to the `House.m` implementation file below the `@implementation` line.

Modify the main function in `main.c` to use the property instead of the accessor methods:

```c
int main (int argc, const char * argv[])
{

    // Declare an array of houses
    House* houses[3];

    // Create houses
    House* redHouse;
    redHouse = [[House alloc] init];
    redHouse.color = @"Red";

    // put the red house into the array
    houses[0] = redHouse;

    Colonial* greenHouse = [[Colonial alloc] init];
    greenHouse.color = @"Green";

    // put the green house into the array
    houses[1] = greenHouse;

    Mansion* yellowHouse = [[Mansion alloc] init];
    yellowHouse.color= @"Yellow";

    // put the yellow house into the array
    houses[2] = yellowHouse;

    for (int i=0;i<=2;i++)
    {
        // Print houses and enter
        NSLog(@"house is %@", houses[i].color);
        [houses[i] enterFrontDoor];
    }
    return 0;
```

CHAPTER 5

1. The root object is NSObject. It is defined in the Cocoa Foundation framework. You should inherit any objects that you create from scratch, which are not subclasses of other objects from NSObject.

2. The *model* is the class or set of classes that represent your data. In general, model objects should encapsulate all of your data.

The *view* portion of the MVC architecture is your user interface; the graphics, widgets, tables, and text boxes present the data in your model to the user.

The *controller* is the glue that binds your model to your view. The controller is responsible for telling the view what data from the model to display.

In summary, the model is your application data, the view is the user interface, and the controller is the logic code that binds the view to the model.

3. Outlets link the controls to your code by defining variables in your code that represent the controls. Actions link the controls to your code by defining methods that are called when a user interacts with a control.

4. You cannot append text to an NSString because the NSString class is immutable. To concatenate strings, you should use the appendString: method of the NSMutableString class.

5. NSArray can hold objects that inherit only from NSObject. Since the scalar types do not inherit from NSObject, you cannot store them in an NSArray. To get around this shortcoming, you can wrap scalar types in a wrapper class like NSNumber.

6. A simple command-line program that accomplishes this is:

```
int main (int argc, const char * argv[])
{

    // Initialize array
    NSArray *arr = [[NSArray alloc] initWithObjects:
                    @"This", @"is", @"my", @"word", @"list",nil];

    // Print list
    for (int i=0; i<[arr count]; i++)
    {
        NSLog(@"%@",[arr objectAtIndex:i]);
    }

    // Print list in reverse
    for (int i=(int)[arr count]-1; i>=0; i--)
    {
        NSLog(@"%@",[arr objectAtIndex:i]);
    }

    return 0;
}
```

I've included the code for this in a project called Test.

7. The steps for using a timer are creating an instance, configuring it to send a specific message to a specific object, and associating the timer with a run loop. When you are finished using the timer you need to invalidate it so that it stops sending the timed message.

8. Start a new View-Based project. Using Interface Builder, add a UILabel control to the view controller XIB. Add an outlet for this UILabel to the view controller header file. Also, add an instance variable for a timer and an int variable to keep track of the number of seconds. My view controller header looks like this:

```
@interface TestTimerViewController : UIViewController {

    IBOutlet UILabel *timerLabel;
    NSTimer* timer;
    int time;
}
@end
```

Add code to the `viewDidLoad` method of the view controller to initialize the label and the time variable. Add code to start the timer and add it to the run loop. My `viewDidLoad` method looks like this:

```
// Implement viewDidLoad to do additional setup after loading the view, typically from a
// nib.
- (void)viewDidLoad
{
    [super viewDidLoad];

    timerLabel.text = @"0";
    time=0;

    // Start the timer
    timer = [NSTimer scheduledTimerWithTimeInterval:1.0
                                             target:self
                                           selector:@selector(timerFired:)
                                           userInfo:nil
                                            repeats:YES];

}
```

Add a `timerFired:` method to update the time variable and the label when the timer fires. My `timerFired:` method looks like this:

```
- (void)timerFired:(NSTimer*)theTimer
{
    time++;
    timerLabel.text = [NSString stringWithFormat:@"%i",time];
}
```

I've included the code for this in a project called TestTimer.

CHAPTER 6

1. UIKit is a high-level, Objective-C graphics wrapper built on top of Core Graphics. Core Graphics is a low-level C API that you can use to do advanced drawing that you cannot do with UIKit.

2. It is easy to write drawing code based on an un-rotated coordinate system with an origin of 0,0. Then, you can use that code to draw the shape that you defined anywhere on the screen, at any rotation and scale by moving the coordinate system instead of recalculating the position of each point at runtime.

3. No. You should never call `drawRect:` directly. If you need to update the display manually, you tell UIKit that the display needs to be updated by calling the `setNeedsDisplay` or `setNeedsDisplayInRect:` method. The `drawRect:` method should only be called by UIKit.

4. The context is a state machine meaning that it maintains the current state of the drawing environment. Typically, you want to wrap any drawing operations in `CGContextSaveGState` and `CGContextRestoreGState` calls. That way, any changes that you make to the context, like changing drawing colors, transforming the coordinate system, or setting up shadows, are contained only where you need them and do not affect any additional drawing after you make these changes to the context.

5. Sprites are most useful when the graphics are extremely complicated or you have artists drawing your graphics. Writing custom drawing code is the only way that you can write code that modifies the individual vertices of your graphics at runtime.

6. Follow the first seven steps that you did to start the GraphicsStart program in the first example in the chapter. Then, use this `drawRect` method instead of the one in GraphicsStart:

```
- (void)drawRect:(CGRect)rect
{
    // Seed the random number generator
    srandom( time( NULL ) );

    int randomX, randomY, randomDiam;

    UIBezierPath* path;

    // Draw 10 circles
    for (int i=0; i<10; i++)
    {

        randomX = random() % 270;
        randomY = random() % 430;
        randomDiam = random() % 50;


    // Make a 40 x 40 pixel square at 0,0
        CGRect aRectangle = CGRectMake(randomX, randomY, randomDiam, randomDiam);

    // Make a path for a circle with the rectangle
    path = [UIBezierPath bezierPathWithOvalInRect:aRectangle];

    // Fill the circle
    [path fill];
    }
}
```

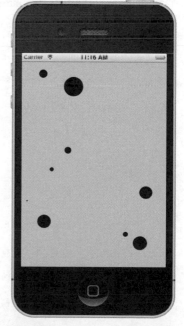

In this code, I used a `for` loop to create the 10 circles. I used the random function to get random x and y coordinates for the circles and to generate a random diameter. I used the `CGRectMake` function to create the `CGRect` object that defines the rectangle in which to inscribe each circle. Finally, I created the circle paths using the `bezierPathWithOvalInRect:` method of the `UIBezierPath` object and then filled the path.

My output looked like Figure A-1.

CHAPTER 7

1. First, UIKit performs a hit test by calling the `pointInside:withEvent:` method recursively on each view in the view hierarchy to determine the objects that

FIGURE A-1: Circle Exercise Output

were touched. Then, the UIKit works its way back up the responder chain, giving each potential responder a chance to respond to the event.

2. You typically implement the `touchesBegan:withEvent:`, `touchesMoved:withEvent:`, and the `touchesEnded:withEvent:` events.

3. When you are processing the set of touches that you receive in the touch events, you can ask the touch for its location by using the `locationInView` method of the `UITouch` object.

4. Start a new Single View Application project. I used the `ball.png` image from the Roller project, so add that image to your new project. In the `viewController` class, add two new instance variables to hold your image and its position:

```
UIImageView* ball;
CGSize ballSize;
```

In the `viewDidLoad` method, add code to draw the ball and add it as a subview to your view:

```
// Draw the ball
ball = [[UIImageView alloc] initWithImage:
        [UIImage imageNamed:@"ball.png"]];

ballSize = [ball.image size];

[ball setFrame:CGRectMake(180.0, 220.0,
                          ballSize.width, ballSize.height)];

[self.view addSubview:ball];
```

Implement the `touchesBegan:withEvent:` and `touchesMoved:withEvent:` methods to move the ball to correspond with the user's touches:

```
- (void)touchesBegan:(NSSet *)touches withEvent:(UIEvent *)event
{
    for (UITouch* t in touches)
    {
        CGPoint touchLocation;

        touchLocation = [t locationInView:self.view];

        // Move the ball by setting its frame to the touch position
        [ball setFrame:CGRectMake(touchLocation.x, touchLocation.y,
                                  ballSize.width, ballSize.height)];

    }
}

- (void)touchesMoved:(NSSet *)touches withEvent:(UIEvent *)event
{
for (UITouch* t in touches)
    {
        CGPoint touchLocation;

        touchLocation = [t locationInView:self.view];
```

```
                    // Move the ball by setting its frame to the touch position
                    [ball setFrame:CGRectMake(touchLocation.x, touchLocation.y,
                                        ballSize.width, ballSize.height)];
    }
}
```

5. You need to set the `multipleTouchEnabled` property of the view to YES. By default, multitouch is not enabled for a view.

6. You need to create an instance of the concrete `UITapGestureRecognizer` class, configure it to respond to two taps, and add it to the view. You also need to code the action method that the gesture recognizer will call when it recognizes the gesture.

The following code creates and configures the gesture recognizer:

```
UITapGestureRecognizer *doubleTap = [[UITapGestureRecognizer alloc]
                            initWithTarget:self
                            action:@selector(handleTap:)];
doubleTap.numberOfTapsRequired=2;
[self.view addGestureRecognizer:doubleTap];
[doubleTap release];
```

This sample implementation of the `handleTap` method logs that a double tap was detected:

```
- (void)handleTap:(UIGestureRecognizer *)sender
{
    NSLog(@"Double tap detected");
}
```

CHAPTER 8

1. To perform animation in forward and reverse, you load all of the images into your `UIImageView` twice. First, you load all of the images in the correct order. Then, you add the images again, in reverse order. Here is a modified version of the `viewDidLoad` method from the ImageAnimation project that solves the problem:

```
- (void)viewDidLoad
{
    [super viewDidLoad];
    // Do any additional setup after loading the view, typically from a nib.

    // Set up the image view
    UIImageView* animatedImages = [[UIImageView alloc]
            initWithFrame:CGRectMake(10, 10, 100, 100)];
    [self.view addSubview:animatedImages];

    // Load the images into an array
    NSMutableArray *imageArray = [[NSMutableArray alloc] initWithCapacity:10];
    NSString* fileName;

    // Add the forward images
    for (int i=1; i<=10; i++) {
        fileName = [NSString stringWithFormat: @"Clock%i.png",i];
```

```
        [imageArray addObject:[UIImage imageNamed:fileName]];

    }

    // Add image 1 because we want to show the hand going to the 12 o'clock
    // position
    [imageArray addObject:[UIImage imageNamed:@"Clock1.png"]];


    // Add the reverse images
    for (int i=10; i>1; i--) {
        fileName = [NSString stringWithFormat: @"Clock%i.png",i];
        [imageArray addObject:[UIImage imageNamed:fileName]];

    }


    // Configure the animation
    animatedImages.animationImages = imageArray;
    animatedImages.animationDuration = 1;

    // Start the animation
    [animatedImages startAnimating];

}
```

2. You set the `animationDuration` property to control the duration of an image animation. The shorter the duration, the faster that the animation will run. You can figure out the frame rate of the animation by dividing the number of frames in the animation by the duration.

3. When you want to animate changes to certain properties of a view, you use property animations. When you want to transition between two views or when you need to make radical changes to a view, you use a transition animation.

4. You can organize your layers by implementing a layer hierarchy. You build a layer hierarchy by adding sub layers to a layer. Each layer can have only one parent, or super layer, but a layer can have many sub layers.

5. I built my version of the solution by starting with the CoreAnimationPlay example.

First, I changed the `addShipLayers` method to only display one ship:

```
-(void) addShipLayers
{
    // Create ship layers
    UIImage *shipImage = [UIImage imageNamed:@"SpaceShip_1.png"];
    ship1 = [[CALayer alloc] init];
    ship1.frame =
    CGRectMake(0, 0, SHIP1_WIDTH/3, SHIP1_HEIGHT/3);
    ship1.contents = (id)[shipImage CGImage];

    // Add ship1 layer to the view's layer
    [self.view.layer addSublayer:ship1];

}
```

Then, I modified the `handletap` method to set the position of the ship1 layer to the location in the view where the user tapped:

```
- (void)handletap:(UIGestureRecognizer *)gestureRecognizer
{
    // Move ship1 and the other sublayers move too
    ship1.position = [gestureRecognizer locationInView:self.view];
}
```

CHAPTER 9

1. You should use System Sound Services to provide feedback for user events. Using System Sound Services is not an option if you need to play more than one sound at a time, play sounds longer than 30 seconds, or if you need precise control of the playback.

2. AV Foundation allows you to create many instances of the `AVAudioPlayer`, allowing you to play many sounds simultaneously. Additionally, you have programmatic control over the timing of the sound, so you can play only portions of a sound file if you choose.

3. The `prepareToPlay` method preloads the buffers for the audio player allowing it to start more quickly when you ultimately call the play method to start audio playback. This reduces lag time from the time that you call the play method to the time that the sound actually starts playing.

4. The `AVAudioPlayer` class has a property called "playing" that you can interrogate to determine if a sound is playing. Playing will return YES if a sound is playing and NO if it is not.

CHAPTER 10

1. First, you need to indicate that you will implement the NSCoding protocol.

```
@interface ScramblerModel : NSObject <NSCoding> {
```

Then, you need to implement the `encodeWithCoder:` and `initWithCoder:` methods to encode and decode the member variables:

```
- (void)encodeWithCoder:(NSCoder *)aCoder
{

    [aCoder encodeObject: computerPlayer forKey:@"ComputerPlayer"];
    [aCoder encodeInt:time forKey:@"Time"];
    [aCoder encodeInt:score forKey:@"Score"];
    [aCoder encodeObject: currentWord forKey:@"CurrentWord"];

}

- (id)initWithCoder:(NSCoder *)aDecoder
{
    computerPlayer = [aDecoder decodeObjectForKey:@"ComputerPlayer"];
    time = [aDecoder decodeIntForKey:@"Time"];
```

```
        score = [aDecoder decodeIntForKey:@"Score"];
        currentWord = [aDecoder decodeObjectForKey:@"CurrentWord"];
        return self;

    }
```

2. Start a new project and add a `UIButton` to the View by using Interface Builder. Add an action for the button so that when a user presses the button, the string is sent to the peers.

In the `ViewController` header, indicate that you will implement the `GKPeerPickerControllerDelegate` protocol:

```
@interface ViewController : UIViewController<GKPeerPickerControllerDelegate>{
```

Add an instance variable so that you can hold a reference to the session:

```
GKSession* theSession;
```

In the `ViewController`, `viewDidAppear:` method, initialize and show the peer picker:

```
- (void)viewDidAppear:(BOOL)animated
{
    [super viewDidAppear:animated];

    GKPeerPickerController* picker = [[GKPeerPickerController alloc] init];
    picker.delegate = self;

    [picker show];
}
```

Implement your button's action method to send a string to peers:

```
- (IBAction)buttonPressed:(id)sender {
    NSData* theData = [[[NSStringalloc] initWithString:@"Test"]
        dataUsingEncoding:NSASCIIStringEncoding];
    NSError* error;
    [self.theSession sendDataToAllPeers:theData withDataMode:GKSendDataReliable
        error:&error];
}
```

Implement the `peerPickerController:didConnectPeer:toSession:` method to store the session, set the data receive handler, and dismiss the peer picker:

```
- (void)peerPickerController:(GKPeerPickerController *)picker
    didConnectPeer:(NSString
*)peerIDtoSession:(GKSession *)session
{
    // Store off the session
    self.theSession= session;

    // Set the receive data handler
    [session setDataReceiveHandler:self withContext:nil];

    // Dismiss the picker
    [picker dismiss];

}
```

Implement the `receiveData:fromPeer:inSession:context:` method to log the data that you received:

```
- (void) receiveData:(NSData *)data fromPeer:(NSString *)peer
    inSession: (GKSession *)session context:(void *)context
{
    NSLog(@"The data was: %@", [[NSString alloc] initWithData:data
    encoding:NSASCIIStringEncoding]);
}
```

3. The `NSCoding` protocol defines how to serialize your classes into binary data, `NSData`, for transfer to peers across a network. Archivers call the methods of the `NSCoding` protocol to perform the serialization.

INDEX

N

W

Y

Z

X